49 14

Counseling
across Cultures

Counseling
across Cultures

REVISED AND EXPANDED EDITION

Edited by
Paul B. Pedersen,
Juris G. Draguns,
Walter J. Lonner,
and Joseph E. Trimble

ꜰ *An East-West Center Book*
from The East-West Culture Learning Institute

Published for the East-West Center
by The University Press of Hawaii

Library of Congress Cataloging in Publication Data

Main entry under title:

Counseling across cultures.

   Some chapters are based on papers presented at a
symposium held during the 1973 meeting of the
American Psychological Association in Montreal.
   Bibliography: p.
   Includes indexes.
   Contents: Counseling across cultures / Juris G.
Draguns—The cultural inclusiveness of counseling /
Paul B. Pedersen—Cultural sensitivities in
counseling / Edward C. Stewart—[etc.]
      1. Counseling—Congresses. 2. Psychiatry, Trans-
cultural—Congresses. I. Pedersen, Paul, 1936–
BF637.C6C63   1981   616.89'14   81–2961
ISBN 0–8248–0725–1 (pbk.)   AACR2

Contents

Preface to the Revised
and Expanded Edition

Mental health professionals are generally in agreement that the cultural background of both the client and the counselor influences the way counseling is conducted and the way it is received. There are, as yet, however, extremely few training opportunities for counselors who work with culturally different clients. There is instead the tendency to deliver mental health services as though clients and counselors shared the same value assumptions in spite of abundant evidence to the contrary. Almost no mental health training programs are available where mental health professionals can receive credentials in cross-cultural therapies. No validated tests, scales, or measures of intercultural counseling exist to gauge effectiveness. Disproportionately few minority members are trained as mental health workers even though minorities contribute a high share of clientele. Prominent mental health professional journals contain but few articles on cross-cultural counseling and therapy. Professional mental health associations, likewise, ignore these issues at their annual meetings. And until recently there was a dearth of textbooks attempting to present a comprehensive overview of cross-cultural counseling.

During the 1973 meeting of the American Psychological Association in Montreal, a group of seven psychologists organized a symposium on "Counseling across Cultures." The symposium was well attended and positively received by its audience. The presenters were so enthusiastic about their shared interest that the papers were elaborated upon, revised, and organized into a manuscript which, with the addition of several more chapters, was published in 1976 by the University Press of Hawaii as an East-West Culture Learning Institute monograph entitled *Counseling across Cultures*. The first edition went through five printings. This resulted in a need to update certain chapters and to add new ones.

This revised and expanded edition, therefore, builds both on the earlier version and on the body of literature on cross-cultural counseling and therapy which has emerged since the first volume was published.

In articulating the implications of the cultural issues of counseling, we make several assumptions: (1) Mental health has been heavily influenced by a narrow range of cultural values representing the dominant cultures in formulation and description. (2) Mental health services are organized according to these nonrepresentative assumptions resulting in culturally inappropriate counselor interventions and culturally misunderstood client needs. (3) The cultural biases in mental health have favored those most conforming to a dominant system of value assumptions and have penalized those groups least conforming to that dominant system. (4) In order to describe accurately the mental health priorities of a culturally differentiated population, the basic assumptions of counseling and therapy need to be reexamined to identify the *specific* impact of cultural differences.

The chapters in this volume, divided into four general categories, deal with ethnic and cultural considerations as they emerge both in recurrent universal themes and in their unique ethnic characterizations. Consideration has been given, for counselors and therapists, to the basic issues, previous research, and practical applications in delivering culturally sensitive mental health services.

Part One provides an introduction and overview to cross-cultural counseling and therapy. Draguns reviews the five basic issues that mental health professionals face regarding cultural differences, briefly developing areas of importance for counseling across cultures. Pedersen surveys much of the widely ranging literature about cross-cultural counseling to document the conclusion that to some extent the cultural dimension is included in all counseling and therapy. In addition to cultural differences of ethnicity and nationality, differences of age, life-style, sex roles, and socioeconomic status mediate and distort communications between counselors and clients. The principles and insights of cross-cultural counseling apply then to the wider field of mental health services.

Part Two describes some general concerns in counseling across cultures. Stewart offers a conceptual model for understanding the difference between empathy and sympathy, similarity and dissimilarity, in cross-cultural counseling, demonstrating how dissimilarity might facilitate the development of empathy by counselors. Vontress reviews racial and ethnic barriers in counseling, such as lack of rapport, language differences, transference, countertransference, and resistance. Wintrob and Harvey, a white male and a non-white female from different academic disciplines, detail some practical issues they encountered in their effort to provide culturally appropriate counseling services. Wohl addresses the problems of transplanting systems of psychotherapy characterized by Western assumptions to non-Western cultures, showing how intercultural counseling and therapy assists in identifying cultural biases that might otherwise have been overlooked.

Part Three identifies specific ethnic and cultural considerations of counseling across cultures. Kitano and Matsushima point out how counseling Asian Americans is frustrated by the inapplicability of either Asian or American models. They suggest reasons why Asian Americans have tended to avoid mental health service agencies and discuss some of the alternative support systems that are preferred. Ruiz and Casas present a bicultural model for counseling Chicano students, a model which might easily be applied to other cultural groups as well. Trimble attacks the tendency to stereotype all American Indians without regard to the significant differences between tribes, nations, and cultures within the inclusive category of American Indians. Alexander et al. draw their conclusions from counseling research among foreign students, finding that the complications of counseling foreign students are characterized by their widely diverse cultural backgrounds, their temporary residence, political vulnerability, and the confusion concerning the purpose of "talk-therapy."

Part Four reviews the problems of cross-cultural research and practical considerations of cross-cultural counseling. Higginbotham and Tanaka-Matsumi's chapter is perhaps the first comprehensive attempt to relate the perspectives of behavioral counseling to culturally different clients. Lonner points out the problems of cross-cultural testing and measurement and suggests means for developing new and more adequate measures. Sundberg identifies a series of research hypotheses which would build on available research findings.

What are the different ways that cultural backgrounds shape a counseling relationship? How can counselors evaluate their own cultural bias? How do problems and appropriate solutions vary from one culture to another? Is counseling itself, as a "talk-therapy," culturally encapsulated? These are important questions that relate to the whole field of mental health. Whether or not counselors are working with culturally different clients, it is critical that counselors and therapists be sensitive to the culturally biased assumptions that profoundly affect our perceptions of the world around us.

We would like to acknowledge the contributions of our colleagues who revised and rewrote their chapters with extraordinary care. We express our appreciation to the East-West Culture Learning Institute for its support in encouraging the publication of the first edition and for the considerable secretarial assistance which allowed the editors to coordinate a revised and expanded edition of this book. We want to thank the staff of the University Press of Hawaii for their encouragement and assistance in assembling both these editions. We also want to thank the many people, our readers, who showed interest in the original *Counseling across Cultures*. It is their response that resulted in this revised edition, and we sincerely hope that it will prove to be an important addition to the professional counselor's bookself.

PAUL B. PEDERSEN
JURIS G. DRAGUNS
WALTER J. LONNER
JOSEPH E. TRIMBLE

PART ONE
Introduction
and Overview

1

Counseling across Cultures: Common Themes and Distinct Approaches

Juris G. Draguns

Edited volumes containing contributions by many authors tend to provide a diversity of outlooks and content. At the same time, such collectively authored contributions are often lacking in integration. This chapter is written to enhance the former and to counteract the latter feature. To this end, I will first seek to articulate a number of commonalities despite the very different approaches and themes of the several contributors. Once this is done, I will focus my attention on some of the topics that remain underemphasized in this volume. In the process, I will take the opportunity to bring my own point of view to bear upon the issues of cross-cultural counseling, even when it may be discrepant from the positions of some of my fellow contributors.

Five Common Themes

As I take a bird's-eye view of the twelve chapters that follow, I am struck by the recurrence of five basic concerns. Authors differ in the stands they take on these five general issues. They also vary in the explicitness with which they address them. Yet, I would contend, most of them in one way or another have come to grips with every one of these five issues. It is my task to articulate them.

Theme one *The Emic-Etic Distinction: How to Balance the Culturally Unique and the Humanly Universal in the Counseling Process?*

Whether we are doing cross-cultural research or planning a practically oriented intervention across cultural lines, we are faced with the question: Where to begin, and how? In cross-cultural experiences, this question assumes a more specific form: Shall we start from within the unique and different culture which we have set out to study, that is, emically; or shall we proceed etically, that is, on the basis of the assumption that all human beings are, in some important respects, alike? These two approaches, the emic and the etic, constitute the points of departure of cross-cultural research in psychology. Introduced by the linguist Pike (1954), widely analyzed in reference to the task of basic cross-cultural information gathering by Berry (1969), Malpass (1977), and Price-Williams (1974), reviewed in relation to their application to empirical cross-cultural research by Triandis, Malpass, and Davidson (1973), and criticized by Jahoda (1977), these concepts have become the conceptual and methodological pivotal points of cross-cultural psychology. Yet rarely, outside of this volume and a number of closely related recent sources (Atkinson, Morten & Sue, 1979; Henderson, 1979; Walz & Benjamin, 1978), have the implications of the emic-etic dichotomy been brought to bear upon the cross-cultural counseling process.

Concerned as it is with subjective experience, cross-cultural counseling inevitably brings the counselor in contact with the personal world of persons of different social backgrounds. This personal world, again, cannot help reflecting the culture of the counselee. The dilemma the counselor faces is to what extent the different, distinctive, or exotic in the counselee's communications and reactions should be focused upon. And conversely, to what extent should the counselor emphasize the generally human, the intuitively understandable? Stewart in chapter 3 has recaptured the distinction between empathy and sympathy, a distinction lost in much of modern psychology. Empathy, according to Stewart, is the sharing of feeling based on differences between the observer and the communicator; sympathy, by contrast, is the affective reaction experienced in the observer on the basis of perceived similarity with the communicator. These two bonds between the self and the other provide the means of implementing the etic and the emic approaches, respectively, in interpersonal encounters including counseling and other helpful services.

As Pedersen reminds us in his historical and conceptual review in chapter 2, explicit cultural awareness in counseling is a relatively recent development. From this recognition it follows that a major share of cross-cultural counseling over the years has been slanted in the etic or universalistic direction. In fact, this recognition provides one of the justifications for the present book. In the wider and more general sense, cross-cultural encounters between the counselor and the counselee are, as Pedersen asserts, ubiquitous. The awareness of the cross-cultural nature of these contacts is, however, by no means universal or automatic. Even when culture as a component of the counseling contact is self-evident and cannot be dismissed—as in working with sojourners from abroad (see chap. 10 by Alexander, Klein, Workneh, & Miller) or with foreign nationals in a distant and culturally different country (see chaps. 5 and 6 by Wintrob & Harvey and Wohl)—it is possible to gloss over the cultural aspects of the counseling experience as trivial or irrelevant to the tasks at hand. This tendency corresponds to the universalistic fallacy described by Collomb (1973): the belief that human distress is the same regardless of context and site and the conviction that the techniques to counteract it are effective everywhere. This fallacy is closely related to what, on the plane of empirical research, Triandis, Malpass, and Davidson (1973) have called the pseudoetic orientation: the assumption that the observer's own culturally bound experience is an adequate guide to what is humanly universal. The earlier history of cross-cultural psychology is replete with instances confounding the Western and the generally human features of experience. On the plane of counseling, this tendency may take the form of equating that which is culturally alien from the counselor's point of view with the humanly aberrant, "change-worthy," or even pathological or sick. The case recapitulated in the opening paragraph of chapter 9 by Trimble provides an eloquent and dramatic illustration of the pitfalls of implicitly assuming that one's cultural experience is an adequate yardstick for judging behavior in another culture. Much less dramatically, a recent comparison of white and Chinese American therapists (Li-Repac, 1980) documents some loss of accuracy in assessing clients outside the therapist's cultural group. At the same time, there is the tendency to attribute greater severity of disturbance to clients of the "outside" culture. "The clinician's prized tools, his empathy and sensitivity, may suffer impairment when carried across cultural lines" (Li-Repac, 1980, p. 339). The challenge to the cross-cultural counselor is to differentiate sharply between that which is different from the framework of experience and that which is maladaptive on its home grounds.

The chapters by Vontress, Trimble, Kitano and Matsushima, and Ruiz and Casas provide a wealth of information on important research findings, clinical observations, and social features of several major population groups in the United States. It is these groups that, historically, have been among the most likely victims of the pseudoetic, universalistic approach to counseling. The temporary sojourners from abroad on the United States college campuses, discussed in the chapter by Alexander et al., find themselves in a special situation. On the one hand, they are called upon to interact with Americans on a daily basis. On the other, they are not expected to become part of the American culture on a permanent basis. The dangers of underadaptation to the host culture are counterbalanced by the dangers of overadaptation and consequent estrangement from their culture of origin. It is probable that much of the counseling done with international students has been pseudoetically slanted; Alexander et al. provide some useful antidotes to this overemphasis. Finally, Wintrob and Harvey have been exceedingly frank in sharing their experiences of doing therapy with members of cultures other than their own and outside of their accustomed social milieu, Wintrob as a Canadian psychiatrist in West Africa, Harvey as a therapist from Korea responding to the needs of American patients in Hawaii. Such experiences powerfully counteract the pseudoetic assumptions that all too many counselors, as a result of their limited cultural exposure, bring to the counseling situation. They are also, as Wintrob and Harvey point out, a source of considerable emotional stress. In different ways, all of these chapters provide the kind of concrete, specific information that the counselor needs in order to operate effectively and efficiently within new and different cultural contexts.

Yet this information, even if useful, is probably not sufficient. Each counselor, in crossing a cultural line, is on his or her own in attempting to counteract a natural etic slant in the delivery of counseling services. As pointed out elsewhere (Draguns, 1981), there are several steps the counselor may take in counteracting the pull towards an etic imbalance. First, the counselee may be enlisted as a valuable, even indispensable, informant of cultural experience. Second, anthropological and other relevant sources on the cultural group in question may be consulted and used to fill gaps in the counselor's knowledge. Third, various formal or informal approaches may be utilized to obtain culturally relevant information from informants and intermediaries. This should be done in such a fashion as not to violate the client's confidentiality. Finally, and most generally, the counselor should approach the experience of counseling across culture lines with openness and flexibility and should be prepared to modify approaches in the service of greater cultural sensitivity.

On a general plane, how to reconcile general and unique elements in the delivery of counseling services across cultural lines remains the problem. Two chapters in this book have come to grips with this problem. Wohl, surveying experiences of counselors applying Western techniques of psychotherapy in the non-Western world, arrives at cautiously pessimistic conclusions. In paraphrase of Wohl, it might be fair to say that verbal psychotherapy, especially of the psychodynamic and psychoanalytic orientation, has not traveled well beyond international and cultural frontiers. Although to deny absolutely its applicability with any and all of non-Western clients would be rash, the range of usefulness of verbal psychotherapy as we know it in our customary Euro-American settings is narrow, subject though it may be to extensive and far-reaching modifications and adaptations. It would be well to note that Prince (1976, 1980) arrived independently at similar conclusions on the basis of his extensive reviews of psychotherapy around the world.

In another chapter in this book, Higginbotham and Tanaka-Matsumi apply a universal and etic framework par excellence, the cognitive social learning approach, to the problem of cross-cultural intervention and the delivery of counseling services. What is remarkable and novel about their contribution is the attention devoted to accommodating the culture which is the target of such intervention. On the basis of ethical considerations, Higginbotham and Tanaka-Matsumi contend that only needs explicitly voiced by members of the culture in question may be met and that only services actually requested may be delivered. The concrete form that the implementation of this principle has taken is the development of the Ethno-Therapy and Culture Accommodation Scale. Higginbotham and Tanaka-Matsumi feel that there is a unique fit between the cognitive social learning approach they espouse and the principle of culture accommodation. Indeed, the parallel between the modus operandi of the practitioner of behavior modification on the individual plane and the planned, culturally sensitive blueprint of intervention on the scale of a culture is clear. Nonetheless, readers who do not abide by the theoretical approach of Higginbotham and Tanaka-Matsumi may still find useful both the culture accommodation scale and the principle that underlies it.

The bulk of this section has been devoted to the dangers of an etic imbalance and possible ways of redressing it. Equal attention should be allocated to the pitfalls of an emic overemphasis. If the swing of the pendulum towards the etic extreme results in cultural insensitivity, a lopsided emic emphasis brings with it the dangers of exoticism and cultural stereotyping. As Trimble reminds us, a tremendous range of individual differences is encompassed under the rubric of American Indian; the same statement can be made about most other cultural groups discussed in this volume, or outside of it. Moreover, the step from cultural sensitivity to cultural stereotyping is as short as it is ominous. In the final paragraph of his chapter, Trimble explicitly cautions counselors against excessive fascination with the culture at the expense of sensitivity to the needs and feelings of the person. The penchant for seeing the counselee only as a group member—a ghetto black, a migrant Puerto Rican, a Sioux Indian—is destructive of the counselor's ability to deal with a unique person. As Sundberg in chapter 13 properly emphasizes, in counseling it is the individual who is in focus, not the culture. Cultural factors alone do not provide the answers to the dilemmas that a counselor faces. An emic overemphasis then is conducive to two pitfalls: of seeing all members of a cultural group as being alike and of glossing over the personal in concern for the socially shared experience.

What the counselor must do then is to strive for an equilibrium between the etic and the emic. Every counseling venture beyond cultural lines becomes a succession of steps, not unlike those described by Berry (1969) in reference to cross-cultural research, involving shifts in emphasis from the humanly universal to the culturally particular, and vice versa.

THEME TWO   *The Autoplastic-Alloplastic Dilemma: What Are the Goals of Cross-Cultural Counseling?*

In coping with the environment, all humans respond either autoplastically, by changing themselves to accommodate the external circumstances, or alloplastically, by imposing changes upon the world at large (cf. Vexliard, 1968). Applied to the counseling situation, this dichotomy sparks the question: How much should the counselee be helped to adapt to a given situation and how much should he be encouraged to shape and change the situation? Historically, counseling with persons who are not native to the United States and/or are culturally atypical has been slanted in the autoplastic direction. The message to the counselee has, implicitly or explicitly, been this: Fit in by becoming more like the people in the cultural mainstream and by changing yourself in the process.

Recently, the counseling situation has come to be seen as one of the avenues of emancipation and liberation—a way of freeing the individual to restructure the situation that has brought him into counseling in the first place. Several of the chapters in the book document this reversal of the autoplastic trend. The chapters by Vontress, Trimble, and Ruiz and Casas are concerned with the importance of fostering and preserving distinct identities in harmony with their characteristic values. Alexander et al. highlight the maintenance of ties with fellow nationals as a critical factor in promoting the adjustment of international students. Ruiz and Casas maintain that problems within the individual must be distinguished from those in the environment. Kitano and Matsushima perhaps go furthest of the authors in this book in articulating the necessity of preparing minority group members through counseling for struggle against, and change of, the oppressive features of the social environment.

Outside of this book, Berman (1979) has brought to light some noteworthy differences in the outlooks of white and black counselors. The former, in an analogue study, offered explanations predominantly in terms of individual behavior; the latter proposed individually as well as socially focused explanations. To translate these orientations into our terms, white counselors showed an almost exclusive preference for autoplastic formulation of problems; their black counterparts placed a greater weight on alloplastic factors. Sue (1978) has proposed an elaborate typology of counseling encounters, recapitulated in Pedersen's chapter. At this point, all that will be said about Sue's scheme is that it is based on the counselor's and client's notions of the sources of attribution of responsibility and control and on the compatibility of these notions. Sue, in particular, cautions counselors against imposing across cultural lines their own culturally bound notions of who and what is responsible.

What these innovative formulations challenge is the ingrained habit of many counselors to look for sources of the client's problem exclusively inside the person. The environment is often at least a part of the problem, especially so in the life space of many minority group members who are burdened by prejudice and social disadvantage, or sojourners and new-comers.

The reversal of the autoplastic bias in cross-cultural counseling is thus to be welcomed. The swing of the pendulum in the alloplastic direction, however, brings with it serious problems. Two issues, in particular, need to be resolved. One of these has to do with counselees' choices; the other involves the bases for counselors' actions. On the former issue, the Aus-tralian psychologist, Taft (1966), identified a trichotomy of adaptive op-tions open to a person whose membership spans two cultural reference groups. The choices range from encapsulation in the community of one's compatriots to a headlong plunge into the social world of the host cul-ture or an integration of elements of host and original cultures into a complex web of personal behavior and experience. This general scheme was developed in reference to immigrants, but it is probably applicable, with variations, to other types of culturally distinct persons. In fact, the fourfold scheme proposed by Ruiz and Casas for Chicano students over-laps with Taft's classification. It provides an additional category of rele-vance to counseling: that of an individual with a tenuous hold on either the "in-group" or the "out-group" culture. Such a person can be de-scribed as marginal and is susceptible to problems of living that may re-quire counseling. In any case, where the counselee stands on the issue of adaptation to the host or majority culture is an important personal deci-sion and concomitantly of great moment in the counseling process. To the extent that the counselee is conflict-torn on this issue, the goal of counseling must be to help him find the personally most satisfying solu-tion of how much to change self and environment and how to define himself in reference to the minority "in-group" and majority "out-group."

The other issue focuses on the bases of alloplastic orientation on the part of the counselor. What is the empirical justification for a social pre-scription for change? And what is the power of an individual counselor or counselee to implement these prescriptions? My own view in this mat-ter is that our knowledge of how to change persons by far exceeds our knowledge of how to change societies. To be sure, prescriptions for social change abound, but their sources are for the most part ideological and not factual. The counselor's legitimate role as an agent of social change is thus limited by the state of knowledge, on the one hand, and by the eth-ical imperative against imposing one's convictions and beliefs upon a counselee, on the other.

In their hypothetical extremes, the alloplastic bias degenerates into revolutionary rhetoric and bombast, and the autoplastic bias, into the jargon and scholasticism of the most rigid variants of the medical model misapplied to the social scene. The alloplastic mode refers any personal problem to its putative social and political causes and the autoplastic traces it to personal pathology. Wohl, in his review of pioneering contributions to intercultural psychotherapy, provides a few glaring examples of accepting the social situation as immutable. From the vantage point of the current political and social climate, examples of such an orientation by the therapist would strike many readers as reactionary politically and rigid clinically. I would add, however, that a similar lopsidedness results if solutions to personal problems are sought exclusively in institutional or social change. Steering clear of these two extremes, the counselor must help the counselee both to act upon people, objects, and situations and to be acted upon—to accommodate to the environment. Combining these two modes realistically and creatively is the goal of all counseling, a measure of its success, and a criterion of the counselor's skill and sensitivity.

THEME THREE   *Relationship Versus Technique: What Stays Constant and What Changes in Cross-Cultural Counseling?*

The several chapters of this book make it readily apparent that the actual techniques of counseling do not remain immutable as they are applied across cultures. On the basis of their research and experience, Alexander et al. provide a number of generalizations on what works and does not work with their international student clientele, most of whom came from the Far East. Vontress performs a similar service in reference to a number of prominent American minority groups. Discussion of the limitations of traditional counseling techniques with American Indians is also found in Trimble's chapter. On a more general plane, Wohl addresses the question of what features of psychotherapy, as we know it in the West, might be exported to other regions and cultures. The rather elaborate system of techniques of psychoanalysis poses special problems of application and adaptation outside of the Western cultures of its origin and development, both in Wohl's view and in those of a number of other contemporary authors (Prince, 1980). Sundberg's objective is equally general although different. He has attempted to link cultural characteristics and the modes of delivery of mental health services. What emerges from all of these perspectives is the conclusion that the techniques of counseling must be plausible and believable to be effective (see also Goldstein, 1962; Higginbotham, 1977). In different cultures, and even within the culturally distinct components of the same population, techniques may differ in the extent to which they are believed and accepted. This realization underscores the importance of cognitive factors in counseling across cultural lines. Even the supposedly immutable techniques of behavior modification discussed by Higginbotham and Tanaka-Matsumi in their chapter may be differently mediated and conceptualized, in part due to cultural influences.

All of these considerations suggest a need for flexibility and innovation in extending counseling services to new and different groups. Does nothing remain constant then as counseling is modified through new adaptations? An affirmative answer to this question is, on an empirical basis, premature and, on conceptual grounds, unlikely. It is plausible, however, that the putative universals of counseling in a cross-cultural perspective are general and broad, more on the plane of inclusive attitudes than of specific behaviors. Sundberg in his chapter confronts this issue in greater detail; other recent treatments of this subject have been provided by Draguns (1975, 1981), Prince (1976, 1980), and Torrey (1972).

A general précis addressed to the cross-cultural counselor might then be as follows: be prepared to adapt your techniques (e.g., general activity level, mode of verbal intervention, content of remarks, tone of voice) to the cultural background of the client; communicate acceptance of and respect for the client in terms that are intelligible and meaningful within his cultural frame of reference; and be open to the possibility of more direct intervention in the life of the client than the traditional ethos of the counseling profession would dictate or permit. Thus, parallel to recent formulations based on psychotherapy research literature (Strupp, 1970, 1973), the non-specific attitudinal and relationship factors appear to be the most robust ingredients of the counseling experience regardless of site or context.

THEME FOUR   *The Bilaterality of the Client-Counselor Relationship: What Demands Does Cross-Cultural Counseling Place upon the Counselor?*

The importance of this theme has already been alluded to under several of the preceding headings. The contributions of several authors converge in suggesting that counseling across the cultural gulf is a personally demanding and involving experience. Yet, the counselor's reactions to a cross-cultural counseling encounter have until recently remained a neglected, if not a taboo, topic in the professional counseling literature. Similarly unshared have been the personal experiences of the observer or investigator in the more inclusive body of cross-cultural psychological literature.

In this volume, silence on this subject has been broken. The counselors' personal feelings and their countertransference occupy a prominent place in Vontress's chapter on counseling members of minority groups. Experiential aspects of cross-cultural therapeutic reactions also constitute an important theme of Wohl's chapter. Alexander et al. allude to countertransference reactions in their chapter on services to international students. Sundberg broaches the question of bilaterality of involvement between counselor and counselee in several of his hypotheses. Wintrob and Harvey's chapter is specifically focused upon the subjective, experiential aspects of the cross-cultural helper-helpee relationship. In the process, they not only provide vivid and candid accounts of personal experience of cross-cultural intervention, but they also offer plausible explanations of why the intensity of countertransference is magnified in cross-cultural applications of counseling and psychotherapy.

Beyond Wintrob and Harvey's explanations, it may be well to add that immersion into a new and different culture powerfully stimulates experiences of ambiguity, dependence, and helplessness. Not coincidentally, these are also the experiences that are fostered in certain traditional, especially psychodynamic, types of psychotherapy. Here, such experiences are crucial contributors to the development of transference reactions as a result of the attendant intensification and distortion of relationships between the therapist and the client. A parallel development takes place when attempting to render counseling or therapeutic services in a new cultural milieu, with the added feature of the culture becoming an object of the therapist's countertransference reaction.

On a more concrete plane, Wintrob and Harvey share with us two particular perspectives: that of a North American mental health specialist offering his services at various distances from his accustomed habitat and that of a Korean immigrant professional operating within the American cultural and institutional milieu. The latter perspective is clearly underrepresented in the literature. Reading Harvey's observations, we catch glimpses of American culture which, as insiders, we might have overlooked.

THEME FIVE *The Future of Cross-Cultural Counseling: What Is Known and What Is Not?*

In terms of its explicit recognition, cross-cultural counseling is a young field, although it appears to be a great deal older in practice. It is therefore striking, although by no means surprising, to what extent the authors in this volume are concerned with the future. As Pedersen and Sundberg point out in their chapters, research on cross-cultural counseling as yet occupies a modest place indeed in the contemporary counseling, psychotherapy, and cross-cultural psychology literature. Hypotheses have prevailed over findings, impressions over data, and formulations over substance. This does not mean that the contemporary practitioner of cross-cultural counseling has to proceed blindly and in ignorance. The particular merit of Pedersen's and Sundberg's chapters, thus, is that they bring to the fore bodies of data which are only in small part based upon cross-cultural counseling but are yet relevant to it. Pedersen has reviewed and integrated the literature of six or seven quasi-independent culturally oriented social science disciplines and fields of professional application. In the process, he has brought these formulations and results to bear upon the concerns of cross-cultural counseling. Sundberg has culled the primarily research-based literature on counseling, psychotherapy, and social interaction in order to derive from it a set of closely reasoned hypotheses. These hypotheses can be put to the test in the investigation of actual cross-cultural counseling. Pending the realization of these research objectives, Sundberg's fifteen statements can be accepted as the closest approximations to truth deduced from intracultural psychotherapy and social psychology research.

In addition to these two chapters, Wohl provides a careful conceptual analysis of psychotherapy in different cultural contexts. He supplements his analysis with a selective review of clinical studies of interventions both indigenous to the cultures in which they are practiced and "imported" from the West. This body of formulations and observations constitutes another foundation for systematic cross-cultural psychotherapy and counseling research that would vary the agents of intervention, the techniques, and the recipients of such services.

Lonner's chapter stands alone in its emphasis upon experiences just prior to counseling: the collection of information relevant to, and to be used in, the actual delivery of counseling services. As such, Lonner's task is analogous to Sundberg's in that what Sundberg attempts in reference to the generic understanding of counseling across cultures, Lonner tries to implement on the plane of understanding a culturally distinct client. As in the case of counseling research, the availability of hard and directly applicable information remains sadly limited. Despite this fact, Lonner has succeeded in marshalling a great deal of pertinent evidence on sensitive and culturally appropriate modes of assessment. The pendulum appears to have swung in the last few years from reiterating the emic desideratum of constructing specific assessment measures for each culture—a program that is impossible to implement for practical reasons—to promoting sensitive, cautious use of existing tools of assessment in a variety of cultural and social conditions. Some empirical findings, such as the high degree of cross-cultural constancy in the factorial structure of some questionnaire and projective tests, bolster this point of view. These developments are recounted at greater length by Lonner. They provide the foundation for further, more systematic research which is necessary in cross-cultural counseling as well as in cross-cultural assessment.

Meanwhile, the user of tests in the cross-cultural context is left with the option of creative, yet critical, improvisation. It is inevitable that, in the cross-cultural setting, test interpretation will involve going beyond the information given. As a consequence, the test is viewed not as a solidly validated psychometric instrument but as an additional avenue of communication beyond the direct and open sharing of personal experience.

Besides these chapters, the cross-cultural counselor or prospective investigator has available to him a more general body of knowledge accumulated in the last decade. There has been a veritable explosion of reviews on abnormal behavior across cultures: Dohrenwend and Dohrenwend, 1974; Draguns, 1973, 1977a, 1977b, 1977c, 1980; Dunham, 1976; Favazza and Oman, 1977, 1978; Guthrie and Tanco, 1980; King, 1978; Kleinman, 1979; Marsella, 1979, 1980; Sanua, 1980; Tseng and Hsu, 1980; and Wittkower and Dubreuil, 1973. Their sheer number and variety in outlook, scope, and style are indicative of the complexity of this pertinent body of information.

Additional Themes: Some Preliminary Considerations

The chapters of this volume encompass a considerable diversity in content, orientation, and style. Collectively, they come close to the goal of comprehensive coverage of issues and findings relevant to cross-cultural counseling. My intention here, thus, is to provide a brief description of themes and topics pertinent to our concerns but which have not been discussed in full.

Counseling on the International Scene

The reader will notice that the focus of this volume is upon cultural diversity within the United States. The two exceptions to this are the chapters by Wohl and Wintrob and Harvey. Several other authors—Pedersen, Sundberg, Higginbotham and Tanaka-Matsumi, Lonner, and Vontress—have included in their coverage pertinent sources from outside the United States. Nonetheless, this volume deals primarily with cross-cultural counseling as it is practiced in America.

To what extent the observations, findings, and conclusions contained in this volume are generalizable beyond the United States is an open question. On the one hand, the general principles embodied in Sundberg's hypotheses are probably applicable regardless of culture and site as are the general laws of learning and cognition from which Higginbotham and Tanaka-Matsumi proceed. On the other hand, the specific recommendations contained in the chapters by Alexander et al., Vontress, Trimble, Ruiz and Casas, and Kitano and Matsushima are in the main reflective of the groups with whom the authors have worked. There remains, however, an undetermined degree of universal validity in the statements made in the context of minority groups and sojourners in America. Generically, some issues of counseling do not change whether one is working with a Chinese student on an American campus or a Turkish guest worker in a West German city. It is, consequently, left to the practitioner to extricate what is culturally unique and what is universally applicable.

Such is one of Stewart's concerns in his chapter on cultural sensitivities. His emphasis is on the similarities rather than the differences in interpersonal relations, which he maintains is characteristic of the United States culture. According to Harvey in chapter 5, another elusive feature of the American culture is the belief in the changeability of maladaptive behavior. Not all cultures share this optimistic conviction which in its extreme manifestations, Harvey points out, leads to the rejection of chronicity and of the people who exhibit it. Readers may wish to supplement the material in this book with other studies of related counseling services on the international scene (Prince, 1976, 1980; Sanua, 1966; Wittkower & Warnes, 1974; Wohl, 1978).

Counseling and Ethnic Units in Pluralistic Cultures

The present book contains chapters which address issues regarding most of the major officially recognized minority groups in the United States. These minorities have been the concern of many social scientists and public policy makers because of their history of social, political, and economic disadvantage—often in the form of official or semiofficial discrimination. These groups probably represent a major share of the cultural diversity in the United States, but they do not exhaust its scope.

This diversity can be further viewed by the multitude of so-called ethnic groups which, over the years, have preserved their identity and at least some of the characteristics of their parent cultures. The problem of what constitutes, conceptually and operationally, an ethnic group is a difficult one; Berry tackled it in 1979. Suffice it to say, some Americans whose origins can be traced to Italy, Ireland, Greece, or Lithuania, for example, are to some extent influenced daily in their social and personal outlook by the culture of their European forebears. Very likely this influence is both detectable and relevant as these persons find themselves in some sort of counseling. Yet, we know all too little of the specifics of such influence, and a chapter on, say, counseling Polish Americans is at this point a lot more difficult to write than one on counseling Asians or Hispanics. In the latter case, a body of pertinent writing exists; in the former, clinical observations that practitioners have gathered remain for the most part unrecorded. One exception to this lack of documentation is provided by the writings of Giordano and Giordano (1976), who compiled a practical list of characteristic values and attitudes of several American ethnic groups for use by mental health professionals.

How far culturally characteristic attitudes extend and how they impinge upon the design and delivery of counseling services is illustrated in a recent study by McLatchie (1977). She investigated attitudes towards mental health services of rural traditionalist Protestants, a group rarely considered either "minority" or "ethnic." The pattern of her findings, however, suggests that the rural Protestant constellation of views on mental health matters is detectably different from more "typical" populations imbued with the modern American liberal secular ethos. What these results highlight is the validity of Pedersen's conclusion that cultural differences are all around us and that we constantly stumble upon them in the course of counseling, unless we anticipate them. Some cultural-ethnic groups then are recognizable, others less so, but their culture-ethnicity is in either case basic to the delivery of appropriate counseling services.

Additional Theoretical Perspectives: The Psychodynamic

Higginbotham and Tanaka-Matsumi bring to bear the principles of behavior modification, in both its traditional and innovative varieties, upon the practice of cross-cultural counseling. Stewart shares with us the relevance of a cognitive and phenomenological outlook for the conduct of counseling across cultures. What is lacking in this volume as well as elsewhere in the literature is the treatment of potential and actual contributions of the third major framework of therapeutic psychology, the psychodynamic. What is the relevance for the delivery and implementation of cross-cultural counseling services of this theoretical perspective, especially of its emphasis upon intrapsychic conflict and unconscious determinants of behavior? To be sure, the psychodynamic perspective is not altogether unrepresented here. Wohl's chapter is informed by this theoretical framework, and concepts of Freudian derivation, such as transference and countertransference, occupy a prominent place in Vontress' contribution. Wintrob and Harvey rely, at least in part, on psychoanalytic notions in dealing with the subjective experience of delivering therapeutic services in another culture. Kitano and Matsushima provide interesting glimpses of dynamics different in content from, although perhaps equal in function to, those described in classical Freudian theory within the Japanese and Japanese American cultures.

What all of these instances suggest is that the psychoanalytic framework is as difficult to banish entirely from cross-cultural counseling as it is to apply systematically. As already pointed out, the modern therapeutic and counseling literature is replete with admonitions against automatically transposing the concepts, the techniques, and the trappings of traditional psychoanalysis to culturally different clienteles. While extended accounts of successful application of psychoanalytic approaches are available (e.g., Devereux, 1969), these are paralleled by skepticism, both conceptual and empirical, of psychoanalysis as a technique of intervention in other than a few Western social settings where it was developed and grew (e.g., Prince, 1980; Torrey, 1972). Yet, one may ask, if the tenets of psychoanalysis have empirical validity (a question of continued, unresolved controversy), how can they be therapeutically applied in other milieus? Again, in keeping with the principle of cross-cultural variability in therapeutic techniques, the challenge is to find a way of dealing with the unconscious that does not mimic techniques developed in turn-of-the-century Vienna.

Culture Contact Situations and Their Individual Effects

With the exception of the chapter by Alexander et al., the volume devotes relatively little attention to culture-contact situations as a source of stress and trauma. Yet, in this age of mass voluntary and involuntary migrations—among them refugees, immigrants, sojourners, and tourists—these culture-contact situations, often summarized under the heading of culture shock, assume a great clinical and practical importance. Information has been gathered and reviewed on the characteristics of the individual, his or her culture of origin, the host culture, and the circumstances of culture contact that promote, inhibit, or modulate the traumatic effects of culture shock (Bennett, 1977; Oberg, 1960; Pintér, 1969; Taft, 1977). Concurrently, a body of literature has been developed to prepare individuals for contact with, and immersion into, a new culture without the adverse effects that often accompany such experiences (e.g., Brislin & Pedersen, 1976; Brein & David, 1971; David, 1976). A general conclusion is that culture, including its subjective aspects, can be systematically taught and learned. In the optimal case, such learning effectively cushions the newcomer against disruptive emotional states and loss of perceived personal effectiveness such as visitors to other cultures often report. Moreover, the implications that these programs hold are not restricted to international migration and travel. In pluralistic cultures, they also apply to adopting a different framework of implicit rules and expectations that is involved, for example, in leaving the ethnic community for a "mainstream" environment of a large city or major university.

A special problem is posed by the psychological sequelae of migrations that are involuntary or occur under duress. Migrations that are in some way related to war or political upheaval are often stressful and traumatic. Yet, accent is often one-sidedly placed on the physical care and rehabilitation of refugees and expellees to the slight or neglect of psychological needs and problems.

Conclusion

It is apparent then that the scope of cross-cultural counseling is wide, that choices and problems confronting its practitioners are numerous, and that the perspectives that can be brought to bear upon these tasks are diverse. This volume encompasses many, although not all, of the approaches to counseling persons across some kind of a cultural gulf. Generally this objective can be accomplished by combining human and cultural sensitivity with flexibility and openness to new approaches. What would be critical to this end is an information base on the cultural group in question. Subject to those specific cultural groups considered and the state of current knowledge, the several contributors to this volume have striven to provide exactly this. What the cross-cultural counselor also needs is an understanding of the generic nature of cultural influence upon counseling interaction. Certain leads in this direction—again limited by the present store of accumulated information—are to be found in several chapters of this book.

Collectively, the articles in this book should help the counselor avoid the pitfalls of "counseling as usual," oblivion to the culturally shaped expectations of counselees and immobility because of fascination with the exotic cultural backgrounds of the clientele. On the one hand, the counseling process is obstructed by cultural insensitivity; on the other, it is complicated by stereotypes and the resultant loss of sensitivity to the person. As one of the authors has reminded us, all of us are like all other persons, like some other persons, and like no other person. Effective counseling is based on the recognition and appropriate use of all of these three components of human experience.

References

Atkinson, D., Morten, G., & Sue, D. W. *Counseling American minorities: A cross-cultural perspective.* Dubuque, Iowa: William C. Brown Co., 1979.

Bennett, J. Transition shock: Putting culture shock in perspective. *International and Intercultural Communication Annual,* 1977, *4*, 44–52.

Berman, J. Individual versus societal focus: Problem diagnoses of black and white male and female counselors. *Journal of Cross-Cultural Psychology,* 1979, *10*, 497–507.

Berry, J. W. On cross-cultural comparability. *International Journal of Psychology,* 1969, *5*, 119–128.

Berry, J. W. Research in multicultural societies: Implications of cross-cultural methods. *Journal of Cross-Cultural Psychology,* 1979, *10*, 415–434.

Brein, M., & David, K. H. Intercultural communication and the adjustment of the sojourner. *Psychological Bulletin,* 1971, *76*, 215–230.

Brislin, R. W., & Pedersen, P. *Cross-cultural orientation programs.* New York: Gardner Press, 1976.

Collomb, H. L'avenir de la psychiatrie en Afrique. *Psychopathologie africaine,* 1973, *9*, 343–370.

David, K. H. The use of social learning theory in preventing intercultural adjustment problems. In P. Pedersen, W. J. Lonner, & J. G. Draguns (Eds.), *Counseling across cultures.* Honolulu: University Press of Hawaii, 1976.

Devereux, G. *Reality and the dream: Psychotherapy of a Plains Indian.* Garden City, New York: Doubleday, 1969.

Dohrenwend, B. P., & Dohrenwend, B. S. Social and cultural influences on psychopathology. *Annual Review of Psychology,* 1974, *25,* 417–452.

Draguns, J. G. Comparisons of psychopathology across cultures: Issues, findings, directions. *Journal of Cross-Cultural Psychology,* 1973, *4,* 9–47.

Draguns, J. G. Resocialization into culture: The complexities of taking a worldwide view of psychotherapy. In R. W. Brislin, S. Bochner, & W. J. Lonner (Eds.), *Cross-cultural perspectives on learning.* New York: Sage Publications, 1975.

Draguns, J. G. Advances in methodology of cross-cultural assessment. *Transcultural Psychiatric Research Review,* 1977, *14,* 125–143.(a)

Draguns, J. G. Mental health and culture. In D. S. Hoopes, P. B. Pedersen, & G. Renwick (Eds.), *Overview of intercultural education, training, and research, Vol. 1: Theory.* Washington, D.C.: Society for Intercultural Education, Training, and Research, 1977.(b)

Draguns, J. G. Problems of defining and comparing abnormal behaviors across cultures. *Annals of the New York Academy of Sciences,* 1977, *285,* 664–675.(c)

Draguns, J. G. Psychological disorders of clinical severity. In H. C. Triandis & J. G. Draguns (Eds.), *Handbook of cross-cultural psychology, Vol. 6: Psychopathology.* Boston: Allyn & Bacon, 1980.

Draguns, J. G. Cross-cultural counseling and psychotherapy: History, issues, current status. In A. J. Marsella & P. Pedersen (Eds.), *Cross-cultural counseling and psychotherapy.* Elmsford, New York: Pergamon Press, 1981.

Dunham, H. W. Society, culture, and mental disorder. *Archives of General Psychiatry,* 1976, *33,* 147–156.

Favazza, A. R., & Oman, M. *Anthropological and cross-cultural themes in mental health: An annotated bibliography: 1925–1974.* Columbia: University of Missouri Press, 1977.

Favazza, A. R., & Oman, M. Overview: Foundations of cultural psychiatry. *American Journal of Psychiatry,* 1978, *135,* 293–303.

Giordano, J., & Giordano, G. P. Ethnicity and community mental health. *Community Mental Health Review,* 1976, *1*(3), 4–14, 15.

Goldstein, A. P. *Therapist-patient expectancies in psychotherapy.* New York: Pergamon Press, 1962.

Guthrie, G. M., & Tanco, P. P. Alienation and anomie. In H. C. Triandis & J. G. Draguns (Eds.), *Handbook of cross-cultural psychology, Vol. 6: Psychopathology.* Boston: Allyn & Bacon, 1980.

Henderson, G. (Ed.). *Understanding and counseling ethnic minorities.* Springfield, Illinois: Thomas, 1979.

Higginbotham, H. N. Culture and the role of client expectancy. *Topics in Culture Learning,* 1977, *5,* 107–124.

Jahoda, G. In pursuit of the emic-etic distinction: Can we ever capture it? In Y. H. Poortinga (Ed.), *Basic problems in cross-cultural psychology.* Amsterdam: Swets & Zeitlinger, 1977.

King, L. M., Social and cultural influences on psychopathology. *Annual Review of Psychology*, 1978, 29, 405–433.

Kleinman, A. *Patients and healers in the context of culture.* Berkeley: University of California Press, 1979.

Li-Repac, D. Cultural influences on clinical perception: A comparison between Caucasian and Chinese American therapists. *Journal of Cross-Cultural Psychology*, 1980, 11, 327–342.

Malpass, R. S. Theory and method in cross-cultural psychology. *American Psychologist*, 1977, 32, 1069–1079.

Marsella, A. J. Cross-cultural study of mental disorders. In A. J. Marsella et al. (Eds.), *Perspectives on cross-cultural psychology.* New York: Academic Press, 1979.

Marsella, A. J. Depression. In H. C. Triandis & J. G. Draguns (Eds.), *Handbook of cross-cultural psychology, Vol. 6: Psychopathology.* Boston: Allyn & Bacon, 1980.

McLatchie, L. R. *The relationship of Protestant traditionalism to concepts of mental illness and of mental health services.* Master's thesis, The Pennsylvania State University, 1977.

Oberg, K. Culture shock: Adjustment to new cultural environments. *Practical Anthropology*, 1960, 7, 177–182.

Pike, K. L. *Language in relation to a unified theory of the structure of human behavior* (Part 1: Preliminary Edition). Glendale, California: Summer Institute of Linguistics, 1954.

Pintér, E. Wohlstandsflüchtlinge. Eine sozialpsychiatrische Studie an ungarischen Flüchtlingen in der Schweiz. *Bibliotheca Psychiatrica et Neurologica*, 1969, No. 138.

Price-Williams, D. Psychological experiment and anthropology: The problem of categories. *Ethos*, 1974, 2, 95–114.

Prince, R. H. Psychotherapy as the manipulation of endogenous healing mechanisms: A transcultural survey. *Transcultural Psychiatric Research Review*, 1976, 13, 115–134.

Prince, R. H. Variations in psychotherapeutic experience. In H. C. Triandis & J. G. Draguns (Eds.), *Handbook of cross-cultural psychology, Vol. 6: Psychopathology.* Boston: Allyn & Bacon, 1980.

Sanua, V. D. Sociocultural aspects of psychotherapy and treatment: A review of the literature. In L. A. Abt & B. F. Riess (Eds.), *Progress in clinical psychology.* New York: Grune & Stratton, 1966.

Sanua, V. D. Familial and sociocultural antecedents of psychopathology. In H. C. Triandis & J. G. Draguns (Eds.), *Handbook of cross-cultural psychology, Vol. 6: Psychopathology.* Boston: Allyn & Bacon, 1980.

Strupp, H. H. Specific or nonspecific factors in psychotherapy and the problems of control. *Archives of General Psychiatry*, 1970, 23, 393–401.

Strupp, H. H. On the basic ingredients of psychotherapy. *Journal of Consulting and Clinical Psychology*, 1973, 41, 1–8.

Sue, D. W. World views and counseling. *Personnel and Guidance Journal*, 1978, 56, 458–463.

Taft, R. *From stranger to citizen.* London: Tavistock, 1966.

Taft, R. Coping with unfamiliar environments. In N. Warren (Ed.), *Studies of cross-cultural psychology* (Vol. 1). London: Academic Press, 1977.

Torrey, E. F. *The mind game: Witchdoctors and psychiatrists.* New York: Emerson Hall, 1972.

Triandis, H. C., Malpass, R. S., & Davidson, A. R. Psychology and culture. *Annual Review of Psychology,* 1973, *24,* 355–378.

Tseng, W. S., & Hsu, J. Subclinical disorders. In H. C. Triandis & J. G. Draguns (Eds.), *Handbook of cross-cultural psychology, Vol. 6: Psychopathology.* Boston: Allyn & Bacon, 1980.

Vexliard, A. Tempérament et modalités d'adaptation. *Bulletin de Psychologie,* 1968, *21,* 1–15.

Walz, G. R., & Benjamin, L. (Eds.). *Transcultural counseling.* New York: Human Sciences Press, 1978.

Wittkower, E. D., & Dubreuil, G. Psychocultural stress in relation to mental illness. *Social Science and Medicine,* 1973, *7,* 691–704.

Wittkower, E. D., & Warnes, H. Cultural aspects of psychotherapy. *American Journal of Psychotherapy,* 1974, *38,* 566–573.

Wohl, J. Counseling and guidance in Asia: Impressions about a developing profession. *International Journal for the Advancement of Counseling,* 1978, *1,* 209–223.

2

The Cultural Inclusiveness
of Counseling*

Paul B. Pedersen

Counselors are increasingly confronted with pressures from culturally different clients who challenge their basic assumptions about mental health. Questions of ethnic and racial identity have increased consumer demand for awareness of special mental health needs from many cultural perspectives. Counseling has responded to these pressures from both within and without the field to include cultural awareness in counseling. From within the field of counseling, publications have begun to acknowledge the importance of cultural variables in all counseling activities (Atkinson, Morten, & Sue, 1979; Draguns, 1980, in press; Henderson, 1979; Kinzie, 1978; Marsella & Pedersen, 1981; Sue, 1981; Tapp, 1980; Walz & Benjamin, 1978). Influences are also felt from the developing field of "cross-cultural psychology" (Marsella, Tharp, & Ciborowski, 1979; Segall, 1979) and from literature in other disciplines such as anthropology, psychiatry, nursing, and sociology (Favazza & Oman, 1977; Driver, 1965; Hsu, 1972; Leininger, 1978). The National Institute of Mental Health (Fields, 1979), the American Psychological Association (APA, 1979; Korman, 1974), and the recent President's Commission on Mental Health (Fields, 1979) have emphasized the ethical responsibility of all counselors to *know and attend to* their client's cultural values. Cultural awareness is an inclusive requisite that permeates the whole field of counseling and is not limited to exotic populations. Non-Western alternative modes of counseling are also gaining prominence (Higginbotham, 1979; Marsella, 1979; Pedersen, 1977; Tart, 1975; Torrey, 1972; Watts, 1961); these developments have highlighted the cultural

*Supported by National Institute of Mental Health Grant No. 1T24-MH15552-01.

bias in mental health based upon services originated in dominant Western cultures (Diaz-Guerrero, 1977; Pande, 1968; Sampson, 1977).

The topics of culture and personality, intercultural adjustment, cultural bias in counseling, counselor-client relationships, special populations, and research-training needs are discussed in this chapter. I will try to show how these topics emphasize the relevance of cultural awareness to all counseling relationships. Cultural awareness protects the counselor against either underemphasizing or overemphasizing cultural differences in counseling. It promotes compatibility of the world views of clients and counselors. The boundaries of cross-cultural counseling extend into all aspects of counseling and therapy, and the resulting insights are not limited to persons from different ethnic or nationality groups. As will become more apparent later in this chapter, the insights derived from counseling across national and ethnic boundaries provide an analogy for counseling with each special interest group or affiliation.

We are experiencing a social revolution that has brought about an expectation of equality among nations, races, sexes, and generations. We have been taught that only those who made use of their opportunities and developed special skills could be assured of their fair share. Dreikurs (1972), however, contends that the concept of equality is thus diluted to a doctrine of "equal opportunity," which simply defends the equal right to become unequal by competing with one's fellows. Bryne (1977) provides additional discussion on how the perception of equality has politicized the delivery of mental health services. This equal-opportunity doctrine has the potential for setting groups against one another rather than bringing them together. Social harmony depends on cooperating together as equals without reliance on autocratic principles where one group seeks to overpower and control the others (Segall, 1979). The basic issues of mental health focus on the adjustment of individuals within their own sociocultural context, requiring that we reexamine the basic assumptions of our own culturally biased perspective.

Cultural Systems, Personality Types, and Mental Health Services

The interrelationship between culture and personality has been systematically studied more often by anthropologists than by psychologists (Favazza & Oman 1977). The literature is polarized into two opposing ways of looking at personality in relation to culture. One position takes the view that there is a fixed state of mental health where observation is obscured by cultural distortions and which relates cultural behaviors to some universal, or etic, definition of acceptable behavior. This position assumes that there is a single, universal definition of mental health, whatever the person's origin. A contrasting position views intercultural differences as clues to divergent attitudes, values, and assumptions that differentiate one culture from another in a relativist framework based on emic perspectives. Berry (1969, 1980) discusses the logic of integrating both an emic and an etic perspective which is the more common contemporary view. There is a tendency to take culture-specific emic norms and apply them universally as etic values by the dominant culture.

1. *Theories of Culture and Mental Health*

Anthropologists have tended to take a relativist position when classifying and interpreting behavior. Typically, they have identified diverse behaviors as specific to each culture, allowing multiple notions of acceptable behavior to coexist with one another in the intercultural situation, and have examined each culture as a separate configuration (Sears, 1970). Psychologists, on the other hand, have tended to link social characteristics and psychological phenomena, while giving only minimum attention to the different intercultural values. Draguns and Phillips (1972) claim that only with the recent emergence of social psychiatry as a discipline have systematic observations been applied to studying the influence of social and cultural factors upon psychopathological systems. The interface between psychology and anthropology has been dealt with more extensively by Edgerton (1974) and Price-Williams (1974).

Psychiatry has produced the most systematic literature in which conditions of mental health are described in a way that will accommodate both the universal and relativist view (Caudill & Lin, 1969; Fromm, 1955; Kaplan, 1961; Lebra, 1972; Opler, 1959; Pedersen, 1974). Psychiatry has tended to emphasize in-depth study of culture-bound disorders, those unique to isolated areas of the world, from the point of view of the medical (biochemical, neurophysiological, and physiological) models (Yap, 1969). The common assumption that cultural factors condition the basic form and structure of problems makes this literature valuable and relevant to counseling. The overlapping categories of anthropological psychiatry, ethnopsychiatry, transcultural psychiatry, and intercultural psychiatry demonstrate the interdisciplinary coverage shared by psychiatry, social science, and public health that lacks coordination and often confuses persons interested in intercultural counseling.

The annotated bibliographies by Favazza and Oman (1977) and Driver (1965) review thousands of publications on anthropological and cross-cultural themes in mental health. They conclude that normative behavior is an abstraction and that people rarely conform to all the culturally defined rules of their society. Triandis and Draguns (1980) review the essential themes from a clinical perspective to separate and identify both culturally specific and culturally general issues. Therapy has been perceived as enforcing conformity to dominant culture rules. Although the majority of articles, books, and dissertations on cultural influences agree that social and cultural factors are highly relevant to individual thoughts, personality, and psychopathology, there is no adequate paradigm to facilitate research nor a set of consistent theories to guide the cross-cultural counselor. In his review of the literature King (1978) reported typically divergent findings based on identical questions, contradictory explanations for the same set of findings, or the same explanation for two entirely different outcomes. King tentatively summarized his findings that "psychopathology is universal; that its prevalence across countries is roughly the same, although special groups within social structures may have a higher or lesser frequency; that manifestations of psychopathological signs and symptoms differ from culture to culture; that the basic etiologic process with exceptions like the culture-bound syndrome, are generally the same for all cultures but also contain their basic expressive differences; that minority groups (class or race) and women in every society studied were overrepresented in the general mental illness category" (1978, p. 165).

In spite of the extensive literature on intercultural adjustment and mental health, there are few guidelines for the cross-cultural counselor. The observed differences in types, rates, and outcomes of mental illness may be due more to the social labeling and belief systems than to social causes (Waxler, 1975). The lack of a theoretical and conceptual framework for studying cross-cultural adjustment has tended to isolate the field of cross-cultural counseling from the mainstream of counseling psychology. The implication is that cross-cultural questions are remote from and irrelevant to the preoccupations of practitioners although there is a "new clinical orientation" in interdisciplinary specializations such as cross-cultural psychiatry and psychiatric anthropology which emphasize intercultural relevance (Kleinman, 1978).

2. Intercultural Adjustments and Relationships

Amir (1969) reviewed the social psychology literature on intercultural adjustment and concluded that merely getting members of different groups together is not enough to produce understanding and harmony. The direction of change depends on whether it occurs under favorable conditions that tend to reduce prejudice, or unfavorable conditions that tend to increase it. Amir's review of the literature on intercultural relationships suggested that favorable conditions occur under six circumstances: (1) when there is equal status contact between the members of the various ethnic groups; (2) when the contact is between members of a majority group and higher status members of a minority group; (3) when the social climate is likely to promote intergroup contact; (4) when the contact is intimate rather than casual; (5) when the contact is pleasant or rewarding; and (6) when the members of both groups interact in functionally important activities towards superordinate goals. Amir also listed six unfavorable conditions which apply: (1) when the contact situation produces competition between the groups; (2) when the contact is unpleasant or involuntary; (3) when the prestige or status of one group is lowered as a result of the contact; (4) when members of a group perceive themselves as being victims of ethnic "scapegoating"; (5) when one group in the contact has moral standards that are objectionable to the other; and (6) when the minority group members are of lower status in their own community. Unfortunately, intergroup contact typically does not occur under favorable conditions, and intercultural prejudice often is increased.

Brein and David (1971), Roberts (1970), and Stening (1979) reviewed the literature on intercultural adjustment from the perspective of intercultural communications. They discovered very little integration of the various approaches for explaining, understanding, or for predicting a sojourner's adjustment in a host culture. Social patterns of behavior and personality traits were not able to augur adjustment, although social interaction background and situational factors appeared the most promising variables. Whatever facilitates intercultural communication seems to emerge as the crucial factor. If we view counseling as a form of specialized communication, then the cultural barriers that prevent accurate communication become extremely important.

Barna (1970) cited five barriers to accurate intercultural communication. First, there is the obvious barrier of language. Language is much more than learning new sound symbols, and knowing a little of a foreign language only allows one to make a "fluent fool" of oneself if the implicit meanings behind highly subtle linguistic symbols are not understood. Secondly, there is the area of nonverbal communication such as gesture, posture, and other megamessages on which we depend for communication (Ekman, Friesen, & Ellsworth, 1972). Nonverbal messages are often less articulate and more emotional. Boucher (1979) elaborates on the universal aspects of emotional expression across cultures. It is difficult to recognize the unspoken codes that are utilized so automatically in a given culture that they may not even be consciously recognized by members of that culture. Such codes communicate definite attitudes which may emphasize, harden, soften, or contradict the spoken messages. The stereotypes that provide structure to the scrambled raw experiences of our own or other cultures are the third barrier of preconceptions. We perceive pretty much what we expect to perceive, screening out whatever does not fit into our expectations. The stereotype, then, has a tendency to become realized through the self-fulfilling prophecy of the communicator. A fourth barrier is the tendency to evaluate what others say or do as either intrinsically good or bad. Evaluation frequently interferes with understanding the other person's point of view of himself. It leads the counselor into patronizing the counselee. Stewart's distinction between empathy and sympathy in this book deals with this theme. A fifth barrier is the high level of anxiety that is particularly obvious in intercultural encounters where neither person is certain what is expected of him.

Coffman and Harris (1978) have applied the features of culture shock to the problems of "de-institutionalization" that mentally retarded and other individuals experience in extreme disruption through relocation or "role shock." These features, which apply to culture contact situations as well, include identifying cue problems (where familiar cues are missing and important cues are not recognized), recognizing value discrepancies (where alternative values apply in the new setting), accepting heightened emotional awareness (where relocation might result in depression, uneasiness, or even hostility), diagnosing symptom patterns (where dissatisfaction with the new environment and idealization of the previous setting develop), planning for adjustment of behaviors (where learning new coping strategies is required), and accepting a period of prolonged adjustment (where disruption continues even after the initial adjustment).

Therapy systems need to adjust their mental health services in a systematic way to better accommodate culturally diverse clients, both by giving special attention to cross-cultural variables and by integrating services to all clients' needs.

The Cultural Bias in Counseling

Many of the basic assumptions of counseling and therapy reflect the social, economic, and political context of Western cultures as well as imply the universal applicability of these assumptions in non-Western cultures (Pedersen, 1977, 1979). Challenging the universality of Western-based psychology is not to deny psychology's scientific character (Diaz-Guerrero, 1977) but rather to recognize alternative assumptions from other cultural perspectives. Sampson (1977), for example, cites the androgynous ideal of normality as reflecting an individualistic social science in which persons need to be self-contained and self-sufficient to be successful. Rotenberg (1974) and Draguns (1974) describe how the influence of the Protestant ethic's enhancement of a scientific, rational approach to psychopathology in Western psychology idealizes active adjustment rather than passive acceptance in striving for success. The acceptance of the Protestant ethic has contributed historically to the separation of people into categories of good/bad or sick/healthy, predestined by the dualistic labels of therapy to reject the mentally ill. Hsu (1972) rejects individualism and describes mental health in terms of an interpersonal nexus in his theory of psychosocial homeostasis as an alternative which emphasizes the individual-in-context and the relationship between persons as primary.

1. Cultural Differences

There are many discussions of cultural bias in the literature. Marsella (1978) points out that non-Western cultures have tended to emulate the West as a social model, adopting Western assumptions in the process of modernization. Capra (1975) contrasts the mechanistic Western view with the organic Eastern view. In this alternative view, all events are interrelated, connected, and manifested in the same ultimate reality. Capra concludes that modern quantum physics leads us towards a view more similar to the assumption of Eastern mysticism regarding the nature of reality: "The further we penetrate into the submicroscopic world the more we shall realize how the modern physicist, like the Eastern mystic, has come to see the world as a system of inseparable, interacting and ever-moving components with man as an integral part of this system" (1975, p. 11). Pande (1968) is critical of Western notions of development where adulthood is the symbolic goal where one attains values of self-reliance, power, achievement, responsibility, work, and sexual fulfillment and where dependence on others is classified as childish and excessively emotional. Tart (1975) discusses dozens of examples where non-Western cultures include extrasensory information about human experience beyond the normal boundaries of psychological analysis. To communicate with a wider cultural range of clients will require counseling that includes supernatural as well as natural and sociopsychological and biomedical data in understanding human behavior more comprehensively.

There are models of adapting counseling services from other cultures. Watts' Oriental prescription (1961) which provides a "way of liberation" resembles the processes of liberation described by Jung, selfactualization described by Maslow, functional autonomy described by Allport, and creative selfhood described by Adler. Although Watts was a Westerner writing about Asia, he did make a point valuable to Western psychologists: Each individual is a participant in the social game that is based on conventional rules and that defines boundaries between the individual—an ego—and his environment—a hostile and alien world. Watts went on to say that the duty of the therapist is to involve the participant in a "counter-game" that restores a unifying perspective of ego and environment and that results in the liberation of the person. In many ways the skills required of a counselor parallel the insights resulting from Zen training (Leung, 1973). A counselor working with a client in a crisis must be able to understand or empathize with what is happening to the client and at the same time concentrate on outside factors relevant to the client's problem. Whereas Western psychology has studied the psyche or mind as a clinical entity, Eastern cultures have regarded mind and matter, soul and body, as interdependent. Numerous writings on Eastern thought and culture have been done by Asians themselves from the point of view of Asian culture and religion (Pedersen, 1977).

Oriental religious training shares some similar goals with counselor education in our culture. Fromm, Suzuki, and Martino (1960) described some of these similarities, as did Watts (1961) and Pande (1968). Kiev (1964) compiled an edited volume of articles in which a wide range of cultures is described and in which is shown how mental health services are maintained outside the Westernized cultures. Berger (1962) wrote of an interesting adaptation of Zen's "no-thought" to counseling, a technique in which the mind can function on its own, free of established forms and practices. The object of Zen-influenced counseling is to separate abstractions in the form of case descriptions, diagnoses, or test results from the total reality of the counselee as a person.

Sinclair (1967) described the sequence of indigenous healing rituals in New Guinea where first, at the impact of a crisis, the victim becomes fearful and anxious. Second, a cause of the misfortune is sought through divination in the supernatural. Third, the responsibility for the crisis is transferred to a supernatural agency so that the personal anxiety that threatens the psychological equilibrium becomes identified as the energy. There are many other examples of societies, like New Guinea, where the supernatural is seen to contain hostile forces capable of acting upon the individual (Weidman, 1969; Weidman & Sussex, 1971; Yap, 1969). Wittkower and Weidman (1969) described the psychologically integrative function of magic in which something that is ill-defined, anxiety-arousing, and disruptive is given a name.

2. Cultural Similarities

To compare counseling processes as we know them in the West with functionally similar experiences in other cultures (Torrey, 1972) is an enlightening exercise. Both therapists and indigenous healers use the process of "naming" in their treatment. An attempt is made to identify the unknown element of illness by giving it a name. The therapist must know the right name to treat a destructive behavior appropriately. The effect of treatment either by Western therapists or by indigenous healers is to lessen the ambiguity of the crisis and to identify a "cause" that will allow the crisis to be explained in the culturally normal order of things. Both systems depend on the culturally determined personal qualities and credibility of the therapist to establish rapport with the person seeking help. Without the cooperation of the person seeking help, both types of healers recognize themselves as operating under severe and sometimes impossible handicaps. Some kind of a coalition between the help-giver and the help-receiver must be developed if an effective relationship is to be nurtured. Both systems depend on the client's expectation that he will get better as a result of working within this relationship. By demonstrating one's own legitimacy and effectiveness as a help-giver, a counselor can often raise a client's expectations. Demonstrations of prestige and status are used for this purpose as are expensive equipment and elaborate ceremony. The magical techniques of divination have a functional purpose in much the same way as training and certification of skill serve to display a counselor's credentials in the community. Any counselor who has tried to function in a nonaccepting culture recognizes the importance of his first being accepted in the role of help-giver. There are few techniques used in Western therapy that are not also found to some degree in other cultures, but there are techniques practiced in other cultures that are only rarely used by Western psychotherapists.

3. *Counselor Encapsulation*

Seward (1970) provided an early but very useful review of the ways in which classical psychotherapists have been caught up in their own social milieu. Seward's point was that each of the traditional theories of psychotherapy emphasizes the individual as an isolated biosocial unit. These theories do not touch on the complexity of personality development in a plural society in which each person is in a feedback relationship with several cultures at the same time. Seward also provided useful case studies of patient/therapist encapsulation where "normal" behavior for the patient's subculture group was mistakenly interpreted as pathological.

As counselors work with persons belonging to a life-style different from their own for any length of time, they participate in and contribute to a process of acculturation. The counselor may assist a client in choosing cultural assimilation, where the dominant culture enforces its adoption and integration, and where its "best" elements are incorporated; or adaptation, where the individual or group accommodates the dominant environment. Counselors who are undergoing acculturation must first recognize those characteristics of their own style of behavior, attitudes, beliefs, and personal assumptions that will allow them to experience another culture as a means of learning about that culture. Otherwise, therapists may substitute their own "self-reference" criteria of desired social effectiveness for alternative criteria more appropriate to the client's environment (Kanfer & Phillips, 1970). Bloombaum, Yamamoto, and James (1968) have presented data showing that psychotherapists are also culturally conditioned in their responses. They have demonstrated that therapist responses were culturally conditioned at about the same rate as the general public in patterns of response on social distance and cultural stereotyping as judged by interviews with sixteen practicing therapists.

There are many possible models defining the optimal personality. These alternative models have long histories, developing historically from the variety of cultures. Within this range of alternatives, the Western-based tradition reflects its cultures of origin (Coan, 1977) but not to the exclusion of the other alternatives. Although there are similarities of human needs across cultural boundaries, the evaluative labels which define counseling goals must not exclude alternative views. There is a tendency to look for the pathology in the client while overlooking the pathology of the surrounding environment (King, 1978) and to neglect the larger network of persons within which the client is located (Sampson, 1977). Our goal should rather be maintenance of the natural support system networks in the client's environment to mediate mental health. The alternative approach to cross-cultural counseling ignores the client's cultural context and allows culturally encapsulated counselors to assume their culturally limited views can accommodate the broad range of cultural variations with validity.

Wrenn (1962) described encapsulation as a process affecting the counseling profession by substituting symbiotic model stereotypes for the real world, disregarding cultural variations among clients, and dogmatizing a technique-oriented definition of the counseling process. Kagan (1964) and Schwebel (1964) further suggested that counselor education programs may actually be contributing to the encapsulation process by implanting a cultural bias, however implicit, in their curricula. Morrow (1972) introduced but did not develop the hypothesis that counselors tend to become "addicted" to one system of cultural values in a dependency that is counterproductive to effective counseling. Counselors who allow cultural values and biases to become the primary integrating force in decision making experience the same distortion of perception and dependencies as other addicts. Counselors require more self-awareness and testing of cultural assumptions in their training to overcome the disabilities of "cultural addiction."

Professional encapsulation is a result of at least four basic processes of our life activity (Kagan, 1964; Schwebel, 1964; Wrenn, 1962). First, we define reality according to a monocultural set of assumptions and stereotypes which then become more important than the real world. Second, we become insensitive to cultural variations among individuals and assume that our views correspond to reality. The assumption that "I know better than they do what is good for them," not surprisingly, is offensive to the target audience. Third, each of us harbors unreasoned assumptions that we accept without proof. When those assumptions are threatened by alternative religion, political view, or cultural value, we can easily become fearful or defensive. When the minority culture is perceived as threatening, it quickly becomes an enemy to be opposed and ultimately defeated for the sake of self-preservation. Fourth, a technique-oriented job definition further contributes towards, and perpetuates, the process of encapsulation. Each relationship is evaluated according to whether or not it contributes towards solving problems rather than helping persons. However, when counselors seek to escape encapsulation by blindly accepting the problem as resulting from the client's culture, they only succeed in absolving themselves of any responsibility to interpret the behavior of others as being relevant and meaningful.

Counselor-Client Relationship Variables

In addition to the other cultural variables which might stand between a client and a counselor, Kleinman (1978, 1980) points out the difference in perspective between the ethnomedical model of patients and the bio-medical model of practitioners, with each defining their own "clinical reality." This disparity can result in patient noncompliance, dissatisfaction, missed diagnosis, and inappropriate treatment. Kleinman points out that the orientation of most clinicians is biomedical treatment of *disease* or the malfunctioning of biological or psychological processes, even as most patients and families are oriented towards the personal and social significance of *illness* and the consequent problems created by the experience of perceived disease. While patients evaluate treatment in terms of healing illness with improved management of life problems, the clinical evaluation is more likely to depend on curing disease. Here exists a significant difference in perspective between the client and therapist which is further exaggerated by any cultural differences.

1. *Matching Counselors and Clients*

Carkhuff and Pierce (1967) concluded that counselors who are most different from their clients in ethnicity and social class or who are not of the same sex have the greatest difficulty effecting constructive changes, whereas helpers who are most similar to their clients in these respects have the greater facility for empathic interpersonal relationships. LeVine and Campbell (1972) reviewed the literature on ethnocentrism and concluded that groups or individuals who perceive themselves as similar are more likely to relate harmoniously. Along the same lines, Mitchell (1970) suggested that the great majority of Caucasian counselors cannot effect a solution for a black client since so frequently they are part of the problem. Williams (1970) likewise asserted that the Caucasian mental health worker cannot successfully counsel the "black psyche." The very notion of counseling is too frequently seen as demeaning, debilitating, patronizing, and dehumanizing (Russel, 1970), particularly when the counselor's implicit or explicit bias is communicated to the contrast-culture client (Ayres, 1970). Stranges and Riccio (1970) likewise found that counselor trainees preferred counselors of the same racial and cultural backgrounds. Harrison (1975) concluded that clients, and particularly blacks, prefer counselors of the same race, and Berman (1979) demonstrated how blacks used more active expression skills and less attending skills than whites.

There is another side to the issue, however. Muliozzi (1972) discovered that Caucasian counselors felt more genuine and empathic with Caucasian than with black clients; whereas black clients did not see Caucasian counselors as less understanding, less genuine, or less unconditioned in their regard, although they did *not* feel that Caucasian counselors "like them as much," relative to a sample of Caucasian clients' perceptions on the same measure. Muliozzi (1972) suggested that Caucasian counselors may be unrealistic in their fear of not being accepted by black clients as therapeutic helping agents.

Ewing (1974) indicated that black students tended to react more favorably to black and to white counselors than white students, suggesting that racial similarity by itself was not a crucial factor. Bryson and Cody (1973) likewise indicated that black counselors understood black clients best and white counselors understood white clients best. White counselors, however, understood both white and black counselors better than black counselors. Acosta and Sheehan (1976) provided data that both Mexican Americans and Anglo Americans attributed more skill, understanding, and trustworthiness to therapists who were either Anglo American professionals or Mexican American nonprofessionals. It would appear that other variables such as active intervention for positive change through counseling activity emerge as more important than racial similarity in assessing counselor effectiveness (Atkinson, Maruyama, & Matsui, 1978; Peoples & Dell, 1975).

Stewart's chapter on holographic analysis presents an interesting argument for limiting the principle of similarity as the basis for establishing interaction between counselor and client. The preference is for empathy which reaches across cultural differences.

Cultural differences highlight the need for a person-oriented match between counselor and client in all therapy relationships, including primary prevention as well as therapeutic treatment. These findings relate to class differences as well as cultural ones. For example, middle-class therapists are members of a different cultural group than are lower-class patients. A counselor's suggested solutions based on middle-class values are likely to be inappropriate and ineffective for a patient coming from and returning to a lower-class environment (Ruiz et al., 1978). Therapist attitudes about sex roles and socioeconomic status are important to consider in similarity studies. Erickson (1975) maintains that "co-membership" might be more important than either ethnicity or racial similarity. Similarity in cultural communication style, intelligence, temperament, social class, and social identity had a strong effect on the character and outcomes of counseling interviews of students by "gate-keepers." Erickson uses the concept of "cooling out the mark" (con men convincing suckers that the fault was theirs for allowing themselves to be deceived) in judging counselor attitudes. In his data Erickson saw a few instances of "cooling out" in intra-ethnic encounters, more instances in inter-ethnic encounters, and even more in encounters with low co-membership. "Cooling out" rarely occurred in encounters with high co-membership.

2. *Credibility of Counselors*

Variables such as treatment style and competence in dealing with cultur-ally different clients appear more crucial for successful counseling. The counselor's flexibility is put to the test when he must match technique to client. In his chapter Wohl discusses ways in which the counselor might adjust to culturally different counseling situations. Sue (1981) describes counselor credibility for the client as an important precondition for trust and understanding between counselor and client. Credibility includes both expertise and trustworthiness. Expertise is an ability variable assessing whether the counselor is perceived as informed, capable, or in-telligent, while trustworthiness is a motivational variable dependent on whether the client can believe what the counselor is saying.

Westermeyer (1976) suggests that the therapist can best develop credi-bility when working with culturally different clients by learning from the children in the host society and in a sense imitating "child-like" learning behavior. Sue (1978) suggests that the cross-cultural counselor must integrate the client's world view without losing the counselor's own integrity as a culturally influenced person. The counselor experiences a great variety of alternative roles besides the office-based therapeutic en-counter. Some of these alternatives include the roles of outreach consul-tant, ombudsman, change agent, and facilitator of indigenous support systems any or all of which might be appropriately matched to the cul-turally different client's need (Ivey, 1977).

Some of the research has attempted to relate personal qualities of the counselor to effectiveness in intercultural counseling. We might expect counselors who are open-minded to have less difficulty than would coun-selors who are dogmatic. Indeed, Kemp (1962) and Mezzano (1969) did find that open-minded counselors excel in the supportive understanding and self-exploration that are usually associated with counseling effec-tiveness; whereas Russo, Kelz, and Hudson (1964), Millikan (1965), and Millikan and Patterson (1967) discovered that prejudice or factors relating to prejudice are associated with less effective counseling (as assessed by counseling supervisors).

3. Cultural Misunderstandings

In intercultural counseling there is a greater danger of mutual misunderstanding (McFayden & Winokur, 1956), failure to understand another culture's unique problems (Kincaid, 1969), and a spontaneous hostility that destroys rapport and increases the chances of greater negative transference towards the counselor (Vontress, 1969). Thomas (1962) pointed out the pitfalls of confusing a client's appropriate cultural response with neurotic transference.

In much of the world, professional counseling is only available to the economic and social elite (Drapela, 1977). Psychological help to other segments of the population is supplied through informal networks of family and friends (Brammer, 1978). Counselors can learn a great deal through these informal networks to facilitate outreach services and to identify modal characteristics of the informal helper who is accessible, credible, empathic, caring, practical, and in direct touch with the client.

Cross-culturally, many healers and healing institutions build on the self-righting mechanisms of the client's natural support system, while also providing alternative supports when these endogenous mechanisms break down. Prince (1976) describes the importance of these frequently overlooked endogenous elements of healing as opposed to the more popularly studied exogenous factors. Under conditions of stress, these self-healing mechanisms might take the form of altered states of consciousness such as dreams, dissociated states, religious experiences, even psychotic reactions. Healing techniques tend to manipulate and elaborate these endogenous resources and self-righting mechanisms so that dissociated states can become healing resources rather than pathological phenomena.

Kiev (1969) cited studies demonstrating that factors which have been culturally institutionalized have an important role in influencing established behavior. The internal systems of social control were discussed in the context of shame and guilt resulting from internalized cultural values. Guilt was described as the internalized conscience, which prevents deviation from cultural norms and enforces conformity. Shame is less dependent on internalized norms and depends on real or projected power by others in the community to punish deviation from cultural norms.

How does a person come to do what one "ought" to do in preserving one's own cultural system? Weidman (1965) described these control mechanisms as supporting the development of a superego constellation of internalized pressures, pressures which are more effective in some cultures than in others. Naroll (1969) described societies where rules or practices involve rupture of, or strain on, social ties in ways that suggest that the society rather than the individual is "sick." Cultural identity is not always a barrier to intercultural counseling and may serve as a resource for maintaining mental health. Giordano and Giordano (1977) summarized the literature on how ethnicity among whites in the United States also involves conscious and unconscious processes that fulfill deep psychological needs for security, identity, and historical continuity for white as well as non-white peoples. This support system is implemented, for example, through the family and other affinity units in the cultural community.

4. *Client Expectations*

Should the client be forced to adapt to the expectations of the culturally different therapist or should the therapist be expected to adapt according to client cultural expectations? Goldstein (1981) suggests that the *conformity* prescription, which expects the client to conform, is less desirable but more frequently encountered than the *reformity* prescription, where the treatment is reformulated to fit the client's cultural expectations. There is some increased agreement in the literature that therapy should be shaped to fit client expectations (Gomes-Schwartz et al., 1978; Higginbotham, 1977). The previous research suggests that therapy opportunities have favored the YAVIS group (Youthful, Attractive, Verbal, Intelligent, and Successful) and disfavored the QUOID (Quiet, Ugly, Old, Indigent, Dissimilar culturally) and the HOUND (Homely, Old, Unattractive, Nonverbal, and Dumb) (Krumboltz et al., 1979).

Hollingshead and Redlich (1958) and Torrey (1972) have presented evidence showing how professional mental health services are class-bound, relating the expectancy and type of psychiatric disorder to a person's position in society's class structure. Clients from different social classes were given different treatments and diagnoses. Lower-income persons were less likely to be in therapy, or, if they were, they remained in therapy for shorter periods of time, even though similar symptoms were described as more severe. Likewise, lower-income persons were treated by less experienced staff and were treated with short-term somatic therapies generally considered to be less valuable. Norms for adjustment were defined according to the middle-class values favoring conformity, thrift, respectability, control of emotions, and future orientation.

Some confusion exists in the literature between social class differences and racial affiliation as they influence adjustment. Menacker (1971) and Sweeney (1971) have discussed guidance for persons from a lower-income environment, emphasizing that years of neglect, even benign neglect, are not eradicated by a few hours of counseling. A lower-income population must be viewed within the total context of its unique home and community environment. Gordon and Smith (1971) likewise have maintained that the guidance specialist should be concerned with changing the environment as well as with changing the student being counseled. There is a danger that the counselor will stereotype a lower-income client, disregarding individuality. This tendency is particularly dangerous when the counselor comes from an upper-class or middle-class background. Carkhuff and Pierce (1967) concluded that patient-counselor *similarity* produces *greater* self-exploration by the client, and patient-counselor *dissimilarity* results in *less* self-exploration.

Higginbotham (1977) developed a model describing the individually diverse role expectations, client preferences, forms of anticipated support, types of advice sought, or medical care requested from the client's "expectancy" perspective. Higginbotham and Tanaka-Matsumi discuss this approach in their chapter in this book as favoring the behavioral therapy approach to cross-cultural counseling. The client's expectancy emphasizes the importance of maintaining culture-relevant role behaviors during client contact to establish a helper-client bond. Culture accommodation assumes the therapist is sensitive to the client's conceptions of problem behavior, treatment goal, therapeutic expectations, and legitimate social influence agents. Congruent expectations between the client and counselor depend on agreement in naming the problem, confidence in techniques used, and acceptance of the therapist's personal attributes as appropriate.   /

5. World Views

A group perceives subjectively the social interpersonal part of its environment (Triandis, Vassiliou, Vassiliou, Tanaka, & Shanmugam, 1972). In their interrelationships, members of the same subjective culture share a way of using concepts and role titles. The perception of these values is similar. Where persons do not share similar perceptions there is not much harmony. Similarities are likely to make it easier for two individuals to be attracted to each other and to work together.

We need models for describing the client's point of view. Sue (1977, 1978) describes four possible orientations of client "world view" in a classification of psychological orientations towards counseling which reflects cultural upbringing and life experiences. One dimension of this world view is based on Rotter's (1966, 1975) distinction between internal control (IC), where reinforcement is contingent on the person's own actions, and external control (EC), where consequences are perceived to result from luck, chance, fate, or powerful others. High internality is associated with greater job efficiency, higher need achievement, school success, mastering environment, satisfaction, less anxiety, social action involvement, and personal responsibility—all valued by Western societies as characteristic of mental health. Next Sue develops his own dimension which distinguishes the internal locus of responsibility (IR), where success is attributed to a person's skills, resulting in "person blame," from the external locus of responsiblity (ER), where the sociocultural environment is more potent than the individual, resulting in "system blame." In Sue's classification, the IC-IR world view exemplifies American cultural values, the EC-IR view describes minority persons likely to have little control over how others define them, the EC-ER view is prevalent among minorities who blame their problems on an oppressive social system in which they are powerless, and the IC-ER view assumes the belief in one's ability to achieve personal goals if given a chance. The IC-ER client will seek out self-help approaches, the EC-IR client will experience self-hatred and marginality, the EC-ER client needs coping skills to deal with the institution, and the IC-ER client will demand that counseling become activist and separate oneself from the oppressive system.

A Western-trained counselor might be discredited by a client in India, for example, if the counselor sought an egalitarian relationship with village patients, did not include the family in treatment, or failed to make and guarantee medicines. In Japan the client expectations might favor disengagement from problems and devotion to concrete and constructive pursuits as opposed to the exploration of feelings. Demands for openness and expressiveness might threaten a Chinese client who would expect clear guidelines and assurances of confidentiality from the therapist. Lower-class patients in North America might expect the therapist to prescribe pills or give shots rather than to explore insights in a more drawn out verbal exchange. Higginbotham (1977) further examines other examples of client expectations to demonstrate the importance of appreciating a client's viewpoint. Stewart's discussion of empathy in this book provides additional support to the need for congruence in client/therapist expectations.

Counseling Special Populations

The coexistence of various racial groups and economic classes in our society has favored a Caucasian middle class over non-white populations. Counselors, in working with members of minorities, have occasionally been accused of maintaining or protecting the status quo. Counseling with these special populations requires a sensitivity to the issues of economic imbalance. There has been an implicit assumption by Caucasian middle-class society that other cultures do not advance themselves because of the "deficit hypothesis"—an assumption that a lower-economic-class community is disorganized and that the disorganization results in various forms of deficit. Cole and Bruner (1972), who have discussed this point of view, see the deficit hypothesis as a distortion.

One source of alleged deficit is inadequate mothering. Children in less affluent families are assumed to lack adequate parental attention, following the stereotype which implies illegitimacy and the phenomenon of the "absent father." The mother is assumed to be less occupied with rearing her family, to have less time to develop a warm, supporting relationship, and to give less guidance to her children in establishing their goals. A second manifestation of the deficit hypothesis is that children growing up in that environment lack a seldom-defined "early stimulation," the absence of which is thought to result in lower test scores and poorer academic performance later in life. The implication is that lower-economic-class communities are somehow not only different in their cultural values but also inferior by comparison to middle-class communities, although few counselors would openly admit to making that assumption. Minority classifications sometimes go beyond ethnicity.

Kitano's chapter in this book describes a classification of minority populations according to physiological types (non-whites, women, young students, aged), cultural types (according to ethnic group), economic types (poor, low socioeconomic status, powerless) and behavioral types (legal and social deviants, criminals, mentally ill, and others) (Kinloch, 1979). Until the 1960s the counseling profession demonstrated little interest in racial, ethnic, or other minority groups (Atkinson et al., 1979). Counseling focused on the average person more than on the special needs of persons who because of special characteristics of class, color, or physical ability found themselves disadvantaged in a culturally biased society. By the 1970s the roles of special populations gained needed attention (Aubrey, 1977). Distinctions were made between race, which describes biological and genetic but not social behavior differences, ethnic, which refers to the shared social and cultural heritage of a group, and culture, which may include ethnic and racial differences (Atkinson et al., 1979).

Some of the models of counseling minority group members have provided nondiscriminatory services on the faulty premise that the same service meets everyone's need; special conditions and values of the minority client were disregarded. A more appropriate alternative attempts to design a "cultural fit" between the differentially defined service and the minority client's special situation. Higginbotham and Tanaka-Matsumi's chapter in this book discusses the "guidance nurturant"-oriented intervention where the helper takes an active authoritarian role rather than relying on introspection, reflection, and extensive client verbalization over a long period of time. Sundberg's chapter in this book likewise describes minority counselor characteristics for differentially achieving rapport, empathy, interest, and appreciation of the minority culture, the special language, and the problems of living in a bicultural world. Other chapters in this book will focus on many of the special populations in detail.

1. Black Cultures

Vontress's chapter in this book discusses the research about counseling black minority clients. The early attempts to define a process of minority identity development in the community were based almost totally on the work of black intellectuals and highlighted the process of black identity transformation (Atkinson et al., 1979). At the pre-encounter stage, blacks are programmed to view the world as non-black, anti-black, or the opposite of black. In the next stage, encounter, a black person becomes aware of the meaning of being black and is validated as a black person. The third stage, immersion, results in black persons rejecting all non-black values and immersing themselves in black culture. The final stage, internalization, results in a sense of inner security focused on issues besides self and ethnic-racial needs. The Minority Identity Development model proceeds through the stages of conformity, to dissonance, to resistance/immersion, to introspection, and finally to synergetic articulation and awareness. Several authors already cited (Pine, 1972) provide comprehensive reviews of the literature on counseling minorities with an emphasis on black-white differences and sources of black values (Jackson, 1976).

2. Hispanic Cultures

Martinez (1977) provides a comprehensive review of the research on social psychology, bilingualism, testing, mental health systems, and the foundations for a uniquely Chicano psychology which identifies the basic issues of mental health from within the Hispanic perspective. The problems specific to the Chicano, or Mexican American, community are probably best described by LeVine & Padilla (1980), who contend that Westernized systems of mental health care services can be described as being largely irrelevant to the needs of the Mexican American population that he studied. First, problems of transportation, family responsibilities, and cost factors make those services relatively inaccessible to lower-income populations. Second, Mexican Americans typically were required to use English, which was not their first language. Third, the services were perceived as class-bound, with better service provided to the more affluent and powerful clients. Fourth, the services were perceived as culture-bound, guided by middle-class, Anglo-Caucasian values in the defining of problems as well as of solutions. Fifth, the services were perceived as protecting the status quo point of view. Sixth and finally, the services were considered to be less effective than those provided by traditional healers such as the *curanderos*, who were readily available to each local population. Madsen (1969), Pollack and Menacker (1971), Karno and Edgerton (1969), Aguilar (1972), and Morales (1970, pp. 257–262) have provided additional examples of the problems confronting Mexican Americans and of their resources for coping. Wagner and Haug (1971) have produced what may be the best comprehensive basic text of edited articles on the problems of adjustment among Chicanos.

Ruiz, Padilla, and Alvarez (1978) suggest that "Spanish speaking/ surnamed" (SSS) clients receive comparatively less mental health care than the general population although they actually need more of such services. The SSS clients are faced with pressures for additional acculturation and economic integration resulting in personality disintegration and need for treatment intervention. SSS clients are characterized by limited communication skills in English, poverty, limited economic power, rural values, seasonal migration, and contact with a frequently hostile host culture.

3. American Indian Cultures

American Indian cultures present their own unique requirements for effective counseling (Dinges et al., 1981). When counseling American Indian youth, the counselor is likely to be confronted with passively nonverbal clients who listen and absorb knowledge selectively. A counselor who wishes that all counselees would verbalize their feelings cannot expect to have much success with American Indian clients. The American Indian will tend to withdraw and, using the advice he has received, work out problems by himself. They are conscious of the need to make their own decisions and may resist being pushed in a particular direction by persons seeking to motivate them. Bryde (1971), in an insightful treatment of American Indian students, found one of the chief problems to be the rapid turnover of counselors. Some kind of ongoing relationship is necessary for counseling to be effective. Saslow and Harrover (1968) have gone so far as to say that school experiences inhibit rather than facilitate the American Indian's psychosocial adjustment because of culturally insensitive counselors and teachers.

The American Indian community shares many of the problems facing other contrast-cultures in American society. There are, however, unique values present in each tribal group of American Indians that make a tremendous difference in how American Indians perceive one another. At the same time, there is the attempt to develop a universal American Indian culture, as Trimble points out in his chapter.

Beauvais (1977) discussed the learning characteristics and special problems of Navajo students in training. Jilek-Aall (1976) described the problems relating to Canadian Indian patients. Gustafson (1976) addressed the loss of omnipotence felt by American Indians as a result of psychological separation from the group. Beiser (1974) found that the most frequent false assumptions outsiders make about American Indians are that they are hard to understand, that they have big psychological problems, that their culture is destroyed, and that they have no mental health service. In his chapter here, Trimble emphasizes the multiplicity of cultures and nations which constitute what is known as American Indian culture—a multiplicity that challenges any stereotype.

4. *Asian American Cultures*

Until fairly recently, the issue of counseling Asian Americans received little demand for special insights or skills. Sue and Kirk (1972) described how Chinese American students have different psychological characteristics than the larger population. Sue and Sue (1972) and Sue (1973) then listed the following options as those which are open to Asian Americans: traditionalism (resulting in problems of isolation and self-hate) and Asian-Americanism (resulting in problems of racism). Fantl (1959) discussed the problems of a Chinese family, as Kitano (1969) those of Japanese Americans.

Counseling Asian Americans can be quite different than counseling non-Asians. Kitano's chapter later in this book emphasizes the importance of indirection in counseling as a preferred style. The family as a crucial resource is seen by Pedersen (1977) as a major emotive support in the Asian personality system. Many Japanese, for example, idealize the mother-child relationship of *amae* as a model for all relationships. Higginbotham (1977) suggested further that Asian clients, in particular, expect directive, nurturant, and practical results from therapy, although going to counseling at all may be considered a severe loss of face. Neither Asian nor American models for counseling are completely appropriate for the Asian American, and the development of new, eclectic approaches is needed to fit special and unique combinations of values.

5. *Foreign Student Cultures*

Foreign students in the United States likewise constitute a population with its own special requirements for counseling services. Spalding and Flack (1975) provide a comprehensive review of the research on foreign students' perceptions of counselors as authority figures, advice-givers, and sources of information. Some more than others view counselors as authoritarian (Tan, 1967).

Goldsen, Suchman, and Williams (1956) attributed the absence of close foreign student-host relationships to the cultural distance between the two groups: Europeans interact more intimately and with greater satisfaction with American hosts than do Asians. Studies by Bennett, Passin, and McKnight (1958) among Japanese students, by Lambert and Bressler (1956) among Indians, and by Sewell and Davidson (1956) among Scandinavians similarly suggest that the greater difference in customs, values, and life-styles between Asians and Westerners creates barriers to communication.

A functional acculturation by foreign students requires that they develop new skills in both formal classroom and off-campus peer relationships. In their off-campus relationships, foreign students preserve their own identity and protect themselves against the "foreign" culture in a variety of ways. Although the quality of a foreign student's interaction with his host has been determined by Gezi (1965) to be a significant factor in the student's adjustment, other research by Klein, Alexander, Tseng, Miller, Yeh, and Chu (1971), elaborated in this book, contends that psychologists overestimate the value of person-to-person contact between visitors and hosts and understimate the importance of maintaining relationships with the visitor's co-nationals. Herman and Schild (1961) and, more recently, Antler (1970) also have concluded that harmonious interaction with fellow countrypersons is of greater importance to a foreigner's adjustment than is interaction with host nationals. Hull (1978), however, maintains that contact by foreign students with American host nationals is a factor that relates to the wide area of satisfaction with the whole sojourn experience, academically and nonacademically. Torrey, Van Rheenan, and Katchadourian (1970) pointed out that academic pressures rather than cultural frustrations complicate adjustment in the unique aspects of a university community; accordingly, foreign students should first be seen as students.

Research among Chinese students at the University of Wisconsin (Chu et al., 1971) revealed three major implications of dependence on countrypersons for support: (1) International students associate most with fellow nationals because warm, intimate, dependent, personally satisfying contacts are almost exclusively limited to members in their co-national group. (2) Their relationships with host country nationals rarely go beyond superficial pleasantries. (3) They become discouraged about prospects for deep intercultural friendships and do not expect such friendships to develop. The result is a virtual distrust of Americans and a distance which tends to increase over time. Chu et al. (1971) concluded that Chinese students returned home with considerably less favorable impressions of the United States than they had had before leaving.

6. Cultural Differences as Resources

In summary, counselors might fail when working with foreign students for the following reasons: students from another culture are unfamiliar with American counseling services, they have relied on other back-home resources, they may not consider themselves as having a problem, they are reluctant to get outside assistance for problems of internal conflict, or they would expect a counselor to be authoritarian in advice and direct action.

Atkinson et al. (1979) review the evidence that minorities are diagnosed differently and receive less preferred forms of treatment than do

majority clients. The model of time-bound, space-bound cathartic counseling is not appropriate to minority life experiences and needs. It is important that counselors get out of their offices and meet minority clients
on the client's ground and within the client's cultural setting. The intrapsychic model of client problems is not always effective or appropriate
and has instead taken on the trappings of an oppressive establishment to
the discredit of counseling as a profession. Rather than focusing exclusively on a client's pathology, we should be researching the survival
skills of minorities, women, and oppressed client populations in our
society to learn more about the strengths of these individuals that allow
them to function competently even at a disadvantage (King, 1978). Personalities may be shaped early in childhood by the values and norms of
primary groups internalized through socialization, but people are flexible. They can acquire an amazing number of new responses as the culture around them changes. Thus, value conflicts and acculturative stress
are the exception and not the rule of intercultural contact (Segall, 1979).

Research and Training Priorities

In an attempt to deal appropriately with cultural differences, Flaugher,
Campbell, and Pike (1969) discovered the need for closer attention to the
underlying assumptions of predictive studies. Their study observed that
unrecognized and uncontrolled combinations of influences on these assumptions may determine results as fully as the predictive measures
under evaluation. Freeberg (1969), for example, described many of these
"unspecific biases" in the use of tests. In the academic setting, where
achievement is most frequently measured by the ability to write well and
to do well in written tests, the cultural loading of measurement criteria is
most immediately obvious. Freeberg isolated these "unspecific biases"
and found that (1) the format, entirely verbal at a relatively high reading
level, is without the complement of pictorial information when the syntax of expression and impression is culturally loaded; (2) the content is
often culturally biased, favoring middle-class concepts, language, or experiences that tend to be foreign and unrelated to contrast-culture activities; (3) most of the formal measures are lengthy, which contributes to
distraction and poor test-taking motivation; (4) oral presentation is
seldom used, although performance of disadvantaged youth on intellectual ability measures has been found to be superior in certain respects
when oral presentation is utilized; (5) tests are designed to be administered to large, highly structured groups in which the disadvantaged
youth is not likely to seek clarification or assistance when appropriate;
and (6) tight time restrictions are themselves detrimental to noncompe-
titive individuals who have not become "test-wise" through previous experience in test taking.

   Gardner Lindzey (1961) considered the extent to which Western tests, such as the Rorschach and Euro-American norms, have been useful in providing information about persons from other cultures. Spain (1972) has discussed the more recent contributions. Cronbach and Drenth's edited volume (1972), which resulted from a conference on mental tests and cultural adaptation, addresses the following question: Should tests be used to adapt people individually and collectively to the current dominant model of Western industrial society rather than to uncover human potentialities in their own non-Western cultures? Brislin, Lonner, and Thorndike (1973) have provided a most recent and comprehensive review of interculturally viable tests and inventories, along with data from intercultural validation of these instruments. Lonner's chapter in this book discusses the assessment of test data across cultures with reference to constructs, equivalence, verbal and nonverbal test stimuli, norms, response sets, inferred deficits, and cultural isomorphism of Western-based tests. These problems are further discussed by Butcher and Pancheri (1976), who sought to demonstrate that the factor structure of the Minnesota Multiphasic Personality Inventory (MMPI) is stable cross-culturally (Butcher & Clark, 1979).

While published research on cross-cultural counseling and therapy is available, it is often published outside the better known journals in psychology. An analysis of articles from the *Journal of Abnormal Psychology*, the *Journal of Consulting and Clinical Psychology*, the *Journal of Counseling Psychology*, and *Professional Psychology* shows that only 2 or 3 percent of the ninety article titles in the last five years indicate cultural or ethnic materials (Sundberg, 1981). Cross-cultural research in these major counseling and therapy journals was mostly assessment or general correlational rather than therapy-related, mostly about blacks and Hispanics, little about Asian Americans, nothing about American Indians, and nothing on the cultural effects in either outcome or process variables of cross-cultural counseling.

1. Research on Symptoms

Research in culture and mental health has been predominantly a basic research enterprise, which has been unwittingly, yet effectively, separated from the practical concerns of program development, service delivery, and techniques of treatment (Draguns, 1977). The study of abnormal behavior in other cultures is isolated from studies of normal behavior, although increased interdisciplinary collaboration of mental-health related fields has penetrated these professional and historical barriers (Samuda, 1975). Empirical research on culture and mental health has overemphasized the symptom as the basic variable while neglecting both the personal subjective intercultural experience and the social network of client, professional, institution, and community. There is a need for data on indigenous therapies, comparisons of therapy styles across cultures, comparative effectiveness of indigenous and foreign therapies, and outcomes of indigenous therapies.

Cross-cultural counseling research has demonstrated that race variables alone cannot account for the prevalence of mental illness and are perhaps less accurate than socioeconomic status as a predictive variable (Warheit et al., 1975). Leininger (1978) describes a more comprehensive culturological nursing assessment procedure to include cultural beliefs, values, and practices in an ethnographic appraisal of the cultural context as a guide for nursing care plans and intervention modes. Leininger's work with the culturological nursing assessment has identified research priorities in differences between caring values and behaviors for technologically dependent and nontechnologically dependent societies, the role of the professional in culturally different health services, the effect of culture-specific caring practices, the rates of group support and kinship behavior contrasted with individual health care, the conflicts of interest between care givers and care receivers, and the effect of ethnocentric stereotypes among health care professionals. Yamamoto (1978) likewise suggests the need for research on why some minorities, like Asian Americans, underutilize mental health services, for the development of culturally acceptable mental health measures that avoid stigmatized labeling, for a comparison of therapy styles according to culturally determined needs, and a study on the misinterpretation of cultural data by inappropriate labeling of culturally different behavior.

2. Training Guidelines

One of the problems in coordinating the research and training on cross-cultural counseling is that there is no current established constituency for a program in ethnicity and mental health. One of the mental health professions is actively seeking opportunities to develop a multicultural approach (Spiegel, 1976). Cross-cultural counseling must deal with the obstacles of competing with other training priorities for time, money, staff, and resources. It encounters covert ethnocentricity that sees little or no need for research and training on cross-cultural counseling. It faces a lack of knowledge on how to match training, research, and therapy models in mental health with specific cultures. When cultural material is introduced into the training or educational curriculum, it is usually seen and analyzed from a dominant culture (white middle-class) perspective (Atkinson et al., 1978). In their chapter Higginbotham and Tanaka-Matsumi discuss behavioral applications of cross-cultural training, emphasizing the functional relationships between individual and cultural variables. Vontress' chapter emphasizes the importance of direct exposure to culturally different populations as a necessary part of training counselors. The cognitive awareness of intercultural ideas is not sufficient to help counselor trainees understand their own biases or to appreciate the experience of a culturally different life-style from the subjective as well as objective perspective (Atkinson et al., 1979).

Ivey and Authier (1978) described several cross-cultural counselor training programs. Jackson's "Black Identity Theory" described by Ivey involves the training of counselors through four stages of black consciousness—from passive acceptance through active resistance and redirection to internalization resulting in an increased sense of personal and cultural identity. Jackson is critical of transferring counseling insights from black to white clients without prior training in cultural identity. Ivey also described a program by McDermott which used a direct training modality through peer counselor training in the Lower East Side of New York. Through microcounseling and cocounseling under supervision, Jaslow (1978) wrote of peer training approaches in several secondary schools. Another training approach described by Ivey has been developed by Pedersen (1977, 1978) who matches a counselor from one culture with a client and an "anti-counselor" from the same other culture for simulated interviews. These interviews are videotaped and used in debriefing trainees. The counselors are trained to perceive the problems from the client's cultural perspective, to recognize cultural resistance in specific rather than general terms, to reduce counselor defensiveness working with culturally different clients, and to develop recovery skills for getting out of trouble after a culturally inappropriate intervention (Pedersen, in press). In all these designs Ivey emphasizes the necessity of matching an appropriate process with an appropriate goal in training counselors. If either the process or the goal is inappropriate, the training is not likely to succeed (Carkhuff & Banks, 1970; Lewis & Lewis, 1970).

3. Training Priorities

Cross-cultural counselor education offers the advantage of helping students see the cultural limitations of favored counseling approaches. While rapport might be important in all counseling, the methods of establishing rapport will be specific to the cultural context. While learning theory principles might be universally applied, each culture may require a different reinforcing stimulus. It is unlikely that trained counselors will be able to avoid working with minority or culturally different clients in today's pluralistic environment or that an adequate counselor training program can evade the responsibility of teaching culturally different viewpoints. Atkinson et al. (1978) discuss the dilemma of meeting federal standards for admitting minority applicants to counseling programs while maintaining a single admission standard on test scores and selection procedures. The United States Supreme Court Bakke decision prohibiting reverse discrimination against a Caucasian applicant to a medical school demonstrates a need to revise admission criteria to consider strengths represented by minority candidates as well as weaknesses and thereby avoid the condescension of preferential categories against *any* cultural group. An interculturally comprehensive training program seeks to increase the intercultural awareness of graduates. Curricula could be specifically designed with cross-cultural or multicultural counseling courses; other counselor education courses could be revised to include minority-relevant topics. The adequate training program needs to consider the resources of culturally different peoples to be relevant for both the minority and the majority group counselor graduate. Leininger (1978) has developed such a comprehensive program for a Ph.D. in transcultural nursing at the University of Utah, and Sanders (1977) is developing a comprehensive intercultural training program in the School of Social Work at the University of Hawaii.

Conclusion

There is enough evidence from intercultural studies of counseling and psychotherapy to raise many questions about our system of selecting, training, and certifying therapists, with middle-class values dominating the field. Increasing evidence suggests that professionally trained counselors may not be prepared to deal with persons from different racial, ethnic, or socioeconomic groups whose values, attitudes, and general life-styles are different from their own and perhaps threatening.

The literature on cultural systems and mental health services is confusing, contradictory, and complex although several theoretical systems have been formulated to apply the insights derived from intercultural research to wider situations. The cultural bias in counseling psychology has become more visible as alternative mental health service delivery systems are developed to deal with the variety of culturally different groups. Therapy and the counselor-client relationship must be adjusted appropriately to the situation. Each special population maintains a unique perspective, and cultural identity is an essential component of mental health. Increased attention to minority needs has helped sensitize the counseling profession to the wide range of individual needs in both dominant and minority populations. The cultural variable has been difficult to investigate because of its complexity and political volatility. The lack of a clear constituency has inhibited the emphasis of cross-cultural counseling in education and training. Inasmuch as comprehensive research designs are being developed, there are few graduate programs where a student of counseling can develop a major, minor, or specialization in cross-cultural counseling.

The question of how to provide increased attention to cross-cultural counseling is not only an ethical one—how to eliminate cultural bias in counseling—but also professional—how to deliver mental health services to a culturally diverse population appropriately and effectively. Counseling as a profession stands before us as an "individual" requiring guidance in its own life crises, occasionally deluded about reality, full of contradictions and ambivalence about the future. By analogy we may best serve "counseling" as a field by specifying the multiple cultural identities of its constituency beyond the cultural boundaries of counseling.

References

Acosta, F., & Sheehan, J. Preferences toward Mexican American and Anglo American psychotherapists. *Journal of Consulting and Clinical Psychology*, 1976, *44*, 272–279.

Aguilar, I. Initial contacts with Mexican-American families. *Social Work*, 1972, *17*(3), 66–70.

American Psychological Association. Council of Representatives minutes from the meeting of January 19–20, 1979.

Amir, Y. Contact hypothesis in ethnic relations. *Psychological Bulletin*, 1969, *71*(5), 319–342.

Antler, L. Correlates of home and host family acquaintanceship among foreign medical residents in the United States. *Journal of Social Psychology*, 1970, *80*, 49–57.

Atkinson, D., Morten, G., & Sue, D. W. *Counseling American minorities: A cross-cultural perspective*. Dubuque, Iowa: William C. Brown Company, 1979.

Atkinson, D., Staso, D., & Hosford, R. Selecting counselor trainees with multicultural strengths: A solution to the Bakke decision crisis. *Personnel and Guidance Journal*, 1978, *56*(9), 546–549.

Atkinson, D. R., Maruyama, M., & Matsui, S. Effects of counselor race and counseling approach on Asian Americans' perceptions of counselor credibility and utility. *Journal of Counseling Psychology*, 1978, *25*, 76–83.

Aubrey, R. F. Historical development of guidance and counseling and implications for the future. *Personnel and Guidance Journal*, 1977, *55*, 288–295.

Ayres, C. *The disadvantaged: An analysis of factors affecting the counselor relationship*. Paper presented at the Minnesota Personnel and Guidance Association Mid-Winter Conference, Minneapolis, February 1970.

Barna, L. M. Stumbling blocks in interpersonal intercultural communications. In D. S. Hoopes (Ed.), *Readings in Intercultural Communications* (Vol. 1). Pittsburgh: University of Pittsburgh Intercultural Communication Network of the Regional Council for International Education, 1970.

Beauvais, F. Counseling psychology in a cross-cultural setting. *Counseling Psychologist*, 1977, *7*(2), 80–82.

Beiser, M. Indian mental health. *Psychiatric Annals*, 1974, *4*(11), 6–8.

Bennett, J. W., Passin, H., & McKnight, R. K. *In search of identity: The Japanese overseas scholar in America and Japan*. Minneapolis: University of Minnesota Press, 1958.

Berger, E. M. Zen Buddhism, general psychology and counseling psychology. *Journal of Counseling Psychology*, 1962, *9*(2), 122–127.

Berman, J. Individual versus societal focus in problem diagnosis of black and white male and female counselors. *Journal of Cross-Cultural Psychology*, 1979, *10*(4), 497–507.

Berry, J. W. On cross-cultural compatibility. *International Journal of Psychology*, 1969, *4*, 119–128.

Berry, J. W. Social and cultural change. In H. Triandis and J. Berry (Eds.), *Handbook of cross-cultural psychology, Vol. 5: Social Psychology*. Boston: Allyn & Bacon, 1980, pp. 211–281.

Bloombaum, M., Yamamoto, J., & James, Q. Cultural stereotyping among psychotherapists. *Journal of Consulting and Clinical Psychology*, 1968, *32*(1), 99.

Boucher, J. D. Culture and emotion. In A. J. Marsella, R. Tharp, & T. Ciborowski (Eds.), *Perspectives on cross-cultural psychology*. New York: Academic Press, 1979.

Brammer, L. M. Informal helping systems in selected subcultures. *Personnel and Guidance Journal*, 1978, *56*(8), 476–479.

Brein, M., & David, K. H. Intercultural communication and the adjustment of the sojourner. *Psychological Bulletin*, 1971, *76*, 215–230.

Brislin, R. W., Lonner, W. J., & Thorndike, R. M. *Cross-cultural research methods*. New York: John Wiley & Sons, 1973.

Bryde, J. F. *Indian students and guidance*. Boston: Houghton Mifflin Co., 1971.

Bryne, R. H. *Guidance: A behavioral approach*. Englewood Cliffs: Prentice-Hall, 1977.

Bryson, L., & Cody, J. Relationship of race and level of understanding between counselor and client. *Journal of Counseling Psychology*, 1973, *20*, 495–498.

Butcher, J., & Clark, L. A. Recent trends in cross-cultural MMPI research an application. In J. Butcher (Ed.), *New developments in the use of the MMPI*. Minneapolis: University of Minnesota Press, 1979.

Butcher, J., & Pancheri, P. *A handbook of cross-national MMPI research*. Minneapolis: University of Minnesota Press, 1976.

Capra, F. *The Tao of Physics*. New York: Bantam, 1975.

Carkhuff, R. R., & Banks, G. Training as a preferred mode of facilitating relations between races and generations. *Journal of Counseling Psychology*, 1970, *17*, 413–418.

Carkhuff, R. R., & Pierce, R. Differential effects of therapist race and social class upon patient depth of self-exploration in the initial clinical interview. *Journal of Consulting Psychology*, 1967, *31*(6), 632–634.

Caudill, W., & Lin, Tsung-yi (Eds.). *Mental health research in Asia and the Pacific*. Honolulu: East-West Center Press, 1969.

Chu, H. M., Yeh, E. K., Klein, M. H., Alexander, A. A., & Miller, M. H. A study of Chinese students' adjustment in the U.S.A. *Aeta Psychologica Taiwanica*, No. 13, March 1971.

Coan, R. *Hero, Artist, Sage, or Saint?* New York: Columbia University Press, 1977.

Coffman, T., & Harris, M. *Transition shock and the de-institutionalization of the mentally retarded citizen*. Paper presented at the 102nd annual meeting of the American Association on Mental Deficiency, Denver, May 18, 1978.

Cole, M., & Bruner, J. S. Cultural differences and inferences about psychological processes. *American Psychologist*, 1972, *26*, 867–876.

Cronbach, L. J., & Drenth, P. J. D. *Mental tests and cultural adaptation.* The Hague: Mouton, 1972.

Diaz-Guerrero, R. A Mexican psychology. *American Psychologist*, 1977, *32*, 934–944.

Dinges, N., Trimble, J. E., Manson, S. M., & Pasquale, F. L. The social ecology of counseling and psychotherapy with American Indians and Alaskan Natives. In A. J. Marsella & P. Pedersen (Eds.), *Cross-cultural counseling and psychotherapy: Foundations, evaluation and ethnocultural considerations.* Elmsford, New York: Pergamon, 1981.

Draguns, J. G. Cross-cultural counseling and psychotherapy: History, issues, current status. In A. J. Marsella & P. Pedersen (Eds.), *Cross-cultural counseling and psychotherapy: Foundations, evaluation and ethnocultural considerations.* Elmsford, New York: Pergamon, 1981.

Draguns, J. G. Values reflected in psychopathology: The case of the Protestant ethic. *Ethos*, 1974, *2*, 115–136.

Draguns, J. G. Mental health and culture. In D. S. Hoopes, P. B. Pedersen, and G. Renwick (Eds.), *Overview of intercultural education, training and research, Vol. 1: Theory.* Washington, D.C.: Society for Intercultural Education, Training, and Research, 1977.

Draguns, J. G. Psychological disorders of clinical severity. In H. C. Triandis and J. G. Draguns (Eds.), *Handbook of cross-cultural psychology, Vol. 6: Psychopathology.* Boston: Allyn & Bacon, 1980.

Draguns, J., & Phillips, L. *Culture and psychopathology: The quest for a relationship.* Morristown, New Jersey: General Learning Corporation, 1972.

Drapela, V. J. (Ed.). *Guidance in other countries.* Tampa: University of South Florida, 1977.

Dreikurs, R. Equality: The life-style of tomorrow. *The Futurist*, August 1972, 153–155.

Driver, E. D. *The sociology and anthropology of mental illness.* Amherst: The University of Massachusetts Press, 1965.

Edgerton, R. B. Cross-cultural psychology and psychological anthropology: One paradigm or two. *Reviews in Anthropology*, 1974, *1*, 52–65.

Ekman, P., Friesen, W., & Ellsworth, P. *Emotion in the human face.* New York: Pergamon, 1972.

Erickson, F. Gatekeeping and the melting pot. *Harvard Educational Review*, 1975, *45*, 44–71.

Ewing, T. N. Racial similarity of client and counselor and client satisfaction with counseling. *Journal of Counseling Psychology*, 1974, *21*, 446–449.

Fantl, B. Cultural factors in family diagnosis of a Chinese family. *International Journal of Social Psychiatry*, 1959, *5*, 27–32.

Favazza, A. R., & Oman, M. *Anthropological and cross-cultural themes in mental health: An annotated bibliography 1925–1974.* Columbia & London: University of Missouri Press, 1977.

Fields, S. Mental health and the melting pot. *Innovations*, 1979, *6*(2), 2–3.

Flaugher, R. L., Campbell, J. T., & Pike, L. W. Prediction of job performance for Negro and white medical technicians. *Research Bulletin*. Princeton, New Jersey: Educational Testing Service, April 1969.

Freeberg, N. E. Assessment of disadvantaged adolescents: A different approach to research and evaluation measures. *Research Bulletin*. Princeton, New Jersey: Educational Testing Service, May 1969.

Fromm, E. *The sane society*. New York: Holt, Rinehart & Winston, 1955.

Fromm, E., Suzuki, D. T., & Martino, R. *Zen Buddhism and psychoanalysis*. New York: Harper & Row, 1960.

Gezi, K. I. Factors associated with student adjustment in cross-cultural contact. *California Journal of Educational Research*, 1965, *16*(3), 126–236.

Giordano, J., & Giordano, G. P. *The ethnic-cultural factor in mental health: A literature review and bibliography*. New York: Institute on Pluralism and Group Identity, 1977.

Goldsen, R. K., Suchman, E. A., & Williams, R. M. Factors associated with the development of cross-cultural social interaction. *The Journal of Social Issues*, 1956, *12*, 26–32.

Goldstein, A. Expectancy effects in cross-cultural counseling. In A. J. Marsella & P. Pedersen (Eds.), *Cross-cultural counseling and psychotherapy: Foundations, evaluation, and cultural considerations*. Elmsford, New York: Pergamon, 1981.

Gomes-Schwartz, B., Hadley, S. W., & Strupp, H. H. Individual psychotherapy and behavior therapy. *Annual Review of Psychology*, 1978, *29*, 435–472.

Gordon, E. W., & Smith, P. M. The guidance specialist and the disadvantaged student. In D. R. Cook (Ed.), *Guidance for education in revolution*. Boston: Allyn & Bacon, 1971.

Gustafson, J. P. The group matrix of individual therapy with Plains Indian People. *Contemporary Psychoanalysis*, 1976, *12*(2), 227–239.

Harrison, D. K. Race as a counselor-client variable in counseling and psychotherapy: A review of the research. *The Counseling Psychologist*, 1975, *5*(1), 124–133.

Henderson, G. (Ed.). *Understanding and counseling ethnic minorities*. Springfield, Illinois: Charles C. Thomas, 1979.

Herman, S. N., & Schild, E. O. The stranger group in a cross-cultural situation. *Sociometry*, 1961, *24*, 165–176.

Higginbotham, H. N. Culture and the role of client expectancy. *Topics in Culture Learning*, 1977, *5*, 107–124.

Higginbotham, H. N. Culture in the delivery of psychological services in developing nations. *Transcultural Psychiatric Research Review*, 1979, *16*, 7–27.

Hollingshead, A. B., & Redlich, R. C. *Social class and mental illness*. New York: John Wiley & Sons, 1958.

Hsu, F. L. K. (Ed.). *Psychological Anthropology*. Cambridge, Massachusetts: Schenkman, 1972.

Hull, W. F. *Foreign students in the United States of America: Coping behavior within the educational environment*. New York: Praeger, 1978.

Ivey, A. Toward a definition of the culturally effective counselor. *Personnel and Guidance Journal*, 1977, *55*, 296–302.

Ivey, A., & Authier, J. *Microcounseling.* Springfield, Illinois: Charles C. Thomas, 1978.

Jackson, G. G. The African genesis of the Black perspective on helping. *Professional Psychology,* 1976, *7,* 292–308.

Jaslow, C. Exemplary programs, practices and policies. In G. R. Walz & L. Benjamin (Eds.), *Transcultural counseling: Needs, programs and techniques.* New York: Human Sciences Press, 1978.

Jilek-Aall, L. The Western psychiatrist and his non-Western clientelle: Transcultural experiences of relevance to psychotherapy with Canadian Indian patients. *Canadian Psychiatric Association Journal,* 1976, *21*(6), 353–359.

Kagan, N. Three dimensions of counselor encapsulation. *Journal of Counseling Psychology,* 1964, *11*(4), 361–365.

Kanfer, F. H., & Phillips, J. S. *Learning foundations of behavior therapy.* New York: John Wiley & Sons, 1970.

Kaplan, B. (Ed.). *Studying personality cross-culturally.* New York: Harper & Row, 1961.

Karno, M., & Edgerton, R. B. Perception of mental illness in a Mexican-American community. *Archives of General Psychiatry,* 1969, *20,* 233–238.

Kemp, C. Influence of dogmatism on the training of counselors. *Journal of Counseling Psychology,* 1962, *9,* 155–157.

Kiev, A. (Ed.). *Magic, faith and healing: Studies in primitive psychiatry today.* New York: Free Press of Glencoe, 1964.

Kiev, A. Transcultural psychiatry: Research problems and perspectives. In S. C. Plog & R. B. Edgerton (Eds.), *Changing perspectives in mental illness.* New York: Holt, Rinehart & Winston, 1969.

Kincaid, M. Identity and therapy in the Black community. *Personnel and Guidance Journal,* 1969, *47*(9), 884–890.

King, L. M. Social and cultural influences on psychopathology. *Annual Review of Psychology,* 1978, *29,* 405–433.

Kinloch, G. *The sociology of minority group relations.* Englewood Cliffs: Prentice-Hall, 1979.

Kinzie, J. D. Lessons from cross-cultural psychotherapy. *American Journal of Psychotherapy,* 1978, *32,* 510–520.

Kitano, H. H. Japanese-American mental illness. In S. C. Plog & R. B. Edgerton (Eds.), *Changing perspectives in mental illness.* New York: Holt, Rinehart & Winston, 1969.

Klein, M. H., Alexander, A. A., Tseng, K. H., Miller, M. H., Yeh, E. K., & Chu, H. M. *Foreign students in a big university: Subculture within a subculture.* Mimeographed, 1971.

Kleinman, A. Clinical relevance of anthropological and cross-cultural research: Concepts and strategies. *American Journal of Psychiatry,* 1978, *135,* 427–431.

Kleinman, A. *Patients and healers in the context of culture.* Berkeley & Los Angeles: University of California Press, 1980.

Korman, M. National conference on levels and patterns of professional training in psychology: Major themes. *American Psychologist,* 1974, *29,* 441–449.

Krumboltz, J. D., Becker-Haven, J. F., & Burnett, K. F. Counseling psychology. *Annual Review of Psychology,* 1979, *30,* 555–602.

Lambert, R. D., & Bressler, M. *Indian students on an American campus.* Minneapolis: University of Minnesota Press, 1956.

Lebra, W. P. (Ed.). *Transcultural research in mental health* (Vol. 2 of Mental Health Research in Asia and the Pacific). Honolulu: The University Press of Hawaii, An East-West Center Book, 1972.

Leininger, M. *Transcultural nursing: Concepts, theories and practices.* New York: John Wiley & Sons, 1978.

Leung, P. Comparative effects of training in external and internal concentration on two counseling behaviors. *Journal of Counseling Psychology,* 1973, *20*(3), 227–234.

LeVine, E. S., & Padilla, A. M. *Crossing cultures in therapy: Pluralistic counseling for the Hispanic.* Monterey, California: Brooks/Cole, 1980.

LeVine, R., & Campbell, D. T. *Ethnocentrism: Theories of conflict, Ethnic attitudes and group behavior.* New York: Wiley, 1972.

Lewis, M. D., & Lewis, J. A. Relevant training for relevant roles: A model for educating inner-city counselors. *Counselor Education and Supervision,* 1970, *10*(1), 31–38.

Lindzey, G. *Projective techniques and cross-cultural research.* New York: Appleton-Century-Crofts, 1961.

Madsen, W. Mexican-Americans and Anglo-Americans: A comparative study of mental health in Texas. In S. C. Plog & R. B. Edgerton (Eds.), *Changing perspectives in mental illness.* New York: Holt, Rinehart & Winston, 1969.

Marsella, A. J. The modernization of traditional cultures: Consequences for the individual. In D. Hoopes, P. Pedersen, & G. Renwick (Eds.), *Overview of intercultural education, training and research* (Vol. 3). Washington, D.C.: Society for Intercultural Education, Training and Research, 1978.

Marsella, A. J. Cross-cultural study of mental disorders. In A. J. Marsella, R. Tharp, & T. Ciborowski (Eds.), *Perspectives on cross-cultural psychology.* New York: Academic Press, 1979.

Marsella, A. J., & Pedersen, P. (Eds.). *Cross-cultural counseling and psychotherapy: Foundations, evaluation and ethnocultural considerations.* Elmsford, New York: Pergamon, 1981.

Marsella, A. J., Tharp, R., & Ciborowski, T. (Eds.). *Perspectives on cross-cultural psychology.* New York: Academic Press, 1979.

Martinez, J. L. *Chicano psychology.* New York: Academic Press, 1977.

McFayden, M., & Winokur, G. Cross-cultural psychotherapy. *Journal of Nervous and Mental Disorders,* 1956, *123,* 369–374.

Menacker, J. *Urban poor students and guidance.* Boston: Houghton Mifflin Co., 1971.

Mezzano, J. A note on dogmatism and counselor effectiveness. *Counselor Education and Supervision,* 1969, *9*(1), 64–65.

Millikan, R. L. Prejudice and counseling effectiveness. *Personnel and Guidance Journal,* 1965, *43,* 710–712.

Millikan, R. L., & Patterson, J. J. Relationship of dogmatism and prejudice to counseling effectiveness. *Counselor Education and Supervision,* 1967, *6,* 125–129.

Mitchell, H. The Black experience in higher education. *The Counseling Psychologist*, 1970, 2, 30–36.

Morales, A. The impact of class discrimination and white racism in the mental health of Mexican-Americans. In N. N. Wagner & M. Haug (Eds.), *Chicanos: Social and psychological perspectives*. St. Louis: C. V. Mosby Co., 1970.

Morrow, D. L. Cultural addiction. *Journal of Rehabilitation*, 1972, 38(3), 30–32.

Muliozzi, A. D. *Inter-racial counseling: Does it work?* Paper presented at the American Personnel and Guidance Association meeting, Chicago, 1972.

Naroll, R. Cultural determinants and the concept of the sick society. In S. C. Plog & R. B. Edgerton (Eds.), *Changing perspectives in mental illness*. New York: Holt, Rinehart & Winston, 1969.

Opler, M. K. The cultural backgrounds of mental health. In M. K. Opler (Ed.), *Culture and mental health*. New York: Macmillan Co., 1959.

Pande, S. K. The mystique of "Western" psychotherapy: An Eastern interpretation. *Journal of Nervous and Mental Disorders*, 1969, *146*, 425–432.

Pedersen, P. *Cross-cultural counseling: Readings in intercultural communications* (Vol. 4). Pittsburgh: The Intercultural Communication Network of the Regional Council for International Education, 1974.

Pedersen, P. Asian theories of personality. In R. Corsini (Ed.), *Contemporary theories of personality*. Itasca, Illinois: Peacock, 1977.

Pedersen, P. Four dimensions of cross-cultural skill in counselor training. *Personnel and Guidance Journal*, 1978, 56, 480–483.

Pedersen, P. Non-western psychologies: The search for alternatives. In A. J. Marsella, R. Tharp, & T. Ciborowski (Eds.), *Perspectives on cross-cultural psychology*. New York: Academic Press, 1979.

Pedersen, P. The Triad model: A cross-cultural coalition against the problem. In R. Corsini (Ed.), *Innovative psychotherapies*. New York: Wiley Interscience, in press.

Peoples, V. Y., & Dell, D. M. Black and white student preferences for counselor roles. *Journal of Counseling Psychology*, 1975, 22, 529–534.

Pine, G. J. Counseling minority groups: A review of the literature. *Counseling and Values*, 1972, *17*(1), 35–44.

Pollack, E., & Menacker, J. *Spanish-speaking students and guidance*. Boston: Houghton Mifflin Co., 1971.

Price-Williams, D. R. Psychological experiment and anthropology: The problem of categories. *Ethos*, 1974, 2(2), 95–114.

Prince, R. H. Psychotherapy as the manipulation of endogenous healing mechanisms: A transcultural survey. *Transcultural Psychiatric Research Review*, 1976, *13*, 155–233.

Roberts, K. H. On looking at an elephant: An evaluation of cross-cultural research related to organizations. *Psychological Bulletin*, 1970, 74(5), 327–350.

Rotenberg, M. The Protestant ethic versus Western people-changing sciences. In J. L. M. Dawson & W. Lonner (Eds.), *Readings in cross-cultural psychology*. Hong Kong: University of Hong Kong Press, 1974.

Rotter, J. Generalized expectancies for internal versus external control of reinforcement. *Psychological Monographs*, 1966, *80*(1, Whole No. 609).

Rotter, J. Some problems and misconceptions related to the construct of internal versus external control of reinforcement. *Journal of Consulting and Clinical Psychology*, 1975, *43*, 56–67.

Ruiz, R. A., Padilla, A. M., & Alvarez, R. Issues in the counseling of Spanish-speaking/surnamed clients: Recommendations for therapeutic services. In G. Walz & L. Benjamin, *Transcultural Counseling: Needs, Programs and Techniques*. New York: Human Sciences Press, 1978, pp. 13–56.

Russel, R. D. Black perspective of guidance. *The Personnel and Guidance Journal*, 1970, *48*, 721–729.

Russo, R. J., Kelz, J. W., & Hudson, G. Are good counselors open-minded? *Counselor Education and Supervision*, 1964, *3*(2), 74–77.

Sampson, E. Psychology and the American ideal. *Journal of Personality and Social Psychology*, 1977, *11*, 767–782.

Samuda, R. J. *Psychological testing of American minorities: Issues and consequences*. New York: Dodd, Mead & Co., 1975.

Sanders, D. Developing a graduate social work curriculum with an international cross-cultural perspective. *Journal of Education for Social Work*, Fall 1977, *13*(3), 76–83.

Saslow, H. L., & Harrover, M. J. Research on psychological adjustment of Indian youth. *American Journal of Psychiatry*, 1968, *125*(2), 224–231.

Schwebel, M. Ideology and counselor encapsulation. *Journal of Counseling Psychology*, 1964, *11*(4), 366–369.

Sears, R. R. Transcultural variables and conceptual equivalence. In I. Al-Issa & W. Dennis (Eds.), *Cross-cultural studies of behavior*. New York: Holt, Rinehart & Winston, 1970.

Segall, M. H. *Cross-cultural psychology: Human behavior in global perspective*. Monterey, California: Brooks-Cole, 1979.

Seward, G. *Clinical studies in cultural conflict*. New York: Ronald Press Co., 1970.

Sewell, W. H., & Davidson, O. M. The adjustment of Scandinavian students. *Journal of Social Issues*, 1956, *12*(1), 9–19.

Sinclair, A. *Field and clinical survey report of the mental health of the indigenes of the Territory of Papua and New Guinea*. Port Moresby: Government Publication, 1967.

Spain, D. H. On the use of projective techniques for psychological anthropology. In F. L. K. Hsu (Ed.), *Psychological anthropology*. Cambridge, Massachusetts: Schenkman Publishing Co., 1972.

Spalding, S., & Flack, M. *The world's students in the United States: A review and evaluation of research on foreign students 1967–1974*. Pittsburgh: Department of State Contract 1742-32009, 1975.

Spiegel, J. Prospectus for the Brandeis/Heller School Training Program in Ethnicity and Mental Health, Brandeis University, Waltham, Massachusetts, September 1976.

Stening, B. W. Problems in cross-cultural contact: A literature review. *International Journal of Intercultural Relations*, 1979, *3*, 269–313.

Stranges, R., & Riccio, A. A counselee preference for counselors: Some implications for counselor education. *Counselor Education and Supervision*, 1970, *10*, 39–46.

Sue, D. W. Barriers to effective cross-cultural counseling. *Journal of Counseling Psychology,* 1977, *24,* 420–429.

Sue, D. W. World views and counseling. *Personnel and Guidance Journal,* 1978, *56*(8), 458–463.

Sue, D. W. Evaluating process variables in cross-cultural counseling/therapy. In A. J. Marsella & P. Pedersen (Eds.), *Cross-cultural counseling and psychotherapy: Foundations, evaluation and cultural considerations.* Elmsford, New York: Pergamon, 1981.

Sue, D. W., & Kirk, B. A. Psychological characteristics of Chinese-American students. *Journal of Counseling Psychology,* 1972, *19,* 471–478.

Sue, D. W., & Sue, S. Counseling Chinese-Americans. *Personnel and Guidance Journal,* 1972, *50,* 637–645.

Sue, S. Training of Third World students to function as counselors. *Journal of Counseling Psychology,* 1973, *20*(1), 73–78.

Sundberg, N. Evaluation research in cross-cultural counseling and psychotherapy: A review. In A. J. Marsella & P. Pedersen (Eds.), *Cross-cultural counseling and psychotherapy: Foundations, evaluation and cultural considerations.* Elmsford, New York: Pergamon, 1981.

Sweeney, T. J. *Rural poor students and guidance.* Boston: Houghton Mifflin Co., 1971.

Tan, H. Intercultural study of counseling expectancies. *Journal of Counseling Psychology,* 1967, *41*(2), 122–130.

Tapp, J. L. Studying personality development. In H. C. Triandis & A. Heron (Eds.), *Handbook of cross-cultural psychology, Vol. 4, Developmental Psychology.* Boston: Allyn & Bacon, 1980.

Tart, C. Some assumptions of orthodox Western psychology. In C. Tart (Ed.), *Transpersonal psychologies.* New York: Harper & Row, 1975, pp. 59–113.

Thomas, A. Pseudo-transference reactions due to cultural stereotyping. *American Journal of Orthopsychiatry,* 1962, *32,* 894–900.

Torrey, E. F. *The mind game: Witchdoctors and psychiatrists.* New York: Emerson Hall, 1972.

Torrey, E. F., Van Rheenan, F. J., & Katchadourian, H. A. Problems of foreign students: An overview. *Journal of the American College Health Association,* 1970, *19,* 83–86.

Triandis, H. C., & Draguns, J. G. *Handbook of cross-cultural psychology, Vol. 6, Psychopathology.* Boston: Allyn & Bacon, 1980.

Triandis, H. C., Vassiliou, V., Vassiliou, G., Tanaka, Y., & Shanmugam, A. V. *The analysis of subjective culture.* New York: John Wiley & Sons, 1972.

Vontress, C. E. Culture barriers in the counseling relationship. *Personnel and Guidance Journal,* 1969, *48,* 11–17.

Wagner, N. N., & Haug, M. J. (Eds.), *Chicanos: Social and psychological perspectives.* St. Louis: C. V. Mosby Co., 1971.

Walz, G. R., & Benjamin, L. *Transcultural counseling.* New York: Human Sciences Press, 1978.

Warheit, G. J., Holzer, C. E., & Arey, S. A. Race and mental illness: An epidemiological update. *Journal of Health and Social Behavior,* 1975, *16,* 243–256.

Watts, A. W. *Psychotherapy east and west.* New York: Mentor Press, 1961.

Waxler, N. Culture and mental illness: A social labelling perspective. *Journal of Nervous and Mental Disorders*, 1975, *159*, 379–395.

Weidman, H. H. *Shame and guilt: A reformulation of the problem.* Paper presented at the meeting of the American Anthropological Association, Denver, November 1965.

Weidman, H. H. The self-concept as a crucial link between social sciences and psychiatric theory. *Transcultural Psychiatry Research Review*, 1969, *6*, 113–116.

Weidman, H. H., & Sussex, J. N. Cultural values and ego functioning in relation to the typical culture-bound reactive syndromes. *International Journal of Social Psychiatry*, 1971, *17*(2), 83–100.

Westermeyer, J. Clinical guidelines for the cross-cultural treatment of chemical dependency. *American Journal of Drug and Alcohol Abuse*, 1976, 3(2), 315–322.

Williams, R. L. Black pride, academic relevance, and individual achievement. *The Counseling Psychologist*, 1970, 2, 18–22.

Wittkower, E. D., & Weidman, H. H. Magic, witchcraft and sorcery in relation to mental health and mental disorder. *Social Psychiatry*, 1969, *8*, 169–184.

Wrenn, G. C. The culturally encapsulated counselor. *Harvard Educational Review*, 1962, *32*(4), 444–449.

Yamamoto, J. Research priorities in Asian American mental health delivery. *American Journal of Psychiatry*, 1978, *135*, 457–458.

Yap, P. M. The culture-bound reactive syndromes. In W. Caudill & T. Y. Lin (Eds.), *Mental health research in Asia and the Pacific.* Honolulu: East-West Center Press, 1969.

PART TWO
General
Considerations

3

Cultural Sensitivities in Counseling

Edward C. Stewart

Counselors of college students often adopt the view that the counseling situation should be expanded into an event embedded in the wider context of the total life of the student. The need for this humanizing perspective arises spontaneously when one counsels foreign students. The problems foreign students convey to the counselor frequently bring to the surface cultural values and patterns of thinking that undermine common assumptions in counseling. These assumptions usually are considered universal and, though seldom examined for their cultural limits, they deserve scrutiny if the counseling of foreign students is to be effective.

When counselors and counselees share the same culture, counselors intuitively rely on shared assumptions to flesh out intentions of counselees, and on personal knowledge to fill in gaps in the clients' backgrounds. When the cultures of the participants in counseling differ, counselors often lack implicit inferences to create coherent images of counselees. Significant aspects of perceptions, memories, and histories remain silent. The slice of time of counseling sessions should be extended horizontally to include the clients' histories and futures, and vertically, to incorporate cultural meaning. Counselors should structure the sessions so that counselees can perceive themselves as total persons (Hampshire, 1973), beyond temporary rewards and punishments, and sensitive to unexpected cultural assumptions, values, and patterns of thought. The cultural perspective gives a focus to counseling but also introduces a knot of complexity. Counseling becomes another event of intercultural interaction, resembling other events in which persons of different cultural backgrounds participate. Intercultural communication then appears as the key to the problems of counseling, and simplifies the role of the counselor, who applies knowledge and experience from the field of intercultural communication.

The counselor sacrifices some of the objectivity usually associated with behaviorism, but the loss is more apparent than real. Current trends from objective psychology in decision making, problem solving, evaluation criteria, and behavior modification propose three ideas. First, actions are probably judged by their consequences; therefore, students should practice adjusting to norms that provide benefits from attending school, thus fulfilling the purposes which brought them to the foreign country. Along with this stress on practicality (utility), there is, second, the assumption that both rewards and punishments can be combined in a calculus that yields choices. Priorities are established according to an unspecified criterion. Finally, the time frame for making choices is brief. Choices refer to relatively immediate objectives, which tend to be practical and concrete, in comparison to more long-range goals, even those which have implications in the present. The implication of these three factors is that the individual is given limited choices that diminish the dignity and sensibilities which so many students, both American and foreign, expect.

In counseling, the counselee should be perceived as going beyond the limits of temporary behavioral contingencies and making choices according to values, patterns of thinking, and other predispositions which shape him as a cultural being. For this purpose objective measures of psychology fall short. Decision theory has failed to explain how the decision maker, combining subjective estimates of his own situation, makes a rational choice from among conflicting options. The experimental evidence, after fifteen years of investigation, is inconclusive (Tversky, 1967). Reviews of decision making in social contexts have fared no better. The theory of utility provides no way to compare the preferences of one actor with those of another (McIntosh, 1969).

In his review of how people combine individual preferences into social choices, Lieberman (1969) ended on an inconclusive note, very similar to the positions of Tversky and McIntosh—they all drew attention to an area that has not been studied. He stated that "one set of processes that undoubtedly have great influence on the social choice problem, but have been virtually unstudied, are the processes involving the effect of past commitments and decisions, and anticipations of the effect of future social choice situations and commitments on the present problem" (1969, p. 110). Although the workings of the past and anticipations of the future are largely unknown, the counselor can gain some insight into these processes by remembering typical errors committed by decision makers in laboratory studies (Slovic et al., 1977), and in real life. We shall consider counseling as a process of decision making and apply the typical errors to counselors. First, vivid and recent experiences exercise a greater influence on the counselor than expected by an objective assessment. Perhaps this result is natural and requires only vigilance to guard against mistaken decisions in counseling. Second, the value placed on securing all available information, a strong tendency in Americans, leads to an emphasis on *quantity* of information and imperceptibly degrades the standards for assessing the *quality* of information. The rejection of "theory" or "selectors" to classify information according to quality leads to reliance on practicality and facts and incurs one of the errors identified in decision-making theory. Degraded information, that is, unreliable, unverified information, influences the decision, and its effect on decision making remains even when the counselor is aware the information is degraded. Although the research on decision making has not been applied directly to the counseling situation, the second error seems to apply where knowledge of the client is gleaned from hearsay and incorporates stereotypes. The role of degraded information in counseling is potentially subversive of the objectives of the client. A third decision-making error looms large in counseling and supplies the problem for this chapter. Decision makers typically rely on similarities of superficial features to make predictions and assign cases to appropriate categories (Kahneman & Tversky, 1973). Many errors of this kind, e.g., misuses of stereotypes, lead to conclusions that Latins are emotional and Japanese are polite, which in turn evoke certain actions by the counselor. Perhaps the most important example of the error of similarity in counseling is the assumption that Western approaches are universal, permitting the counselor to disregard cultural differences. The fallacies of this assumption are discussed by Wohl in this volume.

Acquaintance with the typical errors he might commit in making counseling decisions forearms the counselor with certain rules of thumb. Neither decision-making theory nor behaviorism, however, supplies the counselor with explanations of everyday behavior. Reviews of decision-making research concur that when these theories are adequate, the conditions and issues are highly artificial. If we use decision making as a guide in counseling, we affirm a narrow perception of the foreign student. We perceive a stranger from another culture and see only a small part, with the larger, more important body of unshared experiences buried in his own unique culture. We judge and counsel him on only the small part we see and how it looks to us, rather than on how it looks to him. The reverse view is likewise limited. For our purposes it is necessary to describe actions and choices in a context of the person's total environment and identity, discarding the time-exclusive models of stimulus-response explanations. Since an analysis of theoretical terms is beyond the scope of the present chapter, it suffices to note the need for theoretical concepts—for example, *intention*—that incorporate freedom of choice, complexity of intention, direction of behavior, and temporal characteristics such as delay and duration (Ryan, 1970, p. 30). In the field of counseling, behaviorism no longer acts as a model or theory. Higginbotham and Tanaka-Matsumi in their chapter in this volume display this view when they discuss the functional analysis of behavior. Although some of the language habits of behaviorism remain, particularly the phrasing of behavior in stimulus-response terms and the use of reinforcement, the center of attention is in social and cognitive variables and not behavior as such. Acceptance of the "person," stress on "skills for regulating their own behavior," and "cognitive-behavioral status" demonstrate the need to interpret behavior and clothe it with meaning. Behaviorism becomes an analytical discipline.

Basis of Interaction: Similarities and Differences

The interaction between counselor and client may be seen as a deliberate intervention in the activities of the client—conducted and constructed to yield insight, understanding, and benefits for the client's satisfaction and improved effectiveness. The participants must create an interface which will sustain the counseling relationship and which will benefit the client. It is widely accepted that the interface that is needed should be genuine and warm and should generate empathy. The last concept is critical for intercultural communication, since empathy suggests establishing a bond, a link, based on a state of similarity between the two participants. Intercultural counseling, by definition, does not permit a totally accurate interaction, since empathy, defined as understanding others on the basis of shared qualities, cannot occur. Before abandoning the possibility of intercultural counseling, we should look into the similarities needed to sustain empathy.

Experienced counselors develop impressions of clients from other societies and may change their style of counseling to accommodate to the perceived "cultural" qualities of the client. Changes usually adapt to social and cultural customs and preferences and seldom take into account the deep culture of clients such as values and patterns of thinking. The result is that changes in counseling style typically are superficial and are designed to encourage the client's entry into the counseling process. The traditional assumptions and practices of the counselor generally remain intact. Perhaps it is fair to say that counselors derive most of their beliefs and methods from a body of values in American society, from a residue of clinical insights, and from conventional wisdom in education. The conceptual and emotional supports of the counseling process are deeply embedded in American culture. Counselors, furthermore, do not appear to be much affected by systematic research findings in psychology and anthropology. For these reasons we shall first discuss the importance of similarity in American life, then of its status in the culture, and conclude with research findings.

Similarity has been an important influence in American life since the colonial days, when travelers to the New World were already aware of the uniformity of the American language (Boorstin, 1958). In social relations similarity is expressed as conformity, and by the 1830s Tocqueville had perceived the "tyranny of the majority" in the United States, believing that public inquiry had already intruded more deeply into the private affairs of Americans than in those of the French. Nearly every observer of the United States has commented on the conformity and standardization of American life. Most of these observations have been made on the basis of European cultures and can be summarized by the observation of Richard Müller-Freinfels, who stated in 1929 (in Williams, 1970, p. 484) that "distance, uniqueness, and originality are European values, which are foreign to the American. His values are the very reverse of these: adherence to type, agreement, similarity."

Robin Williams (1970) associates conformity in American life with several themes, chief among these being the economic order and the heterogeneity of American culture. Equality and the stress on activity probably also contribute to the predisposition for conformity in American culture. Despite such general agreement on conformity, the opinions of these observers should not end the matter. It would be desirable to obtain more objective comparisons with other societies, for to some degree all men must conform with standards in society if any kind of social existence is to take place. It would be crucial to determine not only the degree of conformity, but also the nature of it, whether there is full compliance and whether a J-curve can be found in which a few comply fully while others deviate. Although Americans are perceived as conformists by Europeans, are they also seen as conformists by non-European societies?

Although research may modify the significance of similarity, the principle continues to influence values in American society. Its importance perhaps is great enough for it to qualify, for Americans, as an assumption in thought, in social life, and in communication. Thus, the more similar two persons are, the better they should be able to communicate, whereas differences impede communication. In some other cultures, however, differences may be assumed to be necessary for communication to take place, and the degree of success is not measured by agreement and conformity as it tends to be in American life.

Research of diffusion of innovation provides a critical "incident" for demonstrating the effects of similarities and differences. For nearly a generation Americans have gone throughout the world and developed programs to stimulate economic and social development. Their efforts have invariably involved working and living with people of a different cultural background. Innovators have developed two ideas that have widely influenced innovation. These are homophily and heterophily.

The concept of homophily/similarity apparently originated with Tarde (1903), who stated that social relations are closer among people who are similar in occupation and education. The term now is used primarily in the literature on innovation, and homophily or similarity is declared to underscore the adoption of innovations (Rogers & Shoemaker, 1971). A crucial comment from this source states that "when source and receiver share common meanings, attitudes and beliefs, and a mutual language, communication between them is likely to be effective" (1971, p. 210).

This statement underscores the importance of homophily. It is a position which is now undergoing modification as heterophily is discovered to underlie diffusion of innovation (Rogers & Shoemaker, 1971). Dodd (1973) reached a similar conclusion in his study of the spread of Christianity in Ghana. Focusing on nontechnological innovations, he concluded that heterophily prevails in the adoption stages of innovation, while homophily characterizes a sociometric bias of opinion leaders (1973, p. 8). It would seem that diffusion of innovation, by definition, involves heterophily, since innovation requires that change be diffused among dissimilar people. Both similarities and differences are required to understand the process of innovation.

Leaving the level of social theories, we turn to examine the bias towards similarity as a predisposition of the perceiving and thinking person. Similarity and difference may be two separate ways of describing the same situation. A dark gray may be described according to its similarity to black, or its difference from white. Laboratory experiments have shown that sounds judged to be the same and sounds judged to be different are not equivalent obverse aspects of a unitary judgmental process, such as two sides of the same coin. Subjects take longer to decide that two tones are the same than that two tones are different (Bindra, Williams, & Wise, 1965). At the perceptual and judgmental level there exists a difference between perceiving and judging same and different, with difference apparently the easier and preferred response. The experimental results disclose a dual judgment, which is available to all subjects.

Building on this basic psychological process, cultural learning may well establish a perceptual set that will seek out similarities more than meeting differences. If laboratory findings can be extended to levels of social perception, we can hypothesize that in some societies, American, for instance, cultural learning encourages the perception of similarities, while in others, the French perhaps, the predisposition is to perceive differences. These are general observations which need to be confirmed or rejected.

At a more complex level of thinking, it can be said that Americans prefer similarities in their logical rules. Induction and conjunction are clearly American preferences, and both of these aspects of thinking rely more on similarity than deduction and disjunction. In the course of his research, Cole and colleagues concluded that the Kpelle of Liberia were better at disjunctive reasoning, while Americans were better at conjunctive. This result was modified, if not neutralized, by Cole's subsequent research. If sustained, such findings would offer a clear example to the area of cognitive concepts in which American culture predisposes towards similarity (Cole, Gay, Glick, & Sharp, 1971, pp. 197–203). It is not necessary to show that a cultural difference in proficiency exists between styles of thinking, with one being better than the other, to acknowledge a cultural predisposition or preference. It can be demonstrated that Americans in their daily behavior consistently search for similarities and sameness and avoid difference. This tendency is reflected throughout their mental health service systems.

The researcher encounters in the field of interpersonal attraction a final area of research that is relevant to the predisposition towards similarity. Researchers who have examined the psychological bases for social interaction generally conclude that attraction is positively influenced by personality similarities (Byrne & Griffitt, 1973). Studies have usually been conducted with American subjects, but a recent one systematically extends the finding to other cultures and concludes that there is a ubiquitous relationship between attitude similarity and attraction (Byrne, 1973). This and other such conclusions frequently associate similarities of social environment and of learning with transcultural properties of behavior, which view in turn launches the proposition by Byrne (1973) that "our supposition is that the response to attitudes is based on common learning experiences which stress the desirability of being logical and correct in perceiving the world as others do" (p. 205). This statement implies the presence of universal qualities of logic and perception and suggests that there is a "correct" view. The inquiry can be advanced one step further to stress universal similarities in basic processes. In learning, for example, food serves a similar function as a reinforcer. Specific details differ. The effectiveness of chocolate or whale fat varies from society to society (Byrne, 1973, p. 201).

It is clear that at some level of abstraction a general psychological theory shall contain behavioral laws independent of cultural backgrounds and hence be based on similarities. There are universals of human behavior, for example, the basic processes of psychology and physiology. Although attraction theory has revealed some universal qualities in interpersonal interactions, its results usually have been based on experimental studies in which the experimenter limits alternative responses of subjects. These restricted conditions are necessary for collecting responses on the basis of similarity, since it has been shown that strong situational variables will otherwise obscure the role of individual differences (Mischel, 1973, p. 276). In unscrambling the effects of similarity and difference, one must stress the difficulty of attributing behavior to the personalized situation or the global qualities of personality (Mischel, 1973). This is a demanding research task, but a beginning has been made. Mettee and Riskind (1973) have shown that under circumstances of competition the defeated prefer to lose to those who are different, not similar. There are other examples in a useful analysis of similarities and differences from the perspective of attraction theory, but the ways in which human beings are like and unlike other human beings remain a challenge for research. The level of similarity/difference is often combined with the third level of how every human being in some respects is like no other human being. Theory tends to search for similarities, to discover differences, and then to focus on individuality. Fromkin (1973, p. 1) examined "the prevailing theories and research of interpersonal similarity, their limitations, and the ways that the notions of uniqueness limit, clarify and expand upon the range of behavior encompassed by them."

Fromkin's analysis suggests that the experimental basis of most of the research in attraction theory has been too limited in scope. Several important variables, such as the degrees of similarity, number of attitudes compared, and the characteristics of the comparative criteria, have been neglected. When these variables are examined in research, the conclusions reached are more realistic and the claims made for similarity must be revised. Fromkin (1973) concluded that "when a person engages in social comparisons of a *large* number and high proportion of *similar* attributes with a large number of similar comparison others, he will tend to assign himself a position with high degrees of similarity" (p. 51). These are the conditions under which a person experiences a loss of uniqueness, a sense that he or she is not different from others. According to Fromkin (1973), the favorable self-evaluation found under conditions of moderate similarity is replaced by unfavorable self-evaluation (p. 51).

In the paragraphs above, we have attempted to skirt the theoretical hazards of using the principle of similarity, which is usually employed in a literal sense. The contrasting concept, difference, indicates vague and undefined meanings. Since theoreticians and practitioners scarcely acknowledge, let alone apply, the workings of the principles of similarity and difference, almost any analysis of similarity contributes to explanation. But it is necessary to accept the limited theoretical explanation gained and to insist on the continuing inquiry that carries analysis beyond literal similarity and undifferentiated differences (Ortony, 1979; Tversky, 1977). Fromkin's work on the psychology of uniqueness is significant for a revision of the attraction theory. The principle of difference is approached from the viewpoint of individual difference, uniqueness, which is used to limit the applications of similarity. The two limiting conditions of similarity/difference, universal and unique, provide a theoretical basis for intercultural communication, which starts with an assumed cultural difference between communicators.

We have stressed the work on uniqueness because it provides the most relevant research for counseling concerning the significance of differences. It also raises the problem of self-identity of a client in counseling and his relationship to the counselor. In the next section we shall turn to the preferred interface of empathy and examine its appropriateness for intercultural communication. We will have occasion to refer to similarity/dissimilarity and uniqueness, the bases for introducing the self-concept into the discussion of intercultural communication in counseling.

The Interface between Counselor and Client

Empathy has scaled the pinnacle of success and attained an unchallenged nominal status in American society, a status unmarked by a cloud of either a negative connotation or a negative functional meaning. Its history in American psychology goes back to 1909 when Titchener translated the writing of Theodore Lipps (1903), specifically his translation of the concept of *Einfühlung* as "empathy." The original German refers to an aesthetic experience, and its meaning lies close to motor mimicry (Allport, 1968). It was only later that the concept acquired the meaning of the generalized ability to understand others.

The meaning of empathy was transformed in American society, particularly by those values which stress similarity and self-perception. The current definition of empathy is often confused with a second potential interface between persons—sympathy, a concept with a much longer and troubled history. Preceding the time of Adam Smith, it later declined, fell into disrepute, and now is confined primarily to pleas for compassion and to studies of children (Allport, 1968).

The rich history of empathy has yielded several subtle analyses that have been conducted in German, a language which stimulates a rich analysis of emotional states that is difficult to translate into English. The peak of analysis may have been reached with Scheler (Allport, 1968), who distinguished eight different levels ranging from motor mimicry, *Einfühlung*, to a mystical union of all with the One. A quick glance at the eight levels yields an interesting, if superficial, rhythm between differences and similarity. Thus, all the even-numbered levels of Scheler— levels 2, 4, 6, 8—suggest states of similarity, summarized as simultaneous feelings, identification between persons, affiliative fellow feelings though the feelings themselves are separated, and the unity of all. These similarities of the even levels appeal to Americans and contrast with the odd-numbered stages, which refer to differences or at least lack the common bond of the even levels. While *Einfühlung* refers to motor mimicry and is correctly translated as empathy, the concept does not necessarily suggest a similar feeling. The similarity is in terms of the act, not of the persons. The term has even been used to describe the impulse to tilt the head to look at a picture hanging at an angle on the wall. Level 3 refers to the emotional contagion which sweeps from person to person in a crowd. (It is the emotion which brings people together, not the persons themselves as in identity, level 6.) The next two levels reflect increasing degrees of intellectual detachment, feelings that are altruistic but lack the common emotional bond of level 6, characterized by affiliative fellow feelings. Level 5 represents persons who know how others feel, but the understanding of the other is conscious and detached, distinguishing the self from others. The self understands how others feel but does not necessarily endorse their actions. At the final level of empathy, 7, the self senses the state of mind of the other and prizes and respects it.

Scheler's levels easily incorporate the ideas both of sympathy and empathy. Even-numbered levels show a clear progression from a temporary fusion of self with others to the complete unity of Scheler's mystical level 8, often identified with religious feelings. Empathy, in the odd-numbered levels, suggests a separation between self and others. It is a more complex progression than sympathy: uniqueness and difference would appear to have infinite roots. Scheler's analysis is tentative and must be considered suggestive at best. Nevertheless, it draws attention to at least two interfaces that occur in intercultural communication. Wispé (1968) derived the etymological structure of both sympathy and empathy and finds that connotations of negative affect predominate. In sympathy, the simpler of the two interfaces, I (the subject) know that you are in pain and I sympathize with you. I use my own feelings as the barometer; hence, I feel my sympathy and my pain, not yours. You are judged by my perception of my own feelings (Wispé, 1968, p. 441).

Empathy, based on differences, is the more complex interface. Wispé makes an important distinction when he separates empathy as an act from empathic understanding (1968, p. 441). It is possible for the counselor to attain empathic understanding through the mechanism of sympathy. Our discussion will focus on the act itself, identifying four components for the interface: (1) Empathy is the self-conscious awareness of the consciousness of others. (2) The effort to understand the other person encompasses not only the presumed consciousness, but also the perceptions of the others' thoughts and feelings and the muscular tensions of kinesics. The empathizer (at least in the case of the Japanese) also attempts to understand the causes of the other's temporary state of consciousness. (3) The empathizer focuses on the imagination that serves to transpose oneself into another rather than upon *own feelings* as in sympathy. (4) Empathy denotes an active referent: the empathizer attends to the feelings of another and goes so far as to feel the other's pain (Wispé, 1968, p. 441).

The abstract discussion of sympathy and empathy can be relieved and brought closer to the issues encountered by counselors and clients through examples. In a workshop for counselors built around psychodrama, one example involved a police officer who was called to investigate a citizen's threat to kill the president of the local draft board. The officer was informed that the citizen had just learned that his son, a draftee, had been killed in Vietnam. When the officer approached the citizen, he encountered a man possessed by grief and hate. The officer responded by taking great pains to identify his own feelings as a young man and those of others he knew in Vietnam. This is *sympathy*.

An internal monologue of a counselor, corresponding to sympathy, might in part reconstruct the above counseling session thus:

> *I feel good* about this session. He [the client] was speaking more openly about his feelings; that's movement. It has taken a long time. *I felt very good* when he admitted his fear to reveal his inner feelings. *I felt* he took me into his confidence. *I now feel* that we can get to the bottom of this problem. I am sure that he will be a better person because of it.

In the example, reconstructed from many episodes, notice the American value judgment as to the desirability of "let it all hang out," as Alexander et al. describe in chapter 10. It is the counselor's feelings and intuitions that assess the behavior of the client displaying the paradox in psychology: self-assessment relies primarily on intentions and feelings while other-assessment stresses behavior. This psychic asymmetry seems anchored in sympathy while empathy appears more balanced. In the same scene regarding the Vietnamese War, a second police officer entered the house of the citizen, spotted a picture on the wall, began to talk about it, and engaged the man in conversation about the objects that both perceived. Out of this conversation developed information about the family and the son who had been reported killed, without the police officer ever establishing a basis of personal similarity with the man or with the dead son. The officer did respond to the emotions of the citizen but did not use his own emotional identity to guide his responses. This is *empathy*. The Japanese are known for it; an everyday example from Japan serves to illustrate it:

> K. was speaking with her friend but also listening to the conversation between her husband and the foreign guest in an adjoining room. After an hour or so she noticed that the speech of the guest slowed and his voice became a little husky. She remembered that they had talked late into the night after a hard day's journey and another leg of the journey would begin in a few hours. In a few minutes K. left her companion, walked into the adjoining room and spoke

with her husband in Japanese. He translated to the guest that his wife had said that his [the guest's] conversation now revealed that he was tired and that she would serve refreshments.

The two interfaces, sympathy and empathy, may be approached from another direction and described in relation to defense mechanisms. Sympathy, encircling personal responses and emotions, is part of the domain of introjection. The outward movement of empathy, in which the person engages the emotions of the other, clearly brings the interface close to the mechanism of projection. The distinctions between the two concepts seem to match, so that we can refer to sympathetic introjection and empathic projection. The important question for counseling and communication posed by the matching concepts is whether sympathy goes along with projection and empathy with introjection. The choice in American society seems to have been made both for introjection and sympathy.

Perhaps it is rash to propose sympathy as the interface Americans prefer when it is empathy that has attained a nominal status. Whichever the case, Americans create a sense of understanding and of intimacy with others when they refer to a common experience in the past, as Mead (1964) has pointed out. They search for a place visited in common. They search their lives for people they have known and they examine shared experiences. They identify similar roles in sympathy. For persons who develop interfaces of empathy, however, there is a shared domain but there is no intent or desire to share identities in either time or space or to integrate roles. The sympathetic or empathetic interface exhibited by a person can be seen as an extension of the self-concept, which probably governs the kind of interface that the person habitually employs in social exchanges. In American society, the confusion between sympathy and empathy can be explained as a confusion between *acts* and understanding and can also be associated with the dominant concept of the self which has prevailed in the society.

The dominant pattern of the American self-perception lacks clearly recognized structures of values and beliefs (McClelland, Sturr, Knapp, & Wendt, 1958). There are motivating needs and required responses, but the self is known by actions and by fears of dependence, a core value called self-reliance (Hsu, 1972). Each individual should be his own master, control his own destiny, and attribute his successes and failures in society to his own efforts (Hsu, 1972). As a general rule, individualism prevents Americans from forming deep and abiding bonds with others. Typically Americans establish a general belongingness with other persons while retaining a private inner core of the self (Rogers, 1964), inaccessible and isolated in a subjective world from the "selves" of all other persons. Others are not usually given the same subjective existence so that the "self" is different from other selves in a sweeping subjective sense that cannot be matched by differences between any two "others." The American self is unique: it is the quantum of the culture (Stewart, 1971b). The meaning of identity derives from the individual's happening, his doings and attainments. Americans put little stress on the individual as a link between ancestors and progeny and give little thought to an individual's membership in family, clan, or some other collectivity. Aspects of the political, social, or economic orders likewise leave the self vacant and do not flesh it out. There is no reason for the existence of the American self other than in itself. Simone de Beauvoir remarked that Americans consider their existences as accidents (1964). Meaning and values are derived from an almost impersonal affiliation in social groups. The only bond for persons whose real selves are inarticulate and inaccessible—since there is no reason or "cause" for them—is a common purpose or goal in action, in groupings that accommodate persons on the basis of needs which are seen as universal.

The reluctance of Americans to perceive themselves as members of a category or a class has been often noted. It is reflected in the lack of ideology in political parties, relative disengagement from philosophies, and constant stress on performance. Pragmatism replaces abstractions, theories, and even *a priori* values as criteria for choice and decisions. The high value placed on concepts of decision, choice, and preference in American society suggests that the favored terms employed to describe personality ideals have the effect of severing the individual from the group.

It is doubtful that the self exists as an empirical phenomenon completely separate from attitudes, values, or other psychological constructs. At the same time the subjective feeling of a self exists as an empirical phenomenon, although it is often taken for granted (Epstein, 1973, p. 405). These aspects of self-perception have led to the view that the self is a theory held by the individual about himself, even though he may not necessarily be aware of the significant features in his own self theory (Epstein, 1973). The individual also holds theories about the nature of the world, the nature of the self, and the interaction between the two. These are subjects that have been treated as aspects of the culture of the individual (Stewart, 1971a) and that open up the area of cultural differences in personal theories about the self.

The undifferentiated notions of American identity, dependent on social norms for direction, help to explain the confusion of empathy and sympathy while still maintaining the label empathy as a historical relic. The tendency among Americans is to insist on their own individual feelings, choices, and preferences and to use their evocation to establish a bond, i.e., a similarity basis, with another person. Thus the distinctions between the two interfaces seem appropriate. Sympathy has been the ideal of conventional wisdom in American society, while empathy is the necessary interface in intensive interactions of intercultural communication.

Model for Counseling Session: The Hologram

The counseling process symbolizes a condensation of the individual's total life experiences, emphasizing some experiences more than others. The counseling situation is a "simulacrum" of the client's life space. This description is timeworn and difficult to analyze, but we have had occasion to turn to technology and to use the hologram principle as a model for the counseling situation. "In a hologram the information in a scene is recorded on a photographic plate in the form of a complex interference, or diffraction, pattern that appears meaningless. When the pattern is illuminated by coherent light, however, the original image is reconstructed. What makes the hologram unique as a storage device is that every element in the original image is distributed over the entire photographic plate" (Pribram, 1969, p. 73). The hologram represents an image that is not intelligible; the original can be obtained only through a reconstruction. This process parallels the process of reconstruction in the interaction between a counselor and the client in the intercultural situation.

There are several characteristics of a hologram which are important for the model of counseling. First, the usual hologram resembles intricate patterns of contour lines on a map. The observer cannot identify the objects it represents from the incomplete holographic image, since there is no photographic similarity between the two. Thus, the principle of similarity, which often functions in both perception and thinking, does not operate to represent the object in the hologram. By analogy there is no reason to find in the counseling situation superficial resemblances to the other life experiences of the client. Second, every aspect of the hologram reproduces the entire image and, inversely, the image spreads over the entire surface of the hologram. We can again draw an analogy with counseling and suggest that any aspect of a counseling session can be enlarged, elaborated, and decoded to yield the basic patterns of life experiences.

The correspondence between a counseling situation and other life experiences of the individual is not one of similarity or of representativeness. Counseling is a deliberate intervention, analogous to a pattern of interference encoded in the hologram, which serves to bring out in counseling that which is meaningful and to link it to other life experiences of the individual. Interference—a term which seems too strong for counseling—is used in holography. When the interaction in counseling involves cultural differences, cultural concepts can be used to illuminate the process of interaction and its relationship to the life experiences of the student.

The hologram provides an accurate analogy for the "deliberate interaction of counseling." The recorded light patterns of the hologram represent the meaningless reflected light from an object recorded with a reference beam of light from the same source. The image, the hologram, records the interference pattern from the two beams (Leith & Upatnieks, 1965). It does not represent distinctive features of the object. To make sense of the meaningless hologram and to identify the object contained, one needs to flash a coherent light, which in optics is defined as a narrow wave, ideally monochromatic, as provided by laser lights. In counseling we lack the precision of narrow-band laser lights, but we have the developing field of cultural differences in values and thinking that can be used as a coherent light to cast on the interactions and problems of the foreign client.

There is one final point of analogy which is important—the relationship of the hologram to time. The hologram represents light waves stopped in an instant of time. Two light waves are frozen and recorded in their interference patterns. In counseling, time is brief; meaning is concentrated and reconstructed in cultural terms. Identifying the counseling session with the model of a hologram permits us to isolate a brief slice of time and yet accept the client as a person existing in the broader landscape of his cultural existence. The analogy suggests a holographic analysis of what happens in the counseling situation—a reconstruction in relation to other life experiences which clarify the meaning of counseling. The model draws attention to the crucial issue of how the student can be assisted to live and function more effectively out there through the mediation of events in counseling. How does counseling generalize to affect the actions and adjustment out there? An answer to this question requires the drawing of a link between counseling and the life experience of the cultural client.

The holographic model for intercultural counseling provides a perspective on the relationship between a segment of behavior and other aspects of behavior. It also suggests a criterion for success which is reached when counseling attains holographic meaning. The criterion of success, it must be stressed, is inseparable from the model itself, which introduces criteria for choices in counseling that contrast with other principles of explanation. First, the principle of similarity assumes that each individual is in search of immediate behavioral reinforcements. It is difficult for the counselor to generalize from the counseling situation to the life experiences of the client. There is no link other than that found in similarities. Inasmuch as the counseling situation is not the same as other life events, then the two are mutually exclusive and similarities are misleading.

A second principle of explanation is derived from information theory. The central idea is that any item of information about a topic used in communication is meaningfully related to other items from the same domain of total information about that topic. Information selected for communication implies items not selected. Thus, a student coming to the counselor has ruled out going to friends or others for assistance at this time when he states that he has made the decision to come. The two kinds of resource persons, selected and not selected, are inextricably linked. An acceptance of the counselor implies a rejection of the friend. The problem with this view in counseling is that all items of information may be related, but some of the alternatives are less meaningful to the student. Any decision assumes the ability to make alternative choices in the abstract. The information on which any given choice is made refers to events or situations that may not be meaningful to the student. This pattern of thinking uses utility as the criterion of choice. It does not allow for the decision-maker with a past, present, and future. The decision between information selected and not selected is not made exclusive of experience, perception, or values of the student. The atomism of simplistic decisions is artificial. It should be noted that the counseling event is connected to other life experiences of the individual in terms of the potential choices which he or she may make. The client's own experiences or history does not necessarily provide the connecting link.

Turning to the holographic explanation, we consider a fusion of abstract ideas and concrete emotions that occur in a field of past, present, and future relationships. Holography illuminates both counseling and outside events in an aesthetic relationship rather than a logical or statistical one. The psychology of both counselor and client is approached through layers and embeddedness. In addition, this principle of the hologram allows us to look at the individual's cognitive processes, the relationship between the individual and culture, and the connection between cultural influences and the total environment.

The counselor adopts a fixed illumination to perceive the counseling of foreign students as an intercultural experience. This view of counseling does not apply to all counseling situations, since foreign students may have problems that do not require a cultural interpretation. Because counselors should not overreact to cultural differences, the model presented is not intended to cover all counseling situations with foreign students, only those in which the coherent light of culture does provide resolving insight to the student and the counselor.

Leaving theory behind, we find that this model of counseling leads to several practical consequences. First, it focuses attention on counseling as an event in the life experiences of the client and compels the counselor to discard the stereotype of foreigners prevalent in American society. The stereotype might otherwise lead Americans to respond in the same way to a Japanese as to an Arab. The counselor should be aware of his own foreignness in the eyes of the client. Cultural perception influences perception of physical features to the extent that all those who are foreign seem to resemble one another.

Second, the approach places the various methods and beliefs with respect to counseling in a different perspective. The traditional definition of counseling is discarded and we are able to see where role playing, aesthetics, and simulations could be used together with dialogue between the counselor and the client. The hologram model has been used in part to demonstrate the contributions of these other methods, which at times seem merely to enliven counseling techniques but appear in their therapeutic effect more central and significant than the traditional dialogue or psychometric approach. These approaches, as well as any other innovative technique in counseling, should be carefully evaluated, since both the methods and content of counseling convey cultural assumptions.

In leaving the hologram model, we shall proceed to two main effects of using this model in counseling situations. We will first turn to the resistance or interference in the interface between client and counselor and then to culture.

The emphasis in counseling on the analogy of the hologram and the reference to aesthetics leads to a conception of counseling as drama. It is important to stress that the drama is internal; it occurs in the perception, feelings, and emotions of the participants. The relationship between the counselor and the client is transitory and cannot become a permanent aspect of the resolution of the counseling problem. The purpose of the drama is to use counseling to bring about a change in the client. The change and the drama in counseling are internal to the persons involved. For this reason, it will be necessary later on to develop a view of cognitive structures.

Natural Empathy

The theoretical and the practical clarification of empathy still leaves one question standing: how one person, the counselor, can have an understanding of consciousness of another person, the client. Some have claimed for empathy an intuitive primordial existence (Stein, 1964). The idea is not new. Vico (in Bergin & Fisch, 1969) stressed something akin to it, and many persons today subscribe to "gut feelings"—the acceptance of the outcome of a blind process, similar to empathy, obfuscating objective understanding. A natural explanation of empathy in intercultural counseling is essential, since the counselor cannot use sympathy for an interface and hence cannot freely employ his own emotions to understand the client. To grasp natural empathy, one should understand what happens in the perception of an event.

The layman usually assumes that what one perceives is stored in the brain in the form of a fair replica of what really happened. Inaccuracies intrude and the original perception fades, but the trace retains features of the original. The brain, in this view, is assumed to be an automatic storing box from which memory may later be retrieved. Any explanation of how the individual knows or learns from his experience assumes that all stored traces derive, in all of their essential features, from original perceptions. If the original perception has not been stored in all of its essentials, then the automatic storing box has lost traces, and the person has forgotten. On the other hand, if the individual can act on "understandings," which cannot be associated with stored traces and, in turn, with original perceptions, then the psychologist is confronted with the problem of discovering the source of the understanding. The problem resides with the assumed identity between perceived reality and stored traces—the knowledge, information, and feelings acquired by the person. The gap between "nonperceived" reality and stored traces is bridged by "empathy," "gut feeling," and extrasensory perception, which, in the last, reveals in some undisclosed way understandings that do not stem from original perceptions.

This model of the brain, accepted by many psychologists until recently, resembles that conceived by conventional wisdom. Within the subdiscipline of behaviorism, the brain was treated as a master muscle or gland. Behaviorists focused on stimuli, the input, and on responses, the output. They paid scant attention to what intervened when they described or explained behavior. Mind did not exist. Within the last ten years, however, this view of the brain has changed drastically; advances in neurophysiology, the pressures of internal disagreements in psychology, the development of computers, information theories, and the contributions of linguistics (Segal & Lachman, 1972) have contributed to that change. The intervening stage, called mind, has been reinstated, inasmuch as the previous concept of the brain made no provision to store and transform deep structures of language, organization of information, consolidations in memory, or various other aspects of perception. For these reasons it became necessary to insert mind between stimuli and response and also to suggest a causal system.

The model that is gaining in favor describes the mind as being much more active than was previously believed. Because the brain senses and scans the outside world, Gyr (1972) has described the process of perception as taking place from inside out as well as outside in. A given stimulus that impinges upon the sensory organs is abstracted or modified before it is transmitted to the brain, where the incoming impulses are again modified as they are encoded and stored (Weimer, 1973). A replication of reality, the *eidola* theory of perception held by the Greeks (Boring, 1950) never arrives at the brain, which can only know the ends of its nerve, so to speak. The act of storing in the brain, or memory, establishes a new order of events with its own principles governing that which is stored. This world of mental representation, or subjective space, does not correspond directly to the physical world of objects. One of the startling implications of this idea is that the only thing which a person can know directly is a mental representation which corresponds to an abstraction rather than to a concrete manifestation in the physical world of objects (Pylyshyn, 1972; Weimer, 1973). Whereas the influences on mental representations from the outside are severely limited by time, those from the inside regulate subjective space in a timeless order.

The world of mental representation, however, is not a static condition, since what is stored does not remain impervious to other cerebral events which take place and which further modify the stored perceptions according to principles largely unknown. At some future time the original perception may be retrieved and brought to conscious awareness, but this process itself distorts what is recognized as past experience. Memory is dynamic and changing. As in a hologram, something remembered is distributed over wide parts of the mind. Remembering is an active process of reconstruction, one that is holographic in nature, as Pribram (1969) has suggested. Conscious memory seems to match this process of holographic memory. In keeping with the holographic principle, any of many fragments of the experience can serve to reconstitute the entire experience. The same experience probably can never be recovered, however, since the act of retrieving and bringing an original perception to conscious awareness distorts what is recognized as a past experience.

This view of the brain and mind involves one additional factor which again is related to the holographic principle or, perhaps more accurately, the gestalt principle. It is the consciousness (Sperry, 1969) that assumes a role in the causal sequence of a complete explanation of the cerebral process (Sperry, 1970, p. 588). This view of consciousness, attained from the field of psychobiology, resembles conclusions reached from information-processing models (Shallice, 1972). The data on consciousness have only begun to appear and the issue is far from settled. Whatever the eventual resolution, it is clear that in this complex process there is plenty of room for the past experience of the individual to provide "input" into a raw perception so that, when it is served up, the retrieved outcome, perceived as the original event, may well reveal features which are novel to the original perception. Thus, we have an instance of understanding which differs markedly from original observations. When the understanding refers to others, we have an example of empathy, and it does not seem to require an intuitive primordial process to explain it. The sources of information and knowledge are quite sufficient to provide the mysterious source of insight so frequently associated with empathy. Our task ahead is to show that the influences from the past and from the immediate present are shaped at least in part by culture, and that intercultural sensitivity in counseling implies knowing and observing the appropriate cultural forms.

The essential point in the analysis of empathy given in these pages consists of the source of the understanding, which is the experiences and the memory of the person himself. Such understanding is not derived from external sources of stimulation but comes instead from memories and traces of language, images, emotions, and unformulated perceptions in the present. They may be fleeting sensations and experiences which lend their flow to the empathic understanding. It is a knowledge obtained from the inside, constructed by imagination and memory, and it depends on participation to take root. It is a way of knowing, discovered by Giambattista Vico (in Bergin & Fisch, 1969), that assigns to memory, to imagination, and to the immediate apperception of human interaction and communication a modality of knowing which is radically different from thought formed as induction or deduction (Berlin, 1969).

Empathy leads to understanding of another individual. In an intercultural situation, empathy should generate regressions towards cultural assumptions, values, and patterns of thinking. This kind of understanding through empathy is cultivated by inducing the mind to contribute its past experience to encoding traces and revealing the assumptions and the categorizations used in encoding and decoding perceptions.

Empathic understanding should be assisted by quick, fleeting perceptions which register stimulation from another's body language, tone of voice, smells, touches, etc. These are encoded as symbols and as information close to the perceptual domain. They are quick, often peripheral, perceptions that come close to revealing the deep structure of thought and values. The patterns of thought, the use of analogies, and the train of thought all contribute to a latent level of communication which is the basis of empathy. These assumptions and values should be understood in the ways in which they function to guide behavior and not necessarily according to the operational definitions they receive when employed to collect research data. Operational definitions often have little in common with the way in which the "concept" is stored and in which it functions to guide behavior. Apparently a natural conflict exists between firm research parameters and operational categories or stereotypes as applied in psychology, such as is evidenced by encoding strategies and personal constructs (Mischel, 1973, pp. 267–268).

If we define empathy as response to the latent level of communication, and if we accept it as the desired interface, then there follows an important consequence for the use of intercultural communication in counseling. In behavior modification or in sensitivity training, the client examines his personal constructs, style of life, and feelings. He runs the risk of surrendering his privacy. When counseling is conducted as an intercultural communication, however, the counselor attempts to ascertain and work with cultural values. The client examines qualities in himself which he shares with an ethnic reference group. He is provided with a safety factor if he personally believes that he has encountered unpleasant or undesirable qualities or aspects of his behavior that he is unprepared to accept as self-descriptive. He can assign them to qualities of the cultural group to which he belongs without necessarily subscribing to them. The counselor also has a clear task. He should consider the behavior of the client within a cultural context. He is not required to make a choice or even to impose a change on the client. Both participants work with cultural factors and are partly spared from making moral or ethical judgments. At least the freedom for choice would seem to be clearer.

Cultural References in Empathic Understanding

The use of the holograph as the model for the counseling situation implies that the interaction between the counselor and the client is not directly meaningful. It is necessary to establish a cultural reference as a backdrop for the description and the analysis of intercultural counseling. An analysis of culture provides the analogy of counseling to the reference beam in the hologram. The hologram is understandable, is coded in a meaningful manner only in reference to the beam of light whose characteristics are known. Thus the objectives, motives, action, and, in general, the dimensions of the problem of the client should be perceived as particular manifestations of cultural predispositions. Attention given to cultural dimensions acts as reference lights to the counseling situation and provides a personal understanding of the client. Interpreting the counseling event means transforming an abstract (etic) into a specific (emic) analysis.

A successful counseling session implies that the client has attained meaning at three levels: abstract, from reference to culture; general, from the interaction with the counselor; and personal, from the internalized personal constructs and strategies of encoding that provide the particularized meaning of counseling (Lounsbury, 1955). Accordingly, the etic analysis is followed by an emic one, which eventually yields to a personal analysis. Developed in cultural terms, all three levels are fused as in a hologram.

The analysis of culture yields abstractions of code, patterns of thinking, emotions, values, motivation, roles, and events—concepts that we can call *deep culture*, since they most appropriately refer to values defined as the "criteria" or the "rules" used to reach conclusions. Deep culture is uneasily tied to the personal constructs of clients, referring instead to cultural collectivities from which clients derive. Wohl, in chapter 6 of this volume, uses a similar concept, calling it "world view," while Ruiz and Casas speak of "value system" in their chapter. In both chapters, as in this one, the writers converge on the view that the human services of-

fered in counseling and therapy are embedded in the process of communication. The exchanges between "counselor" and "client" require
shared deep cultures, but these are, for us, imbricated deep cultures. The
success of counseling depends on how the results are encoded or represented in the perceptions of the client. The problem is how to express
results of counseling with the imagery, verbal representations, and acts
that will guide and govern positive actions. This is a problem which has
not received very much empirical attention. To put the problem square-
ly as a question: If the counselor and the client establish that it is
desirable for the client to pursue a course of action, how is the result to
be represented to the client? As procedures and schedules? As purposes
and utilities? As visual images? Kinesthetics, as associations with the
time and place of action? How is the action represented, that is, how is it
encoded in the client's thoughts, emotions, and values?

There is need to examine the methods used to impart information,
knowledge, and attitudes so that encoded knowledge should guide and
govern behavior accurately. The analysis of deep culture yields abstract
concepts which do not readily engage the personal constructs of Americans. The concepts of culture and cultural differences are, for this reason, frequently conveyed in the context of human relations training. The
patterns of interaction provide experiences that can be used to define the
nature of cultural differences. The combination of culture and human
relations training is not always successful, since human relations training tends to assume a goal of sympathy, i.e., similarity, whereas in the
area of intercultural situations, empathy should be the preferred interface.

There are other methods, such as simulations and exercises, that can
be employed successfully to convey cultural predispositions. Implications must be drawn from analyses of similarities and differences. Those
differences that are important for communication and those that are not
must be identified. Although there are many intuitive studies and analyses, at this time neither theory nor field experience yields conclusive
answers. Similarity and the self-concept were advanced as important for
Americans, but the counselor must exercise personal choices until research illuminates the field of cultural differences and reveals the differences and similarities that are most significant for a given client and the
counselor.

Identification of meaningful cultural differences implies that the differences do indeed affect the client or the counseling situation. Working
with the differences requires that they be perceived as relevant by the
client, that they be grasped intellectually and accepted emotionally. Finally the client should derive benefit from counseling that will lead to
actions guided by the insights obtained in counseling. One measure of
success can be attained by drawing concrete examples to the attention of

the client. These examples can be related to a single principle which the client, in turn, can use as a guide to behavior under different situations.

Summary

There is the need in intercultural counseling to consider the client as a person, perceived as the sum total of his or her experiences. The counseling context should be expanded to include an awareness by the counselor of both the client's past and future; it should be treated as an intercultural event embedded in the total life and cultural experiences of the client.

The literature on counseling usually assumes that the interface between the client and the counselor should generate empathy. The interface implied, however, more correctly describes sympathy, which reposes on similarities between the two concerned individuals. Because intercultural counseling assumes cultural differences, sympathy may be an ineffective interface.

The apparent necessity of similarity to undergird the process of communication in counseling may be associated with conformity in American life, a conformity observed by Europeans and persons from other cultures. Recent research in the diffusion of innovations, in perception, and in patterns of thinking has begun to distinguish between similarities and differences in psychological and social processes. It is in the field of attraction theory—how people make social comparisons—that recent research has begun to disclose the complex relations between similarity, uniqueness, and the self-concept. An individual needs to be different and unique, as well as similar to others. The unique attribute is associated with differences and with empathy, similarity with sympathy.

Intercultural counseling can be analyzed as possessing the qualities of a hologram. Each counseling event can reconstruct and symbolize the life pattern of the client. Nevertheless, these overlapping counseling and life events do not necessarily resemble one another. It is necessary to analyze counseling with a cultural perspective to reconstruct the meaning of the counseling event for the client as applied to experience.

The holographic analysis of counseling draws attention to the limits of the principle of similarity as the basis for establishing an interaction between the counselor and the client. It points to the need for empathy based on differences. The holographic model can provide a way of conceptualizing intercultural counseling according to intercultural relationships. Accordingly, culture in counseling can be analogized to the reference beam in the hologram.

The two interfaces, sympathy and empathy, are considered to be extensions of self-concepts. The hold of similarity on American culture, the American self-concept, has apparently contributed to the shift in the meaning of empathy, with this current usage generally implying sympathy.

Some have argued that empathy has an intuitive primordial existence, but this view has been derived from problematical analyses of the processes of perception and recall. Empathic understanding requires a sensitivity to experience, personal constructs, and cultural predispositions for an encoded trace to be retrieved. Empathy involves a response to these factors. In the intercultural counseling situation, the interface of empathy relieves both counselor and client from making moral judgments and from evaluating the other's point of view.

There are no firm guides by which to formulate concepts of differences or similarities that are important in intercultural counseling. Cultural variations of the self-concept and of similarity are two likely factors that influence intercultural communication. Insights gained through the process of empathy may be conceptualized within a cultural frame.

References

Allport, G. W. The historical background of modern social psychology. In G. Lindzey & E. Aronson (Eds.), *The handbook of social psychology* (Vol. 1). Reading, Massachusetts: Addison-Wesley Publishing Co., 1968.

Beauvoir, S. de. Adieu to America. In M. McGiffert (Ed.), *The character of Americans*. Homewood, Illinois: Dorsey Press, 1964.

Bergin, T. G., & Fisch, M. H. *The new science of Giambattista Vico* (rev. trans. of 3rd ed.). Ithaca: Cornell University Press, 1969.

Berlin, I. A note on Vico's concept of knowledge. *The New York Review of Books*, April 24, 1969, pp. 23–26.

Bindra, D., Williams, J. A., & Wise, J. S. Judgments of sameness and difference: Experiments on decision time. *Science*, 1965, *150*, 1625–1627.

Boorstin, D. J. *The Americans. Vol. 1: The colonial experience.* New York: Random House, Vintage Books, 1958.

Boring, E. G. *A history of experimental psychology.* New York: Appleton-Century-Crofts, 1950.

Byrne, D. The ubiquitous relationship: Attitude similarity and attraction. *Human Relations*, 1973, *24*, 201–207.

Byrne, D., & Griffitt, W. Interpersonal attraction. In P. H. Mussen & M. R. Rosenzweig (Eds.), *Annual Review of Psychology*, 1973, *24*, 317–336.

Cole, M., Gay, J., Glick, J. A., & Sharp, D. W. *Cultural context of learning and thinking: An exploration in experimental anthropology.* New York: Basic Books, 1971.

Dodd, C. H. *Homophily and heterophily in diffusion of innovations: A cross-cultural analysis in an African setting.* Paper presented at the Speech Communication Association convention, New York, November 1973.

Epstein, S. The self-concept revisited: Or a theory of a theory. *American Psychologist*, 1973, *28*, 404–416.

Fromkin, H. L. *The psychology of uniqueness: Avoidance of similarity and seeking of differentness* (Paper no. 438). West Lafayette, Indiana: Institute for Research in the Behavioral, Economic and Management Sciences, Krannert Graduate School of Industrial Administration, Purdue University, 1973.

Gyr, J. W. Is a theory of direct visual perception adequate? *Psychological Bulletin*, 1972, *77*, 246–261.

Hampshire, S. Morality and pessimism. *The New York Review of Books*, January 25, 1973, pp. 26–33.

Hsu, F. L. K. American core value and national character. In F. L. K. Hsu (Ed.), *Psychological anthropology*. Cambridge, Massachusetts: Schenkman Publishing Co., 1972.

Kahneman, D., & Tversky, A. On the psychology of prediction. *Psychological Review*, 1973, *80*, 237–251.

Leith, E. N., & Upatnieks, J. Photography by laser. *Scientific American*, 1965, *212*, 24–35.

Lieberman, B. Combining individual preferences into a social choice. In I. R. Buchler & H. G. Nuttini (Eds.), *Game theory in the behavioral sciences*. Pittsburgh: University of Pittsburgh Press, 1969.

Lipps, T. Einfühlung, innere Nachahmung und Organe findungen. *Archiv für die Gesamte Psychologie*, 1903, *20*, 185–204.

Lounsbury, F. G. The varieties of meaning. *Georgetown University Monograph Series on Languages and Linguistics*, 1955, *8*, 158–164.

McClelland, D. C., Sturr, J. F., Knapp, R. H., & Wendt, H. W. Obligation to self and society in the United States and Germany. *Journal of Abnormal and Social Psychology*, 1958, *56*, 245–255.

McIntosh, D. *The foundations of society*. Chicago: University of Chicago Press, 1969.

Mead, M. We are all third generation. In M. McGiffert (Ed.), *The character of Americans*. Homewood, Illinois: Dorsey Press, 1964.

Mettee, D. R., & Riskind, J. *When ability dissimilarity is a blessing: Liking for others who defeat us decisively.* Paper presented at the American Psychological Association convention, Montreal, September 1973.

Mischel, W. Reconceptualization of personality. *Psychological Review*, 1973, *80*, 252–283.

Ortony, A. Beyond literal similarity. *Psychological Review*, 1979, *86*, 161–180.

Pribram, K. H. The neurophysiology of remembering. *Scientific American*, 1969, *220*, 73–86.

Pylyshyn, Z. Competence and psychological reality. *American Psychologist*, 1972, *27*, 546–552.

Rogers, C. Toward a modern approach to values. *Journal of Abnormal and Social Psychology*, 1964, *68*(2), 160–167.

Rogers, E., & Shoemaker, F. F. *Communication and innovation*. New York: Macmillan Co., Free Press, 1971.

Ryan, T. A. *Intentional behavior*. New York: Ronald Press, 1970.

Segal, E. M., & Lachman, R. Complex behavior or higher mental process: Is there a paradigm shift? *American Psychologist*, 1972, *27*, 46–55.

Shallice, T. Dual function of consciousness. *Psychological Review*, 1972, *79*, 383–393.

Slovic, P., Fischhoff, B., & Lichtenstein, S. Behavioral decision theory. In M. R. Rosenzweig & L. W. Porter (Eds.), *Annual Review of Psychology*, 1977, 28.

Sperry, R. W. A modified concept of consciousness. *Psychological Review*, 1969, 76, 532-536.

Sperry, R. W. An objective approach to subjective experience: Further explanation of a hypothesis. *Psychological Review*, 1970, 77, 585-590.

Stein, E. *On the problem of empathy.* The Hague: Martinus Nijhoff, 1964.

Stewart, E. C. *American cultural patterns: A cross-cultural perspective.* Pittsburgh: Regional Council for International Understanding, 1971.(a)

Stewart, E. C. *The self: Quantum of American culture.* Paper presented at the American Psychological Association convention, Washington, D.C., 1971.(b)

Tarde, G. *The laws of imitation.* Gloucester, Massachusetts: Peter Smith, 1903.

Titchener, E. B. *Experimental psychology of the thought processes.* New York: Macmillan Co., 1909.

Tocqueville, A. de. *Democracy in America.* New York: Random House, 1945.

Tversky, A. Additivity, utility and subjective probability. *Journal of Mathematical Psychology*, 1967, 4, 175-202.

Tversky, A. Features of similarity. *Psychological Review*, 1977, 84, 327-352.

Weimer, W. B. Psycholinguistics and Plato's paradoxes of the *Meno*. *American Psychologist*, 1973, 28, 15-33.

Williams, R. M., Jr. *American society* (3rd ed.). New York: Random House, Alfred A. Knopf, 1970.

Wispé, L. G. Sympathy and empathy. *International Encyclopedia of the Social Sciences* (Vol. 15). New York: Macmillan Co., Free Press, 1968.

4

Racial and Ethnic
Barriers in Counseling

Clemmont E. Vontress

The racial and ethnic diversity of people in the United States has never been denied. Early observers characterized the nation as a "melting pot," a folksy concept which suggested that culturally different citizens eventually would lose the distinct identities separating them and all would become alike. The concept aptly described many assimilation-oriented immigrants, immigrants so committed to becoming "real Americans" that their social and cultural interests, identities, and allegiances lay predominantly with the host society rather than with the ethnic community or the old country. The least assimilation-oriented immigrants confined themselves to their ethnic enclaves, spoke their languages proudly, worshipped in their own way—in general keeping alive their ethnic subcultures.

As racial and ethnic enclaves grew and became more prominent and annoying to the dominant cultural group, the concept "cultural pluralism" developed a special appeal to Americans verbally committed to the ideals of democracy and tolerance (Zintz, 1969). The concept implied cooperation between majority and minority; it suggested mutual respect, appreciation, and acceptance of cultural differences; and it implied that minorities would not have to fear repression or obliteration of their heritages. Cultural pluralism was put to a severe test during the great push for civil rights in the 1950s and 1960s when the largest and most severely excluded minority in the United States, Americans of black African descent, stood forth as never before with great pride in their racial heritage. Similarly, other racial and ethnic groups—American Indians, Spanish heritage people, American Jews, to name a few—reaffirmed their identities as they decried the inequalities inflicted upon them by dominant group Americans. The demands and demonstrations of racial and ethnic minorities revealed to the world that the United States is composed of numerous subgroups, many of whom, for various reasons, encounter almost insurmountable obstacles to equal participation in the society. The protests for equal rights caused a variety of reactions from mainstream Americans. These ranged from humanitarian concern to overt hostility towards the minorities who had upset the social status quo.

The social phenomenon described above reflects the fact that when human groups exist separately for whatever reason, voluntarily or forced, they, in time, develop different language habits and nuances, personalities, perceptions of themselves and others, and values and norms which guide their behavior. They become culturally different. The differences, in turn, become reasons for exclusion by those in power. In the United States, to the degree that racial and ethnic minorities are different from the dominant group, they are excluded from equal opportunity. In the case of racial minorities, primary exclusion variables are color of skin, curl of hair, and slave heritage. These are genetically transmitted; that is, if one or both parents have the characteristics, the offspring will have them also, at least to some extent. Although "slave heritage" is not a biological trait, the fact that one's forebears were slaves is historically indelible. The dominant group reacts to the primary exclusion variables with varying degrees of curiosity, ignorance, fear, abhorrence, and hostility. These reactions effectively isolate visibly different minorities from equal membership in majority communities and produce numerous potent secondary exclusion variables, such as differences in language, values, income, housing, and general culture and lifestyle—factors generally cited by majority group observers to explain lack of equal opportunity in the United States.

Indeed, citizens in the American society are separate and unequal—a fact evident throughout the social order. Whenever and wherever majority group members meet and greet members of minority groups, the likelihood of misunderstanding and ill will is great. Counseling, the largest helping profession in this country, has not gone untouched by the lack of understanding and goodwill between the majority and minorities. As a process, counseling is a psychological interaction involving two or more individuals. One or more of the interactants is considered able to help the other person or persons to live and function more effectively at the time of the involvement or at some future time. Specifically, the goal of counseling is to assist directly or indirectly the recipients in adjusting to or otherwise negotiating the various environments which influence their own or someone else's psychological well-being. In order to accomplish this goal, counselors must relate and communicate with clients, determine their state of adjustment, decide alone or with them the course of action needed to improve their current or future situation, and intervene at some level of competency to assist the clients.

The purpose of this chapter is to indicate the effects of racial and ethnic factors on the counseling process, i.e., to point out how cultural differences affect the ability of counselors to relate and communicate with clients therapeutically, to discuss problems counselors may experience in making a diagnosis of minority group clients, to suggest some difficulties inherent in making recommendations to assist minority group clients, and to consider briefly intervention problems often encountered in cross-cultural counseling.

The Relationship

Counseling is a dynamic process. The psychological environment in which it occurs changes constantly and imperceptibly. It is influenced by the clients—their social, racial, and ethnic background, their expectations, and their experiences with helping professionals; by the counselors —their race, sex, age, professional training, and personality; by the nature of the clients' problems; and by numerous other variables. In spite of the fluid nature of the relationship, an attempt is made here to examine various aspects of the interaction as they relate to assisting minority group individuals.

Rapport

As a relationship between two or more individuals, counseling suggests ipso facto the establishment of a mutual bond between the interactants. The emotional bond between the counselor and the counselee is referred to as rapport, a concept which pervades therapeutic literature. Simply defined, it connotes the comfortable and unconstrained mutual trust and confidence between two or more persons (Buchheimer & Balogh, 1961). In a counseling dyad, it implies positive feelings combined with a spirit of cooperativeness. In therapeutic groups, rapport is the existence of a mutual responsiveness which encourages each member to react immediately, spontaneously, and sympathetically to the sentiments and attitudes of every other member (Hinsie & Campbell, 1960).

Rapport should not be misconstrued as merely initial "small talk" designed to put the counselee at ease. It is a dynamic emotional bridge which must be maintained throughout the interview. During the relationship, the participants continuously take stock of each other. They notice how each individual presents himself: what is said and how it is said. The nature of the communication, explicit or implicit, can cause the counselee to alternate from trust to tacit reserve or even overt hostility. Exploring content that is threatening to the ego generally requires a more positive relationship bridge than is otherwise needed.

It is a matter of common experience that individuals find it more difficult to establish empathy with those unlike themselves than they do with their confreres (Katz, 1963). Differences in racial and ethnic background, in socioeconomic class, and in language patterns—these and other factors singly or interactively create rapport problems in the counseling relationship. Often the differences or similarities are so imperceptible that counselees cannot verbalize them. They can only feel them. For example, they can express good feelings towards the counselor only by the statement "He talks like us," which is equivalent to saying "He is one of us."

However, it is important to indicate that differences make a difference when all other things are equal. In the United States, minorities are so disadvantaged that fellow minorities who succeed are often suspect by members of their own racial or ethnic group. On the one hand, they view achievers as collaborators with the "enemy." How else could they have risen above them! On the other, they are consumed by destructive envy of them, because they are better than they who have not achieved. The ambivalence is aggravated when self-hatred pervades the minority group in question. For example, in order to understand the complex dynamics of the black-black counseling dyad, one must consider the client's ambivalence towards the counselor and the self-hatred of the interactants. Self-hatred causes each to reject the other, as he or she rejects self. This phenomenon helps to explain why white counselors may be more effective counseling some black clients than are black counselors.

Notwithstanding these observations, it is possible to offer some general advice for establishing rapport with minorities, especially with those who have not had a continuing relationship with members of the dominant cultural group. First, counselors should try to avoid extremes in behavior. For example, they should refrain from overdressing or underdressing; they should dress so as not to call undue attention to themselves. American Indians from reservations seem to be extremely suspicious of too much talking, too many questions, and too much "putting on the dog." Similar attitudes are pervasive among Appalacian whites, who historically have been suspicious of the fast-talking, uppity city slicker in foppish clothes.

In general, counselors should curtail their small talk in the beginning of the interview, especially if they do not know what small talk is appropriate. Small talk may be perceived as an attempt by counselors to delay the unpleasant. Therefore, it can be anxiety-producing. Counselors should start interviews with a direct but courteous "How can I help you?" This will allow their clients to chitchat, if they are uncomfortable going immediately into the reason for coming for counseling. Some Spanish heritage clients may annoy Anglo counselors with the penchant to pry into their personal lives. In such cases, the counselor should not be alarmed and reply to such a question as "Are you married?" and get on with the interview.

Structuring

On the whole, disadvantaged minority group members have had limited experience with counselors and related psychotherapeutic professionals. Their contacts have been mainly with people who tell them what they must or should do in order to receive wages, to get well, or to stay out of trouble. Relationships with professionals who place major responsibility on individuals for solving their own problems are few. Therefore, counselors working within such a context should structure or define their role to clients; that is, they should indicate what, how, and why they intend to do what is planned. It is also important to communicate to clients and sometimes to their loved ones what is expected of them in the relationship. Failure to structure early and adequately in counseling can result in unfortunate and unnecessary misunderstanding, simply because the counselor's interests and concerns are unclear to the clients, their parents, and significant others.

Counselors of deprived minorities need to realize that they are working with people who, because of their cultural and experiential backgrounds, are unable or unwilling to participate in introspective explorations. Therefore, techniques such as prolonged silences should be avoided, at least until positive rapport has been established, for their use tends to become awkward and to increase the psychological distance between the counselor and the client (MacKinnon & Michels, 1971).

Counselors may find it particularly difficult to conduct an interview in which personal issues must be explored. Appalachian whites, for example, find personal queries which counselors may perceive as innocuous to be very offensive (Coles, 1971). Often parents of counselees are the first to inform counselors of this, especially if the counselors happen not to be "from 'round here."

In general, more than usual attention should be paid to structuring when the subcultural group is typically suspicious of outsiders and when the socialization patterns in the group encourage a structured, well-ordered approach to life. For example, the well-defined roles and expectations for members of the orderly Chinese American family probably explain why high school and college students from such families prefer concrete and well-structured situations in and out of the classroom (Sue & Sue, 1972). The ambiguity inherent in the counseling process is terribly disconcerting to them, to say the least.

Resistance

The counselee's opposition to the goals of counseling is usually referred to as resistance. It may manifest itself as self-devaluation, intellectualization, or overt hostility. Although counselors may recognize these various manifestations when they counsel middle-class white counselees, they often fail to recognize the phenomenon in minority group clients, possibly because the visible or perceived differences of their clients are so overwhelming.

Although many Spanish heritage clients are unable to converse fluently in English, their command of English is usually quite adequate. This fact, however, comes as a surprise to many counselors. These clients' alleged inability to speak English must be viewed therefore as resistance, either to the counselor, to the Anglo establishment, or to both (MacKinnon & Michels, 1971).

It has been observed also that many young blacks, urban and rural, appear shy and withdrawn in the counseling dyad or group. Counselors unfamiliar with the nuances of black culture may be quick to assess such behavior as just another unfortunate effect of social and economic deprivation. The clients' perception of their own conduct, though, may be very different: they are just "cooling it." They know how to "rap" beautifully about whatever, but are unwilling to do so, until they are convinced that their audience is a person of goodwill. On the other hand, such clients may be so talkative that they refuse to let the counselor get a word in edgeways. Although such deportment may be perceived as an indication of positive rapport and desire for assistance, it can also mean that the client is "playing along" the counselor. It is somewhat similar to a sandlot basketball game in which the ball is being passed to all players but one, the isolate. In this case, the counselor is the outsider.

Many examples of resistance among minorities in the counseling relationship can be cited. A very obvious one is failure to show up for an appointment. American Indians, for example, are reluctant to disagree or be uncooperative, especially with someone of higher status than they. Such reluctance may be observed also among many low status Southern blacks, in counseling situations with whites, although perhaps for different reasons. Therefore, Indians and blacks of all ages may agree to come in for an interview or conference, when, in fact, they have no intention of following through. They promise to do so out of courtesy, respect, or fear.

Transference

Transference refers to clients' reacting to counselors in a manner similar to how they have responded to other persons in their life (Lagache, 1952). In other words, the phenomenon is a repetition or new edition of an old relationship. Whether positive or negative, it is an unconscious form of resistance to the goals of counseling (Harrison & Carek, 1966). Common in most psychotherapeutic involvements, transference is especially knotty in the majority-minority counseling dyad or group because minority group members bring to the relationship intense emotions derived from experiences witn the majority group (Carter & Haizlip, 1972).

In counseling, clients expect counselors to give succor and support or to punish and control (Brammer & Shostrom, 1968). Minority group counselees usually anticipate majority group counselors to exhibit the latter behavior, either because of direct experiences with people of whom counselors remind them or because of socialization which taught them to be suspicious of majority group members or those who identify with the majority group. For example, preschool Pueblo Indian children know better than to tell the "white man" about anything that is happening in the village (Zintz, 1969). In barrios of the Southwest, the Mexican American's fear of and hostility towards Anglos can be seen in the cries of "La migra! la migra!" (immigration official) by four- and five-year-old children when any official-looking vehicle enters their neighborhood (Moore, 1970). Such behavior has been learned by these children before they enter school: Anglos are not to be trusted. It is thus easy to understand why many of them associate a counselor in a private office with "la policía" or some other official who does not have their best interest at heart.

Black children also learn at an early age, usually at the feet of their parents, that white people are not to be trusted. As they mature in decaying ghettos of large cities, they have other experiences which lead them habitually to approach whites with resentment, anxiety, distrust, hostility, and ambivalence. In a similar way, many Appalachian children learn that outsiders, whatever color they happen to be, are people who "mean no good." Their school counselors, especially those perceived as outsiders, then find that mountain children appear to be fearful, shy, and reluctant to talk (Coles, 1971).

Countertransference

Countertransference is the transference of the counselor to the counselee. The counterpart of transference, it may lead to persistently inappropriate behavior towards the counselee, resulting in untold strains in the counseling relationship (Wolstein, 1959). Although counselors are quick to recognize transference as a reality, they find it difficult to admit to the possibility that they may not accept, respect, or like many of their counselees (Harrison & Carek, 1966). Their professional training has inculcated in them aspects of empathy, positive regard, unconditionality of positive regard, and congruence. They, therefore, fail to see that they too are mothers and fathers, voters, property owners, taxpayers, Northerners and Southerners, and Republicans and Democrats—in a word, that they are human beings with a variety of attitudes, beliefs, and values, conscious and unconscious, which invariably affect the counseling relationships with minority group people.

As products of a society which has been characterized as racist, counselors bring to the psychotherapeutic relationship preconceived attitudes and ideas about racial and ethnic minorities. The preconceptions manifest themselves in numerous ways. Because majority group members occupy the most powerful and prestigious positions in society, they are often perceived, rightly or wrongly, by minority group people as "Ugly Americans," as authoritarian and condescending. In counseling, this phenomenon may be described as "The Great White Father Syndrome." The communication conveyed to minority group clients is that counselors are not only omnipotent (because of their membership in the majority group) but that they also mean their counselees nothing but good. Counselors guarantee that they will "deliver," if the clients will put themselves in their hands. Simultaneously, the counselors intimate, albeit unconsciously, that if clients do not depend on them, catastrophe is inevitable. The great white father syndrome may be interpreted as countertransference, because it implies that the counselors are anxious not only to demonstrate their power and authority but also to prove that they are not like all the other majority group people the minority group clients may have known.

Another general manifestation of countertransference is the tendency of counselors to be excessively sympathetic and indulgent with minority clients. For example, their definition of achievement for them may be in wide variance with the achievement yardstick for members of the majority group. Do they view achievement for minorities—educational, social, occupational, and economic—by the same criteria, explicit or implicit, established by or applied to the dominant cultural group? Or do they consider it appropriate to use a different set of achievement criteria for minorities, simply because they are minorities? If the latter is the case, counselors are guilty of saying, thinking, or implying that their minority group clients are pretty good as compared to most blacks, Mexican Americans, or Indians.

In general, countertransference is problematic to the extent that the client and counselor are racially and culturally dissimilar. Differences, real or imagined, pollute the psychotherapeutic environment with misinformation, prejudgment, preconceived expectations, and perceptual distortions.

Language

Language is a significant component of the culture or subculture of a people. Failure to understand their language is, to some degree, failure to comprehend their culture. In order to communicate effectively with minority group clients, counselors should be able to understand the verbal and nonverbal language of their counselees, for both aspects are dependent on each other. Conversers who listen only to spoken words may get as much communicative distortion as they would if they "listened" only to body language. To understand the meaning of gestures, postures, and inflections, it is important to know a people, their institutions, values, and life-style.

Counselors encounter varying degress of difficulty communicating with racial and ethnic minorities. For example, on Indian reservations, variations in ability to use English can be illustrated on the one hand by some of the Pueblos of New Mexico, where no English is spoken in everyday life, and on the other by the Fort Berthold Reservation Indians of North Dakota where almost everybody speaks English. On the Choctaw Reservation in Mississippi, about 4 percent of the families use excellent English, 57 percent good, and 39 percent poor (U.S. Department of Labor, 1968). Although this description is fairly typical of English used among reservation Indians in general, young Indians, as might be expected, having gone to school in English, use that language with greater facility than do their elders. Even so, Indians of whatever age communicate with great economy of language, and they are given to the use of concrete as opposed to abstract words. Counselors, consequently, find Indian clients limited in their ability to express personal feelings—usually considered a requirement by most counselors.

In the Southwest, Spanish heritage people customarily live in enclaves isolated from the English-speaking community. In many counties in Texas and New Mexico, the children enter the English-speaking world for the first time when they enroll in public schools. In classrooms children unable to speak English are threatened often with punishment if they speak in their native language. Badly needed to assist these children and their parents are bilingual counselors who are native speakers of Spanish; Anglo counselors who have studied Spanish may still be unable to communicate with alingual or biculturally illiterate children who speak neither English nor a Spanish that is standard (Moore, 1970).

Counselors are less handicapped in communicating with Appalachian whites than they are with American Indians and Spanish heritage clients. Even so, they usually find therapeutic communication difficult, because mountain people tend to use simple Anglo-Saxon words as opposed to Latinic ones. Their speech is characterized by a reduction in qualifiers, adjectives, and adverbs, especially those which involve feelings (Weller, 1966). Therefore, counselors expecting Appalachian clients to talk a great deal about how they feel are apt to be disappointed. Unique idioms and pronunciations also may constitute communication barriers, at least until counselors become attuned to the language patterns.

Among lower-class blacks, counselors—black and white—often experience difficulty in understanding not only slurred pronunciations but also idioms and slang endemic to the community. Some counselors, not wishing to reveal their inability to understand their clients, continue the dialogue, hoping to catch up later on. Unfortunately, they often discover that the more they allow clients to talk without clarification, the more confused they become. If counselors fail to understand clients for whatever reason, the most honest thing to do is to ask for an explanation or repetition.

Counselors probably experience more difficulty understanding implicit language in the lower-class black community than they do comprehending the explicit (Wachtel, 1967). Language is spoken not with voices alone; entire bodies are used to make a complete statement or to punctuate one (Kris, 1941). For example, the "hip" shuffle of the young urban black male, the slouched sitting position with chin in hand, the erect stance with genitals cupped, the apparently unconscious wipe at the chin or mouth with his hand when there is nothing visible to wipe away—all of these nonverbal expressions are filled with significant meaning if counselors can interpret them (Beier, 1966). To arrive at the correct interpretation, counselors must understand both the general and contextual meanings. They need to recognize that the more emotionally charged the verbal language, the less definite is its meaning and the more important are the accompanying nonverbal expressions (Vetter, 1969).

Occasionally, counselors may need to use an interpreter with clients who do not speak English fluently. In such cases, it is important to select a person who is bicultural and bilingual, who understands language patterns peculiar to socioeconomic groups within each linguistic community, and whom clients respect as they do the counselor (de Galindez, 1969; Mounin, 1976). The interpreter's usefulness is increased considerably if the roles of all interactants are clearly understood in advance of the counseling interview (MacKinnon & Michels, 1971). For example, an interpreter should position himself inobtrusively so as not to obstruct the counselor and client's direct visual contact, allowing them to speak to each other as if they indeed were communicating in the same language. The interpreter should translate the client and counselor's statements instead of giving a personal understanding of their meaning, he should try to capture intonations and other paralinguistic content, and he should resist the temptation to converse directly with the client, either during or between sessions, in order to reduce the possibility of inadvertently usurping the counselor's role (Seleskovitch, 1975).

Ideally, personal fluency in the client's language is desirable, because so many customary counseling techniques require instantaneous comprehension. Paraphrasing, reflection, and interpretation presuppose an understanding of the client's language. In order to reflect accurately what the client is experiencing and feeling, the counselor should be able to derive meaning from the totality of the individual's communicative behavior on the spot.

Psychosocial Barriers

Several psychosocial characteristics of racial and ethnic minorities constitute, singly or interactively, barriers to the achievement of therapeutic goals in the counseling relationship. These barriers are usually unconscious aspects of the personality and derive primarily from the American culture which socializes and oppresses its minorities simultaneously. Current behavior patterns can occasionally be traced back to the old country. Some of the these barriers are discussed below.

Self-disclosure

Self-disclosure, or the willingness to let another person know thoughts, feelings, or wants, is basic to the counseling process. It is particularly crucial in the rapport establishment phase of the relationship, because it is the most direct means by which persons can make themselves known to others and is, therefore, prerequisite to achieving the goals of counseling. People of black African descent are especially reluctant to disclose themselves to others, probably because of the hardships which they and their forebears have experienced in the United States. Many of them, especially males, are devoid of confidence in human relations (Karon, 1975).

Reluctance to disclose is a problem in the white-black dyad, because few blacks initially perceive whites as persons of goodwill. Clients disclose themselves when they feel that they can trust the target person, not necessarily when they feel that they are being understood (Jourard, 1964). In fact, many black clients fear being understood, for it implies engulfment, loss of autonomy, being found out, and that is the same as being destroyed in a society which is perceived as racist. Obviously, the fear of being understood has grave implications for individual and group counseling. It is conceivable that, in the case of some black clients, counselors who understand too much are to be feared or even hated.

Self-hatred

As Allport (1954) indicates, members of an ostracized, excluded, or oppressed group tend not only to despise their group, but also to hate themselves for being a part of it. In the United States, blacks, more than any other minority, have unconsciously identified with the majority group, their perceived oppressors; consequently, they have developed a contempt for, and hatred of, themselves (Vontress, 1971). In view of the generally acknowledged positive correlation between self-rejection and the rejection of others, counselors may expect repulsion, passive or overt, from many black clients for this reason alone. Helping black clients to accept themselves more positively should result in the progressive acceptance of counselors.

Machismo

When counseling the Hispanic male, it is important to understand the meaning of machismo, which refers to one's manhood, to manly traits of honor and dignity, to the courage to fight, to keeping one's word, and to protecting one's name (Steiner, 1969). It also refers to a man's running his home, "controlling" his women, and directing his children. Thus, machismo, which provides respect from a male's peers, is not to be taken lightly. It also suggests a rather clear-cut separation of the sexes. The male ipso facto enjoys rights and privileges denied women, who are generally reluctant to demand equality. Probably because of machismo Spanish heritage boys and girls are often more uncomfortable and uncommunicative in coed group counseling than with groups composed entirely of Anglos. Another implication of machismo is that Anglo female counselors should not be too assertive or forward in the counseling interview with Hispanic males, not even with preadolescents. The right amount of deference should be shown at all times.

Personalism

Personalism is a rather stubborn counseling barrier among Appalachian whites, Spanish heritage people, and blacks. Although a precise definition is difficult, it suggests that individuals are more interested in and motivated by considerations for people than they are by bureaucratic protocol (Lacroix, 1972). Mountain people derive self-identification mainly from relationships with others (Fetterman, 1971). Therefore, they put a lot of stock in being neighborly. For them, it is more important to pass the time of day with friends encountered en route to an appointment than it is to arrive at a destination punctually.

Refusing to be enslaved by clocks, mountain people transact business by feelings, not protocol (Weller, 1966). People who keep appointments, are prompt, and pay attention to protocol are suspect. In counseling, personalism is an obstacle to the counselor's getting clients to make and keep appointments. They prefer to drop by to "pass a spell" and "visit," and may get around to discussing something that has been "bothering my mind" while they are there.

As suggested earlier, asking counselors personal questions may be the way persons of Spanish heritage have for getting close to persons who might otherwise remain distant. Although lower-class blacks are reluctant to ask counselors direct personal questions, they are generally more comfortable relating to them after they have obtained at least a modicum of information about their counselors as human beings; i.e., they are apt to "check out the dude" before "spilling my guts" to anybody.

Listening

Counseling requires, among other things, listening, an area in which many lower-class blacks and Appalachian whites have had little experience. This may be due to their socialization in large families. Often, as Surface (1971) points out, their homes are filled with din and confusion, with everybody talking simultaneously. In such an environment, young people soon learn not to listen to what words mean, but to emotions speakers convey (Weller, 1966). This is why counselors may discern blank stares on the faces of their clients, even when they imagine themselves to be offering much-needed insight. A vacuous facial expression usually means that the client has tuned out the counselor until the talking has ceased. The inability of black and mountain people to listen to a speaker may help to explain why their conversation seems to have little continuity of ideas. Inability or unwillingness to listen hampers more directly group counseling than it does dyadic relationships.

Modesty

Modesty in the presence of superiors is a relationship barrier in counseling Japanese Americans. The phenomenon may be attributed to the total respect customarily paid the father, whose authority in the family is beyond question, and towards whom one is forbidden to express overt negative feelings (Kitano, 1969). Many young Japanese Americans are so imbued with awe of authority that they hesitate to express their feelings on any subject when they are in the presence of higher status individuals or when they are expected to articulate their views in groups. It is easy to understand how their hesitancy intrudes in the counseling relationship, dyadic or group.

Characteristic reserve in the Japanese American personality makes it difficult to determine where cultural patterns end and psychologically debilitating symptomatology begins (Kitano, 1970). The counselor must have two perceptual yardsticks for measuring normal behavior; that is, one must be able to determine what is deviant behavior in the Japanese American subculture as well as what is aberrant in the culture at large.

Reserve among many Puerto Rican females and rural lower-class blacks in general corresponds closely to that of Japanese Americans. The well-bred Puerto Rican girl often avoids eye-to-eye contact, especially with men, a fact which may cause the Anglo counselor to draw false conclusions about her character and personality. Her hesitancy to interact voluntarily in group counseling may be attributed to socialization in the Puerto Rican culture in which boys are expected to assert their manhood, while girls remain retiring. Traditionally, Southern blacks were expected by Southern whites to be nonassertive and passive (Karon, 1975). The residue of such expectations remains today, especially among lower-class blacks in the South, and probably helps to explain why black youngsters are often hesitant to interact in interracial counseling groups.

These, then, are but a few psychosocial barriers counselors may experience in therapeutic interactions with racial and ethnic minorities. Others could be cited to illustrate the importance of counselors' cognizance of subcultural factors when relating to culturally different clients.

Diagnosing

In order to accomplish the goals of counseling, counselors must be able to relate to and communicate with clients, determine their state of adjustment, make therapeutic recommendations designed to assist them, and intervene personally on their behalf. Relating to minority group people is problematic, as has been pointed out, but making an accurate diagnosis of culturally different counselees is probably fraught with more difficulties. Although clients are racially and ethnically different, counselors perforce rely on the same assessment tools and procedures used in counseling majority group clients.

Diagnostic Techniques

Commonly used diagnostic techniques, whether standardized or unstandardized, are generally questionable for assessing minority group clients. The ones most used today are standardized and objective; that is, their procedure, apparatus, and scoring have been regularized to allow replicated administration. Every observer of performance arrives at the same report. Included in this category is a variety of commercially available instruments labeled proficiency, achievement, developmental, intelligence, and personality tests, and a limited number designated as interest inventories.

There are several problems inherent in using these instruments with minorities. The first may be described as situational. To disadvantaged minority group individuals, extended structured situations demanding assiduity are physically and psychologically annoying. Unusual surroundings, formal procedures, and unfamiliar people—characteristics of large group testing environments—may aggravate and account for anxiety sufficient to lower scores of reluctant examinees (American Psychological Association, 1969). In the case of blacks, examiners with regional accents that put them on guard can influence performance. In general, white people with Southern accents are associated with prejudice and discrimination; therefore, they as test administrators are apt to produce in blacks an anxiety which affects test performance (Samuda, 1975).

Steps can be taken to assure an environment most conducive to optimum performance of minority group persons on standardized tests. First, test administrators should prepare the examinees in advance for the test. Individual and group counseling is one vehicle which can be used both to allay apprehension about test taking and to motivate them towards optimum performance. Second, in order to insure the most favorable testing conditions, the size of the testing group should be kept small, for example, ten or twenty examinees to a room. Herding groups of fifty, a hundred, or two hundred students into a large arena is most undesirable. Third, test batteries requiring from six to eight hours to administer should be given in segments extending over several days. Finally, examiners and proctors of the same racial and ethnic background should be used whenever possible.

In general, language constitutes a handicap for minorities taking standardized tests, not necessarily because it serves as a people's vehicle for communication but because of its role in the transmission of culture from one generation to another. As a major aspect of culture, it is also a barometer which reflects changes in cultural demands and expectations, however subtle (Cohen, 1956). Those who observe that minorities are verbally destitute, and somehow connect the destitution with low scores on standardized tests, oversimplify a complex problem. Language differences are simply indicative of more global and significant cultural differences.

The more assimilated a minority group, the fewer problems its members are apt to experience in taking standardized tests. Groups may lose their total cultural identity as many ethnics have done. They may do as Jewish and Japanese Americans have done—that is, to accept selectively achievement-related aspects of the host culture, while simultaneously retaining many components of the old. They may become equicultural, moving comfortably back and forth across the line separating the old culture from the new. Or they may remain cultural isolates. The majority of American Indians, Americans of black African descent, and Mexican Americans can be classified as cultural isolates, because they are excluded physically and psychologically from the cultural mainstream of the American society. The language difficulty which they experience in taking standardized tests is but one of the manifestations of their exclusionary status.

In view of this problem, counselors should determine informally the degree to which clients are assimilated in the American culture before administering them standardized tests. If they are cultural isolates, insisting that they take standardized tests in the idiom of the dominant culture is questionable. The examiner should determine also the reading level of the examinees before subjecting them to tests which demand reading facility. If the readability level of a test is beyond the reading ability of the examinees, there is little to be gained from using the test.

Because of the cultural barriers encountered in using standardized tests with racial and ethnic minorities, it is often felt that substitute procedures should be employed. The obvious alternative is an impressionistic approach; that is, the counselor looks for significant cues by any means available and integrates them into a total impression of the individual's ability, personality, aptitude, and other traits. Unstandardized procedures include observations, anecdotal records, and interviews—assessment techniques well known to counselors, and interviews—assessment techniques well known to counselors. Unfortunately, for minorities, these approaches are probably more unreliable than the objective, standardized techniques, as cultural stereotypes can impair the ability of counselors to diagnose persons from subcultural groups of which they are not members. Culture determines the specific ways in which persons perceive their environment. It influences the forms of conflict, behavior, and psychopathology that occur in members of the culture (Horney, 1966, 1937). This fact helps to explain why, for example, counselors generally find it difficult to determine through an impressionistic interview where the usual Japanese American modesty and reserve end and psychological malady begins (Kitano, 1970). Anglo counselors are also generally inapt in assessing psychological morbidity in blacks, mainly because for so long whites have accepted, expected, or demanded bizarre behavior from Negroes.

Recurrent Problems

Although each minority group counselee should be perceived and counseled as an individual, several common problems plague identifiable minorities in the United States. The severity of each problem depends on, among other things, geographic location and level of assimilation and deprivation. Three recurrent problems are economic deprivation, educational deficiencies, and negative self-concept.

In general, the unemployment rate of minorities far exceeds that of the majority group. On countless reservations and in many ghettos and barrios, more able-bodied people are unemployed than are employed. Economic deprivation, resulting from unemployment and low-paying jobs, in turn leads to a complex of psychosocial problems. For example, inadequate and high density housing fast gives rise not only to family dissension but to increased morbidity as well. Life becomes so difficult that short-run hedonism necessarily becomes one's goal.

Intertwined with economic disability are educational deficiencies so much in evidence in black, Mexican American, and Indian communities. Although there is no consensus on the cause of educational bankruptcy among minorities, it seems clear that a complex of factors such as poor nutrition, inadequate housing, insufficient or improper familial stimuli and role models, poor teachers, and limited school resources interact to constitute a formidable barrier to equal education.

Members of subcultural groups enduring victim status in a country, over an extended period of history, soon come to view themselves negatively (Allport, 1954). An example of this is the blacks who were abducted to this country, stripped of their language, heritage, and religion, and assigned an inferior status from which few have been able to escape. Their lack of identity and consequential self-contempt help to explain their lack of academic achievement, interpersonal conflicts, intragroup hostility, and drug abuse, especially among young black males in urban areas.

Among American Indians, confusion over cultural identity also leads to interpersonal problems that are expressed in terms of jealousy and suspicion of others (Samora et al., 1965). Envy and distrust of one's peers are reflected in the school performance of many Indians who are reluctant to surpass the achievement of their classmates, in their hesitancy to assume leadership roles which might lead to invidious comparisons, and in hostility and conflict between adolescents and their elders. Widespread alcoholism among Indians, even teenagers, may also be attributed to loss of cultural identity and the accompanying institutional and ritualistic restraints which provided significant meaning and direction in life (Kiev, 1972; "White man brings," 1972).

Therapeutic Recommendations

Having made a diagnosis of the client's situation, the counselor must then conceptualize what needs to be done, why it should be done, and by whom it should be done to alleviate, enhance, or insure continuous development of the trait, state, or condition diagnosed. Simultaneously, it is important to anticipate the probable immediate, intermediate, and final consequences of each action recommended. In order to do this, the counselor should know the demands and expectations of the client's subculture, not just those of the dominant cultural group.

In counseling disadvantaged minorities, many of the counselor's recommendations reflect explicitly or implicitly, directly or indirectly, an immediate or long-range attempt to help clients move from their racial or ethnic cultural influences to mainstream status and living style. For example, an Anglo counselor new to the black ghetto may recommend that a child be removed from his or her home which the counselor considers deplorable without realizing that by local community standards the home is quite good. Another counselor insists that a Puerto Rican girl who has scored high on the Scholastic Aptitude Test apply for admission to a college where she can surely get a scholarship, without first consulting with her father who believes that a nice Puerto Rican girl should get married, have children, and obey her husband. Illustrative also is the counselor who directs a black student to a predominantly white college without realizing that the young man in an all-white environment is apt to be very lonely for the culturally familiar.

The examples are cited not to suggest that the counselor should refrain from making what could be termed cross-cultural recommendations. Rather, the intent is to show that most therapeutic recommendations made by counselors are, in effect, slanted towards the mainstream life-style. As such, these recommendations are often antithetical to the demands and expectations of the client's particular subculture. Therefore, the counselor must help clients to make a series of intermediate adjustments prerequisite to becoming comfortable with the demands and expectations of the dominant culture. Often the problems are related to guilt feelings associated with having left behind people who still suffer as they have suffered. There is also fear of achievement which is pervasive among disadvantaged minorities. This phenomenon, upon closer inspection, is essentially fear of the envy of one's racial and ethnic fellows.

Intervention

In cross-cultural counseling, counselors are often unable to intervene effectively on behalf of clients for several reasons. Minority group clients themselves may be resistant to the goals of counseling. Intervention involves change, and that may trigger personal social cataclysms, with which they are unwilling to cope. For example, the mountain boy who is the first in his community to go away to college may worry that his friends staying behind will find him different upon his return. A black youngster from the ghetto may be reluctant to accept a scholarship to a predominantly white university, choosing instead to attend a smaller all-black college, because he fears losing his racial identity, which his friends consider important.

Intervention also can be blocked directly by the client's significant others. Counselors in Appalachia are chagrined sometimes to discover that their counseling is undone by superstitious parents once the child gets home with a report of the counseling interview (Coles, 1971). In extended Asian and Hispanic families, it is important to recognize that family members rarely make individual decisions. In such situations, counselors may need to provide family counseling in order to intervene on behalf of a single member, no matter how old the client is.

That counselors typically work within institutional settings suggests that there are forces outside their offices which can hinder intervention efforts. For example, school counselors may find that they alone cannot help Spanish heritage or black children adjust to a predominantly Anglo school, if janitors, teachers, fellow students, and administrators are hostile to their presence. In government, although personnel counselors place minority group employees in positions commensurate with their experience and skills, they may be unable to control the indifferent reception of other employees or the demeaning tasks assigned by the supervisor.

Intervention on behalf of minority group clients is made difficult and sometimes impossible because the community at large is indifferent to the needs and problems of the minority group in question. For example, in the Southwest, many Spanish heritage children are doomed to failure in the public schools, because English is the sole language of instruction. Although counselors may recognize that some of their Spanish-speaking clients who are failing in school are in fact extremely gifted, they are often unable to scotch their academic demise because the Anglo community, which controls the purse strings, just does not care when it comes to "those kids."

Conclusion

Numerous problems exist in counseling minority group clients. They derive primarily from cross-cultural barriers which cause communication static and distortion in interactions involving individuals from culturally different backgrounds. The fact that clients come from distinct subcultures impairs the ability of counselors to determine not only what difficulties clients are experiencing but also what to do to prevent or alleviate them.

Now that the impediments have been described, what should be done? Concerned counselors ask for special techniques to use with minorities. Others want to know whether it is better for minorities to be counselors to minorities, since racial and ethnic barriers are so threatening and difficult to penetrate. Few counselors ever ask what they can do to change themselves; few want to know how they can become better human beings in order to relate more effectively with other human beings who, through birth, are racially and ethnically different. The failure of counselors to ask these questions indicates why counseling minorities continues to be a problem in this country. Counselors are products of a culture which has been characterized as racist. They, in spite of a few graduate courses in counseling and psychology, are shaped by that culture.

Counselors in service and in training need to be exposed to new experiences if they are to become effective when counseling minorities. Although a course in counseling racial and ethnic minorities may be another exciting and rewarding cognitive exposure, needed most are affective experiences designed to humanize counselors. Therapeutic group activities extending over long periods, practicums and internships in minority group communities, living in subcultural environments, and individual therapy—these are just a few suggestions for helping counselors grow as human beings. Yet, these experiences presuppose that counselor educators and supervisors have achieved enough personal insight and knowledge of minorities to help others develop in the manner suggested.

Finally, research is needed badly. There are so many complex and imprecise dimensions in cross-cultural counseling that they elude traditional empirical scrutiny. Variables such as transference, countertransference, self-disclosure, machismo, and personalism are affective considerations which demand novel research strategies. The investigator should be polycultural in order to perceive clearly across racial and ethnic lines—a prerequisite to designing research which allows rejection or acceptance of the assertions made in this chapter. A glaring research pitfall is the investigator's assumption that racial and ethnic identity is unidimensional. For example, the researcher fails to control for the degree of assimilation in the case of black clients and counselors, or for the extent of prejudice in the case of white clients with black counselors and white counselors with black clients.

References

Allport, G. W. *The nature of prejudice.* Reading, Massachusetts: Addison-Wesley, 1954.

American Psychological Association, Task Force on Employment Testing of Minority Groups. Job testing and the disadvantaged. *American Psychologist,* 1969, 24, 637–650.

Beier, E. G. *The silent language of psychotherapy.* Chicago: Aldine, 1966.

Brammer, L. M., & Shostrom, E. *Therapeutic psychology* (2nd ed.). Englewood Cliffs: Prentice-Hall, 1968.

Buchheimer, A., & Balogh, S. C. *The counseling relationship.* Chicago: Science Research Associates, 1961.

Carter, J. H., & Haizlip, T. M. Race and its relevance to transference. *American Journal of Orthopsychiatry,* 1972, 42, 865–871.

Cohen, M. *Pour une sociologie du langage.* Paris: Éditions Albins Michel, 1956.

Coles, R. *Children of crisis, Vol. 2: Migrants, sharecroppers, mountaineers.* Boston & Toronto: Little, Brown & Co., 1971.

de Galindez, J. *Puerto Rico en Nueva York.* Buenos Aires, Argentina: Editorial Tiempo Contemporaneo, 1969.

Fetterman, J. The people of Cumberland Gap. *National Geographic,* 1971, *140,* 591–621.

Harrison, S. I., & Carek, D. J. *A guide to psychotherapy.* Boston: Little, Brown & Co., 1966.

Hinsie, L. E., & Campbell, R. J. *Psychiatric dictionary* (3rd ed.). New York: Oxford University Press, 1960.

Horney, K. *The neurotic personality of our time.* New York: W. W. Norton, 1937.

Horney, K. *New ways in psychoanalysis.* New York: W. W. Norton, 1966.

Jourard, S. M. *The transparent self.* Princeton, New Jersey: D. Van Nostrand, 1964.

Karon, B. P. *Black scars: a rigorous investigation of the effects of discrimination.*
    New York: Springer, 1975.
Katz, R. L. *Empathy.* New York: The Free Press of Glencoe, 1963.
Kiev, A. *Transcultural psychiatry.* New York: Macmillan Co., Free Press, 1972.
Kitano, H. H. L. *Japanese Americans.* Englewood Cliffs: Prentice-Hall, 1969.
Kitano, H. H. L. Mental illness in four cultures. *Journal of Social Psychology,*
    1970, *80*, 121-134.
Kris, E. Laughter as an expressive process. *International Journal of Psycho-Anal-
    ysis,* 1941, *21*, 314-341.
Lacroix, J. *Le Personnelisme comme anti-idéologie.* Paris: Presses Universitaires
    de France, 1972.
Lagache, D. Le Problème du transfert. *Revue Française de Psychanalyse,* 1952,
    16, 5-122.
MacKinnon, R. A., & Michels, R. *The psychiatric interview in clinical practice.*
    Philadelphia: W. B. Saunders, 1971.
Moore, J. W. *Mexican Americans.* Englewood Cliffs: Prentice-Hall, 1970.
Mounin, G. *Les problèmes théorique de la traduction.* Paris: Gallimard, 1976.
Samora, J., Barrett, D. N., Jones, L. W., Roessel, R. A., Taylor, L., Jones, A. R., &
    Bram, J. Rural youth with special problems—Low income, Negro, Indian,
    Spanish American. In L. G. Burchinal (Ed.), *Rural youth in crisis.*
    Washington, D.C.: Superintendent of Documents, 1965.
Samuda, R. J. *Psychological testing of American minorities: Issues and conse-
    quences.* New York: Dodd, Mead & Co., 1975.
Seleskovitch, D. *Langage, langues, et mémoire; étude de la prise de notes en inter-
    prétation consécutive.* Paris: Lettres Modernes Minard, 1975.
Steiner, S. *La raza.* New York: Harper & Row, 1969.
Sue, D. W., & Sue, S. Counseling Chinese-Americans. *Personnel and Guidance
    Journal,* 1972, *50*, 637-644.
Surface, B. *The hollow.* New York: Coward, McCann, 1971.
U.S. Department of Labor. *Role of manpower programs in assisting the Ameri-
    can Indians.* Washington, D.C.: United States Employment Service, circa
    1968.
Vetter, H. J. *Language behavior and communication.* Itasca, Illinois: F. E. Pea-
    cock, 1969.
Vontress, C. E. The black male personality. *The Black Scholar,* 1971, *2*, 10-16.
Wachtel, P. L. An approach to the study of body language in psychotherapy.
    Psychotherapy, 1967, *4*, 97-100.
Weller, J. E. Yesterday's people: Life in contemporary Appalachia. Lexington:
    University of Kentucky Press, 1966.
White man brings booze, new woes to frustrated western Indian. *Po-ye-da*
    (Friend), 1972, *1*, 11-12.
Wolstein, B. *Countertransference.* New York: Grune & Stratton, 1959.
Zintz, M. V. *Education across cultures* (2nd ed.). Dubuque, Iowa: Kendall-Hunt,
    1969.

5

The Self-Awareness Factor
in Intercultural Psychotherapy:
Some Personal Reflections

Ronald M. Wintrob
Youngsook Kim Harvey

During the past ten years the steady growth of interest in the cultural context of mental health care has led to major cross-cultural studies of psychiatric evaluation and diagnosis (WHO, 1979) as well as to more careful assessment of the cultural specificity of psychiatric treatment (Foulks, Wintrob, Westermeyer, & Favazza 1977). A considerable number of papers have addressed the complex issues of intercultural psychotherapy, that is, counseling conducted under circumstances of significant racial, ethnic, social class, and religious differences between therapist and client. Students of the field have argued that an understanding of these differences is of critical importance in the training of mental health personnel, since a large part of treatment activities must involve working with both staff and patients whose backgrounds are significantly different from our own. National professional organizations and licensing authorities have been slow to recognize this need, however, and are only now responding to reports such as that of the American Psychiatric Association's Task Force on Ethnocentricity among Psychiatrists. Reports of this kind have demonstrated the weakness of training programs in preparing psychiatrists to evaluate and treat people of diverse backgrounds (American Psychiatric Association Task Force on Ethnocentricity, 1979). Both the conceptual and the clinical bases for understanding the issues involved in intercultural psychotherapy have been elaborated upon in recent years: on the cultural dimensions of transference and countertransference, by Spiegel (1964; 1976); on the psychosocial meaning of sickness, illness behavior, and healing practices, by Kleinman, Eisenberg, and Good (1978), Kleinman (1979), and Fabrega (1974); on the common elements of healing relationships in general and psychotherapy in particular, by Frank (1963; 1972) and Torrey

(1972); and on issues specific to intercultural psychotherapy, including verbal and nonverbal communication, stereotyping of patient and therapist roles, interpretation and advice-giving, definition of psychotherapeutic problems and treatment goals, rapport building, and the influence of the therapist's personality, by Hsu and Tseng (1972), Tseng and McDermott (1975), Bolman (1968), Wittkower and Warnes (1974), and Kinzie (1972; 1978). Chapters in this book by Pedersen, Wohl, Sundberg, and Vontress provide a comprehensive review and discussion of the literature on cultural factors in psychotherapy. In this chapter we are centrally concerned with the emotionally charged and comparatively under-reported issue of the interpersonal relationship between therapist and patient. It is a relationship that is, by its very nature, the fundamental vehicle for therapeutic effectiveness and at the same time highly susceptible to misinterpretation, distortion, resistance, and therapeutic stalemate. Tseng and McDermott, among other authors, in observing that the personality of the therapist "is a crucial factor—regardless of culture" (1975, p. 380), point out that this is also an often-neglected factor. Kinzie emphasizes that the therapist needs to have "self-awareness of his own value systems and beliefs about psychiatric goals and treatments" (1978, p. 517) in order for the technical aspects of intercultural psychotherapy to be effective. There is, in fact, little disagreement in the psychotherapy literature about the critical importance of the personality of the therapist in determining outcome of treatment. Frank's summary of the six features common to all psychotherapies begins with "an intense, emotionally charged, confiding relationship with a helping person" (1972, p. 37), and includes the following features: explanation of the cause of the patient's distress and a method for relieving it; provision of new information concerning the nature and sources of the patient's problems and possible alternative ways of dealing with them; strengthening of the patient's expectations of help through the personal qualities of the therapist, enhanced by his status in society and the setting in which he works; provision of success experiences which further heighten the patient's hopes and also affirm his sense of mastery, interpersonal competence, or capability; and facilitation of emotional arousal (1972). Two of these six features apply directly to the personal qualities of the therapist. By comparison, Torrey (1972) noted four common factors in cross-cultural psychotherapy: a shared world view leading to labelling of the disorder; benevolent personal qualities of the therapist; patient's expectations of being helped; and specific techniques of psychotherapy, such as interpretation.

This chapter is an effort by two therapists who have had substantial experience in intercultural psychotherapy to reflect on and evaluate their personal experiences. It is an effort to describe their development of self-awareness in intercultural psychotherapy and is based on the conviction that an understanding of the therapist's feelings about his or her own social class, racial, ethnic, and religious characteristics and their points of congruence with or divergence from a patient is critical to therapeutic effectiveness.

The two therapists come from strikingly different backgrounds and have had different professional training. Their common experience is their role as therapists in intercultural psychotherapy. They also share a broad professional interest in culture and healing. Dr. Harvey was born in Korea, came to the United states at age seventeen and has lived in the United States most of her adult life. Both Dr. Harvey's parents were educators, members of the Korean intelligentsia. Dr. Harvey and her siblings attended elite "public" schools in Korea. It was in America that she first experienced being a member of a very visible ethnic minority, although as a child she had lived as one of the colonized Korean majority under a Japanese administration. Dr. Harvey first trained in nursing in the United States. She later achieved a doctorate in anthropology, with particular interests in medical and psychiatric anthropology, at the same time continuing her professional role as a nurse-therapist, practicing in the multi-ethnic community of Hawaii. Dr. Wintrob was born in Canada, to which his parents had emigrated as children from Eastern Europe. Educated in medicine and psychiatry in Canada, Dr. Wintrob subsequently practiced in the United States, Southeast Asia, West Africa, France, Canada, and New Zealand. He has been living in Connecticut for most of the past ten years.

In the following sections of this chapter, the reflections of each author are reported in turn. Our intention in describing our experiences in this way is that readers may be encouraged to reflect on similar and contrasting aspects of their own background, professional training, and experience in intercultural counseling. It is our hope that by so reflecting on their background and experiences, this chapter may contribute toward increasing self-awareness in intercultural psychotherapy.

Reflections of Dr. Harvey

Until I attained the status of the "privileged," first through marriage to an American who was himself a professional person and then through my own academic and professional achievements, being an immigrant in America was an experience in devolution in social status. I was a curio, usually treated with charm and not infrequently praised for my pluck for going so far from home. But I was seldom taken seriously as a member of American society. In some ways, it proved advantageous not to be taken seriously, for I was not perceived as competition, a threat to the natives.

Even so, the predisposition of Americans as regards foreigners of certain occupations influenced me greatly in my choice of nursing as my undergraduate major and first professional field. Nursing, like medicine or dentistry, was perceived by Americans to be as much a utilitarian service occupation as a profession. Because of this, to have foreigners working in these fields was more acceptable than in some other fields, at least in the early 1960s when I started nursing. Care of the sick was apparently viewed as ministering to the body and therefore not a cultural or psychological matter. In fact, large-scale importation of foreign medical and nursing personnel was an ongoing practice.

For a long time, I felt quietly proud about being a Korean in America. However, I could never openly express my pride, especially since I had arrived in this country as negotiations for a cease-fire of the Korean War were just getting underway. I quickly became sensitive to the fact that Americans felt almost proprietary towards me—I was one of the "rescued," saved, with other South Koreans, from the clutches of the Communist North. One gentle, elderly Italian patient, grateful for the care I had given him and wanting to reassure me, held my hand and said, "Don't worry, sweetheart, one day we'll make Korea a part of the United States, and everything will be okay." I couldn't be angry at him, for, given the circumstances, he was expressing acceptance of me. I think that my security in my own cultural and ethnic identity sustained me through the processes of acculturation, professional education, and clinical experience. It also helped me to realize that I came from an elite background even though I could not expect that recognition and acknowledgment from Americans.

My first experience in a psychiatric setting was at a large public facility in New Jersey, where, for the entire duration of my clinical affiliation, I was filled with anger and protest which I sensed to be culturally motivated and therefore not to be voiced. The source of this disaccord seemed to lie in a basic difference between the world views of Korean and American cultures.

In my treatment of patients, especially chronic psychotic patients, my efforts were directed towards easing their immediate distress. It seemed to me, though, that many of them, with long histories of multiple hospitalizations, were beyond recovery in any essential sense and and that all I could do as their nurse was literally to look after them. That efforts were still made to intensively treat some of these patients by means of occupational, recreational, or psychological intervention in order to restore them to some antecedent level of function struck me as noble but imprudent. The principle that must underlie such expenditure of therapeutic resources, always in short supply, was almost a willful imposition on the patients. That is to say, through their efforts the hospital personnel seemed to confirm, with some desperation perhaps, the American value of the perfectibility of man—that every man is deserving of salvation, whatever the cost. Was the clinical staff daring the broken-of-the-soul-and-body to prove the American philosophical notion that all things are ultimately possible through sheer determination and hard work? By clinging to this belief, especially in the face of overwhelming evidence of its futility, the staff placed on their patients the additional burden of performing as acceptable patients. In order to please their care-givers and therapists, patients had to uphold certain cultural as well as ideological myths about the effectiveness of psychiatric interventions—even though many had become patients precisely because they were unable to live up to these myths (see also Townsend, 1975a, 1975b; Yamamoto, 1972).

Although I was equally aware that, but for such cultural myths, Americans would not expend the resources they do to give everyone the opportunity to realize their personal capabilities, it seemed incredible that in America the "net" seemed to be drawn to catch everyone in the hope of not missing those capable of rehabilitation. I realized that their cultural myths encouraged Americans, including health care personnel, to feel morally superior to East Asians. East Asians have for a long time had to function in the interest of economic efficiency in providing social welfare and health care. The Americans whom I perceived as imprudently wasteful of their scarce resources perceived East Asians as holding individual lives "cheap." Obviously, each value orientation must be judged in its own context to be appropriately understood. For the person moving from one cultural system to another, ethnocentrism is the greatest obstacle; unmonitored ethnocentrism in a therapist working with a client from another culture can be antitherapeutic.

As an immigrant, I paid close attention to the proverbs, axioms, and parables common in America, for it is on a rich diet of similar such distilled wisdom that we in East Asia are socialized as children. But two sayings always confused and disturbed me: "God helps those who help themselves" and "When you smile, the whole world smiles with you, but when you cry, you cry alone." These lines, it seemed to me, suggested values in direct contradiction to the altruistic ones mentioned earlier. They implied that one must show initiative and cheerful countenance in order to deserve help. I could not imagine a more total abandonment of the truly helpless.

Even among the hospital personnel, I sensed an undercurrent of hostility towards the chronically and severely disabled, those who in one way or another invalidated the American myth that everyone can be restored to functional ability, and that it is worth the effort. I also noted that patients had to show resourcefulness and initiative to identify potential sources of help and then were expected to show gratitude for services rendered, however short these fell of their needs. The stress inherent in the role of the identified mentally ill, I felt, was not sufficiently appreciated by those providing care for them. In fact, the American system of psychiatric care seemed to be harder on the "loser" than was the East Asian tradition.

I found it difficult to negotiate these contradictions between therapeutic goals and practices in America. One set of values nourished the "rescue fantasy." Another set of values dictated contempt for the very people in need of rescue, unless they manifested a degree of initiative and resourcefulness inconsistent with their impairment.

As an immigrant therapist, I was often uncertain about my perceptions of American culture and behavior. Whenever I was faced with an apparent contradiction, like the one I have described here, my first tendency was to doubt my perception, to reexamine it obsessively, and then to express my thoughts to my American colleagues in order to elicit their reactions. At times, the exercise led me to the ethnocentric conviction that my own culture was free of such conflicting values.

In the meantime, I lived an uneasy, watchful life. I felt it was my duty to help my patients learn effective strategies for coping with some of their culturally induced stresses which were real and immediate. But I also needed to do so without exciting their defensive ethnocentrism against me. My culturally based wish to be selective about working with only those patients who, I felt, could derive benefit from my professional care often resulted in accusations of favoritism by colleagues. When I explained my selective therapeutic behavior to them, my East Asian world views would be criticized as clinically incorrect. These experiences led me to an awareness of the culture-specific nature of American psychiatry (or perhaps of psychiatry in general).

I mention these experiences not to disapprove, rather to give context to some basically different cultural perceptions that influence the relationship between the therapist and the patient. This situation can be otherwise understood as the "poker-bridge" phenomenon in counseling that takes place interculturally. "Poker-bridge" is an expression current in Hawaii that refers to a cross-cultural situation in which one participant thinks the game being played is bridge and the other thinks it is poker. Each player is upset by the other's departure from the rules of the supposed game.

One clinical example of "poker-bridge" is the case of a Samoan woman who was hospitalized for delivery of her ninth baby not long after her arrival in Hawaii. In Samoa, she had given birth to her eight children at home in the traditional manner, that is, in the squatting position. As she was being positioned on her back in the delivery room, with communication limited to instructive gestures, she put up a furious resistance. She was desperate to find a place where she could squat securely. In the end, she was sedated, "made manageable," and gave birth according to American hospital practice. That this particular patient proved "uncooperative" in postpartum care is scarcely surprising. Fortunately for both staff and patient in this case, help was then sought and effective consultation provided by a bilingual/bicultural Samoan social worker.

An immigrant Korean family seeking psychiatric care provides another example of mutual misunderstanding in intercultural therapy. The family, convinced that one of its members needed psychiatric help, arrived collectively for the first meeting with the psychiatrist, all except the individual identified as disturbed. Given the Korean perception of mental disorders as resulting principally from interpersonal disharmony, it was completely logical, culturally, for the family to present itself to the psychiatrist in the absence of the disturbed family member. The ill member, already under stress, would not be expected to take an active role in initiating changes in the family dynamics. The American psychiatrist, unfamiliar with such cultural logic, was baffled and irritated; consequently, treatment was jeopardized from the outset.

Some time ago, I was asked to assess a Korean patient hospitalized for possible postpartum depression. The woman had become resistant when attempts were made to get her to walk the day following her delivery. As the nurses became more insistent, the patient became more agitated. When the nurses finally succeeded in getting her out of bed, she sat on the floor and went into a temper tantrum. When I spoke with her, it was apparent that the routine of postpartum care in an American hospital was so unexpected that she felt personally assaulted and humiliated. In Korea, where traditionally the young bride or daughter-in-law has the humblest status in the household of her husband, the prescribed twenty-one day postpartum period is marked by extraordinary privileges accorded the young mother, especially by the mother-in-law. For many Korean women, the postpartum period is a cherished reservoir of happy memories that ease the drudgery of daily domestic life. This patient had expected her experience in an American hospital to be different, but was not prepared for the humiliation in terms of her own cultural expectations.

Experiences such as these lead some therapists who are unfamiliar with a multicultural environment to develop a protective retrenchment, firmly consolidating their ethnocentric views. For others, these experiences provoke self-questioning that results in rethinking the culture-bound nature of their psychiatric knowledge, its clinical application, its meaning to patients, and the impact of cultural differences on the patient-therapist relationship.

Even when such self-questioning results in increased awareness and reorientation towards increased intercultural sensitivity, it does not eliminate problems. Some patients, with a history of frustrating experiences with therapists of the ethnic majority, may become more defensive towards those who wish to probe details of their ethnic background.

Such therapists are sometimes perceived as intrusive, demanding to be taken into the cultural and ethnic confidence of the patient and removing from him his control as a gatekeeper of his culture. The patient, and here I can speak as a patient as well, finds the therapist's interest in his culture at once flattering, seductive, and threatening. The patient feels vulnerable to cultural penetration once he shares his culture with the therapist.

It is also important to remember that, just as some men will not go to a female physician and some women will not go to a male gynecologist, some patients will similarly avoid going to an ethnic minority therapist. I can recall a Polish American patient with a marked accent and serious psychiatric problems who, irate at discovering me in attendance, bellowed out that he wanted no "chink" nurse. To him, a man already indignant and feeling betrayed by American medicine, I was the symbolic last straw that broke the camel's back. My foreignness was an insult that aggravated his condition. The immigrant therapist of ethnic minority background may have all too many opportunities for a thorough examination of his self-identity on the personal, ethnic, and cultural levels.

Another difficulty I experienced as an immigrant, minority, and female therapist was that of not being taken seriously by patients and, sometimes, by colleagues as well. Asians are commonly thought by Americans to be much younger than their actual age; and when I was in my twenties, I had to struggle to be treated as an adult, let alone as a therapist. This was a serious problem in my professional development, for people seemed to refuse to take what I did seriously—even my errors. There were much lower expectations of my performance. I was perceived, above all, as an exotic "China-doll" who could talk in English. The situation also conferred upon me the dubious advantage of *not* being considered a threat to other therapists.

Because of my minority ethnicity and immigrant status, I experienced difficulty asserting professional authority. Many Americans have never dealt with Asians who are professionals and find it psychologically disorienting, even disturbing, to do so, particularly when the professional is a young Asian female immigrant. For therapists like myself, there are problems that must be dealt with that may be absent from the usual therapist-patient relationship involving American-born therapists of the majority culture. I have, for example, treated patients who move from a seemingly conversational interest in my accent to a persistent interest in my life history, causing me considerable anxiety as I search for an uncontentious way to regain control of the process of treatment.

On occasion, my married Anglo surname has attracted similar curiosity. The simple answer that I am married to an American can cause some male patients to reminisce about their military tour of duty in Korea and to assume that I met my husband when he was stationed in Korea. In Hawaii, the fact that I am Korean can provoke some patients, again usually male, into extraneous commentaries on "hostess bars" (called "Korean bars" in Hawaii). With some male patients, these statements sometimes signify a seductive attempt to render me ineffective as a therapist. Such stereotypic responses from patients introduce unexpected ramifications into the therapist-patient relationship and carry with them a strong temptation for me to respond with similarly stereotypic defenses. Then I feel guilty, vulnerable, and anxious. The fine balance I must strike in both my roles as a therapist and as a representative of my ethnic group and gender requires a constant effort at self-awareness.

Experiences of this kind convinced me that I needed to structure my relationships with patients much more formally than might otherwise have been my inclination. I came to recognize and to accept the greater necessity for distance, achieved through formal structure, that a visibly different minority female therapist must maintain.

The emotional task for me was to learn *not* to take these problems personally while giving them careful attention in the context of therapy. I had to will into my consciousness a certain level of trust; that just as I would not judge all of America by the behavior of any one American or take to task any one American on behalf of the entire society, so also would my American patients come to trust in my professional authority and integrity. This was helpful in keeping my therapist's role foremost not only with patients but also with colleagues.

As an immigrant therapist, I had to cope with the lingering doubt of many American-born patients that a foreigner can understand their culture and language in sufficient depth to understand the scope and complexity of their personal problems. That such doubt exists becomes ironically apparent at that moment in therapy when the patient feels reassured that it was an unnecessary source of concern. Patients, usually the more sophisticated ones, make comments such as: "For a foreigner, you have an exceptional grasp of American society. Did you go to school over here?" Or "Your English is almost better than mine. Where did you learn to speak so well?" They seem to be searching for an "American" explanation for my credibility as a therapist. Or else they seek an acceptable explanation by identifying me as a member of an elite class in my own society, to make me an exception to a cultural stereotype.

Cross-culturally sophisticated patients can be an unexpected source of complication in other ways. They tend sometimes to be hypercritical of America and to romanticize other cultures on the basis of isolated aspects, brief experiences of living there, or simply reading about them. In working with such patients, I have found myself rising to the defense of American culture, trying to provide proper cultural contexts that deromanticize their notions of other cultures. I have done this especially to discourage a concomitant propensity for "locating" their problematic behaviors in alien cultural norms and thereby justifying them. Some patients also try to second-guess the cultural context of the therapist, whether out of a desire to be accommodating, to uphold their self-image as cross-culturally sophisticated, or out of a subconscious distrust of an immigrant, minority therapist. That is, the patient tries to be bicultural in his interactions with the therapist who is officially operating monoculturally during therapy. This can result in wasteful confusion. Patients like these can be exhausting to work with and have left me at times longing to treat those who represent the absolutely "standard" American mainstream culture.

Another difficulty I have encountered in intercultural therapy is a culturally influenced therapeutic style and strategy. Coming from a culture heavily reliant on proverbs, riddles, and parables as vehicles for socialization, I naturally incorporated the use of these in therapy and came to grief thereby, particularly in group therapy sessions. More accustomed to the analytical approach to problems and the confrontational, interpersonal style, my American patients viewed my use of parables and proverbs as oblique—confirmation of me as an "inscrutable Oriental"!

I have learned that in working with immigrant or minority patients, whether from my own background or another, some basic teaching of cross-cultural equivalences in reference and meaning is necessary before proceeding with therapy for the personal problems of the patient. This is a common recognition among intercultural therapists and others involved in delivering health care in multiethnic, multicultural environments.

The role of the "culture-broker" is almost naturally foisted upon the bicultural therapist working with patients from ethnic minorities, especially one's own. Such patients tend to seek validation of their perceptions of American values and norms. Some have sought my endorsement of their censorship of American culture and people, or expect—sometimes even demand—that I make sense of aspects of American life that confuse and frustrate them. Because many of the difficulties they experience can be traced to their limited understanding of the dominant culture or to the conflicts generated by cultural differences, and because I had similar experiences when I came to America, the temptation is to give them "tips" on how to get through the "mazeway of America." I have had to become watchful of this tendency in me, for, while it may facilitate the acculturation of immigrant or minority patients, it can also erode their ethnic identity and their need to learn for themselves. Rescue fantasy born of empathy can be as detrimental to effective therapy as that born of ethnocentrism. The ideal approach in these cases seems to be to help patients achieve bicultural competence rather than assimilation; in this context the bicultural immigrant therapist may have an advantage.

A minority therapist is sometimes regarded inexplicably by his colleagues as an expert on the behavior of clients from his background, when such behavior escapes their grasp. In such situations, I have sometimes felt myself isolated in the "demilitarized zone" of the bilingual and bicultural. Even though my comparative knowledge of the two cultures may be greater than that of my colleagues, to impart it is no easy matter: the intuitive character of much of this knowledge makes verbal exposition difficult. Bicultural competence evolves through intensive and extensive immersion in the cultures involved and through both formal and informal processes. Stating one's comparative assessment of behavior as it may be influenced by culture is easier than demonstrating in their totality the processes by which one has come to one's understanding; even the former is a difficult enough task. It is frustrating to have an audience of therapists, some eagerly willing to be shown cross-cultural equivalencies in constructs and behavior patterns the better to understand their clients, and to find that bicultural and bilingual facility are not readily amenable to intellectual explication and transmission. A minority therapist in such a predicament finds that he must plead for belief in his explanations on the basis of the credibility he has established with his colleagues in other areas.

The same feeling of "cultural loneliness" arises in relating to immigrant patients, particularly from my own country, who expect, however implicitly, that I will serve as their advocate and "culture broker." One such patient was a Korean woman divorced from her American husband, whose refusal to talk to clinic personnel was assumed to be the consequence of a language barrier. When she finally spoke through me as an interpreter, she acknowledged the language barrier but added very astutely that no non-Korean could understand what she meant, even if she had had no language difficulty. She said that the best policy under the circumstances was not to talk, for talking and trying to be understood by Americans—particularly her husband—and trying to understand them in turn, had led to her marital difficulties and psychiatric problems.

I think there is great value for the minority therapist and for me, less discomfort, in serving as a therapist to persons from different but related cultural groups such as the Filipinos, Tongans, or Samoans. The degree of cultural difference and distance allows me to feel more gratified as a therapist, and less taken to task as a "culture broker." There is less expectation of me to serve as a "culture broker" and to understand automatically things about the shared cultural background of the therapist and the patient—which may be distorted in the latter's mind.

A clear advantage of a bicultural therapist is the capacity to view problems from a greater variety of ways than is generally available to the monocultural therapist. For just that reason some patients prefer a foreign or minority therapist in the belief that the therapist will have a more objective view of their culture and society and can, as a result, be more objective in helping them understand their problems.

Reflections of Dr. Wintrob

Toronto in the 1940s and 1950s, when I grew up and went through school, was a multicultural city, but the dominant majority tended to ignore that fact to the same degree that ethnic minority groups were sensitive to their disadvantaged status as non-British immigrants. The differences that impinged on my family and me were ethnic and religious, not race or social class.

Sensitivity to people of different backgrounds was an intrinsic part of my early life experience. Yet, when I finished medical school in Toronto and went to New York as an intern at a large public hospital, I was unprepared for the differences I encountered. The patient population was not only more ethnically diverse, but it was also racially different and less varied in social class than that of the Toronto teaching hospitals. The backgrounds of the professional staff were much more varied than in Toronto as well, and the quality of both professional and social interactions was sufficiently unfamiliar that I experienced a completely unanticipated period of troubled self-scrutiny and an erosion of personal and professional self-esteem. This surprised me because in most respects the organization and functioning of large, public teaching hospitals in Toronto and New York are more similar than they are different. But as I found out, differences do not need to be major to be stress-inducing, even temporarily disorienting. I was painfully aware that I had to communicate with patients and with staff across a cultural gap. I was anxious about measuring up to performance expectations, worried about making stupid and obvious procedural mistakes. It was the familiar story of the greening of another young doctor.

I did the expected thing to cope with my discomfort: I increased my professional efficiency by increasing my social and emotional distance. That kind of defensive distancing can be adaptive; one feels much less conflict and turmoil and more in control of emotional responses. It allows for a brief psychosocial moratorium, for self-reflection, necessary to restore self-confidence. Increasing my social and emotional distance was a regressive adaptation. The cost was diminished expressivity, diminished ability to establish and maintain rapport—to empathize. In short, the cost of affective distancing was a loss of interpersonal sensitivity, the very quality needed for effectiveness as a physician and as a psychotherapist, whether in a monocultural or multicultural environment.

I mention the stressful beginning of my internship because, perhaps naively, I was unprepared for it. After all, there was no reason for me to expect emotionally disorienting differences between two large cities, six hundred miles apart, which shared common cultural and medical traditions. I mention this experience because it generated in me a sense of cultural dysadaptation (Wintrob, 1969). I learned that relatively minor changes in a person's familiar environment and emotional support system can be stressful enough to provoke temporarily regressive dysadaptation responses, and that a phase of self-scrutiny, in which one is preoccupied with personal conflicts and identifications, can be a productive, restorative experience in self-awareness for a therapist. A sensitive and detailed description of this process is recounted by Briggs in her extensive fieldwork with the Utku Eskimos of the Canadian Arctic (1970).

Since my internship in New York, I have conducted psychotherapy in several countries, including two years in Liberia and one year in New Zealand. In those settings, where I functioned primarily in a treatment role, as well as those where I worked in both research and treatment—with Cree Indians in Canada, with physicians in Peru, and with blacks and Puerto Ricans in Connecticut—I again experienced some of that complex of feelings of cultural dysadaptation that I went through during my internship. What has made the greatest impression on me through all of this is the constant need to evaluate my own feelings about the person I am treating: the degree to which I identify with the patient and the extent to which I over-identify with aspects of his racial, ethnic, social class, and religious background, as distinct from his individual psychosocial conflicts. I have learned that the therapist's feelings about patients, especially in the context of intercultural psychotherapy, are greatly influenced by the therapist's own sense of strangeness in an unfamiliar setting, by his positive and negative feelings about the people with and for whom he is working, and by the extent to which he identifies a given patient with a particular group, class, subculture, or society. The tendency of the therapist to react to his own foreignness in other countries and to be affected by cultural stereotypes of patients whose backgrounds are unfamiliar to him is common to everyone. It affects those who are comparatively sophisticated cultural relativists, such as anthropologists and psychologists, just as it does other people (Nash & Wintrob, 1972).

I can illustrate this cultural stereotyping tendency from my own experience. Living in Liberia was difficult for me. Being the only psychiatrist in the country and charged with developing and running the country's mental health services, I felt overloaded with both clinical and administrative demands. I felt increasingly constrained by high-level government officials and inhibited from carrying out the treatment programs we had discussed and agreed upon. At that time (the mid-1960s) in Liberia, most upper-level government officials defined themselves as Americo-Liberians, descendants of those liberated American slaves who settled along that part of the West African coast during the first half of the nineteenth century and founded the first black African republic in 1847.

Americo-Liberians distinguished themselves from Liberians of tribal affiliation. Most of the patients and staff with whom I worked were tribal Liberians. As I sensed a growing resistance from Americo-Liberian officialdom, I began to dichotomize my feelings about my patients, forming a stronger positive identification with tribal patients. I was well aware that this splitting of the images of the two Liberian groups interfered with my ability to sympathize with and evaluate the interpersonal conflicts of Americo-Liberian patients. This realization forced me to monitor my own reactions in order to recognize and separate my own conflicts from those of the patient, to separate stereotype from individual, to make a distinction between psychological conflicts and sociopolitical ones.

I would also point out that it is rare that a therapist in the United States is required to work in close contact with policy makers and the national political process. In many developing countries, that role is thrust on the therapist because of his administrative responsibilities for program development, a role that may be a dangerous "ego-trip," distorting his capacity to draw accurate inferences from clinical data. As several of my patients in Liberia were senior decision makers in government and business, this was another aspect of my self-monitoring. My point here is that while ideological neutrality is neither necessary nor desirable for a therapist, it is essential that the therapist not distort the patient's communications by introducing ideological inferences not intended by the patient. Each patient needs to be considered and treated as an individual, not as a representative of a group, class, race, or ideology.

The therapist must be aware of and keep separate his own feelings of disapproval of the political, ethnic, and social-class biases of a given patient and the interpersonal conflicts of that patient that find expression in prejudiced attitudes and acts. One patient, an Americo-Liberian official, who frequently expressed anger about American companies for their exploitation of Liberian natural resources and Liberian workers, was at the same time demonstrating his ambivalence towards me, the American therapist he needed to consult, towards himself for succumbing to symptoms of emotional distress, and towards the administration in which he was an official for its unwillingness to support the legislative changes he proposed to reduce foreign exploitation. Other patients, members of the limited expatriate community in Liberia, would overgeneralize about their difficulties with Liberian officials, Liberian laborers, and household workers. In this kind of stressful intercultural environment, cultural stereotyping readily occurs and scapegoating reduces the individual's capacity for personal responsibility for problem-solving. This short-term, adaptive, coping strategy becomes increasingly maladaptive and psychologically constricting over time, unless it is reversed by the enhanced self-awareness of sensitive reflection or psychotherapy.

Working in this kind of environment with patients who sometimes seemed like representatives of, if not advocates for, their particular groups, I could not avoid examining my own attitudes and values, my background and interests. Being the only psychiatrist in the country made my need for self-assessment more compelling; there was, except for my wife, a psychiatric nurse, no other psychotherapist to share experiences with or refer patients to. I often had the feeling that I was treading a narrow path between conflicting groups in a rapidly changing society, trying to avoid the traps of my own group identifications in order to keep therapeutic focus on my patients' needs.

Reflecting my own biases and personal commitments, I devoted much of my effort in Liberia to developing counseling services for students. It is widely recognized in Liberia that higher education is the sine qua non to good jobs, and the competition is intense. Anxiety among students is common. It was easy for me to empathize with their struggles and aspirations—a concern that I thought was politically uncomplicated.

I was, however, unaware of the real complication and the extent to which I had sublimated my conflicting feelings about Liberians until I prepared my first clinical paper in Liberia. It was entitled "A Study of Disillusionment" and described the dysadaptation reactions of Liberian students who had returned from advanced training abroad (Wintrob, 1967). The paper contained several case histories of Liberians who had been trained abroad and whose talents were both envied and resented by their colleagues. These colleagues had not had similar opportunities, and their authority was challenged and bypassed by the returning students. On the other hand, some returning students found themselves intensely frustrated by what they perceived to be bureaucratic resistance to changes in the established order, leaving them with a sense of helpless rage at their inability to put to use the skills they had acquired overseas. Since I was functioning under what I felt were similar conditions, I channelled my frustrations into writing about theirs, despite—and to some extent because of—the possibility that publication of my article would have deleterious consequences for the implementation of the treatment programs I had been working towards.

Such distortion of objectivity, as in the Liberian case, is important material from which to learn, material that is all too rarely discussed by therapists. But the same risk of misinterpretation of clinical data also comes from positive overidentification with a group. To some extent, this was the case with me in my treatment of students and tribal Liberians. It was a more striking feature of my approach to Cree Indian patients in Quebec. Influenced by my perceptions of the powerless status of tribal Liberians, and by the anthropologist's proclivity to identify with the people he studies, I knew that I would have to watch my tendency to interpret the conflicts of Cree students as the intrapsychic sequelae of prejudice and Cree political powerlessness. I would have to reevaluate my reactions to the clinical data because the content more often related to interpersonal, intra-Cree concerns than it did to the concerns of the Cree as a Canadian minority subject to discrimination. Of course, the two themes often interdigitated in the expression of Cree students' conflicts, and much of my therapeutic effort was devoted to understanding precisely that interdigitation. That fact did not diminish the necessity for carefully monitoring my own feelings so that I did not incorrectly infer discrimination in every discussion of, for example, a Cree student breaking up with his white girlfriend, or an older Cree woman with very limited ability to communicate in English or French being evacuated to a distant mental hospital for psychiatric treatment by personnel unfamiliar with Cree language or culture.

During recent years, several colleagues and I have been studying how different ethnic groups in Connecticut explain mental illness. We have been particularly concerned with supernatural explanations of emotional disorders—with hexing and rootwork explanations among blacks and spiritism and witchcraft beliefs among Puerto Ricans (Gaviria & Wintrob, 1975, 1979; Wintrob, 1973). This research, growing out of our psychotherapeutic contact with people who share these supernatural explanations of their symptoms, caused us to review our feelings about who would be the appropriate therapist for such people. It was apparent that a majority of both patients and community informants felt that the treatment methods of community healers were more effective than psychiatric treatment, largely because of the closer "fit" between healers' explanations of illness and the community residents' explanations of illness. Accordingly, healers' treatment procedures were more understandable to many patients and their families, involved a greater degree of family and community support for the victim of the illness, and were felt to produce better results on the grounds that indigenous healing techniques could neutralize or remove the spell and thus lead to complete recovery. Psychiatric treatments, on the other hand, could only relieve the distressing symptoms caused by the spell.

Our experience in Connecticut led us to remember that one of the strongest biases we have as therapists is our commitment to what we choose to consider rational, scientific explanation. It was a threat to our sense of professional identity and self-esteem to have our scientific world view neither welcomed nor accepted by a large part of the population we were there to help. Had I not had the Liberian and Cree experiences, I have little doubt I would have felt more defensive about the issue. Therapists who want to work in an intercultural context need to remind themselves, as I again had reason to do in Connecticut, that we tend to be least anxious and feel most effective when we treat people whose world view corresponds with our own. This is certainly the case for the sample of

150 psychiatrists in Canada, the United States, and Mexico interviewed by members of the American Psychiatric Association Task Force on Ethnocentricity (American Psychiatric Association Task Force, 1979).

Nonetheless, there are important limits to that generalization. In our work with black and Puerto Rican patients in Connecticut as well as in the American Psychiatric Association study, we found considerable variation in the degree to which patients and therapists identified with the beliefs and behaviors of their families of origin, neighborhood, ethnic group, or macrosociety. The limits of generalization are the determinants of treatment of a given patient by a particular therapist.

In my own experience, the patients who have caused me the greatest worry about my objectivity were those who are closest to me in background and interest. It is far more difficult for me to be confident about my objectivity or to maintain a degree of emotional distance necessary for a fair interpretation of the patient's conflicts when his life experiences are very similar to my own. This has been particularly apparent to me in my treatment of physicians of similar ethnic background, who are members of the faculty of my own university and who are subject to the same academic conflicts I myself undergo. These cases have taught me that by keeping some affective distance between me and the patient, I can be more helpful in working through the patient's conflicts without my own conflicts interfering with that process. Obviously, the opposite is also true; complete unfamiliarity with the background and personal experiences of a patient makes psychotherapy an enterprise of doubtful value with high potential for frustration of both patient and therapist. That is not to say we should not attempt psychotherapy with people who diverge—even diverge sharply—from our world view, rather that we should carefully assess the objectives and limitations of the therapy we undertake, and just as carefully explain those objectives and limitations to the people who ask for our help. Our patients will help us revise the goals of therapy as the essential relationship of interpersonal trust is consolidated during the course of treatment. With increased openness of communication, the mutual misperceptions, biases, and mistaken interpretations of clinical data can be corrected.

We should recognize too that the fact of the therapist being an outsider may be the very reason he has been asked to fill the helping role. One of the few black psychiatrists in my area, for example, has been told repeatedly by his Caucasian patients that they feel more secure about his maintaining objectivity and preserving confidentiality because of his difference, both of upbringing and experience. (He adds that some of these patients like to use ghetto talk with him "to establish their liberal credentials.") For similar reasons, one of my Jewish colleagues has been selected as therapist by a number of Catholic and Protestant clergymen who feel they can more easily communicate their personal conflicts to a therapist of a different religion. I have had similar experiences with Americo-Liberian patients who were understandably concerned that a breach of confidentiality could have serious repercussions for themselves, their families, and others within their relatively closed society.

This is the kind of situation that comes up time and again in the intercultural context of psychotherapy. In my view, it is an unparalleled challenge to the therapist to enhance his self-awareness in the interest of greater therapeutic effectiveness.

Stresses of Intercultural Psychotherapy: Some Common Themes

Having described and reflected on some of the experiences each author has had in the context of intercultural psychotherapy, we turn now to a review and assessment of themes we feel are particularly common, stressful, and important for therapists to understand as they engage in treatment of people who are different from themselves in racial, ethnic, and social class background, religious conviction, political philosophy, and conceptions of illness and its appropriate treatment.

A shared system of ideas, from a comprehensive cultural understanding to a specific psychotherapeutic ideology, is assumed to exist among therapists working together, just as it is between therapists and those whom they treat. Such an assumption becomes jarringly obvious in situations of intercultural psychotherapy where therapists and patients find themselves at an impasse at the crossroads of their different cultures and world views. As the differences in the authors' personal experiences show, there are many other factors that further influence and complicate the process of intercultural psychotherapy. Among these are the age, gender, physical appearance, and ethnicity of both patient and therapist, the comparative world views of patient and therapist, the relative social prestige of therapists' professions, and even the relative international political status of their countries of origin.

The complexity and multiplicity of these several factors, and the processes through which they exert their influence on the course of intercultural psychotherapy, suggest that in the generally uncharted waters of intercultural psychotherapy, each therapist must discover for himself how best to steer the course of therapy. Reading about the experiences of others cannot immunize the therapist to the need for reflection, for self-awareness, that comes from experiencing the stress—and the exhilaration—inherent in the process of intercultural therapy.

Our experiences suggest certain specific pitfalls inherent in the process of intercultural psychotherapy. Perhaps the most serious, though not the most obvious, is the tendency to interpret behavior appropriate to an unfamiliar culture in terms of one's own culture, distorting in the process the meaning of the behavior sometimes to the point of labelling it psy-

chopathological. Although such distortions are more often the product
of lack of knowledge than of willful ethnocentrism, the effects are the
same: ethnocentric misjudgment of therapeutic goals on the one hand,
and misuse of therapeutic interventions on the other.

There is also a tendency among some patients to manifest a degree of
cross-cultural sophistication that exceeds their actual cross-cultural
knowledge and experience when working with a therapist of immigrant
or minority background. Such patients can complicate the therapeutic
process by making darting excursions out of the American cultural medium, in which the therapy is being conducted, to adopt inadequately
understood, fragmented, and isolated traits of another culture or ethnic
group.

Yet another inherent source of potential difficulty in intercultural psychotherapy arises out of cultural differences in affective styles and interpersonal relatedness. Culturally influenced affective behavior, which appears to be more resistant to intercultural "translation" than cognitive
behavior, can sometimes render the therapist ineffectual.

A clear advantage of an immigrant therapist or one from a cultural
background significantly different from that of the patient has been cited
as that of greater objectivity. For the immigrant or minority therapist,
this advantage is a double-edged sword. He is more likely to comprehend
the contradictions between the ideal culture and the actual culture than
either his native-born colleagues or patients but he also runs a greater
risk of exciting ethnocentric defenses in colleagues and patients as he
tries to suggest to the former alternative perspectives or tries to help the
latter negotiate cultural inconsistencies with greater strategic effectiveness.

A difficulty shared by all therapists in intercultural psychotherapy is
the need to clarify for immigrant or minority patients the cultural norms
of the host country, behavior which patients may find confusing or disorienting. This need is sometimes overlooked in an idealistic over-
identification with the patient and may contribute instead to creating
"interculturally burned out" patients. To such patients, therapists who
are interculturally sensitive and willing to learn the patient's cultural
frame of reference may seem to be, notwithstanding their good will, intrusive, exploitative, and more threatening than therapists who remain
consistently and rigidly ethnocentric.

Generally, therapists can do very little immediately and tangibly to
alter either the cultural or the psychiatric system to meet the needs of minority or immigrant patients, even when these have been accurately
assessed. The empathetic and enthusiastic therapist working with immigrant or minority patients thus risks losing his credibility if he prema-
turely and openly identifies himself as their advocate or culture broker
and fails to be effective in that role. These patients feel doubly betrayed

for having had their hopes raised and for having been made more vulnerable through disclosure and trust. They feel more exposed and vulnerable to psychological penetration, and consequently, may feel more angry and helpless than before.

Some experiences Dr. Harvey described were more specific to her as an Asian, immigrant, and female, and to her as a nurse therapist rather than a psychiatrist. Early in her career she had difficulty being taken seriously as a professional and had to overcome stereotypic attributions in order to assert her professional authority and maintain the kind of social distance expected of therapists in relationship to their patients. At the same time, she had to resist responding defensively to those stereotypic attributions, learning not to take them personally. There is, at the same time, the need on the part of minority or culturally different therapists to recognize that it poses additional stress for some patients, distressed as they are already, to receive care from therapists who are perceived by them and by the larger host society to belong to a less prestigious or even devalued ethnic group or foreign nationality.

For his part, the immigrant therapist is pulled by opposite inclinations. He has a lingering sense of tentativeness, at least in the early stages, about his interpretation of the host culture and is therefore more cautious in his treatment approaches. Or, isolated from the culture of his upbringing, he becomes nostalgically ethnocentric and less sympathetic towards native-born patients. Or he fluctuates between the two poles.

Some experiences described are particularly characteristic of the bicultural therapist who practices in a community where there is a substantial population of his own ethnic background. One common experience may be the roles of the "culture broker" and the "intercultural ombudsman" which native-born colleagues unfamiliar with the therapist's culture of origin, and patients from the therapist's ethnic background unfamiliar with the ways of the host culture may foist upon the therapist. The resulting feeling of "cultural loneliness" may be a significant source of stress for the therapist.

Dr. Wintrob has described the process of social and emotional distancing from colleagues and patients in response to a sharp increase in professional self-doubt, anxiety, and personal insecurity that followed migration and sudden role change from student to responsible therapist. We have conceptualized this kind of distancing as a means of coping with "stranger anxiety" (Nash, 1970), a temporary regression to restore self-esteem and reduce the sense of unfamiliarity. Therapists, like others who must adapt to cultural differences and changes in status and professional role when working in another cultural environment, need to recover from cultural dysadaptation before they can effectively treat people (GAP Report No. 41, 1958; Wintrob, 1969). It is critical, however, that the regressive distancing that is the first stage in adaptation be temporary and that the cultural dysadaptation not be protracted or lead to a more stable state of defensive ethnocentrism and intolerance. Professional maturation and increasing self-awareness, whether derived from intracultural or intercultural experience, are factors directly related to the duration and intensity of the kind of cultural dysadaptation we have described.

We have pointed out the problem of the therapist over-identifying with particular aspects of a patient's background, attitudes, values, or life experiences. Sometimes these over-identifications are positive and supportive, at other times negative and rejecting. In either case, the phenomenon occurs because the patient's life experiences strike a particularly resonant chord in the therapist, often bringing to the surface of consciousness intense emotions that the therapist may not have been aware of or understood. The emotional splitting of ethnic groups within a culture is the most important experience of this kind that the authors have been familiar with. We recognize the need to guard against this natural proclivity of all therapists to over-identify with their patients and to take up their causes without adequate analysis of the patients' distortions in reporting and therapists' distortions in evaluation. As part of the process of splitting and over-identification, our experience suggests a tendency for therapists to displace frustration and resentment derived from both professional and personal dysadaptation onto individuals or groups unconnected with the sources of frustration.

It bears repeating that the processes of over-identification, splitting, and displacement as discussed above are *not* conscious or intentional. On the contrary, these processes occur because of a conscious attempt to maintain professional equanimity and objectivity. By trying not to openly manifest frustration or resentment, one becomes unaware of the complex ways by which we suppress, neutralize, and sublimate our more ambivalent conflicted feelings about certain patients, groups, and aspects of our own personality. Without some self-scrutiny and increased self-awareness, the ambivalent and conflicted feelings of the therapist can jeopardize personal adaptation and professional effectiveness.

We have referred to how the intercultural therapist can be seduced by functioning in close proximity to political power when he is one of the very few therapists in a country whose mental health services are in an early stage of development. Not only may the therapist function in closer proximity to a country's leaders than he is used to, but he may, in the conduct of his professional activities, have access to a range of information that makes confidentiality an issue of ever-present importance. By the same token, having such information increases the therapist's professional and social loneliness in these comparatively small scale and highly personalistic societies. Given these working and living conditions, the importance of the emotional support of a few close friends or family members helps to maintain emotional balance and equanimity of judgment. Perhaps it is equally important for therapists to be aware of their need for confirmation of their worth, a confirmation that usually comes from colleagues with whom one works closely, from peers, supervisors, and students; in an unfamiliar cultural environment, there may be very few, if any, such people.

One of the most ambivalently regarded and conflict-generating problems encountered in intercultural psychotherapy is the need to define the appropriateness of treatment methods and the limitations and expected goals of treatment. To assess these issues adequately, the therapist must consider the degree of "fit" between his conceptual model of the causes, manifestations, and treatment of emotional disorders and that of the patient's, the patient's relatives, and the cultural environment (Torrey, 1972; Kleinman, Eisenberg, & Good, 1978). The therapist needs to determine how the patient "explains" the nature of his symptoms and especially the extent to which the patient's explanation is in accord with a "folk" or a "scientific" world view of sickness and its treatment. This, in turn, will lead the therapist to examine his feelings about treating people whose conceptual models of illness are dissimilar, even in contradiction to his own. Should the therapist expect his intervention to lead to symptom reduction, or psychological insight and conflict resolution, or functional recovery, or cure? How will the patient and the patient's family view the therapist's treatment goals and methods of intervention? Indeed, should the therapist intervene at all, or is it more appropriate for certain patients to be treated by alternative healers? (Kleinman, 1979; Ness & Wintrob, 1980.)

Finally, we have considered the limits of the sensible generalization that most therapists feel most comfortable and clinically effective treating people whose backgrounds and attitudes are similar to their own. One of the limits to the validity of this generalization is that therapists like variety in their professional life; they prefer to treat people with some variation in their backgrounds, attitudes, world views, and life experiences, just as they prefer to treat people with a variety of clinical problems and diagnoses (American Psychiatric Association Task Force on Ethnocentricity, 1979). Therapists may be chosen by certain patients *because* they are dissimilar. Therapists need to be sensitive to the tendency of certain patients to project a broad range of fantasies onto their therapists. Both Dr. Harvey and Dr. Wintrob have cited examples of some of those projected fantasies; other case examples are given by Hsu and Tseng (1972), Kinzie (1972), and Spiegel (1964).

Among the reasons for a patient choosing a therapist of a different background are those that have less projected fantasy and more objective reality. One such belief is that a therapist will be more insightful or more objective in evaluating the patient's conflicts because of his "outsider's view." Or that the therapist can be more confidently entrusted with confidential information because he is less likely to have any social or personal involvement with the people or events the patient is concerned about. Among the reasons for choosing a therapist that have a greater proportion of projected fantasy than objective reality are such ethnocentrically biased notions as Jewish therapists being more perceptive, those of French background being more philosophical, Italians being more emotional and empathetic, Chinese more intellectually precise. It would be easy to list many more such examples. Whatever the details and qualities of these projections, the therapist's task is to identify them and clarify them—first for his own understanding, and then for the patient's.

In considering the limits of the generalization about treating persons of similar background to the therapist, we have emphasized the need for therapists to maintain a degree of emotional distance from their patients; positive or negative over-identification, splitting and displacement of therapists' conflicted feelings may be generated as much by patients whose personal background and life experiences are very similar to those of the therapist as by patients who are strikingly dissimilar and unfamiliar to him.

References

American Psychiatric Association Task Force on Ethnocentricity among Psychiatrists. *Ethnicity and ethnocentricity among psychiatrists.* Paper presented at the American Psychiatric Association Meeting, Chicago, May 1979.

Bolman, W. M. Cross-cultural psychotherapy. *American Journal of Psychiatry*, 1968, *124*, 1237–1244.

Briggs, J. *Never in anger: Protrait of an Eskimo family.* Cambridge: Harvard University Press, 1970.

Fabrega, Jr., H. *Disease and social behavior: An interdisciplinary perspective.* Cambridge: M.I.T. Press, 1974.

Foulks, E. F., Wintrob, R. M., Westermeyer, J., & Favazza, A. R. (Eds.). *Current perspectives in cultural psychiatry.* New York: Spectrum, 1977.

Frank, J. D. Common features of psychotherapy. *Australian and New Zealand Journal of Psychiatry*, 1972, *6*, 34–40.

Frank, J. D. *Persuasion and healing: A comparative study of psychotherapy.* Second edition. Baltimore: Johns Hopkins Press, 1973.

Gaviria, M., & Wintrob, R. M. The foreign medical graduate who returns home after post-graduate training in U.S.A.: A Peruvian case study. *Journal of Medical Education*, 1975, *50*, 160–175.

Gaviria, M., & Wintrob, R. M. Spiritist or psychiatrist: Treatment of mental illness among Puerto Ricans in two Connecticut towns. *Journal of Operational Psychiatry*, 1979, *10*, 40–46.

Group for the Advancement of Psychiatry. *Working abroad: A discussion of psychological attitudes and adaptation in new situations.* New York: International Relations Committee, GAP Report No. 41, 1958.

Hsu, J., & Tseng, W. S. Intercultural psychotherapy. *Archives of General Psychiatry*, 1972, *27*, 700–705.

Kinzie, J. D. Cross-cultural psychotherapy: The Malaysian experience. *American Journal of Psychotherapy*, 1972, *26*, 220–231.

Kinzie, J. D. Lessons from cross-cultural psychotherapy. *American Journal of Psychotherapy*, 1978, *32*, 510–520.

Kleinman, A. *Patients and healers in the context of culture.* Berkeley: University of California Press, 1979.

Kleinman, A., Eisenberg, L., & Good, B. Culture, illness and care: Clinical lessons from anthropologic and cross-cultural research. *Annals of Internal Medicine*, 1978, *88*, 251–258.

Nash, D. *A community in limbo: An anthropological study of an American community abroad.* Bloomington: Indiana University Press, 1970.

Nash, D., & Wintrob, R. M. The emergence of self-consciousness in ethnography. *Current Anthropology*, 1972, *13*, 527–542.

Ness, R., & Wintrob, R. The emotional impact of fundamentalist religious participation: An empirical study of intra-group variation. *American Journal of Orthopsychiatry*, 1980, *50*, 302–315.

Pedersen, P. B. The cultural inclusiveness of counseling. In P. B. Pedersen, J. G. Draguns, W. J. Lonner, & J. E. Trimble (Eds.), *Counseling across cultures* (rev. and expanded ed.). Honolulu: University Press of Hawaii, 1981.

Spiegel, J. P. Some cultural aspects of transference and counter-transference. In F. Riessman, J. Cohen, & A. Pearl (Eds.), *The mental health of the poor.* New York: Free Press, 1964.

Spiegel, J. P. Cultural aspects of transference and countertransference revisited. *Journal of the American Academy of Psychoanalysis*, 1976, *4*, 447–467.

Sundberg, N. D. Research and research hypotheses about effectiveness in intercultural counseling. In P. B. Pedersen, J. G. Draguns, W. J. Lonner & J. E. Trimble (Eds.), *Counseling across cultures* (rev. and expanded ed.). Honolulu: University Press of Hawaii, 1981.

Torrey, E. F. *The mind game: Witchdoctors and psychiatrists.* New York: Emerson Hall, 1972.

Townsend, J. M. Cultural conceptions and mental illness: A controlled comparison of Germany and America. *Journal of Nervous and Mental Disease*, 1975, *160*(6), 409–421.(a)

Townsend, J. M. Cultural conceptions, mental disorders, and social roles: A comparison of Germany and America. *American Sociological Review*, 1975, *40*(6), 739–752.(b)

Tseng, W. S., & McDermott, J. F. Psychotherapy: Historical roots, universal elements, and cultural variations. *American Journal of Psychiatry*, 1975, *132*, 378–384.

Vontress, C. M. Racial and ethnic barriers in counseling. In P. B. Pedersen, J. G. Draguns, W. J. Lonner, & J. E. Trimble (Eds.), *Counseling across cultures* (rev. and expanded ed.). Honolulu: University Press of Hawaii, 1981.

Wintrob, R. M. A study of disillusionment: Depressive reactions of Liberian students returning from advanced training abroad. *American Journal of Psychiatry*, 1967, *123*, 1593–1598.

Wintrob, R. M. An inward focus: Psychological stress in fieldwork experience. In F. Henry & S. Saberwal (Eds.), *Stress and response in fieldwork*. New York: Holt, Rinehart & Winston, 1969.

Wintrob, R. M. The influence of others: Witchcraft and rootwork as explanations of behavior disturbances. *Journal of Nervous and Mental Disease*, 1973, *156*, 318–326.

Wittkower, E. D., & Warnes, H. Cultural aspects of psychotherapy. *American Journal of Psychotherapy*, 1974, 28, 566–573.

Wohl, J. Intercultural psychotherapy: Issues, questions, and reflections. In P. B. Pedersen, J. G. Draguns, W. J. Lonner, & J. E. Trimble (Eds.), *Counseling across cultures* (rev. and expanded ed.). Honolulu: University Press of Hawaii, 1981.

World Health Organization. *Schizophrenia: An international follow-up study*. New York: Wiley, 1979.

Yamamoto, K. A comparative study of patienthood in Japanese and American mental hospitals. In W. P. Lebra (Ed.), *Transcultural research in mental health*, Vol. 2 of *Mental health research in Asia and the Pacific*. Honolulu: University Press of Hawaii, 1972, pp. 190–212.

6

Intercultural Psychotherapy: Issues, Questions, and Reflections

Julian Wohl

In the summer of 1961, a month or so after leaving the Veterans Administration clinic where I had been a staff clinical psychologist, I found myself in Rangoon facing an obviously (from my cultural view) tense university student. He had been referred by his teacher and supervisor, an American anthropologist who had done research in the young man's home district, far up-country from the University of Rangoon. The young man told me in limited but understandable English that he was very nervous and felt considerable distress in the abdominal region. He said that his discomfort was due to some demonic spiritual power that he had offended, a belief consistent with Burmese folk conceptions of psychological disturbance (Spiro, 1967), but it surprised me because he was a university student of anthropology. In my ignorance I thought that university students, especially those in cultural anthropology, would not have such "prescientific" notions. When I asked about his belief in the light of his knowledge of anthropology, I was even more surprised as he calmly indicated that he knew "primitive people" (his term) believed that spirits caused such distress and, since he was one of this class of people, he of course held this belief. At this point the intricate complexity of the relationship between culture on the one side and psychopathology and psychotherapy on the other lost its abstractness and became a reality for me. It was fortunate for both of us that I was not then called upon to continue to satisfy his therapeutic needs.

Several years later I was in Thailand. In the classroom I attempted to teach the theoretical side of clinical psychology, and in the nearby mental hospital I supervised the inaugural efforts of the same students as they strove to engage the inmates in helpful conversation. The memory of the earlier trauma was revived afresh as I was confronted both by the language barrier created by my total ignorance of Thai and their limited

competence in English, and the differences in our thought styles, fundamental ideas about motivation, and assumptions about meaningfulness
and causation in human behavior. It was not only that these students,
who were as intelligent and talented a sample of college seniors as one
could find anywhere, did not know psychological facts, theories, and
methods of clinical intervention. More basically, the difficulty lay in the
fact that the knowledge and skills could not readily be abstracted from a
complex, deeply rooted structure of underlying assumptions about life,
behavior, and nature. Their assumptions about psychological processes
were not consonant with those basic to the psychological techniques,
skills, and theories they were struggling to master (Pedersen, 1978). To
make this framework of Western clinical psychology functional was to
demand from them, it seemed to me later, a substantial degree of internalization of alien ways of thought, belief, judgment, and understanding. In short, it meant not only cognitive change, but drastic cultural
transformation as well (Wohl & Silverstein, 1966; Wohl & Tapingkae,
1970).

The six years between those two experiences in cross-cultural clinical
psychology, and the seven years after the second one, found me ponder-
ing the problems involved in transferring Western ways of counseling
and psychotherapy to Southeast Asian populations, and vacillating between hopelessness and slight optimism about the prospects for success.

In 1976 and again in 1978, brief experiences in Southeast Asia, this
time with professionals in counseling and psychotherapy from several
different parts of Asia, strengthened my optimism but also reinforced my
appreciation of the culturally based difficulties. After participating in
the first two biannual meetings of the Association of Psychological and
Educational Counselors in Asia (APECA), I have concluded that, whatever the obstacles, a vibrant professional counseling movement is being
established in Asia and that a good part of this effort includes adopting
and adapting Western approaches (Wohl, 1978).

Meanings of Intercultural Psychotherapy

The main focus of this chapter on intercultural psychotherapy is the
question of applying Western modes of therapy to non-Western clientele
in non-Western settings. The focal geographic area, based on the experience of the author, is Southeast Asia, although material from other areas
will be used. One general criticism that can be made of much of the literature in intercultural psychotherapy is its failure to define clearly and
categorize explicitly the uses of the concept. Writers select one or two
aspects and proceed to discuss them as if they comprised the whole field.
There are exceptions to this, one of whom is Sundberg who, elsewhere in
this volume, makes a tripartite division of the field of intercultural
psychotherapy. Another is in the work of Wittkower and Warnes (1974a;

1974b), who have a bipartite classification. In a reasonably comprehensive, although not exhaustive, book, Abel and Metraux (1974) have explored and described many of the ramifications of intercultural psychotherapy. This study is unusual in that it is the combined effort of only two authors, a clinical psychologist and a cultural anthropologist, rather than being an edited book with many contributors. Although its coverage of the literature is deficient (very few publications after 1968 are cited and many important earlier ones are omitted), it contains an abundance of case vignettes and examples that could be helpful to intercultural clinical workers.

Intercultural psychotherapy is not an unambiguous concept. Without much difficulty, at least seven different operational meanings of the term can be identified.

(1) The first of these is the situation in which representatives of one culture study the therapeutic modes and practices of another. This is essentially a pure research activity, usually carried out by anthropologists or anthropologically oriented psychiatric and psychological clinicians (Kennedy, 1963). It does not entail the actual practice of cross-cultural psychotherapy, but nevertheless may provide an extremely useful body of information. From it we can get a sense of the relativity of our own theories and practices. We can detect similarities and differences in form and content, in methods, techniques, and values. Looking from the outside at a substantially different culture, one can begin to identify relationships between assumptions made about life, nature, and psychopathology on the one hand, and psychotherapeutic practices that are not apparent to workers immersed in their own culture on the other. This might help to provide understanding which could be applied to discussions of transcultural universality and the cultural individuality of modes of psychotherapy. Although the development of such knowledge could occur with other aspects of cross-cultural work in psychotherapy —and is seen by some scholars as a major justification for such practices (Bolman, 1968; Draguns, 1975)—in this use of the term, research is the main purpose and not a subsidiary one. Most of the studies of so-called culture-bound disorders, traditional healers, and folk treatment procedures that involve observations by outsiders fall into this category (Kiev, 1964; Lebra, 1976).

(2) An increasingly popular and important concern are those problems associated with the existence of culturally heterogeneous groups within a larger cultural unit. Much of the literature on this subject is based on studies within the United States and appears related to the recent "discovery" of minorities and of their neglect or mistreatment by the mental health system. Language or dialect, race, urban as opposed to rural location, ethnicity, socioeconomic status, gender, and even sex preference, have come to be defining characteristics for cultural differ-

ences (Walz & Benjamin, 1978). A paradigmatic situation in the United States is a white middle-class therapist treating a non-Caucasian, usually of lower socioeconomic status. It has been argued that traditional modes of therapy demand from members of non-white, lower socioeconomic groups with their own subcultural characteristics a performance in the treatment situation which is foreign to them and which they neither understand nor find acceptable (Lorion, 1973; Prince, 1964; Stratton, 1975). Yet it is just as unfair to create new cultural stereotypes based upon a patient's group membership, and then to deny the patient the therapy that would otherwise be the treatment of choice (Jones, 1974; Lerner, 1972; Lorion, 1973). A sensitivity to the culturally different within the larger American cultural scene is important and desirable, but one must raise questions about the extent to which therapists, in their efforts to be responsive to cultural differences, might obscure the equally important individuality of personality within cultural commonality.

The next four conceptions of intercultural psychotherapy deal with larger and, from an anthropological point of view, more traditional cultural differences. In these instances, psychotherapists work with clients who are much more foreign to them than in the situation above and use methods that are totally foreign to the cultural context of one of the participants.

(3) In the first of these conditions an immigrant or sojourner within a culture becomes a psychotherapy client of a member of the host culture and is treated using the language and a method of the host culture. This is illustrated by the work of Alexander and his associates with Chinese students in Wisconsin, reported in their chapter in this volume, and Pedersen's (1977) study of foreign students' problems as issues of role learning. Another example would be a Thai physician coming to the United States for psychiatric training and obtaining personal psychoanalytic therapy from an American therapist during his period of residence.

(4) This is the partial reverse of the previous arrangement. Here a visitor or temporary resident brings methods from afar and applies these in a culturally alien society. The primary role of the visitor may be direct service or research, or training and supervision. From the viewpoint of the host society, direct service by a temporary resident has little long-term meaning or practical significance. The long-term practitioner in a culturally foreign realm usually has little lasting impact. The sojourn is long enough only to permit the person to begin to adapt to the local scene and usually there is a primary duty to research or teaching, with clinical service a sideline. When the visitor leaves, little evidence of the visit remains with respect to psychotherapy beyond the few persons who have received some assistance.

A typical example is the American who accepts a one-year assignment to a developing country as a clinical teacher or consultant in a mental health setting. Instead of functioning in an educational role, however, the visitor becomes immersed in service (originally intending only to take a few cases "for experience") and finds no time or opportunity for training. Noteworthy in this situation is that while psychotherapy is being transported to a different cultural setting, it is being applied by someone for whom the therapeutic mode is familiar. Only the context in which the service is delivered is culturally different. This approach leaves unanswerable the question as to whether the therapeutic system at issue can be adopted by the local practitioners.

(5) It seems desirable to distinguish the form of intercultural psychotherapy described immediately above from that which is not tied to the person who delivers the service, but instead focuses upon the psychotherapy itself.

This is the transference of a body of theory and practice from its place of origin and growth to a significantly different cultural climate. Ultimately, the practice must be performed by local persons who have been trained in the foreign methods. This concept is similar to the previous one in that it involves the exportation of a foreign mode of therapeutic practice, but the measure of success will not be whether the outsider can claim progress with local clients, rather that local practitioners can be trained to employ the foreign methods competently. The survey and analysis of the psychotherapy literature presented in this chapter is undertaken with this use of the intercultural psychotherapy concept as a primary frame of reference.

(6) Another, but infrequent, form of intercultural psychotherapy situation is demonstrated by Sundberg in his chapter. He creates a hypothetical situation of an Iranian student, obtaining psychotherapy from a Hungarian emigrant in an American counseling setting. In this instance the methods employed are not named, but theoretically these methods could provide a fourth culture entrant. For example, the therapist might employ the Morita approach from Japan. Here, intercultural psychotherapy refers to a therapist working with a patient from another culture, within yet a third cultural setting, probably employing methods popular in the setting in which they both reside, but possibly utilizing those that derive from a fourth culture.

(7) Finally, a special, but not necessarily rare, cultural interface situation can be described where members of a Western culture have lived for some time in a non-Western developing society and associate to a great extent with select members of that culture (Useem, Useem, & Donaghue, 1963). Through their frequent interaction, dictated usually by the nature of their jobs, the members of the two cultures develop social rules and interpersonal patterns that, although rooted in their respective original cultures, synthesize a new, binational, third culture. As examples, the authors cite in India the Indo-British carry-over from the colonial era,

and the Indo-American third culture, based upon the American commercial and assistance complex. This "third culture" situation can find the Western practitioner or the Western-trained local practitioner working with local Westerners or "Westernized" non-Westerners.

The foregoing seven operational meanings of intercultural or cross-cultural psychotherapy do not exhaust all of its logical possibilities. They do, however, incorporate the vast majority that appear in the literature and that seem of practical import. All of these various usages or "intercultural" are found throughout this volume, and different authors emphasize one or more of them. In this chapter the basic concern is with the fifth item above, the transfer to a non-Western society of Western modes of intervention.

Doubts About Cultural Transplants

If there exists a world trend towards cultural homogeneity, then it can be argued rationally that even as technologies from the West move to Eastern, African, or other non-Europeanized culture areas, traffic could to the same degree flow from them to the West. This ethically pleasing position, though, fails to consider the triumph of the West in the international struggle for power and riches, and imposes a construction of history which distorts the imbalance between the "haves" and "have nots." This imbalance is a reality that has led to the West's applying its technology to the rest of the world and not the other way around. Like it or not, the overall direction is towards the Westernization of the world with respect to transformation of technology and the cultural changes that come from it (Marsella & Sanborn, 1977).

Counseling or psychotherapy, although perhaps a limited and puny manifestation of Western technology when compared with such obvious achievements as electronic communication, high-powered fertilizer, and life-preserving pharmaceuticals, no less represents a technological intervention developed in Western society as a response to Western problems. As with the implantation of any body part, the risk of rejection is real. Psychotherapy's universal functionality cannot be safely assumed, and knowledgeable observers, both Western and non-Western, are skeptical about this peculiar institution of Western culture surviving a transplant unless it undergoes drastic change.

Torrey (1972), in his broad survey, judged certain attempts at transplantation as failures or exceptionally difficult. Neki (1975) found Western psychotherapy at best suitable only for the few highly Westernized Indians. Lambo's (1974) description of the cultural context of African psychology leads one to conclude that Western individual psychotherapy would barely be recognizable to the Western practitioner observing it in Africa, if it could be applied at all, while Olatawura (1974) used case material also to argue its unsuitability, without considerable modification, for Nigerian patients. Penningroth and Penningroth (1977) listed a number of modifications that make psychotherapy feasible in Guam, but the degree and kind of change suggested was substantial. An optimistic picture was presented of Korea (Chang & Kim, 1973; Kim & Rhi, 1976), but there was more evidence of hope than accomplishment in their surveys. Even in a European country such as Greece, individual psychotherapy seems hardly to have had an opportunity to be tried (Kokantzis & Ierodiakonou, 1975). Pande (1968) was decidedly negative in his claim that psychotherapy was a Western reaction to peculiarly Western problems of living rooted in the Western style of life. The cautions and strictures for its use with Chinese patients were so abundant (Hsu & Tseng, 1972; Singer, 1976; Tseng, 1978) that one must wonder how much of Western psychotherapy was left and how much of what was offered was but that residue of psychiatric wisdom, or common sense, sometimes intraculturally characterized as "eclectic." In a recent contribution to the cross-cultural literature, Doi (1976) noted the reluctance of the Japanese to participate in the "hide and seek" game which he finds to be characteristic of all psychotherapy.

It appears that a sound basis in clinical and scholarly research exists for questioning the cultural portability of at least that one expression of Western science, technology, and that practical art known as individual psychotherapy. Rational analysis must strengthen these doubts. While all such foreign forms can have far-reaching and complex ramifications within the societies into which they are introduced, the impact upon lives is indirect. A new fertilizer is intended to transform an economy and its immediate or even long-term effects upon the lives of individual farmers are incidental. But psychotherapy is intended directly to change the lives of those who avail themselves of it. While it might ultimately affect many aspects of the culture into which it is introduced, such macrocultural effects are secondary to its immediate microcultural purpose.

Not only does psychotherapy impinge directly upon its individual clients, but it strikes at the center, not at the periphery. It confronts and arouses fundamental personal attitudes, values, feelings, beliefs, and standards about the conduct of life and the interrelationships of people. All technological innovation has sociocultural and interpersonal implications, but the concerns of counseling and psychotherapy seem pervaded by them. In this context, Draguns' (1975) observation about the centrality of sociocultural purposes and interpersonal methods in psychotherapy is particularly apt. He conceives of psychotherapy as a means of facilitating the return of alienated persons into more complete societal participation and functioning, a position which highlights psychotherapy's cultural focus.

Psychological Disorders and Psychotherapy as Cultural Universals

At the same time that we question the utility of Western psychotherapy in non-Western contexts, we must acknowledge that the category of human concerns at which psychotherapy is aimed is not really restricted to Western settings. Problems in living, or mental illness, or intolerable deviancy, or whatever else we choose to call such problems apparently exist universally, and all cultures creat social institutions in response (DeVos, 1974; Kennedy, 1963; Torrey, 1972). They also create their own criteria for intervention. In his extensive social and historical study, Rosen (1968) emphasized how the diagnosis or categorization of psychological disorders is a function of both the extent to which a person's actions are disturbed and the standards set by the social group performing the evaluation. In our own era, we are seeing this relativity extend even to the notion of mental illness itself, as criticism of the euphemism mounts on scientific, legal, and social grounds (Kittrie, 1973; Szasz, 1961).

The concept of adaptation provides a framework from which to view psychopathology and psychotherapy in worldwide perspective (Draguns, 1975). Adaptation, which has moved into a central position in modern psychoanalytic ego psychology (Hartmann, 1958), lends itself to a very simple, yet universal conception of psychological disorders. People are either *troubled*, by internal conflicts and pressures, or they are *in trouble*, with the world around them. Interventions, of which psychotherapy or counseling is only one mode, are introduced to modify conditions of maladaptation. Either an alloplastic adaptation (one which frees the individual internally to permit more effective acting upon and modification of the environment) or an autoplastic adaptation (one which aims at internal change to permit more flexible functioning within the environment) would be emphasized (Hartmann, 1958; on this point, see also Draguns' chapter in this volume). But basic to each is the common feature that both are reactions to maladaptedness which the psychotherapy is designed to remedy (Draguns, 1975).

The quest for a universalistic or transcultural framework for psychological disorders encourages the parallel effort to identify transcultural, universal features of psychotherapy. These serve as reference points from which to consider problems of applying Western psychotherapy to non-Western societies. One such bedrock universal is that psychotherapeutic activities are found historically and contemporaneously in virtually all societies, although they may be performed by people not narrowly defined as mental health specialists. In his exhaustive study of the "cure of souls" in religious and philosophic traditions, McNeill (1965) notes that healing includes a caring and concern on the part of the healer—features considered intrinsic by most psychotherapies today. These caring activities have not always been the specialized, discrete functions that they are in the Westernized world today. McNeill observed that the separation of mental healing from its source in religious and philosophic thought and its conversion to a specialized scientific discipline are relatively recent developments. Theological distinctions among various churches and religions tend to obscure their common function of soul healing. To this group of "physicians of the soul," referred to by McNeill as a "spiritual elite" (p. 330), must be added the modern psychotherapists of all persuasions who, despite their chronic squabbling, are joined in this specialized brotherhood and together enjoy its special status.

Although the partisans of each cult may believe that theirs is the best way to cure or care for the troubled who consult them, collectively they comprise what Meadows (1968) referred to as the "mediatorial elite." In discussing ancient Greece, Meadows noted that "therapy was an act of mediation between the sufferer and the superordinate world of powers and values . . . [T]he mediatorial role of the priesthood was that of the cure of souls, whether by divination, exorcism, absolution, expiation, orgiastic dance, ritual mysteries, teaching, revealing, directing" (p. 497) —each of these are techniques used in psychotherapeutic practice throughout the world today. All cultures, he added, have members who play this mediatorial role. One is tempted to add that, while all practitioners in all cultures have successes and failures, the existence of the "mediatorial elite" is not dependent, even in the scientific West, upon its ability to demonstrate understanding of causes, ability to predict outcome of intervention as against nonintervention, or empirical measures of efficacy of treatment. Rather, the survival of the healing class depends upon its socially sanctioned (licensed, "degreed") role, and the continued willingness of society to believe in the efficacy of treatment by the specialist.

The fact that activities or functions which we refer to as psychotherapy appear to have been universally performed provides some hope to those who assert that Western psychotherapy can be useful in non-Western societies. This is qualified, however, by a consensus expressed in the literature (Draguns, 1975; Torrey, 1972) that the specific form psychotherapy takes in any culture must harmonize with the broader cultural ethos. It should not violate those implicit values and unarticulated presuppositions that constitute the culture's "world view."

In his "Eastern interpretation" of Western psychotherapy, Pande (1968) argued that fundamental processes of therapy are provided with a cultural cosmetic to achieve this compatibility. He looked at Western concepts in psychotherapy in the manner of an anthropologist examining the strange rituals of some exotic group and found a covert collusion between patient and therapist. Under a cover of manifest content couched in the language of science and medicine is the latent fact that therapy provides a special, close, love relationship. Pande argued that for Westerners to admit that they deliver and derive emotional gratification in therapy is not consistent with their valued conception of psychotherapy as a scientific, intellectual, objective healing process, and, therefore, they are forced to conceal this fact from themselves.

After having demonstrated that many modes of psychological intervention stand at great variance from Western methods, Kiev (1964) suggests that we should get at the essentials of psychotherapy, those features that are universally present regardless of local idiosyncrasies. This challenge has been accepted by a number of investigators both interculturally and intraculturally. One of the difficulties which is not commonly made explicit in this search for commonality is that simply to identify functions in other societies which are fulfilled by psychotherapy in our society does not mean that they are performed in the same ways.

Defining Psychotherapy

The mere universal existence of activities that, if construed broadly, fit the concept of psychotherapy does not demand the conclusion that all such practices are basically similar to each other, as some writers assume (Tseng & McDermott, 1975). Part of the problem is definitional. If one begins with the assumption that all activities aimed at emotional healing, cultural reintegration, or improving someone's mental state are psychotherapy, it will be easy to find universal or common features. For example, Tseng and McDermott (1975) cite identifying a problem, setting a goal, developing a relationship, prescribing and executing a course of action, and ending the work as universal features of psychotherapy. Another such broad characteristic is Torrey's (1972) "Rumpelstiltskin Principle." But these could apply equally easily to accounting, dentistry, surgery, or teaching tennis. If, however, a more restricted conception is selected, then fewer transcultural qualities will be found.

A simple working definition, which is not tied to any particular theory of psychotherapy, needs to be used. From my own experience, a functional definition of individual psychotherapy or personal counseling would see it as a two-person situation in which a trained, socially defined expert and a client (or patient) agreed formally to discuss the client's difficulties in order to alleviate the client's distress and improve the client's effectiveness in living. This formulation is similar to that of Draguns (1975), and without taking space to discuss each of the elements systematically, it can be noted that both limit psychotherapy to its traditional medium of conversation. This eliminates drugs, medicines, potions, synthetic or natural mind altering products, somatic interventions, and bodily contacts from the realm of psychotherapy, although all of these are used in psychiatric and other healing rites which this formulation does not include as psychotherapy. Despite restricting psychotherapy to conversation, which not all other psychologists and psychiatrists follow (Prince, 1976), these formulations are comprehensive enough to be umbrellas under which many modes of psychotherapeutic intervention could find shelter.

A close and systematic scrutiny of psychotherapy aimed at isolating its essential, basic, and shared features has been undertaken by Strupp. In a series of important studies, only some of which are cited here (1972; 1973a; 1973b; 1975), he has articulated clearly two themes emerging in psychotherapy's recent history. One theme places great emphasis upon the "non-specific" healing aura hovering over the psychotherapeutic relationship. Since all psychotherapy includes a therapist and a client interacting in some special way in the therapeutic situation, one is tempted to identify the common factors in this relationship as the essential ingredients. This can help to account, for example, for why all therapies can rightfully claim to be helpful (Karasu, 1977). The emphasis upon the curative power of the relationship has been greatest in the work of Carl Rogers and followers of the "humanistic" approaches. But the relationship is itself complex and probably not all of the elements of the relationship are shared by all therapies, nor are all equally essential as has been noted by Garfield (1973) in his critique of Strupp (1973a). In general, psychologists who favor applying to one culture, methods originating in another, follow the trend which emphasizes universal features and focuses heavily on the significance of the relationship and various facets of it. An example of this is the belief in the power of the therapist to influence the client who believes in the therapist's capacity to promote change.

The second major theme is the emphasis upon technical skill and specific therapeutic techniques combined with a deemphasis of importance of the "human relationship" in psychotherapy. Until recently, behavioral and psychoanalytic approaches have been seen as minimizing the human aspect of the therapist-patient relationship (Karasu, 1977), but Greenson (1967) and Langs (1976a; 1976b), two outstanding writers on technique in psychoanalytic psychotherapy, clearly demonstrate that this is no longer true of psychoanalysis (if it ever was). Strupp (1976b) remarks that Freud did not consider human relationship variables unimportant, but rather took for granted that therapists would be humane and caring people with their patients.

Strupp has sought to identify the specific features of therapeutic influence, originally with the hope that it would be possible to devise specific techniques for individual persons and their unique symptoms. He relinquished this mechanical conception when he wrote that "we are beginning to recognize and take seriously the extraordinary complexity of the therapeutic influence" (1973b; p. 275). With some reluctance, he acknowledged that generally "the search for highly specific techniques . . . is probably futile" (p. 313). His final position was that the therapeutic influence is composed of two fundamental factors: one consists of the non-specific, basic, or general effect, which inheres in the interpersonal relationship; the other consists of specific techniques employed by the therapist. The techniques, however, are operative only through the medium of the relationship and all effects can be attributed, at least in part, to the human qualities of the therapist, such qualities being "interest, understanding, respect, dedication, empathy, etc. . . . which instill trust" (1973b, p. 283). He underscored this by asserting "the equivalence of therapeutic techniques," all of which can achieve results and are "anchored in, and potentiated by . . . the establishment and maintenance of a proper healing relationship" (1973b, p. 283). The core of this proper healing relationship is the "emotional experience" made possible by the therapeutic relationship.

Another landmark effort aimed at establishing the essentials of psychotherapy is the work of Frank (1963, 1971). His approach was to look at psychotherapy as one among many ways to get people to change their minds or mend their ways. Since there is perhaps nothing in human affairs as ubiquitous as this, Frank hit upon a useful approach from the interculturalist's point of view. His work is frequently cited in the cross-cultural literature, and indeed many of the recent papers seem to use or paraphrase his definition of psychotherapy. Like Strupp, Frank places great emphasis on the power conveyed by the personal influence of the helping person in the special situation socioculturally defined as psychotherapeutic. He attributes the major curative value to the contextual arrangements, to the socially defined power, and to the emotional arousal in the relationship. From this point of view, it matters less just what therapists do (technique and methods) but that they are endowed with culturally defined therapeutic qualities and conduct themselves as their clientele expect that they will (relationship factors).

The issues of belief, suggestion, and expectation of help are seen in much of the cross-cultural literature as vital to the efficacy of treatment. Calestro (1972) in an extensive survey of non-Western methods argues for the importance of suggestibility and the therapist's capacity to mobilize this endogenous factor. The same general position is taken by Prince (1976). He first summarizes the nonspecific, universal factors previously identified by such contributors as Frank (1963), Torrey (1972), Calestro (1972), Draguns (1975), Mendel (1972),Tseng and McDermott (1975), and Singer (1976). These nonspecific, universal factors include the "special relationship," "shared world view," "expectant hope of the patient," "naming the illness," "attribution of cause and prescription of treatment by the healer," and the "central role of suggestion" (Prince, 1976, p. 115). He characterizes these factors as "exogeneous" since they come from outside the patient, and states that many psychotherapy methods involve mobilization of internal mechanisms and processes, among which he includes dreams, mystical and ecstatic states, trance and dissociation phenomena, and other altered states of consciousness. Prince asserts that these latter experiences may themselves provide cures if the therapist can activate them. The material that he provides, which is basically from non-European societies, is used to argue that the manipulation of such mechanisms offers an opportunity for successful intervention where more conventional Western approaches are not feasible.

An unusually thorough scrutiny of one nonspecific factor, the expectations held by the patient about therapy, has been made by Higginbotham (1977). After a careful, scholarly evaluation, he concludes that expectations on the part of the patient about the nature of the treatment can have powerful effects upon the development of the therapeutic relationship. He recommends that because cultural conditioning is a critical determinant of expectations about therapy, psychotherapy across a cultural gap should be preceded by an assessment of those expectations and an attempt to reduce the disparity between what the patient expects and the actual therapeutic procedures.

Working within a pan-cultural framework, Torrey (1972) has tried to obliterate any distinctions among psychotherapies, arguing that there are a few basic features which all psychotherapies share. But at the same time he argues that cultural commonality within these aspects is so critical, that a cultural gap of any distance between the participants of a therapeutic interaction provides almost overwhelming barriers to the therapeutic work. His four universals include a world view shared by therapist and patient, a close interpersonal relationship, the patient's expectation of being helped, and specific techniques. His position, well known as evidenced by the frequency with which this work is cited, is one of the most extreme with respect to its assertion of the universal existence of psychotherapy and its insistence on basic common factors all over the world. Torrey is also certain in his belief that overcoming cultural barriers between therapists and patients is extremely difficult.

Tseng and McDermott (1975) likewise consider the crucial elements in therapy, but present a more detailed breakdown of operations and processes. They too emphasize the "nonspecific" factors of expectancy and belief, the therapist's personal qualities in developing a good therapeutic relationship, and an appropriate atmosphere within which the work can go on. They also stress the importance of introducing individual cultural variations upon the universals so as to make the treatment useful and relevant in various sociocultural contexts.

Singer (1976) in a long paper on the "dynamics of cross-cultural psychotherapy" describes some of the culturally shared components, although much of his article is also a warning of the dangers and difficulties in doing Western psychotherapy with non-Western (Chinese) patients in Hong Kong. He finds universality in personal qualities of therapists such as warmth, interest, and caring, general technical factors such as suggestion and catharsis, and cognitive aspects such as naming and defining problems, with the clients deriving some understanding and control of their problems.

Culture and the Therapeutic Relationship

Although it is not always expressed in the same words, the theoretical and scholarly literature on psychotherapy and its cross-cultural potentialities converge on the therapeutic relationship where the minimal necessary basis for any psychotherapeutically meaningful work is found. Few people experienced in personal counseling or psychotherapy would take issue with the position that at least one universal, fundamental feature of psychotherapy is an emotionally special interpersonal relationship created and managed to foster personal change in the client. Despite this universality, it is possible, and even probable, that the constituent elements of the "good human relationship" are different in one culture than they are in another. Presumably, specific techniques such as interpreting, advising, or reassuring would not be equally appropriate in all cultures. Some would be consistent with the norms of a specific culture while others would be alien. But the greater question remains: To what extent is our general Western conception of the good therapeutic relationship universally valid? Even if in all cultures most people respond well to "acceptance," "respect," "interest," "concern," "wish to help," and the other components, we still must ask whether the outsider can deliver, express, and communicate these factors in terms understandable and acceptable to the client.

Aside from these "internal" aspects of therapy, there are other aspects that are usually taken for granted when both parties share the same culture. Frank emphasized the requirement that patient and therapist share an acceptance of the social trappings and the framework of meaning within which disorder and treatment are understood and confronted. Strupp followed him in recognizing the necessity for a rational system that both parties can use to make sense out of therapeutic events. Is it possible for two people of different cultures to achieve a reasonable degree of agreement and understanding about this superstructure?

Not always sufficiently explicit in this literature is that the two participants in the therapeutic relationship interact with each other primarily through conversation and that the effectiveness of their communication is a major variable in determining productiveness. Whether the patients change their expectations about therapy or the therapists change theirs to fit those of their patients, the recommendation that they reduce the size of their conceptual difference (Higginbotham, 1977) speaks to the same issue expressed in much broader terms by Torrey (1972) when he stressed the difficulty of cross-cultural therapy where the participants do not share a common world view

The essence of the psychotherapeutic process is human communication. More importantly, much of the activity in therapy consists of communication about communication. A great deal of psychotherapy includes efforts directed towards clarifying meanings and making conscious and explicit what is indirect, subtle, and unwitting in the client's communication. Participants in any conversation, therapeutic or otherwise, are able to communicate to the extent that they employ a common referential symbol system. They must achieve agreement on what they are discussing and on the manner in which they are to discuss their subject matter (Sullivan, 1953). On this point, the discussion in the chapter by Alexander et al. on the therapist's difficulty in understanding the communication signals of a patient is informative. In such a situation the patient, of course, has the same problem.

An anecdotal study (Vassiliou & Vassiliou, 1973) has described difficulties arising in the training of therapists in a foreign culture because of different connotations of the same words. If this happens in training, one can imagine the difficulties in practice. Bickley (1978), although not writing specifically about psychotherapy, demonstrates how misunderstandings can arise in delicate negotiations because of language barriers, again where the "same" word has different connotations for speakers from two different cultures.

Seminal work on the language and communication aspects of social class (Bernstein, 1964) reinforces one's appreciation of the problems in psychotherapeutic discourse presented by participants who believe they speak the same language but have unconsciously disparate semantic worlds. A series of papers by Marcos (Marcos, 1976a, 1976b; Marcos & Alpert, 1976) has described problems in psychotherapy associated with bilingualism, even when participants are able to use the same language.

Ultimately, communication in a special kind of human relationship is fundamental to achieve the effects that will be seen as psychotherapeutic. If communication is to develop within a tolerable limit of error, the framework of understanding within which it occurs requires the sharing of a set of assumptions about the world and its working, about the nature of mankind and its relation to natural events and supernatural influences, and about the physical and social circumstances within which this healing function goes on, something which has come to be known as a "world view."

The therapeutic relationship can tolerate some disparity between the participants and, indeed, this always exists. Part of the therapeutic work is mutual learning about such gaps and the negotiation of them; but if the gap between the participants is too great, there is no basis for understanding and the "noise" becomes too loud to permit a working alliance (Greenson, 1967). For example, the gap may occur because of personal characteristics of the therapist. It is possible that the much-researched trinity of warmth, empathy, and genuineness might appear in a Burmese context to be evidence of weakness and incompetence. Or perhaps client-centered or psychoanalytic positions, with egalitarianism, mutuality, and openness as part of their value orientations, may not mesh effectively with the hierarchically ordered Thai society. Alexander et al., in their chapter, indicate how a fundamental therapeutic stance of the therapist, such as nondirectiveness, can be misinterpreted as lack of interest.

Thus, while the fact of a special kind of human relationship is a mark of psychotherapy, the particular expression of such a relationship and the distinct qualities required of the therapist to create the desired hope, trust, and faith on the client's part may not be universally applicable. Furthermore, it is quite possible that the sounds and gestures that are intended to convey certain meanings may actually convey other meanings which do not create the desired attitudes in the patient. All of this should give pause to those of us who argue the case for cultural transferability of psychotherapy. The problems can be seen in better relief when some of the reports of those who have attempted to engage in intercultural psychotherapy are examined.

Examples of Intercultural Psychotherapy

This section presents a selective, evaluative survey of accounts in intercultural psychotherapy. The articles were chosen because of their focus upon the encounter of psychotherapeutic issues within cultural contexts and their emphasis on technical problems. They involve Western or Western-trained therapists applying their skill to members of social groups upon which Western psychotherapeutics constitute a foreign graft. The patients involved are American Indian, Canadian Indian, Chinese, Cuban and Afro-Cuban, Turkish, Indian, Japanese, and Malaysian.

In what he states is the "first study devoted specifically to the technical problems of a culturally oriented individual psychotherapy," Devereux (1951, p. 422) wrote of his experiences in psychoanalytic psychotherapy with Plains Indians (1951, 1953). He concluded that three major features—transference, dream utilization, and therapeutic goals—require a significant appreciation of the patient's cultural background. To understand and interpret appropriately transference communications, the therapist must comprehend the cultural context of the patient's family life. Similarly, to understand dreams in therapy, the therapist must know the cultural framework of dream interpretation. But the greatest problem for Devereux was therapeutic goals. His solution was that the therapist must want "to restore the patient to himself" (1951, p. 420). Other goals of therapy provide some understanding of his dilemma. He states that the "patient must be helped to handle the realities of the reservation, which is his predictable future environment" (1951, p. 421), as well as to learn selectively to use traditional Indian values and means in the white world.

This issue of appropriate therapeutic goals in the context of therapy appears commonly with any member of a restricted or oppressed group. Devereux's solution was an acceptance of the current social situation, a political act which would seem to reinforce that situation. His decision to do so was especially poignant because his patients were acculturated to the degree that they considered their "Indian heritage peripheral" (1951, p. 411). Today's "radical therapists" would resolve the dilemma of goal selection by supporting or promoting social change. It was not as obvious to Devereux in 1951 as it is for us today that psychotherapy has inevitable political implications. In certain societies this could be a particularly sensitive factor, one which would require careful consideration before an attempt is made to embark on any major programmatic importation of foreign therapy.

Western psychotherapies which are premised upon personal growth through self-exploration could well lead to increased adaptational difficulties in patients as they become more aware of and hence more dissatisfied with the oppressive context of their lives (Halleck, 1971). Moreover, counselors working in university settings in countries with authoritarian regimes where students may be regarded as a threat to the established order might themselves be seen as subversive in their practice of Western psychotherapy (Wohl, 1978).

Devereux's patients were all well educated, relatively well acculturated, and, by their own account, partly removed from their Indian heritage. The gap here between the therapist and the patient is less than the unmodified term "Plains Indian" might suggest. Is therapy possible here only to the extent that patients are acculturated and can share the therapist's world view to a considerable degree?

Bishop and Winokur (1956) reported therapy that took place in the United States between a Japanese male physician and an American female psychiatrist. The authors asserted that, in general, knowledge of the cultural background increases the therapist's understanding of the patient's problems and also helps in goal selection. Such knowledge can help avoid "guiding him into patterns" that, although acceptable in the therapist's culture, would create trouble "when the patient returns to his own group" (p. 369). The authors admit to seducing the prospective patient into therapy through a three-week warm-up period in which the therapist befriended the patient and expressed interest in Japan and of the patient's current work in an American hospital.

Without going further into this apparently successful treatment, it is evident that the "warm-up period" was a substantial departure from any conventional therapeutic procedure. Furthermore, the east-west cultural gap was narrower than it might have seemed at first glance. The authors reinforced this point by saying that "there was practically no difficulty with language" and that the patient "has lived so long in a cosmopolitan society and had associated extensively with Americans" (p. 372).

Abel (1956) advocated the learning of cultural facts in order to improve the therapist's understanding of the patient and to present formulations in a useful manner. The argument is supported by clinical illustrations—vignettes of her own and others' experiences with cultural differences. Although the points she makes about the advantage of cultural understanding by the therapist are valuable, it must be noted that all of her material refers to therapy in the United States with indigenous or immigrant subcultural groups, largely European in origin. Her own work with a Chinese patient was done in English, and his degree of acculturation was considerable, as Abel reported in a later article (1962).

The kind of intercultural therapy she discusses is a predecessor to the wave of interest that began in the 1960s—problems provided by middle-class, mainstream, Americanized helpers working with educationally and economically impoverished and discriminated-against members of ethnic minorities. Problems in that domain are today probably the center of activity in intercultural counseling and psychotherapy, and as Kinzie (1972) maintains, there are continuities between applying Western psychotherapy in Malaysia and applying it to "nontraditional" target populations within the United States. Abel's work reflects psychotherapeutic interests and issues existing within the cosmopolitan climate of New York City in the 1930s and 1940s with its vast heterogeneity of national and ethnic groups, varying in extent of assimilation, but all tending towards Americanization. Intercultural therapy in this chapter is concerned with members of a foreign population who will stay foreign, so to speak, and be treated in their own lands, not ours. Vontress, in his chapter, also speaks of the importance of accounting for variations in degree of cultural assimilation among members of the same cultural group.

A paper by Bustamente (1957) is similar to that of Abel in its focus upon patients within one society who are treated by a therapist of different cultural or subcultural background, and it makes the same reasonable points as does Abel's paper. "A psychiatrist must be able to assess the cultural background of his patient, and have a thorough knowledge of his own culture as well, to be effective with polycultural patients" (p. 811). By "polycultural," he meant patients who shared or participated in Cuban, European, and Afro-Cuban traditions.

Information gathering, research rather than therapy, is the interview function discussed by Carstairs (1961), whose conclusions derive from work done with villagers in India. He indicates that a clinician engaged in research may be obligated to employ his therapeutic skill, even though his interest lies in research. The act of drawing forth information may open up problems for the informant which the clinician cannot ignore. The reverse of this situation was described by Devereux (1953) who wrote that his professional interest in culture was an obstacle to therapy when he became too interested in cultural features at the expense of clinical involvement with the patients. Such an anthropological preoccupation is dangerous in any intercultural endeavor where service rather than science is the basic purpose. There is always a tendency to use the subject as an informant so as to provide a window to the culture; in psychotherapy more than in other fields involvement of this kind can become an impediment to productiveness.

The article by Carstairs contains a number of useful suggestions and observations. Carstairs is insistent that interviewing be done in the native language of the informant or in the one that he or she normally uses. The use of an interpreter is not adequate, because this interferes with the establishment of a relationship. Carstairs also points out that as an outsider one is not expected by the members of the culture to have a full knowledge of cultural facts. This position of acknowledged ignorance can be used to promote openness and clarity of communication because it provides a good justification for asking people to explain themselves. He warns against premature interpretations, formulations, or diagnoses: "It is only after a gradual process of feeling one's way into the accepted values and expectations of the group that one learns to recognize behavior which *they* regard as abnormal . . ." (p. 545).

The problem of goal setting has been raised by Hsu and Tseng (1972). They make the same point that Devereux made—that goals need to fit the cultural realities or what is culturally possible for the patient. They emphasize that the therapist needs to know the patient's cultural context very well so that he or she can engage in this goal-oriented activity. Indeed, if the therapist is to set goals and judge what goals are suitable, then this knowledge must be possessed by the therapist. But one can also display the ignorance of Carstairs' (1961) cultural explorer who, by focusing upon the patient's background, makes the patient explain the culture to him. Ultimately then, perhaps sufferers can define their own suffering and participate in determining what must be done to terminate it.

Hsu and Tseng confront a fundamental issue of psychotherapy, that of a communication problem beyond the basic knowledge of a common language. Verbal localisms, facial expressions, and special cultural nuances of symbols distort communication even when words and sentences are understood literally. Metaphoric communication illustrates this problem well. Communication in therapy constantly employs metaphor, and metaphor represents an almost impassible cultural barrier. A sad, yet humorous, example of this occurred in connection with a patient admitted to a Midwestern mental hospital. One of the allegations made about him upon admission was his delusion that there was a radio in his stomach. Inquiry about this revealed that the admitting physician, a recent immigrant to the United States whose knowledge of English was very limited, interpreted literally the patient's complaint about his neighbor's constant loud playing of a radio. The patient said, "I got a belly full."

Hsu and Tseng also point out that, beyond the problems of language and communication, there can be other complications in the relationship, particularly that of the danger of mutual projection of cultural stereotypes. This was noted with respect to subcultural differences by Thomas (1962). These authors conclude by offering a collection of therapeutic aphorisms, highly desirable as criteria for excellence in performance but probably greatly limited in actual fulfillment. These include awareness of the importance of culture in a general sense, knowledge of the patient's culture, mutual acknowledgment and discussion by patient and therapist of differences as they appear, search for the meaning of a patient's history, and provision of a good relationship. These praiseworthy features of therapy could be used as standards applicable to any psychotherapy. But apart from intercultural therapy with the relatively intelligent, educated, and culturally aware patients in this survey, it seems unrealistic to expect these criteria to be more realizable in intercultural therapeutic ventures than in the simpler intracultural efforts.

An informative paper by Kinzie (1978) supports both hopes and doubts about intercultural psychotherapy. He reiterates many of the items mentioned earlier that he sees as helpful in surmounting the cultural barriers in psychotherapy. These include self-awareness and awareness of the patient's culture, an open attitude, continuing mutual checking on the adequacy of communication, and readiness of the therapist to adjust action and style to the patient's conception of a healer. Recognizing that language difficulties can make fine and subtle communication impossible, he suggests the use of an interpreter where necessary. Although he acknowledges that this seriously complicates the situation, he feels it has proven its worth. This is similar in concept to the suggestion of Bolman (1968) that where cultural gaps are very wide, people who are able to act as links between the two cultures should be used. Jilek-Aall (1976) provides an enlightening tabular presentation of differences between typical Western psychotherapists and non-Western patients, arguing that successful interaction demands a degree of acculturation of the patient. Her case material shows also a substantial degree of modification of Western methods.

In clear detail Ozturk (1978) gives an extended description of a case in which the circumstance of the treatment rather than the cultural background of the patient seemed most critical in determining the means of psychotherapy. Essentially, he seemed to establish a long-term dependent tie which provided direction and support for the patient in a therapy carried out by mail, with intermittent periods of personal contact. That the treatment was successful is not as relevant as that it was far removed from any conventional Western mode of psychotherapy, and that the variations were not particularly "culturally" based, but demanded by geography. The circumstances of treatment could just as easily have occurred in the West. Of special interest is the therapist's reporting of similarities between the patient's background and his own and the importance of this in managing the treatment.

On the topic of goals in therapy, Kinzie (1972) approaches more closely than any other the position suggested earlier that goals "will be primarily determined by the patient himself and by his culture" (p. 226). He notes that after therapy the patients may well have achieved a broader perspective of themselves in their cultural contexts and have better recognition of their choices. The positive point here is that the therapist must recognize the danger of foreign cultural values being imposed as goals or criteria for successful therapy; he must combine this knowledge with the therapeutic position that such criteria are determined by a patient in a cultural framework. The therapist needs to worry less about what criteria to set and more about guarding against setting foreign ones or making any other inappropriate interventions. The arbitrary imposition of the therapist's beliefs and values violates the rules for proper conduct of most traditional Western psychotherapy. It should be assumed that the same principle of good technique would apply interculturally as well and that goals therefore are not to be determined unilaterally by the psychotherapist.

The paper by Kinzie (1972) provides three case examples of psychotherapy in Malaysia, uniquely qualified to exemplify the point that intercultural therapy is possible only if the cultural gap between patient and therapist, especially the language and world-view aspect of it, is not overly wide. The first case was a rural, uneducated woman who saw her "problem in magical and medical terms" (p. 227), not in concepts of family and interpersonal stress. She was treated with medication which brought relief. The second patient who had a moderate degree of Western (English-language) background asked for hypnosis and advice on his interpersonal inadequacy. He was treated with a hodgepodge of behavioral and medical methods which produced little change until he was able to discuss his feelings openly. From that point on he improved, more because of the relationship rather than the technique. The third patient was apparently at home in the European world, had already some experience in marital therapy, and was able to participate in a cathartic-supportive, self-exploratory relationship. The author pointed out that "because of his previous experience, this patient quickly became involved in therapy" (p. 228).

In two of the three case examples of successful intervention, the patient shared conceptions with the therapist about the usefulness of Western psychological methods of helping, whereas in one, these methods were not attempted. This is really not a very substantial demonstration of intercultural psychotherapeutics. One could just as well argue that the first case suggests the utility of working with traditional healers to make them more effective or the futility of trying to impose Western therapeutic approaches where they are incomprehensible or unknown.

These three cases demonstrate a continuum of readiness to accept psychotherapy which seems to correlate with the patient having had previous experiences that reduce the cultural gap between the Western therapy and the patient's expectations. Furthermore, it is plausible to suggest that, had the therapist been less quick to fire a shotgun of manipulative techniques at the second patient, a therapeutic relationship might more readily have developed.

One criticism commonly made of traditional (now something of pejorative expression) Western psychotherapists is that they prefer and are able to work only with young, intelligent, sophisticated, verbal, middleclass persons who are similar to themselves. It is striking that the same statement might be applied to the successful psychotherapy described in the above studies. In almost all cases, patients have deviated from their cultural background in ways that make them more like the desirable American patients and less like other people in their own culture. If psychotherapy is to be aimed at this population, perhaps one problem is less cultural and more clinical: we must account for those who have the same level of cultural sophistication as do those people who have accepted therapy but who do not themselves accept it. Cultural provincialism after all is not limited to Americans. Among equally educated people of any culture there are degrees of awareness and openness—of tolerance or acceptance of novelty and of foreignness. It may be that one variable not accorded sufficient respect in our fascination with cultural problems and resistance to novel forms of helping is the individual personality of the sufferer. It should be recognized in intercultural therapy as in any other therapy that one significant set of variables is the psychological structure and dynamics of the individual.

Some Conclusions

If one employs sufficiently broad concepts and definitions to describe its fundamental character, then psychotherapy can be reasonably viewed as a cultural universal. Many such elements have been identified. First is the existence of social support, a cultural context that is generally known and understood and by which the healer and his activities are defined.

There are societal rules, which govern or regulate the healing rituals with respect to their social and physical environmental aspects. Second are the sets of variables internal to the process of therapy. Included here are concepts dealing with the personal qualities of the therapist and of the therapeutic relationship. Third are the so-called technique variables, those characteristics traditionally seen as most directly involved in the change-inducing process but which are now seen as dependent upon the existence of a working therapeutic relationship.

Without a fitting external societal context and without therapist and relationship suitability, the magical power of technique is lost. Not only must these sets of variables coexist, they must be harmoniously related to each other. The physical setting, social rules, therapist's style, the relationship the therapist tries to establish, and the techniques used must be such as to fit in with the general expectations of the patient concerning what healers will do. Finally, all of these fundamentals in their concrete manifestations require that communication occur between the participants. They must be able to achieve some agreement and understanding about what they are doing together.

The literature suggests that intercultural psychotherapy is possible if the patient's expectations, based upon some aspects of cultural, subcultural, or intercultural experiences, make him at least minimally receptive to Western psychotherapy. The successful clinical examples are generally of people who are inclined towards accepting Western psychotherapy, whose world views are, even if fundamentally different, open enough to permit some new scenery to be examined. Yet paradoxically, these cases have been used to argue for the feasibility of applying Western psychotherapy to non-Western cultures, and even then always with the stipulation that some highly idealistic standards of therapist quality and competence be met. One could, with at least equal justification, suggest that if the therapist must be a paragon of therapeutic skill in order to deal with patients who are only marginally definable as intercultural, then the enterprise has very limited value.

In many of these cases, both the therapist and the therapy were foreign to the patient. The real test of intercultural psychotherapy, the carry-over to a different cultural environment of alien modes of psychotherapy, will come in the effort to work with non-Westernized patients only minimally familiar with Western ways. By this selection criterion, therapeutic communication will have to go on in the patient's language either with an interpreter or a therapist who is very much at home in that language. If that end is to be achieved in any practical way, members of the local culture must be able to identify with Western culture sufficiently to understand its psychotherapies; they must be sufficiently flexible in their own culture to sense how these therapies can be made to work. This means that the Westerner engaging in occasional intercultural therapy will do well to learn the culture in the interests of research or to perform training and consultative functions for the direct deliverer of service.

References

Abel, T. M. Cultural patterns as they affect psychotherapeutic procedures. *American Journal of Psychotherapy*, 1956, *10*, 728–739.

Abel, T. M. The dreams of a Chinese patient. In W. Muensterberger & S. Axelrad (Eds.), *The psychoanalytic study of society* (Vol. 2). New York: International University Press, 1962.

Abel, T. M., & Metraux, R. *Culture and psychotherapy*. New Haven: College & University Press, 1974.

Bernstein, B. Social class, speech systems, and psychotherapy. In F. Riessman, J. Cohen, & A. Pearl (Eds.), *Mental health of the poor*. Glencoe: Free Press, 1964.

Bickley, V. Cross-cultural, cross-national education: The greatest resource. *Culture Learning Institute Report*, 1978, 5(4), 1–9.

Bishop, M., & Winokur, G. Cross-cultural psychotherapy. *Journal of Nervous and Mental Disease*, 1956, *123*, 369–375.

Bolman, W. Cross-cultural psychotherapy. *American Journal of Psychiatry*, 1968, *124*, 1237–1244.

Bustamente, J. Importance of cultural patterns in psychotherapy. *American Journal of Psychotherapy*, 1957, *11*, 803–812.

Calestro, K. M. Psychotherapy, faith healing and suggestion. *International Journal of Psychiatry*, 1972, *10*, 83–113.

Carstairs, G. M. Cross-cultural psychiatric interviewing. In B. Kaplan (Ed.), *Studying personality cross-culturally*. New York: Harper & Row, 1961.

Chang, S. C., & Kim, K. Psychiatry in South Korea. *American Journal of Psychiatry*, 1973, *130*, 667–669.

Devereux, G. Three technical problems in psychotherapy of Plains Indian patients. *American Journal of Psychotherapy*, 1951, 5, 411–423.

Devereux, G. Cultural factors in psychoanalytic therapy. *Journal of the American Psychoanalytic Association*, 1953, *1*(4), 629–635.

DeVos, G. Cross-cultural studies of mental disorder. In G. Caplan & S. Arieti (Eds.), *American handbook of psychiatry* (Vol. 2, 2nd ed.). New York: Basic Books, 1974.

Doi, T. L. Psychotherapy as "hide and seek." In W. P. Lebra (Ed.), *Culture-bound syndromes, ethnopsychiatry and alternate therapies*. Honolulu: University Press of Hawaii, 1976.

Draguns, J. Resocialization into culture: The complexities of taking a worldwide view of psychotherapy. In R. Brislin, S. Bochner, & W. Lonner (Eds.), *Cross-cultural perspectives on learning*. New York: John Wiley & Sons, Halsted, 1975.

Frank, J. *Persuasion and healing*. New York: Schocken Books, 1963.

Frank, J. Therapeutic factors in psychotherapy. *American Journal of Psychotherapy*, 1971, *24*, 359–361.

Garfield, S. L. Basic ingredients or common factors in psychotherapy? *Journal of Consulting and Clinical Psychology*, 1973, *41*, 9–12.

Greenson, R. *The technique and practice of psychoanalysis*. New York: International University Press, 1967.

Halleck, S. L. *The politics of therapy*. New York: Harper & Row, 1971.

Hartmann, H. *Ego psychology and the problem of adaptation*. New York: International Universities Press, 1958.

Higginbotham, H. N. Culture and the role of client expectancy. In R. W. Brislin & M. P. Hamnett (Eds.), *Topics in culture learning*, 1977, 5.

Hsu, J., & Tseng, W. Intercultural psychotherapy. *Archives of General Psychiatry*, 1972, *27*, 700–706.

Jilek-Aall, L. The Western psychiatrist and non-Western clientele. *Canadian Psychiatric Association Journal*, 1976, *21*, 353–360.

Jones, E. Social class and psychotherapy: A critical review of research. *Psychiatry*, 1974, *37*, 307–320.

Karasu, T. B. Psychotherapies-overview. *American Journal of Psychiatry*, 1977, *134*, 851–863.

Kennedy, J. Cultural psychiatry. In J. J. Honigmann (Ed.), *Handbook of social and cultural anthropology*. Chicago: Rand McNally, 1973.

Kiev, A. (Ed.). *Magic, faith and healing*. New York: Macmillan Co., Free Press, 1964.

Kim, K. I., & Rhi, B. Y. A review of Korean cultural psychiatry. *Transcultural Psychiatric Research Review*, 1976, *13*, 101–114.

Kinzie, J. D. Cross-cultural psychotherapy: The Malaysian experience. *American Journal of Psychotherapy*, 1972, *26*, 220–231.

Kinzie, J. D. Lessons from cross-cultural psychotherapy. *American Journal of Psychotherapy*, 1978, *32*, 510–520.

Kittrie, N. N. *The right to be different*. Baltimore: Penguin Books, 1973.

Kokantzis, N. A., & Ierdioakonou, C. S. Some considerations on the position of psychotherapy in today's Greek culture. *Psychotherapy and Psychosomatics*, 1975, *25*, 254–258.

Lambo, T. A. Psychotherapy in Africa. *Psychotherapy and Psychosomatics*, 1974, *24*, 311–326.

Langs, R. *The bipersonal field*. New York: Jason Aronson, 1976.(a)

Langs, R. *The therapeutic interaction* (Vol. 2). New York: Jason Aronson, 1976.(b)

Lebra, W. P. (Ed.). *Culture-bound syndromes, ethnopsychiatry and alternate therapies*. Honolulu: University Press of Hawaii, 1976.

Lerner, B. *Therapy in the ghetto: Political impotence and personal disintegration*. Baltimore: Johns Hopkins University Press, 1972.

Lorion, R. P. Socioeconomic status and traditional treatment approaches reconsidered. *Psychological Bulletin*, 1973, *79*, 263–270.

Marcos, L. R. Bilinguals in psychotherapy: Language as an emotional barrier. *American Journal of Psychotherapy*, 1976, *30*, 552–560.(a)

Marcos, L. R. Linguistic dimensions in the bilingual patient. *American Journal of Psychoanalysis*, 1976, *36*, 347–354.(b)

Marcos, L. R., & Alpert, M. Strategies and risks with bilingual patients: The phenomenon of language independence. *American Journal of Psychiatry*, 1976, *133*, 1275–1278.

Marsella, A. J., & Sanborn, K. F. *The modernization of traditional cultures: Consequences for the individual.* Paper presented at the Third Annual SIETAR Conference, Chicago, Illinois, February 25–27, 1977.

McNeill, J. T. *A history of the cure of souls.* New York: Harper & Row, Torchbook, 1965.

Meadows, P. The cure of souls and the winds of change. *Psychoanalytic Review*, 1968, *55*, 491–504.

Mendel, W. M. Comparative psychotherapy. *International Journal of Psychoanalytic Psychotherapy*, 1972, *1*, 117–126.

Neki, J. S. Psychotherapy in India: Past, present, and future. *American Journal of Psychotherapy*, 1975, 29, 92–100.

Olatawura, M. O. Psychotherapy for the Nigerian patient. *Psychotherapy and Psychosomatics*, 1975, *25*, 259–266.

Ozturk, O. M. Psychotherapy under limited options: Psychotherapeutic work with Turkish youth. *American Journal of Psychotherapy*, 1978, *32*, 307–319.

Pande, S. The mystique of Western psychotherapy: An Eastern interpretation. *Journal of Nervous and Mental Diseases*, 1968, *146*, 425–432.

Pedersen, P. *Non-Western Psychology: The search for alternatives.* Unpublished manuscript, 1978.

Pedersen, P. *Role learning as a coping strategy for displaced foreign students.* Paper presented at the meeting of the American Psychological Association, San Francisco, August 1977.

Penningroth, P. E., & Penningroth, B. A. Cross-cultural mental health practice on Guam. *Social Psychiatry*, 1977, *12*, 43–48.

Prince, R. H. Psychotherapy and the chronically poor. In J. C. Finney (Ed.), *Culture change, mental health and poverty.* Lexington: University of Kentucky Press, 1969.

Prince, R. H. Psychotherapy as manipulation of endogenous healing mechanisms: A transcultural survey. *Transcultural Psychiatric Research Review*, 1976, *13*, 115–134.

Rosen, G. *Madness in society.* Chicago: University of Chicago Press, 1968.

Spiro, M. *Burmese supernaturalism.* Englewood Cliffs, New Jersey: Prentice-Hall, 1967.

Singer, K. Cross-cultural dynamics in psychotherapy. In J. Masserman (Ed.), *Social psychiatry*, Vol. 2: *The range of normal in human behavior.* New York: Grune & Stratton, 1976.

Stratton, J. G. Cross-cultural counseling: A problem in communication. *The Psychiatric Forum*, 1975, *5*, 15–19.

Strupp, H. On the technology of psychotherapy. *Archives of General Psychiatry*, 1972, *26*, 270–278.

Strupp, H. On the basic ingredients of psychotherapy. *Journal of Consulting Psychology*, 1973, *41*, 1–8.(a)

Strupp, H. Toward a reformulation of the psychotherapeutic influence. *International Journal of Psychiatry*, 1973, *11*, 263–327.(b)

Strupp, H. Psychoanalysis, focal psychotherapy and the nature of the therapeutic influence. *Archives of General Psychiatry*, 1975, *32*, 127-135.

Sullivan, H. S. *The interpersonal theory of psychiatry*. New York: Norton, 1953.

Szasz, T. S. *The myth of mental illness*. New York: Harper & Row, 1961.

Thomas, A. Pseudo-transference reactions due to cultural stereotyping. *American Journal of Orthopsychiatry*, 1962, *32*, 894-900.

Torrey, E. F. *The mind game: Witch doctors and psychiatrists*. New York: Emerson Hall, 1972.

Tseng, W. Traditional and modern psychiatric care in Taiwan. In A. Kleinman, P. Kunstadter, E. R. Alexander, & J. L. Gate (Eds.), *Culture and healing in Asian societies*. Cambridge, Massachusetts: Schenkman, 1978.

Tseng, W., & McDermott, J. F. Psychotherapy: Historical roots, universal elements and cultural variations. *American Journal of Psychiatry*, 1975, *132*, 378-384.

Useem, J., Useem, R., & Donaghue, J. Men in the middle of the third culture: The roles of American and non-Western people in cross-cultural administration. *Human Organization*, 1963, *22*, 169-171.

Vassiliou, G., & Vassiliou, V. G. Subjective culture and psychotherapy. *American Journal of Psychotherapy*, 1973, *27*, 42-51.

Walz, G. R., & Benjamin, L. *Transcultural counseling: Needs, programs, and techniques*. New York: Human Sciences Press, 1978.

Wittkower, E. D., & Warnes, H. Cultural aspects of psychotherapy. *American Journal of Psychotherapy*, 1974, *28*, 566-573.(a)

Wittkower, E. D., & Warnes, H. Cultural aspects of psychotherapy. *Psychotherapy and Psychosomatics*, 1974, *24*, 303-310.(b)

Wohl, J. Counseling and guidance in Asia: Impressions of a developing profession. *International Journal for the Advancement of Counseling*, 1978, *1*, 209-223.

Wohl, J., & Silverstein, J. The Burmese university student: An approach to personality and subculture. *The Public Opinion Quarterly*, 1966, *30*, 237-248.

Wohl, J., & Tapingkae, A. Values of Thai university students. *International Journal of Psychology*, 1970, *7*, 23-31.

PART THREE
Specific Ethnic and Cultural Considerations

7

Counseling Asian Americans

Harry H. L. Kitano
Noreen Matsushima

There is little doubt that at the present time, caseworkers, counselors, psychiatrists, and psychologists can go through their entire professional careers without seeing a single Asian American client. For very few Asian Americans have made use of the services of mental health professionals, even those that have are apt to drop out after their initial visit (Sue & McKinney, 1975). However, it is also highly likely that this situation will change because of such factors as increased numbers, acculturation, the persistence of unsolved problems, the breakup of the ethnic family and community and, if one can be optimistic, the development of more knowledgeable and relevant mental health counseling services.

The meager history of Asian Americans seeking mental health services can be attributed to several reasons: the fragmentation of counseling services, their relative inaccessibility to Asian American clients, the discontinuity of Asian American experiences, the culture of the professional counselor himself, and the lack of accountability of the counseling professions towards non-white communities. By lack of accountability, we suggest that the major reference group for counselors—the white middle class—is not necessarily comparable to the Asian American community (Miranda & Kitano, 1976). In addition, their small numbers are geographically concentrated in California and Hawaii; thus, for most of the country, Asians are unknown except for the stereotype as a group with few problems, if any.

Available material on Asian Americans is scarce, and much of what is available is rife with systematic biases. For example, Hune (1977) has found that most historical studies dealing with Asian immigrants have either ignored or considered Pacific migration unimportant when compared to migration from Europe. This type of parochial thinking has continued to the present day.

The counseling field has not remained immune to these issues so that theories and ways of looking at the world from non-European models are generally unknown, viewed as exotic, or dismissed as minor. Vontress (1981) comments on the mainstream bias of professional counseling, while Pedersen (1979) writes that the underlying assumptions of our mental health delivery systems reflect the social, economic, political, and cultural values of the Western dominant cultures. Further, when there is an acknowledgment of Asian perspectives, there are often paternalistic and racist overtones: the general theme seems to be the contrast of a solid, universal, rational, scientific, and superior knowledge, as typified by European and American thinking, with an irrational, mystical, exotic, and inferior understanding of human behavior, as typified by Oriental thinking.

Asian immigrants and their children have suffered from these perspectives. Europeans who have cultivated an accent are often viewed as charming, sophisticated and continental; Asians with an accent are objects of ridicule and satire ("rots of ruck"). Third and fourth generation Asian Americans are still treated as nationals of a foreign country and are mistaken for visitors, tourists, or aliens, barely able to understand English. There is a general attitude that Asian Americans still have to "prove" their worthiness, that their rights to citizenship are not automatically given.

One other theme which forces a point of view on the Asian American is the assimilationist bias of most counselors. Assimilation and acculturation into the Anglo world is considered necessary, desirable, and functional. The model is often seen as unidimensional so that "becoming American" is encouraged at the sacrifice of the immigrant culture. In cases of "cultural clash," reinforcement is given for the "American way" over the "ethnic way" without adequate knowledge and understanding of the latter alternative. Or there may be a tendency to err in the opposite direction, in which a romantic and uncritical acceptance of the immigrant culture assumes a higher priority than the realities of the problem.

Asians as a Minority Group

There are a number of ways of looking at minority groups. Kinloch defines minority groups as "products of power elites on the basis of perceived physical, cultural, economic and behavioral characteristics" (1979, p. 196). He further differentiates minority groups into (1) physiological types (non-whites, women, young people, students, and the aged); (2) cultural types (non-Anglo Europeans such as Italians and Greeks); (3) economic types (the poor, the lower classes without power); and (4) the behavioral types (the legal and social deviants including criminals and the mentally ill).

Asians fit into both the physiological non-white and the cultural types of minorities, with a scattering of persons in categories three and four.

The one common denominator among the different types of minority groups is their lack of power when compared to the dominant, white male majority. Their needs, expectations, values, and behaviors are generally secondary to the perceptions and wishes of the more powerful. The issue is significant if the majority of counselors are drawn from the dominant group and the majority of counseling clientele come from the dominated group. We have no empirical data concerning this breakdown except to note that it is our impression that the described situation is highly likely.

Asians in America

The Asian American minority was initially created by migration to the United States. From this contact there developed a wide variety of responses—some acculturated and attempted to assimilate, others reacted to discrimination and prejudice by retreating to their own ethnic communities, others returned to their mother country. Very few turned to professional counseling for assistance and it can be hypothesized that very few counselors could have provided much assistance in solving their problems.

The most prevalent model concerning Asian American interaction with the American system is that of immigration, contact, acculturation, integration, and assimilation. Although there may be minor disagreements over the precise definition of some of the terms, the sequence, its desirability, and its stages are commonly accepted. Because of the unequal power relationships between the dominant culture and that of the Asian groups, the interaction is primarily one way, so that very little of the immigrant culture remains or is considered important by the majority. But, many of the problems of the immigrants and their progeny revolve around the processes of acculturation and integration, culture conflict and stresses created by different ways of looking at the world. Kuo (1976) in a study of Chinese Americans found that of the four major theories analyzing the relationship between migration and mental health (social isolation, culture shock, goal-striving stress, and cultural change), social isolation and culture shock were correlated with measures of mental health.

In addition, there is the critical factor of physiological visibility. The fact that Asians look different from the mainstream American has led to discrimination, prejudice, and social inequality. The problem of inequality is a major one, especially since minority groups by definition are less equal and have less opportunity to achieve mobility than members of the majority. By virtue of minority membership, most Asian Americans have received proportionately less of the rewards of the system such as material comforts, power, prestige, privilege, and wealth. Or if they do achieve a degree of autonomy and power, there is a belief among them that they have to expend twice the time and effort as their white peers.

What models do counselors use to explain and to deal with the inequality of minority groups? Possibly the worst strategy is to ignore the fact of social inequality and to pretend that it does not exist. The "you too can become president of this country if you try hard enough" approach and its variations such as "I don't see you as an Asian but only as an individual human being" may be built on good intentions, but they skirt some of the reasons that may have brought the individual into counseling in the first place.

Explanations of Inequality

There are two basic sociological perspectives which address in opposite terms the problem of inequality—the functional model and the conflict model. The "functional approach" sees hierarchical stratification and inequality as necessary in all social structures. The unequal distribution of rewards, power, prestige, privilege, and wealth is characteristic of complex, urban societies (Burkey, 1978, p. 20). Inequality is a consequence of value consensus in these societies. Achievement and performance are judged on the basis of the needs, priorities, and goals of the system. Social inequality results from a differential reward system that encourages able members to fill more difficult positions.

Physiological minorities are generally placed lower in the hierarchical structure than majority group members so that a counselor must ask why this is so and assess his role in maintaining the functional model. It may well be that one of the reasons that Asians are reluctant to use professional counseling is their recognition of the inequality between them and the world of the white counselor, and their lack of power to change the system.

Functional theory can be criticized on a number of grounds. The most important from a minority perspective is its minimization of prejudice, discrimination, and racism as barriers to mobility and participation in the mainstream. Many Asians feel that they cannot gain the full benefits of the system no matter how hard they work or how well they are educated. It is our interpretation that counselors operate primarily from a functional perspective and that their orientation is to urge Asian clients to work hard, do well in school, and get good grades with the implication that such actions will lead to acceptance. Racial barriers are minimized so that those who fail tend to blame themselves and are considered deviant.

Conflict theorists take a different approach. They believe that social inequality arises as a result of the struggle within a society for the "goods, amenities, privileges and rewards which are in short supply"

(Matras, 1978, p. 71). This view emphasizes power and coercion in social life and the exploitation of minority groups by the majority. The ability of the group in power to get what it wants and to prevent less powerful groups from doing the same brings about social inequality. For example, Asian Americans are kept in subordinate positions (e.g., cook, houseboy, gardener) because it is in the interests of the dominant group to maintain such a stratification system. Only those with the "proper" credentials (i.e., college or professional degrees) are allowed to participate in the peripheries of the system, and these individuals are monitored and controlled.

Counselors identified with the conflict model would adopt a different strategy from those following a functionalist perspective. They might aid Asian Americans to question the efficacy of adapting to subordinate positions and help them to achieve a degree of power. They might advise Asians to organize and to attack the structural constraints and conditions which are considered the reasons for inequality. The lady working in a Chinatown sweat shop, for example, might be encouraged to organize to fight for better working conditions under the conflict model; whereas she would be encouraged to work harder and be more productive under the functional model.

The functional model is basically conservative as it suggests that the minority group member adapt to the status quo. The more radical conflict model advocates a change in the societal structure.

Asian American Problems

Most Asian Americans are concentrated on the West Coast and in Hawaii. The 1970 census reports that 38 percent of the total Asian population resides in California and another 27 percent in Hawaii. Counselors who live outside these areas see very few Asians such that the mass media, especially the movies and television, play an important role in filling this vacuum. The present day stereotype of Asians as cooks, houseboys, exotic ladies, and camera-clicking tourists does not cast much light on the unflattering images that most dominant group members have about Asians.

Several problems are held in common by the Asians. One is that of biculturalism and bilingualism—which direction is the more appropriate? Another is that of an ethnic identity in a pluralistic society. A model developed by Newman (1976) analyzes the difficulty of achieving a bicultural identity when the majority community views Asians through negative stereotypes. Problems of immigration, brought about by discriminatory legislation, are also important. In addition, there are culture clashes and intergenerational strains.

The overall Asian experience with the dominant culture has been qualitatively different from that of the Blacks, American Indians, and

Chicanos. First, much of their immigration was voluntary, although there were contract laborers, sojourners, and the recent refugees from Southeast Asia. Second, their cultures were not quickly dismantled. One notable exception to this, however, was the internment of Japanese Americans during World War II—acculturation was encouraged and the repression of "Japanese ways" strongly reinforced. The cohesive ethnic communities of the Chinese and Japanese aided in providing alternative social and economic opportunities when entrance into the mainstream was limited by discrimination and prejudice. Third, ties with a home country were strong, this despite the fact that many Asian countries were victims of colonization. The effects of colonization on a people and their culture are long-lasting; this may account for many of the attitudes and adaptive patterns brought to the United States. Finally, most of the Asian American groups were able to bypass a significant long-term dependency on the United States federal government, although the new refugees from Southeast Asia may be an exception.

Generally, the position of the Asian American has been one of a minority subordinated on the basis of race and culture. Asians' initial presence in the United States was at the lower end of the social structure, and systematic attempts were made to keep them subordinated with legal discrimination as the primary tool. Although there has been improvement over time, Asian Americans remain as unequal minorities. Does counseling have a role in addressing this issue?

An overall picture of the Chinese, Filipino, Japanese, and Korean in the United States can be seen through the 1970 census figures.

TABLE 1
Population of Selected Asian American Groups in 1970

	Chinese	Japanese	Korean	Filipino
Male	226,733	271,453	28,491	183,175
Female	204,850	316,871	42,107	153,556
Total	431,583	588,324	70,598	336,731

SOURCE: U.S. Department of Commerce (Bureau of the Census, 1970), PC(1)-D1.

The Chinese*

The Chinese were the first Asian immigrants to the United States. They arrived in the 1840s and there are many Chinese Americans who have roots in California that go back to the gold rush era. Economic reverses, local rebellions, and social discontent were among the reasons for leav-

---

*Most of the material on the Asian groups is drawn from Kitano, Harry H. L., *Race Relations.* Englewood Cliffs: Prentice-Hall, 1980.

ing China (Purcell, 1965). Most of the early immigrants came from the two Southern provinces of Fukien and Kwangtung.

Initially, the Chinese were welcome because they labored in supplementary occupations rather than as direct competitors (e.g., they took jobs that had to do with the lack of women in California—washing clothes and cooking). However, the Chinese, like other forty-niners, eventually made their way into the gold fields and soon became the targets of anti-Chinese antagonism. The hostility towards them was so extreme that the term "Chinaman's chance," meaning there was no chance at all, was coined. In 1876 a congressional investigating committee visiting San Francisco heard blatantly racist testimony. The Chinese were accused of lowering wages; they were unassimilable; they were heathens; they were disgusting and tended to debauch those around them. Defenders of the Chinese, on the other hand, praised their ability to work hard and their high level of productivity.

In 1882 Congress passed the Chinese Exclusion Act which prohibited Chinese immigration for ten years. The Act was renewed in 1892 and made "permanent" in 1902. These discriminatory actions had their effect on Chinese family life. Although immigration was prohibited, children born of males already in the United States were eligible for legal entry. One common practice of men returning to China was to "father" an impressive number of children who could then be admitted to the United States. There were also the "mutilated marriages" in which men at an early age would leave their wives and families in China to work in the United States, not returning for many years. Then there was the practice of older Chinese men, after years of forced bachelorhood (unless they could find non-Chinese mates), returning to China to marry much younger women. It is difficult to visualize American-trained counselors giving wise counsel to people with problems arising from such situations.

Differences among Chinese

It is important that the counselor identify the various "types" of families and individuals that make up the community. Some families date back many generations while others are newly arrived. Huang (1976) indicates that one type of poor family in the Chinese ghetto is the hard working but lowly paid Chinese male and his "imported" young wife from Hong Kong. Others are the recent adolescent immigrants with problems of language, acculturation, lack of employment opportunities, and who join gangs. Women may be found working in Chinatown "sweatshops" as seamstresses for low wages. Yet others find employment in the numerous Chinese restaurants or in situations which require little skill but entail long hours and few opportunities for advancement. Employment in these labor intensive sectors generally means limited upward mobility and meager chances for acquiring capital.

Then there are Chinese Americans who, with college degree and a house in the suburbs, are more concerned about professional issues than ethnic ones. And there are those whose worries include interracial dating by their children.

Sung (1967, p. 165) reports that Chinese family discipline is strict. Punishment is immediate, and deviant behavior is considered dishonorable and shameful to the immediate family, the extended family, and all who care about the person.

Personality and Counseling

A study by Sue and Kirk (1975) comparing personality differences between Chinese students and those of other ethnic backgrounds at the University of California at Berkeley found the following: (1) Chinese students score higher on quantitative sections than on verbal sections of aptitude tests; (2) they are more interested in the physical sciences, applied technical fields, and business occupations than in the social sciences, aesthetic and cultural fields, and verbal and linguistic vocations; and (3) they prefer the concrete and tangible approaches to life and are more conforming and less socially extroverted than non-Chinese students.

Sue and Sue (1972) suggested that the counseling situation can arouse intense conflicts among Chinese American students. Chinese are taught to obey parents, to respect elders, to value self-control, and to exercise emotional restraint. There may be feelings of guilt and shame at seeking professional counseling help and great anxiety about the matter of confidentiality. Self-worth and self-identity are strongly tied to the family.

The Sues presented the case of a Chinese American client with the following conflicts: loyalty to the family versus personal desires for independence; learned patterns of self-restraint and formality in social interaction leading to lack of social experience and loneliness; and family pressures for academic achievement accentuating feelings of shame and depression in times of failure.

Sue and Sue suggest that the development of rapport and trust is the most critical element in counseling Chinese Americans. A general knowledge of the life experiences of the group is important as well as the ability to work with problems of guilt and shame, the lack of openness, and marginal biculturalism.

In an article entitled "Ancient Needles for Modern Ills," the author Wang (1979) writes of the tendency of Chinese Americans to somatize so that stress and tension are frequently turned into physical complaints. People suffer from headaches, dizzy spells, and stomach trouble; one of the most telling symptoms of serious problems is that of insomnia. Acupuncture is one appropriate form of treatment.

Information on counseling and therapeutic techniques in the home country is not readily available. The major generalization about the use of counseling services is that the family and extended family are likely to handle psychological and emotional problems. The use of indigenous resources (e.g., neighbors, the village seer, acupuncture, and herbal cures) takes precedence over professional counseling, especially in the nonurban areas. It is our understanding that professional counseling as we know it (i.e., the professional with credentials) does not exist in China.

The Japanese

The significant Japanese immigration started after 1890. Material on this group is available: Kitano, 1976; Petersen, 1971; Hosokawa, 1969; and Daniels, 1968. The problems of prejudice and discrimination the Japanese faced were similar to those of the Chinese. Discrimination reached its zenith during World War II with the forced evacuation into concentration camps of more than 110,000 Japanese residing along the Pacific coast.

Groups in the Japanese American community include the Issei, the initial immigrants or the first generation; Nisei, the children of the Issei or second generation; Sansei, or the third generation; and Yonsei, or the fourth generation. Other important groups are the Kibei, who are technically Nisei but who were reared in Japan by their grandparents or other extended family members; war brides; visiting businessmen; students; and the ever increasing number of tourists. There are, as well, differences in ethnic identification, social class, and personality so that although "all Asians look alike," different experiences and life-styles abound.

The major concentration of Japanese is in Hawaii and California. Japanese American proportions are much higher in Hawaii, a fact reflected in the Hawaii political system. The current governor, George Ariyoshi, and United States senators, Daniel Inouye and Spark Matsunaga, are all of Japanese descent.

Problems

Problems which arise frequently in professional counseling include parent-child stresses, care of the aged, and interracial dating and marriage. The group is diverse. A large number appear ready for professional services since their incomes, social status, and problems are appropriate to middle-class concerns. The effect of acculturation, integration and amalgamation has been noticeable: by the 1970s racial intermarriage had reached over 50 percent (Kikumura & Kitano, 1973). There is also some evidence that Japanese American mobility may be to a "middle minority" position (Kitano, 1974), that is, a group that has risen from the bottom of the social structure but may be prevented from reaching much higher than the middle. The Jews were such a minority in Germany prior to World War II, and the Chinese have played a similar role in Southeast Asia.

Counseling and Therapy

Interviews of social workers with Japanese American clients generate several generalizations. Just as with the Chinese and other Asian groups, the Japanese tend to turn towards the family, the extended family, and other local resources for assistance. Feelings of shame and stigma are attached to the use of professional counseling and there is the problem of confidentiality. Major counseling themes include dealing with dependency (the Japanese term *amae* reflects this concern) and culture conflict. The development of confidence and rapport with Japanese clients is often time-consuming, especially since many still communicate indirectly with reliance on inferential messages.

Okano (1977) surveyed a sample of Los Angeles Japanese Americans on their attitudes towards mental health. The major problems facing Japanese Americans included racism, juvenile delinquency, divorce, drug abuse, crime, alcoholism, low self-esteem, depression, identity confusion, and culture conflict. Ministers were the primary resource when emotional problems occurred. Relatives, friends, and the family doctor were mentioned as resources more frequently than professional counselors. Over one-half of the sample indicated that they would prefer to work out emotional problems on their own.

Counseling Techniques with Chinese and Japanese American Clients

A study by Nakao and Lum (1977) provided data concerning counseling techniques for the Chinese and Japanese as compared to a white client population. The authors, using a mail questionnaire, received 70 responses from caseworkers (68 with M.SW and 2 with D.SW degrees) of Asian American background employed in the Los Angeles area. The respondents were asked if they would treat Asian American clients (Chinese and Japanese) differently from Caucasian clients. The results are shown on Table 2.

The findings demonstrate that Asian American professionals used different techniques when dealing with the Chinese and Japanese as compared to white clients. They would treat Asian Americans more formally; would tend to treat them in individual rather than in group sessions; would be less confrontational; and would be hesitant to reinforce the person's competency and expertise. Other variables showed no signifi-

TABLE 2

Differences in Counseling Caucasian and Asian American Clients

Counseling Technique	Asian American Clients		
How Would You Treat Japanese and Chinese Clients in Comparison to Caucasian Clients	Percent in Agreement		
	Japanese	Chinese	Significance
1. More formal	61	62.9	.05*
2. More supportive	42.9	45.7	
3. Individual rather than group sessions	77	67.1	.05*
4. More confidentiality and privacy	57.2	58.6	
5. More structured sessions	57.2	52.9	
6. Less assertive techniques	47.1	45.7	
7. More direct	50	50	
8. Less confrontational	61.5	58.5	.05*
9. Reinforcing person's competency and expertise	30	34.3	.05*

*Statistical significance is between the Asian groups and Caucasians, not between the Chinese and Japanese.
SOURCE: Nakao, Stan, and Lum, Clifford (1977).

cant differences between the groups. There was a high degree of similarity in treating the Chinese and the Japanese.

Models from Japan

There are a number of therapeutic models from Japan that are relatively familiar to American audiences. Morita therapy is probably the best known. Naikan therapy and the Ajase complex are two other ways of treating and understanding human behavior which reflect Japanese views of the world.

Miura and Usa (1974) refer to Morita therapy as a psychotherapy for neurosis; Pedersen (1979) emphasizes its acceptance of phenomenological reality as it is, compared to the Western notion of rationalistic idealism; and Reynolds (1976) and Reynolds and Kiefer (1977) indicate that Morita therapy is group-centered, ritualistic, and behavioristic in contrast to Western therapies which are more talk centered. Morita therapists discourage the verbal rumination of one's problems, place little emphasis on a search for the origins of neuroses, and discourage the client from constructing elaborate plans for recovery. Rather, the concentration is on the here and now, on behavior over moods and feelings, and on the interdependence among individuals. Gibson (1974) remarks on the similarity of Morita with Eysenck's theories of personality. Behavior therapists and Morita therapists, he says, could gain much through cooperation.

Naikan therapy focuses on the important influences in one's life, especially the mother. Under the guidance of a sensei (teacher), the individual gains a better understanding of his or her relationships with these significant others and acknowledges indebtedness. In the process, thera-peutic gain can be observed as the individual becomes more sympathetic to the views of others, including the trouble and problems that the self has created for them (Murase, 1974, p. 432).

Okonogi (1978) writes about the Ajase complex, developed by the Jap-anese psychoanalyst Kosawa (1897–1968) and based on a figure who ap-peared in Buddhist scriptures. The basic concept is that of strong mother-child ties, especially mother to son, and the consequences of this bond. There are strong feelings of love and hostility, with the theme of forgiveness as the child returns to the mother.

Okonogi contrasts the Japanese view of forgiveness to the more puni-tive orientation of Western psychology. Japanese are much more apt to forgive trangressions upon return to the fold than are Europeans. The Ajase complex may be a more fundamental explanation of facets of the Japanese culture than Freud's more widely known Oedipus complex.

The Filipinos

The Filipinos are considered Asians primarily for geographic reasons, but physically and culturally, they are different. The Philippines were a colony of Spain for many years and then of the United States so that col-onization has been a strong part of their history.

The first group of Filipino immigrants were male peasants, brought in to work on Hawaii's plantations and Western agricultural lands. Their numbers were small—in 1920 there were about 5,000 and in 1930, about 45,000. They also faced discrimination. The stereotype was that of "brown men" who had a lust for white women. Most of this group re-mained in agricultural labor; they were known as hard workers and their elderly years have been characterized by isolation, loneliness, and poverty.

New immigrants include the post-World War II group, composed pri-marily of veterans and war victims. The current group includes a number of professionals (i.e., doctors, nurses) with high educational backgrounds. Many of the contemporary group face problems of under-employment, culture clash, identity, and parent-child stresses (Morales, 1974). There is great diversity among the Filipinos and they have not developed the cohesive communities that were a part of the Chinese and Japanese experience. Filipinos are constantly mistaken for Japanese, Chinese, American Indian, and Mexican, especially since many of them have Spanish surnames. Most do not use professional counseling services. As Cordova (1973) notes, the Filipinos are a "hidden minority."

The Koreans

Initial Korean immigration to the United States occurred between 1902 and 1905 at which time the Japanese took over Korea. Koreans in the

United States thus became people without a country. This initial group was small, numbering slightly over 7,000, most of them male. Being cut off from their homeland encouraged a politicization of Korean communities and an involvement in "free Korea" movements aiming to overthrow Japanese rule. There were as many as twenty Korean organizations in Hawaii, often competing with one another, with the theme of solidarity and resistance to Japanese occupation. There were some groups who practiced military drills as a part of their purpose.

New Immigration

The "new" immigration is of relatively recent origin. In the 1970 census there were 70,598 Koreans in the United States, whereas 1978 estimates placed that number in the Los Angeles area alone (Kitano, 1980). Kim (1977) reports that the primary reasons for the new immigration included better opportunities in employment and education as well as reunion with relatives and friends.

The new immigrants reflect current American immigration laws. They tend to be well educated, arriving in the United States with professional skills. However, many of them have to settle for less than what they are capable of. Small business appears as one economic avenue, although Kim and Wong (1977, p. 231) warn that many of these establishments are marginal and reflect the lack of opportunity for the newcomer. The Koreans are pictured as more aggressive than the Chinese and Japanese (Sherman, 1979).

Problems

Major problems for the group include language and underemployment, but they are also making full use of America's educational opportunities. Koreans do well in school and have fierce determination to "make it." Counselors are not likely to see many Korean Americans for intrapsychic problems. Rather, the main contact in the foreseeable future is expected to be as regards vocational and educational choices. As with most Asian groups, the utilization of professional counseling has not been an integral part of their background. Talking about personal problems with strangers has to be learned.

Discussions with staff of the Korean Mental Health Counseling Center indicate other problems, such as marital difficulties (often based on changing roles of husband and wife in the United States), wife beating (as a possible response to the frustrating conditions facing the Korean male), loneliness, and isolation. The majority of these problems were viewed as consequences of migration, and there may be an increase among those Koreans thinking of a return to their homeland. It should be emphasized that there are differences between modern migration and older migration. The present day immigrant tends to be drawn from an educated middle-class background so that he or she is not emigrating from desperate economic circumstances. Further, the relative ease of transportation allows for visits prior to and subsequent to the move so that ambivalence about permanent settlement is greater.

The Vietnamese

Vietnamese migration is drastically different from other Asian groups. Termination of the Vietnam War in April 1975 resulted in a sudden refugee exodus. The refugees were not immigrants who chose to come to America voluntarily; rather, they had left Vietnam because they had no choice. Motivations for leaving had to do simply with survival. Circumstances surrounding the evacuation and resettlement of 120,000 Vietnamese refugees in the United States are tragic and suggest serious adjustment problems for the Vietnamese in America (Liu, 1979).

For most, the evacuation experiences were harrowing. The lack of information about the abrupt military defeat in Saigon resulted in inadequate planning and preparation. Most refugees had thought of locating in countries nearer to Vietnam and were surprised to find themselves in the United States. A detrimental effect of this unplanned flight to safety has been the disintegration of the social fabric—family, community, and cultural ties.

Transitional periods spent at refugee camps and, later, resettlement programs were characterized by the lack of organized planning, insufficient financial input and services. A predominant problem of camp life was the administration; its insensitivity to the cultural values and social networks of the refugees was vast. After material needs, there was a serious lack of concern for mental health (Rahe et al., 1978).

In the resettlement and sponsorship strategy, refugees were dispersed across the United States to facilitate assimilation. Concern for the maintenance of the Vietnamese extended family, however, was meager. Furthermore, the psychological and social support that might have been gained from living in an ethnic community (such as was in camp life) was dissolved.

Demographic data indicates that Vietnamese refugees are young, relatively well educated, and with economic skills. Many have experienced status-deprivation and lowered social positions because of their resettlement. Prejudice and discrimination adds to the sense of status loss.

In general, the reception of the Vietnamese refugee by the American public has been negative. In two national polls conducted in 1975 and 1977, a majority of Americans opposed the immigration of the Vietnamese refugee. The major argument against accepting Vietnamese was the fear of displacement of Americans in their jobs. Additional reasons could be attributed to lingering prejudices against non-Caucasians, interest in economic welfare of self and community as opposed to foreigners, and public reluctance to be reminded of the Vietnamese turmoil.

Several recent "backlash" incidents involving the Vietnamese have received wide publicity. For example, a recent story in *Newsweek* (1979) detailed problems in different areas of the country. In Indiana, a construction union expelled a group of Indo-Chinese for working too hard. In Texas, a conflict over fishing practices led to an alleged killing of an American by a Vietnamese, while boats owned by the refugees were burned. In Denver, tensions between Mexican Americans and the Indo-Chinese in a housing project boiled over into fights and rock throwing, ending in the departure of many refugees. There is bitterness among America's neglected minorities who feel that the Vietnamese receive special treatment.

The plight of the Vietnamese refugee is serious. Disintegration of familiar societal ties, loss of social status, uncertainty of future prospects, and perceived hostility from the host country are factors that contribute to problems that have already been exacerbated by their forced evacuation and resettlement. Language is a constant problem as well, so that for a period of time, most refugees may have to rely upon special assistance before achieving independence in their new country.

Because of their refugee status, most Vietnamese have had contact with the American military and the United States Government, contact which has included life in camps, standing in lines, filling out forms, and following bureaucratic procedures. How they feel about and how they might use voluntary counseling services have yet to be determined.

Other Asian Groups

There are a number of other Asian Pacific groups which have not been covered by the article. They include immigrants from Burma, Cambodia, Guam, India, Indonesia, Laos, Malaysia, Pakistan, Samoa, Singapore, Sri Lanka, Thailand, and Tonga. Each of these groups represents a different nation with their own language and culture.

Conclusion

The most appropriate generalization as regards counseling Asian Americans pertains to the general lack of knowledge about them. The identification of each of the different Asian groups, information as to their respective cultures, the various reasons for migration, a recognition of their unique histories, their reception by the host culture, basic demographic data, their hopes and expectations, their life-styles, and their internal stratification systems are necessary background data before any kind of effective counseling can take place. There should also be a recognition of the social inequality that faces most Asian groups and an introspective look by the counselor at his own feelings about maintaining the status quo. These attitudes often spill out into the counseling situation, which may be one of the reasons why there are so few Asian American clients.

Asian Americans prefer certain cultural styles, although acculturation and time have led to changes. These include indirect communication, deference to authority, emphasis on confidentiality, the importance of the family and community, and group orientation. It is our expectation that Asian models and theories of human behavior will become an integral part of any curriculum which purports to teach students about human behavior.

References

Ancient needles for modern ills. *Innovations*, 1979, 5(2), 14–15.

Brown, W. Japanese management: The cultural background. In T. Lebra & W. Lebra (Eds.), *Japanese culture and behavior*. Honolulu: University Press of Hawaii, 1974, pp. 174–191.

Burkey, R. *Ethnic and racial groups*. Menlo Park: Cummings Publishing Co., 1978.

Caudill, W., & Weinstein, H. Maternal care and infant behavior. In T. Lebra & W. Lebra (Eds.), *Japanese culture and behavior*. Honolulu: University Press of Hawaii, 1974, pp. 225–276.

Cordova, F. The Filipino-American: There is always an identity crisis. In S. Sue & N. Wagner (Eds.), *Asian Americans*. Palo Alto: Science and Behavior Books, 1973, pp. 136–139.

Daniels, R. *The politics of prejudice*. New York: Atheneum, 1980.

Doi, T. Amae: A key concept for understanding Japanese personality structure. In T. Lebra & W. Lebra (Eds.), *Japanese culture and behavior*. Honolulu: University Press of Hawaii, 1974.

Doi, T. *The anatomy of dependence* (trans. J. Bester). Tokyo: Kodansha International Ltd., 1973.

Draguns, J. Cross-cultural counseling and psychotherapy history issues: Current status. Paper presented at DISL Conference on Cross-Cultural Counseling and Psychotherapy Foundations Evaluation and Training, Honolulu, June 12–18, 1979.

Fukuhara, M. Student expectations of counseling: A cross-cultural study. *Japanese Psychological Research*, 1973, *15*, 179–183.

Gibson, H. B. Morita therapy and behavior therapy. *Behavior Research and Therapy*, 1974, *12*(4), 347–353.

Hosokawa, W. *Nisei: The quiet Americans*. New York: Morrow, 1969.

Huang, L. J. The Chinese American family. In C. Mendel & R. Haberstein (Eds.), *Ethnic Families in America*. New York: Elsevier, 1976, pp. 124–125.

Hune, S. *Pacific migration to the United States*. Washington: Research Institute on Immigration and Ethnic Studies, Smithsonian Institution, 1977.

Johnson, C. L. Interdependence reciprocity and indebtedness: An analysis of

Japanese American kinship relations. *Journal of Marriage and the Family,* 1977, *39,* 351-363.

Kasahara, Y. Fear of eye-to-eye confrontation among neurotic patients in Japan. In T. Lebra & W. Lebra (Eds.), *Japanese culture and behavior.* Honolulu: University Press of Hawaii, 1974, pp. 396-406.

Kikumura, A., & Kitano, H. Interracial marriage: A picture of the Japanese Americans. *Journal of Social Issues,* 1973, *29*(2), 67-81.

Kim, B. C., & Condon, M. *A study of Asian Americans in Chicago: Their socioeconomic characteristics, problems and service needs.* Washington, D.C.: Interim Report to the National Institute of Mental Health, U.S. Department of Health, Education, and Welfare, 1975.

Kim, D. S., & Wong, C. C. Business development in Koreatown, Los Angeles. In H. C. Kim (Ed.), *The Korean diaspora.* Santa Barbara, Calif.: ABC-Clio Press, 1977, pp. 229-245.

Kim, H. C. Some aspects of social demography of Korean Americans. In H. C. Kim (Ed.), *The Korean diaspora.* Santa Barbara, Calif.: ABC-Clio Press, 1977, pp. 109-126.

Kinloch, G. *The sociology of minority group relations.* Englewood Cliffs: Prentice-Hall, 1979.

Kitano, H. H. Japanese Americans: The development of a middleman minority. *Pacific Historical Review,* 1974, *43*(4), 500-519.

Kitano, H. H. *Japanese Americans: The evolution of a subculture* (2nd ed.). Englewood Cliffs: Prentice-Hall, 1976.

Kitano, H. H. *Race relations* (rev. ed.). Englewood Cliffs: Prentice-Hall, 1980.

Kuo, W. Theories of migration and mental health: An empirical testing on Chinese Americans. *Social Science and Medicine,* 1976, *10,* 297-306.

Li-Repac, D. *Clinical perception across subcultural lines.* Unpublished paper, no date.

Liu, W. T. *Transition to nowhere.* Nashville: Charter House Publishers, 1979.

Matras, J. *Social inequality, stratification, and mobility.* Englewood Cliffs: Prentice-Hall, 1975.

Miranda, M. R., & Kitano, H. H. Barriers to mental health: A Japanese and Mexican dilemma. In C. A. Hernandez, M. Haug, and N. Wagner (Eds.), *Chicanos: Social and psychological perspectives* (2nd ed.). St. Louis: Mosby, 1976.

Miura, M., & Usa, S. A psychotherapy of neurosis: Morita therapy. In T. Lebra & W. Lebra (Eds.), *Japanese culture and behavior.* Honolulu: University Press of Hawaii, 1974, pp. 407-430.

Morales, R. *Makibaba.* Los Angeles: Mountain View Publishers, 1974.

Murase, T. Naikan therapy. In T. Lebra & W. Lebra (Eds.), *Japanese culture and behavior.* Honolulu: University Press of Hawaii, 1974, pp. 431-442.

Nakane, C. *Japanese society.* Berkeley: University of California Press, 1970.

Nakao, S., & Lum, C. *Yellow is not white and white is not right: Counseling techniques for Japanese and Chinese clients.* Master's thesis, University of California, Los Angeles, 1977.

The Newest Americans. *Newsweek,* 10 Sept. 1979, p. 22.

Newman, W. Multiple realities: The effects of social pluralism on identity. In Arnold Dashefsky (Ed.), *Ethnic identity in society*. Chicago: Rand McNally, 1976, pp. 39–47.

Okano, Y. *Japanese Americans and mental health*. Pamphlet. Los Angeles: Coalition for Mental Health, 1977.

Okonogi, K. The Ajase complex of Japanese (1). *Japan Echo*, 1978, 5(4), 88–105.

Pedersen, P. Alternative futures for cross-cultural counseling and psychotherapy. Paper presented at DISC Conference on Cross-Cultural Counseling and Psychotherapy Foundations Evaluations and Training, Honolulu, June 12–18, 1979.

Petersen, W. *Japanese Americans*. New York: Random House, 1971.

Purcell, V. *The Chinese in Southeast Asia* (2nd ed.). London: Oxford University Press, 1965, ch. 2.

Rahe, R., Looney, J., Ward, H., Tung, T. M., & Liu, W. T. Psychiatric consultation in a Vietnamese refugee camp. *American Journal of Psychiatry*, 1978, *135*(2), 185–190.

Reynolds, D. *Morita psychotherapy*. Berkeley: University of California Press, 1976.

Reynolds, D., & Kiefer, C. Cultural adaptability as an attribute of therapies: The case of Morita Psychotherapy. *Culture, Medicine, and Psychiatry*, 1977, *1*, 395–412.

Sherman, D. Korea Town's extent: Population grows daily. *Los Angeles Times*, 25 Feb. 1979, Sec. 8, p. 1.

Sue, D., & Kirk, B. Asian Americans: Use of counseling and psychiatric services on a college campus. *Journal of Counseling Psychology*, 1975, *22*(1), 81–86.

Sue, D. W., & Sue, S. Counseling Chinese Americans. *Personnel and Guidance Journal*, 1972, *50*, 637–644.

Sue, S., & McKinney, H. Asian Americans in the community mental health care system. *American Journal of Orthopsychiatry*, 1975, *45*(1), 111–118.

Sung, B. L. *Mountain of gold*. New York: Macmillan, 1967.

Tan, H. Intercultural study of counseling experiences. *Journal of Counseling Psychology*, 1967, *14*(2), 122–130.

Vontress, C. Racial and ethnic barriers in counseling. In P. B. Pedersen, J. G. Draguns, W. J. Lonner, & J. E. Trimble (Eds.), *Counseling across cultures* (rev. and expanded ed.). Honolulu: University Press of Hawaii, 1981.

Yamamoto, J., James, Q., Bloombaum, M., & Hatten, J. Racial factors in patient selection. *American Journal of Psychiatry*, 1967, *124*, 630–636.

8

Culturally Relevant and Behavioristic Counseling for Chicano College Students

Rene A. Ruiz
J. Manuel Casas

The purpose of this chapter is to outline a *model* of counseling—one designed for a specific subpopulation—but which can be generalized to others as well. There are two key components to the model. First, it is culturally relevant in the sense it is designed by, delivered by, and delivered to Chicanos or Mexican Americans.[1] Despite the vast heterogeneity found among Chicanos in terms of subculture group membership (differences in area of origin or residence, local custom, dialect, levels of acculturation, and other sociocultural variables), this model has the potential to be applied to Chicanos across the United States. Furthermore, with relatively minor modifications, the model can be adapted for use with other Hispanic groups such as Central or South Americans, Cubans, or Puerto Ricans. The second key component of the model is its behavioristic orientation, a selection based upon the authors' opinion that this theoretical rationale possesses the greatest potential for behavior change with this particular group. Finally, it should be noted that the model is experiential in origin. That is, it has evolved in the context of the delivery of counseling services to Chicano college students. Thus, the model is culturally relevant, behavioristically oriented, and designed for Chicano college students. It also has the potential to be modified to be relevant for other Hispanic cultures, to be based on other theoretical positions, and to involve service delivery to non-college groups.

The Culturally Relevant Component

It is generally acknowledged that Chicanos underutilize the whole range of mental health and other self-help services (Padilla & Ruiz, 1973; Padilla, Ruiz, & Alvarez, 1975; Ruiz, Padilla, & Alvarez, 1978), and this underutilization appears equally typical of Chicano college students (Perez, undated; Ruiz, 1981; Ruiz, Casas, & Padilla, 1977; Sue, 1973). In an attempt to understand why ethnic minority college students at a major West Coast university underutilized counseling services, the directors of four ethnic studies programs arrived at three major conclusions: first, that too few professional therapists were from ethnic minority groups, thus reinforcing minority feelings of powerlessness at having to ask for help from nonminority counselors; second, that many students believed the psychotherapy to be designed for the white middle class; and, third, that the clinic was identified as an "establishment" organization, and students were suspicious that preservation of the status quo would assume priority over the students' needs to develop identity and self-pride.

If one assumes that Chicano college students experience many of the modal problems which plague non-Chicano students, and that counselors and university counseling centers are programmed to help resolve these problems, but that such services are underutilized, then it follows that some problem in communication exists between client and counselor. Clients do not "know," or do not believe, that counseling can help; and counselors are not reaching out to potential clients who "need," or who could benefit from, such help. Furthermore, once client and counselor meet, they sometimes speak at cross purposes. Thus, to facilitate understanding between counselors and Chicano clients, effective client-counselor communication must be established.

Counselors must comprehend the needs and problems of the client, and clients must understand messages from the counselor. These messages are designed to help clients achieve greater self-actualization and self-reliance as a means of ultimately increasing their capacity to function; these goals cannot be met if the messages are not understood. Whenever counselor and client "do not speak the same language," communication is impaired and the quality of the helping relationship declines. This latter point is especially evident in centers where a monolingual English speaking staff attempts to deliver services to a monolingual Spanish, or bilingual, Spanish dominant clientele (Edgerton & Karno, 1971; Karno & Edgerton, 1969; Ruiz, 1981; Ruiz, Padilla, & Alvarez, 1978; Torrey, 1972). Furthermore, it has been noted that successful counseling relationships are much more difficult to establish and maintain when the people involved do not share the same cultural values (Abad, Ramos, & Boyce, 1974; Torrey, 1972; Yamamoto, James, & Palley, 1968).

This problem in "poor" or "weak" communication between Chicano client and counselor, whether Chicano or non-Chicano, is vexing, but neither unsolvable nor permanent. On the contrary, communication is enhanced and the ameliorative effect of counseling is thereby increased, whenever the appropriate techniques are applied. To show when specific techniques are appropriate, and how they should be applied, we begin the outline of the model by identifying related theoretical issues. For example, before deciding whether "culturally relevant" counseling is appropriate for a given ethnic minority client, the counselor must first determine whether the client is "culturally different." This discrimination is based, in turn, on whether the client's primary identification is to the majority or to the minority culture. To clarify this complex decision-making process, we initiate a discussion of "ethnic identification."

Ethnic Identification

We use the term identification to refer to the totality of individual experience and the subset "ethnic identification" to identify that part of the self which includes all those values, attitudes, and preferences which comprise culture group membership (Ruiz, Casas, & Padilla, 1977; Ruiz & Padilla, 1977). If language skill is used as an example, the Chicano who speaks Spanish at home and English at school is bicultural and, by our definition, experiences dual ethnic identification. Language skill in this illustration is merely one index of culture group membership, but there are other equally valid criteria such as custom, tradition, law, religion, costume, and dietary preference. Thus, while language skill helps determine ethnic identification, numerous other variables are operating. A second point is that bicultural group membership creates the *potential* but not necessarily the actual experience of divided group loyalty and confusion about the self. More precisely, the majority of Americans who are members of two cultures almost certainly are neither maladaptive nor psychopathological as a consequence of biculturality. The relatively rare person who is bicultural, who fits smoothly in neither culture, and who consequently develops behavioral patterns which are maladaptive is often referred to as "marginal."

The term marginal stems primarily from the work of Stonequist (1937) and denotes bicultural membership combined with the relative inability to form dual ethnic identification. This complex theoretical statement has significant implications for effective communication and successful counseling of Chicano students. Many Chicano university students are bicultural because they hold simultaneous membership in two different culture groups—the dominant Anglo majority and the Chicano minority.[2] Bicultural membership and dual ethnic identification are in no sense intrinsically pathological. One may argue quite cogently, for example, that multicultural group membership is a normal or expected state of affairs. This is not to imply that all Americans are multi-ethnic, but rather that we all belong to a multitude of groups with different values and attitudes. A related point is that commitment to these "different values and attitudes" varies from "strong" to "weak" as illustrated in Figure 1.

Individuals in Cell A manifest strong commitments to two cultures—

FIGURE 1
Degrees of Ethnic Identification Among Bicultural Chicanos

Majority Anglo Culture

		Strong	Weak
Minority	Strong	A	B
Chicano			
Culture	Weak	D	C

the Anglo dominant majority and their own particular Hispanic sub-group. Using language as an index of ethnic identification, one would expect a person to be fluent in both English and Spanish. And, on the basis of strong commitment to two different cultures, one would anticipate few problems associated with bicultural group membership or ethnic identification. Clients from Cell A would probably present problems manifested in personal life adjustment relatively independent of ethnic group membership.

Now consider individuals in Cell B and Cell D. Cell B people are assumed to manifest a strong commitment to the traditional value system of their minority culture and a weak one to the majority group. Continuing to use language skill for illustrative purposes, one would predict that fluency in Spanish would surpass English. In Cell D, of course, the situation would be reversed. Persons in these two cells may or may not bring problems to the counselor which are related to ethnic identification. The person in transition from one culture to another—who is deliberately attempting to replace one set of cultural values for another—may be experiencing problems in ethnic identification. The Spanish dominant person who is attempting to enter the majority culture by acquiring English fluency, as well as the English dominant individual who is trying to regain contact with his cultural heritage by learning Spanish, will probably experience stress associated with cultural change.

People in Cell C seem to represent the "failures" of Cells B and D; they have surrendered their original commitment, whether minority or majority, but have not yet successfully entered the new culture. Some might minimize Spanish usage to appear more "American." If this occurs prior to the acquisition of English fluency, comprehension may be limited, and they will be forced to remain relatively silent in many situations, or sound ludicrous. If one generalizes beyond language, a variety of situations can be imagined in which the marginal person cannot cope efficiently with the stress of ordinary day-to-day life because the values, attitudes, and social relationships of the original culture have been left behind, and new ones have yet to be acquired. Imagine the intensity of discomfort experienced when a marginal person leaves one culture, tries to enter another, is not fully accepted, and is left in limbo between two different, and sometimes conflicting, value systems.

It should be stressed at this point that any newcomer to a foreign land is bound to be confused by new customs and an unknown language. Most, however, respond to a novel stimulus situation by learning new ways (acculturation) or by residing in neighborhoods in which the old ways retain their adaptive value (barrios, Jewish ghettos, Chinatowns, Little Italys, etc.). The discussion on Cell C, however, has focused on people whose commitment is weak to both the majority and the minority cultures and whose culture group identification is therefore marginal.

The unsophisticated counselor might infer that culturally relevant services are appropriate for all Chicanos since "they are all alike" in terms of degree of ethnic identification and acculturation. Yet Figure 1 belies this inference. To argue further against such a misinterpretation, we note that Chicanos with strong commitments to the majority culture (Cells A and D) seem likely to present for counseling the same kinds of problems monolingual (English-speaking), monocultural non-Chicanos present. The more Anglo-like the person and the problem, the less likely a culturally relevant counseling approach seems called for. On the other hand, the more the client lapses into Spanish, reminisces about culture-specific events, or avoids topics considered sensitive by the criterion of Chicano values, the more appropriate a bilingual, bicultural counseling approach would seem. This seems most likely for Cell A people and least likely for Cell D people.

This approach of determining whether to apply a monocultural or bicultural counseling approach on the basis of the culture-specificity of the problem is extremely important and can be more easily generalized to clients from Cells B and C. With a strong commitment to Chicano culture, and a weak one to Anglo values, Cell B people would seem most likely to present Chicano-specific problems and to respond well to bilingual, bicultural counseling. To predict the behavior of individuals in Cell C is most difficult. Marginal persons seeking to deny Mexican-ness as a means of "becoming American" seem likely to resist any counseling approach which fails to affirm membership in the majority group.

To complete the definition of culturally relevant counseling for Chicano college students, we now turn to the identification of certain counselor characteristics which influence the probability of whether client behavior will change, and whether the change will be positive.

Four Counselor Characteristics

The success of culturally relevant counseling is influenced by four counselor characteristics: bilingualism, biculturality, image, and outreach. The first two are essential, the second two are highly desirable, but the model works best if all four are present. The first two traits are predictable: the counselor must be bilingual in Spanish and English, and the counselor must be bicultural in terms of familiarity with, and comfort in, both the Chicano and Anglo cultures. Without taking the position that ethnic minority clients can be treated only by members of the same ethnic group, it should be clear that most counselors who are "bicultural" (as we have defined the term here) will also be Chicanos and will probably be maximally effective in using this model.

The third and fourth traits, image and outreach, require more elaborate description because they are complex and synergistic. Basically, image refers to how the counselor is perceived by the client. It is generally true that the success of counseling is at least partially dependent upon the image of the counselor, and this may be particularly true of ethnic minority clients (Acosta, 1975, 1977; Acosta & Sheehan, 1976; Herrera, 1977). If the client is bilingual and bicultural, it may be very important that the counselor reflect a similar image. In this context, it is certainly important that the counselor be perceived as a potential change agent who is sensitive and responsive to the unique sociocultural attributes of the culturally different ethnic minority client.

Outreach is the process by which a counselor, and the counseling center which he or she represents, makes a deliberate effort to attract clients. Individual counselors who have left their offices and entered the environment of Chicano college students have improved their image by becoming more accessible. Image and outreach also interact when counseling centers become more responsive to student needs by providing appropriate services—culturally relevant counseling, flexible hours, walk-in appointments, and so on. Basically, high visibility on campus plus participation in activities important to Chicano students increases the positive image of the counselor and the counseling center. The net result is the creation and maintenance of a self-referral system which channels culturally different clients towards culturally sensitive counselors who can decide the culturally relevant counseling approaches with the greatest probability of effecting positive behavioral change.

There is a resemblance between the culturally relevant model of counseling proposed here and elsewhere (Ruiz, 1981; Ruiz, Casas, & Padilla, 1977; Ruiz, Padilla, & Alvarez, 1978) and the so-called "community mental health" or "community psychology" approaches for culturally different people (Padilla, Ruiz, & Alvarez, 1975; Ruiz, 1977; Ruiz & Padilla, 1977). Obvious similarities include the willingness to be innovative, the delivery of relevant rather than traditional services, and the outreach component. The reason for this similarity is that both approaches represent attempts to increase the validity of counseling and other mental health services to a population which differs from the

Anglo majority group and for whom traditional services have proven ineffective.

The Behavioristic Orientation

The basic orientation of the model is behavioristic in terms of philosophy, theory, strategy, and intervention. Furthermore, the theoretical assumptions and principles which define behaviorism permeate this model. Thus, while certain elements which characterize the behavioristic position may be found in many different types of therapeutic interventions, we are defining behaviorism as an intrinsic aspect of this culturally relevant model for Chicanos. More precisely, the number of theoretical constructs is held to a minimum (both in terms of conceptualizing and explaining client behavior), psychodynamic formulation or interpretation is rare, the orientation is to the "here and now." There is great emphasis on specificity and accountability. Major therapeutic efforts are continuously directed towards identification of the problem and the variables which cause or maintain it. If a client complains of anxiety, no time is spent on psychodynamic constructs to explain the anxiety; instead, every attempt is made to identify aspects in the client's life which may be directly causing the anxiety, while teaching the client better coping methods through the use of relaxation exercises.

It is assumed that people possess the potential to change, and that they can decide whether or not to act on that potential. A behavioral intervention strategy which translates these assumptions into therapeutic practice is cognitive restructuring which is based on empirically derived models of cognition (Goldfried, Decenteceo, & Weinberg, 1974; Meichenbaum, 1972). Cognitive restructuring assumes that the act of labeling a situation (e.g., anxiety provoking) determines the emotional reaction to that situation. A client can learn to relabel situations—through the use of a variety of behavioral techniques including modeling and role playing —and subsequently diminish the severity of the anxiety.

Three components of the model are comprised of additional recommendations for techniques of therapeutic intervention. The first recommendation is that the counselor respond to the client in a manner which is *directive*. Counselor input should be straightforward, immediate, and goal-oriented. Second, the number of problems dealt with at any one time should be limited. Clients should be encouraged to list problems and to rank them with regard to the amount of stress each causes. At the very moment the problems are presented by the client, the counselor makes every effort to clarify ambiguities immediately (another illustration of the directive approach). Next, the counselor should actively direct the conversation towards the resolution of these highly circumscribed problems in order of maximum disruptibility. As one problem becomes less stressful, attention is then directed to the next less disturbing one. The client may stray from the problem or set of related problems under discussion, refer to irrelevant problems, raise too many problems to deal with, or introduce unsolvable problems. Under such circumstances, the counselor returns the client to the major issue—the discussion and resolution of the single problem, or the small set of related problems which is maximally disruptive. The third component involves a contract between counselor and client concerning the specific therapeutic objectives (e.g., clear delineation of problems to be dealt with and the methods which will be used in dealing with such problems), as well as the optimal number of sessions to be devoted to the attainment of these objectives. Under conditions of crisis intervention, the contract is typically for one or two sessions, with a maximum of four meetings. When maladjustment is chronic, however, or when the number of problems is relatively large, then more than four sessions may be contracted for. An additional option, although rarely exercised in actual practice, is the possibility of renegotiation to include another series of meetings.

In summary, we have defined the behavioristic component of the culturally relevant and behavioristically oriented model of counseling. The behavioristic component basically refers to minimum use of underlying theoretical assumptions, de-emphasis of psychodynamic formulation, and heavy reliance on principles derived from theories of learning (reinforcement, discrimination, generalization, and others). It is recognized that the behavioristic component may be applied to a variety of clientele and their problems. The directive problem-solving approach may even be preferable for most college students, not just Chicanos. Clearly implied, however, is the proposition that the merger of cultural relevance with behaviorism results in a counseling approach with maximum effectiveness for this particular group. Furthermore, material from other cultures can be merged with behaviorism (or any other treatment modality) to create culturally relevant counseling methods for other culture groups.

High Frequency Problems Reported by Chicanos

This section identifies and discusses modal problems presented by Chicano self-referrals to a university counseling center, the sources of stress Chicano college students experience, the typical skill deficiencies noted, the unique aspects of adjustment to academe, and some potentially troublesome differences between majority and minority cultures.

Subjective Discomfort

The most frequent complaint among people seeking to change their lives through some form of counseling or psychotherapeutic intervention is anxiety or depression. Available evidence indicates this is no less true among Chicanos. One study reports that the most common symptoms reported were anxiety (23.5 percent) and depression (19.6 percent) among a group of Mexican American male and female consecutive admissions to a psychiatric inpatient unit of a barrio mental health clinic. It was also reported that sadness (62.7 percent) and crying (52.9 percent) were present on examination. In all cases, percentages were higher for Mexican American women than men, though no tests of statistical significance were reported. In another relevant study comparing Mexican American and Anglo American women Stoker, Zurcher, and Fox (1968–69, p. 9) identify "a basic disturbance in the sphere of affective functioning which seems to have depression at its core among Mexican-American patients." A third study, on the utilization at a community mental health center in southeast Florida (Valle & Fiester, 1976) reports that the most frequent primary presenting problem was depression (19.6 percent).

The documentation that subjective discomfort is the most frequent complaint among Chicanos and non-Chicanos seeking life changes through self-referral for treatment is consistent with our experiences treating Chicanos at a university counseling center. Typically, subjective discomfort is communicated as some form of low self-esteem or negative self-image. Presenting complaints such as "I don't feel I'm smart enough" (referring to academic work), or "I don't have the nerve to do that" suggest that persons perceive the source of their discomfort as internal; that is, reflecting some type of internal character trait. In other cases, complaints seem to be perceived as having an external etiology. A Chicano student, for example, communicated his perception that the environment was responsible for his unhappy feelings of social estrangement on campus: "The Anglo students and faculty—the whole place makes me feel I don't belong here."

The theoretical dichotomy of intrapsychic-extrapsychic sources of stress are uniquely experienced by Hispanics has been described in detail previously (Ruiz, 1977; Ruiz & Padilla, 1977). The term intrapsychic refers to problems of a personal or individual nature which arise independent of ethnicity or culture group membership. People presenting intrapsychic problems perceive distress as emanating from some aspect of their self-concept, rather than being caused by the external environment. Thus, treatment of choice, prognosis, and response to treatment would be about the same for Chicanos and non-Chicano clients. For example, with the complaint of depression because of not feeling "smart enough," the prognosis seems equally good. Treatment begins with cognitive restructuring and additional supportive techniques for both Chicano and non-Chicano clients.

In the second example, however, the client states that his discomfort stems from the social environment (that is, from other people), rather than from any negative aspect of his self-concept. The strong implication is that the self-perception of this Chicano is his victimization owing to prejudice and discrimination. This client's perception of the source of this particular problem is considered primarily extrapsychic because the source is perceived as external rather than internal. Further, because prejudice and discrimination are typical problems for members of ethnic minority groups, but relatively rare experiences for members of the ethnic majority group, it is an extrapsychic phenomenon.

The intrapsychic-extrapsychic dichotomy is important because it can dictate treatment planning. In the case of the intrapsychic problem cited above, for example, the role of the counselor is to explore the accuracy and dimensions of the client's stated self-concept. Is the client really "not smart enough," or is this negative self-evaluation inaccurate and reflective of a pervasively self-demeaning attitude? Different answers to these questions will result in different counseling approaches. If the client is actually deficient academically, then a tutor or remedial education seems called for. If, however, the problem is due to a self-demeaning attitude, then the counselor might intervene with cognitive restructuring. Using this technique, the counselor could rationally challenge the client's erroneous self-perception, while emphasizing that negative cognitions or labels (e.g., "stupid") shape behavior in a variety of situations. Clients can be taught to take responsibility for their feelings and to use more positive and realistic labels.

On the other hand, if the problem is extrapsychic, the counselor should examine the client's ability to evaluate reality. Is the implied accusation of prejudice and discrimination real, exaggerated, or imagined? Is the client relying excessively and inappropriately on projection? Are reported perceptions essentially valid? Answers to these and similar questions will help the counselor teach the client responsibility for evaluating reality better, to create a more realistic and improved self-concept, and to resist prejudice and discrimination more effectively.

Skill Deficiencies

In relating their difficulties in adjusting to university life, Chicanos frequently identify two deficiencies in skill areas—education and language. With regard to education, a frequent complaint is that the inner city school system has prepared them inadequately for academic competition. Unfortunately, this negative evaluation is sometimes warranted and the attendant self-perception as relatively "undereducated" is accurate. It becomes part of the counselor's responsibility to implement whatever program of supportive education is called for.

In other cases, however, reported skill deficiencies are nonexistent or exaggerated. The Chicano student may be well prepared, but a self-perception of academic ineptitude has been created and maintained. While the origins and maintenance of self-defeatist attitudes tend to be overdetermined, high frequency causal factors may include early encounters with prejudiced teachers who discourage academic effort from Chicano students, underestimates of intellectual ability or academic potential from culturally biased tests, and personal insensitivity to demonstrated competence. Whatever the ultimate cause, this combination of misinformation and misperception sometimes becomes a self-fulfilling prophecy, and the student underachieves because of the false belief that academic success is unattainable. It is the immediate task of the counselor to determine whether or not the Chicano client's complaint of academic skill deficiency accurately reflects the student's potential.

The second high frequency complaint about skill deficiencies concerns language fluency. For example, "I don't speak (or write) English as well as other students do." Limited English fluency may be a valid deficiency and the solution is remedial education. Occasionally, however, some students may misperceive differences in speech patterns as a deficiency. There are suggestions that English spoken with a Spanish accent or with different rhythmic patterns identifies the speakers as bilingual. In addition, among students who are sensitive to identification as Chicano lest discrimination increase, there are also occasional references to differences in physical appearance.

An interesting corollary to the problem of speech deficiency is presented by more than a few students who express discomfort because their grasp of Spanish appears relatively weak! What seems to be occurring is that only the most acculturated Chicanos enroll in college; they also tend to be the most fluent in English and the least fluent in Spanish. As a result, they become distressed because English dominance combined with limited Spanish fluency may be misinterpreted as rejection of Chicano culture.

Adjustment to University Life

It is common for students to encounter difficulty in leaving home and adjusting satisfactorily to a new environment. Nevertheless, it is our clinical impression that a combination of weak adjustment to university life and some form of subjective discomfort occurs more commonly among Chicano students than others. Students whose identification with the university is weak are well aware of their feelings of estrangement and isolation, but they are typically less aware that weak identification hinders acculturation to the university and ultimately affects academic performance adversely. Thus, when counselors hear students complain of alienation from campus life, they should remain alert to the possibility that such a complaint may be prognostic of declining performance and eventual termination of education.

There are many causes for weak identification with the university.

Some are unique to Chicanos and others are typical of any young person away from home for the first time. This is an important distinction to keep in mind as one considers an array of possible etiological factors for weak identification.

First, many Chicano students commute to and from campus, residing a great distance away. This seems to be a more serious problem for Chicano graduate and professional students, as many Chicano undergraduates, like their non-Chicano counterparts, reside in university dormitories. Geographic distance from familiar neighborhoods and family members—for both Chicano and non-Chicano students—can represent the loss of an emotional support system. This may be much more significant for Chicanos, however, because they usually come from ethnically homogeneous neighborhoods with a high Chicano population density. Furthermore, the extended family system, traditional among Chicanos, serves a much greater stress-resistant function than do nuclear family systems (Keefe, Padilla, & Carlos, 1978).

Another factor operates to weaken identification with the university, but it is frequently overlooked, despite its obvious nature and powerful influence. Reliable data document that Chicanos, relative to their numbers in the general population, are significantly underrepresented at higher echelons of education (Padilla, Boxley, & Wagner, 1973; Ruiz, 1971). Less than 1 percent of the undergraduate, graduate, or faculty populations is Chicano; consequently, there are few faculty members of Chicano background to serve as role models. Concomitantly, there are relatively few Chicanos on campus with whom to commiserate, few to encourage continued education, or few to demonstrate by virtue of their own academic success that "it can be done!"

Culture Conflict

Dual-culture group membership can create a unique problem for some Chicano students adjusting to academic life. To provide a base for a discussion of cultural conflict as experienced by the Chicano, it is necessary to reiterate the following points: to some extent, culture group membership determines values, attitudes, and customs as well as overt behavioral responses; Chicanos and Anglos demonstrate somewhat different patterns of behavior even in seemingly similar situations because they are members of different culture groups (although obviously there are similarities between Chicano and Anglo groups and individual differences within the Chicano and Anglo groups); and finally, colleges and universities are under control of the Anglo culture and operate under an Anglo value system. Thus, when Chicano students enter institutions of higher learning, one has a classic paradigm for culture conflict. This is exactly what happens, and this is how it operates.

Like everyone else, Chicanos are familiar with their own sociocultural environment and have acquired coping mechanisms that are maximally efficient in that setting. To illustrate the point, and at the risk of implicitly advocating continued cultural stereotypes, assume that the Chicano culture "expects" youngsters to treat older people who have achieved status with passive and silent deference. Such behavior is remarkably dysfunctional in academic settings where students are rewarded for active participation in class discussions, including seemingly aggressive interrogation of their professors (who have achieved both age and status). Some Chicano students modify their behavior to suit the new environment and become "good students." Other Chicano students, however, may be less skillful in making these shifts or may be less sure about these differences in cultural values. To respond aggressively in the classroom would be disrespectful. This response of inert passivity or ready surrender in stress situations has been studied in depth under the label of "learned helplessness" (Seligman, 1975). Still other Chicano students may overreact and respond with excessive aggression towards professors because they are less familiar with the guidelines of Anglo culture. In some of these cases involving "excessive deference" or "excessive aggression," counseling intervention may become necessary, or at least helpful, in teaching "new" assertive behaviors which are more facilitative for attaining desired goals in a new cultural milieu.

The very same behaviors which are appropriate in the Anglo classroom may nonetheless create disharmony if generalized inappropriately to the Chicano culture. The Chicano student who questions his elders assertively at home as he does professors at school could be perceived as aggressive and insolent rather than as a "good student." Thus, the Chicano student who wants to make the most of both Anglo and Chicano cultures has the burden of acquiring coping mechanisms which are situation-specific to two different cultures.

Cooperation and Competition

Research on cooperation-competition demonstrates differences between Chicanos and Anglos (Kagan & Madsen, 1971; Madsen & Shapira, 1970; Nelson & Kagan, 1972). Much of this material appears in a recent summary (Werner, 1979). The research shows that Chicanos tend to be more cooperative and less competitive than Anglos in game-playing situations. Generalizing from playing games to the academic situation (which may be overgeneralizing), one would expect Chicanos to be especially cooperative within the family, less competitive than Anglos in the classroom situation, and noticeably reluctant to compete academically with other Chicanos. While experimental data are as yet unavailable to confirm or reject these inferences, the impression gleaned from counseling sessions with Chicano clients essentially confirms this. For example, numerous Chicano students enrolled in graduate or professional programs experience extreme difficulty in adjusting to the competitive environment. These students manifest the ability to succeed academically but find intense competition aversive.

Perceived Differences from the Non-Chicano Majority Group

Some Chicano clients perceive themselves as "different" from non-Chicano clients. These perceived differences warrant detailed consideration because they bear directly upon treatment planning and the ultimate success of counseling. Some of these differences are real, while others are exaggerated or imagined. Some appear to be directly related to ethnicity and culture; others do not. In counseling Chicano clients, the counselor must examine complaints of perceived differences, determine if these are real or imagined, and then begin to formulate an appropriate treatment plan. We illustrate this process by discussing "physical appearance" as it might come up in counseling.

Some Chicano clients note they differ in physical appearance from the North American stereotype of the tall, blue-eyed blond. Physical appearance illustrates clearly a perceived difference which is real, relatively unchangeable, related to ethnicity through genetic inheritance, independent of culture, but generally not an appropriate problem for counseling. For example, a swarthy Chicano may complain of prejudice and discrimination from the majority group because of ready identifiability associated with darker skin color. With this kind of problem, the first task is to explore the complaint. If the client erroneously associates feelings of personal inferiority with a swarthy complexion, then the task of the counselor is to direct attention to and challenge the client's negative cognitions (labeling process, beliefs, and attitudes)—the "real" cause of the problem—and subsequently restructure the cognitions in a more positive light. If, on the other hand, the client is singled out for discrimination as reported, then the counselor has a much different task. The client will benefit from learning to respond more appropriately to unfair treatment. This recommendation does not mean that counseling should be perverted to encourage Chicanos or other minority group members to accept continued social injustice passively. On the contrary, we advocate counseling as a means of teaching people how to resist prejudice assertively and to eliminate unfair practices effectively.

Chicano clients also report differences between themselves and non-Chicano students which are predictable if one is familiar with the Chicano culture. The most obvious and frequent examples include closer ties to the family, more cooperative and less competitive behavior, and less obsessive concern with punctuality. In addition, counselors can sometimes infer differences on the basis of census and other demographic data; for example, Chicanos are more often bilingual, impoverished city dwellers than are non-Chicanos.

Group differences—such as those reported in the preceding paragraph —actually exist. The existence of these differences should not be distorted, however, to imply that all Chicanos share all these group characteristics to the same degree. In a similar vein, it should not be inferred that these differences always represent problems in adjustment. On the contrary, there is a vast diversity among Chicanos with regard to individual differences, and as affirmed previously, some of these are assets in a variety of situations. Bilingualism, defined as Spanish fluency, for example, facilitates the acquisition of a second Romance language because of similarities in lexicon, phonetics, syntax, gender, and idioms. As always, the task of the counselor presented with an array of perceived cultural differences is to decide which are real for a particular bicultural client, which are problems (if any), which problems can be changed, and what techniques to apply to change them.

Differences Versus Problems

One of the advantages of the bilingual-bicultural model is that it helps the counselor decide which differences should be treated as problems. To illustrate how this discrimination process operates, we examine "closer ties to the family," a well-known characteristic of Chicanos. This is an excellent example of a real difference which can be documented empirically. It is also a perceived difference since both Chicanos and non-Chicanos recognize its existence. It is clearly a group characteristic of Chicanos, which is strong evidence for its relationship to culture group membership. Finally, because "closer ties" are continually reinforced by the Chicano culture in many ways, the behavioral pattern is extremely resistant to extinction. Thus, even though this difference is real, perceived, and cultural, it does not necessarily reflect pathology or maladjustment among Chicanos any more than less "close ties" among non-Chicanos would.

At the risk of generalizing beyond known information and thereby inadvertently introducing spurious stereotypes, it seems generally accurate to state that the non-Chicano dominant majority of the United States shares certain traits. Among the best documented are adherence to the Protestant ethic of achievement through personal effort, more competition as a means of achieving personal goals, less reliance on the family for support, advice or encouragement, and more striving towards personal autonomy (Kagan, 1977; Kagan & Madsen, 1971; Keefe, Padilla, & Carlos, 1978; McClintock, 1974). This is the middle-class value system out of which many, if not most, of the counselors and other helping personnel emerge. And this is why monolingual-monocultural, majority group counselors can create problems for Chicano clients where none previously existed. Without knowledge of differences between Chicano and non-Chicano values, counselors could encourage Chicano clients to "stop being a mama's boy . . . cut the apron strings . . . make your own decisions." The purpose of such advice would be to weaken family ties as a means of encouraging greater personal autonomy. While Chicanos obviously have "family problems" as do non-Chicano clients (cf. U.C.L.A., 1975), advice contrary to cultural values would have anti-therapeutic effects.

Counseling Process and Counselor Intervention

Culturally relevant counseling for Chicanos is unique compared to other methods of counseling. It requires fluency in both Spanish and English, plus a high degree of familiarity with both the minority Chicano culture and the majority Anglo culture. The counselor must be able to maintain comprehension as clients shift from one language to another ("code switching"), and must be able to tolerate, sometimes initiate, transfers from one language to another. Typically, bilingual clients tend to discuss emotionally laden topics in one language (e.g., Spanish: the family and home) and to discuss less emotional topics in another (e.g., English: work and school). Furthermore, the bilingual-bicultural counselor must be sensitive enough to know when culturally relevant "self-disclosure" will be most therapeutic. Under certain conditions, details of the counselor's personal life or background history are deliberately reported to make a point.

Clients often verbalize feelings of estrangement and alienation in statements such as, "I just feel different. You know I wasn't born in this country and obviously I have an accent." A response from a bilingual-bicultural counselor using self-disclosure might be some variation of a statement such as, "Okay, fine! I wasn't born in this country either and I have an accent too." In this particular case, the counselor went on to document other obvious similarities such as skin color, physical appearance, impoverished background, and a history of discrimination from the majority group. The application of cognitive restructuring (defined earlier as a therapeutic technique which places the responsibility upon the client for both causing and alleviating certain psychological problems) is demonstrated by the following example:

> Much of the unhappiness you are experiencing is self-caused. Your thoughts . . . your cognitions are largely responsible for the emotions you experience. If your thoughts are negative . . . if you label a situation negative, you will experience negative feelings. For instance, if you continue thinking and complaining about how bad things have gone for you, you are going to feel negative . . . unhappy and bitter. On the other hand, if you are more positive in your thinking, you will also experience more positive feelings which may in turn facilitate your attaining positive goals in your life. For example, taking the same negative perspective, it is possible to generate completely different feelings and outcomes. Yeah, things were bad for you. So what? You could

continue to complain about them. On the other hand, these negative experiences could be used as a base from which to move forward. Say to yourself: Things were bad, but I do have certain skills, abilities, and a determination to make things better for myself and my family. The only one who is really holding me back is myself. I can do it . . . ! Following this more positive vein will in turn alter your negative outlook, your negative feelings and ultimately facilitate your reaching your goal . . . I know that trying to understand and work with your thoughts in this way can be rather difficult. However, if we think of thoughts as internal speech, then we are dealing with a behavior which is more tangible and easier to redirect towards more positive objectives. All right . . . let's identify some of your negative statements.

The above (or similar) counselor exhortations may seem impersonal, or even cold, when seen in print rather than when actually experienced. Several factors, however, operate to transform such words into a firm and direct, but caring, message. In this particular instance, the counselor and the client had agreed on counseling objectives and on the directive technique to attain these objectives. Furthermore, the counselor had already used self-disclosure to communicate that he shared certain experiences and characteristics with the client but had modified his life-style to improve his overall adjustment.

Continued use of cognitive restructuring, combined with the directive approach, can soften even further the seemingly harsh component of the message. In this particular case, the counselor identified a tendency on the part of the client to retain a negative self-image by constantly reminding himself of past failures. As an alternative, the counselor directed the client to substitute statements which enhanced, rather than derogated, self-esteem. The client was directed to remind himself repeatedly of a message which went something like this:

It's up to me, I've got the ability and the drive to move towards objectives which will be beneficial to me and my family. I've taken the first steps towards these objectives, towards a more satisfactory life adjustment by identifying my major problems. Next, I'll review alternative resolutions, select the most appropriate one, and go ahead to it. I'm confident I'll succeed because I won't give up trying.

In another case, a Chicano student complained of difficulty in relating to and communicating with his father. While father-son strife is not uncommon among college-age males, note the relatively unique influence exerted by culture group membership. The counselor unfamiliar with Hispanic culture values might misperceive the father in this scenario as overbearing and complaining, and the son as passive-submissive. This particular client stated, "My father never asks me for help around the house . . . but he expects me to be around every weekend in case there's something to be done. He doesn't understand that going to school and studying is a full-time job." After the weekend, the son was often informed by the father that his help had been needed to complete a task, but that completion had been delayed because of the son's absence. This complaint by the father was frequently accompanied by a phrase the client found extremely painful, "I get no respect around here."

Assertion training was used to teach more direct and assertive behaviors. The basic assertive message to be communicated by the client to his father was that he was "more than willing" to help around the house, but needed "advance notice" because of academic commitments. The client agreed to use this more assertive response but later reported he had been unable to do so. The counselor's knowledge of Chicano culture, combined with direct and intensive interrogation, revealed the reason. When the son had gone to his father for a face-to-face encounter, he had decided that the recommended approach was too direct and might be misperceived by his father as "disrespectful." In a very real sense, neither the client nor his father recognized that they were evaluating the same series of events using different criteria. Neither seemed to recognize fully that the two opposing commitments were equally valid.

The counselor responded in a culturally aware manner to the frustration of a client who did not act on a recommendation both had agreed upon. The counselor was sensitive to the intensity of the Chicano value that sons do not show "disrespect" towards their father. Assertion training was supplemented by role modeling and role playing. The counselor's opening statement was, "Well, if that were my father, I might deal with his problem something like this . . . ." When the counselor and client were able to agree verbally on an approach which achieved closer communication without apparent disrespect, the counselor played the role of the father and encouraged the client to initiate interaction. The drama was repeated until the client's anxiety diminished to the extent he felt comfortable in approaching the father surrogate.

A week or so later, the client again reported an inability to complete the terms of the second counseling contract. The counselor inquired again after the client's perception of his interaction with his father. The purpose was to identify variables which were inhibiting communication with the father, with special focus on the client's recall of his thoughts and feelings at the time of the interaction as well as any outstanding aspects of his father's behavior. The response from the client was "I realize now I would feel like a 'bad son' if I did that. I shouldn't talk that way to my father." The counselor emphasized that thinking of himself as a "bad and disrespectful son" made him feel bad and suppress the assertive response. Yet the label was independent of a realistic and appropriate request for advance notice for help around the house on weekends. That is, academic commitments and family obligations were both significant; neither had to be sacrificed for the other since the basic problem seemed to be one of improving father-son communication and ultimately agreeing on some type of schedule. The client achieved these insights and went on to work out an arrangement with his father which he described as equally satisfying for both.

Bilingual-bicultural counseling is not always necessary for bilingual-bicultural clients. When both Chicano and non-Chicano clients report a similar etiology for a given problem, and when the nature and severity of the reported problem appears equivalent, then it is likely that the same treatment approach will be equally effective, regardless of the ethnic identification or culture group membership. For example, both Chicano and non-Chicano clients complain of "anxiety." When anxiety levels are high enough to inhibit communication, the counselor may utilize the same type of relaxation training with both Chicano and non-Chicano clients and expect more or less the same result.

Summary

This chapter has attempted to develop and present a model of counseling based on components of cultural relevance and behaviorism. The model has been designed for Chicano college students who represent a population different from the Anglo majority culture. Cultural relevance refers to the idea that the language, values, customs, traditions, and other sociocultural variables of clients who are culturally different should be given the highest priority in the planning and implementation of a counseling program. In this context, Chicanos are both like and unlike non-Chicanos, and it behooves the counselor to determine when a culturally relevant counseling method is called for.

Behaviorism refers to a process of counseling based on the assumption that positive behavior change is achieved most efficiently when there is heavy reliance on principles derived from learning such as reinforcement, discrimination, and generalization. Behavioristic counseling also involves a minimum of underlying theoretical constructs concerning etiology or remediation. It favors overt behavior change over psychodynamic formulation, and the counselor has available several models for translating these principles into actual counseling practice.

These two components—cultural relevance and behaviorism—have been merged in this chapter into a single model of counseling appropriate for a specific, culturally different population: Chicano college students. Anecdotes and case histories illustrate how the model can be applied to high frequency problems, as well as typical defenses. Knowledge about a culture is thus merged with counseling skill to create an atmosphere in which positive behavior change is more likely to occur among culturally different clients. Nothing, however, in this model is inviolate.

It may be modified in terms of the culture being examined, the theoretical rationale for counseling intervention, or the target group of clients.

Notes

1. Labeling continues to be a problem for residents of the United States whose roots lie in Mexico. While Mexican American and Chicano are conceptual equivalents in terms of denoting area of origin, the connotations are vastly different. The former is preferred by older Mexican Americans since the latter was originally pejorative. In contrast, the young tend to self-identify as Chicano, almost certainly on the basis that the label implies pride in heritage combined with insistence on equal rights.

2. To complicate this situation further, Chicanos are also members of subgroups with very different cultural attributes. Chicanos in northern New Mexico have resided in the same place for more than four centuries and have developed a "Hispano" subculture that is very different from that of Chicanos living on the border, in different states, or who are recent immigrants. In a very real sense, one may refer to many Chicanos as "tricultural." At the present state of knowledge, however, such refined subdivisions do not yet seem to contribute to valid distinctions in counseling.

References

Abad, V., Ramos, J., & Boyce, E. A model for delivery of mental health services to Spanish-speaking minorities. *American Journal of Orthopsychiatry*, 1974, *44*, 584–595.

Acosta, F. X. Mexican American and Anglo American reactions to ethnically similar and dissimilar psychotherapists. In R. Alvarez (Ed.), *Delivery of services for Latino community mental health* (Monograph no. 2). Los Angeles: Spanish Speaking Mental Health Research Center, U.C.L.A., April 1975.

Acosta, F. X. Ethnic variables in psychotherapy: The Mexican American. In J. L. Martinez (Ed.), *Chicano psychology*. New York: Academic Press, 1977.

Acosta, F. X., & Sheehan, J. G. Preference toward Mexican American and Anglo American psychotherapists. *Journal of Consulting and Clinical Psychology*, 1976, *44*(2), 272–279.

Edgerton, R. B., & Karno, M. Mexican-American bilingualism and the perception of mental illness. *Archives of General Psychiatry*, 1971, *24*, 286–290.

Goldfried, M. R., Decenteceo, E. T., & Weinberg, L. Systematic rational restructuring as a self-control technique. *Behavior Therapy*, 1974, *5*, 247–254.

Heiman, E. M., & Kahn, M. W. Mexican-American and European-American psychopathology and hospital course. *Archives of General Psychiatry*, 1977, *34*, 167–170.

Herrera, A. E. *Therapist preferences of bilingual Mexican American psychotherapy candidates*. Unpublished doctoral dissertation, University of Southern California, 1977.

Kagan, S. Social motives and behaviors of Mexican American and Anglo American children. In J. L. Martinez (Ed.), *Chicano Psychology*. New York: Academic Press, 1977.

Kagan, S., & Madsen, M. C. Cooperation and competition of Mexican, Mexican-American, and Anglo-American children of two ages under four instructional sets. *Developmental Psychology*, 1971, 5, 32–39.

Karno, M., & Edgerton, R. B. Perception of mental illness in a Mexican-American community. *Archives of General Psychiatry*, 1968, *20*, 233–238.

Keefe, S. E., Padilla, A. M., & Carlos, M. L. Emotional support systems in two cultures: A comparison of Mexican American and Anglo Americans (Occasional Paper no. 7). Los Angeles: Spanish Speaking Mental Health Research Center, U.C.L.A., 1978.

Madsen, M. C., & Shapira, A. Cooperative and competitive behavior of urban Afro-American, Anglo-American, Mexican-American and Mexican Village children. *Developmental Psychology*, 1970, *3*, 16–20.

McClintock, C. G. The development of social motives in Anglo-American and Mexican-American children. *Journal of Personality and Social Psychology*, 1974, *29*, 348–354.

Meichenbaum, D. H. Cognitive modification of test anxious college students. *Journal of Consulting and Clinical Psychology*, 1972, *39*, 370–380.

Nelson, L. L., & Kagan, S. Competition: The star-spangled scramble. *Psychology Today*, 1972, *6*, 53–56.

Padilla, A. M., & Ruiz, R. A. *Latino mental health: A review of the literature.* Bethesda, Maryland: National Institute of Mental Health, 1973.

Padilla, A. M., Ruiz, R. A., & Alvarez, R. Community mental health services for the Spanish-speaking/surnamed population. *American Psychologist*, 1975, *30*, 892–905.

Padilla, E. R., Boxley, R., & Wagner, N. N. The desegregation of clinical psychology training. *Professional Psychology*, 1973, *4*, 259–264.

Perez, M. S. *Counseling Services at UCSC: Attitudes and Perspectives of Chicano Students.* Unpublished manuscript. Undated.

Ruiz, R. A. Relative frequency of Americans with Spanish surnames in associations of psychology, psychiatry, and sociology. *American Psychologist*, 1971, *26*, 1022–1024.

Ruiz, R. A. The delivery of mental health and social change services for Chicanos: Analysis and recommendations. In J. L. Martinez (Ed.), *Chicano psychology*. New York: Academic Press, 1977.

Ruiz, R. A. Hispanic history and culture as background for the counseling of Chicanos. In D. W. Sue (Ed.), *Cultural perspectives in counseling*. New York: John Wiley, 1981.

Ruiz, R. A., Casas, J. M., & Padilla, A. M. *Culturally relevant behavioristic counseling* (Occasional Paper no. 5). Los Angeles: Spanish Speaking Mental Health Research Center, U.C.L.A., 1977.

Ruiz, R. A., & Padilla, A. M. Counseling Latinos. *Personnel and Guidance Journal*, 1977, 401–408.

Ruiz, R. A., Padilla, A. M., & Alvarez, R. Issues in the counseling of Spanish speaking/surnamed clients: Recommendations for therapeutic services. In

G. R. Walz & L. Benjamin (Eds.), *Transcultural counseling: Needs, programs and techniques.* New York: Human Sciences Press, 1978.

Seligman, M. E. P. *Helplessness: On depression, development, and death.* San Francisco: W. H. Freeman & Company, 1975.

Stoker, D. H., Zurcher, L. A., & Fox, W. Women in psychotherapy: A cross-cultural comparison. *The International Journal of Social Psychiatry,* 1968–69, *15,* 5–22.

Stonequist, F. U. *The Marginal Man: A Study in Personality and Culture Conflict.* New York: Russell and Russell, Inc., 1937.

Sue, S. Training of "Third World" students to function as counselors. *Journal of Counseling Psychology,* 1973, *20,* 73–78.

Torrey, E. F. *The mind game: Witch doctors and psychiatrists.* New York: Emerson Hall, 1972.

University of California at Los Angeles, *Psychological and counseling services annual report.* Los Angeles: U.C.L.A., 1975–76.

Valle, J., & Fiester, A. R. *Utilization patterns of mental health services by the Spanish Speaking/Spanish Surnamed population and services rendered by a community mental health center of southeast Florida.* Presented at the First Annual Southeast Hispanic Conference on Human Services, February 6, 1976.

Werner, E. E. *Cross-cultural child development: A view from the planet earth.* Monterey, California: Brooks/Cole, 1979.

Yamamoto, J., James, Q., & Palley, N. Cultural problems in psychiatric therapy. *Archives of General Psychiatry,* 1968, *19,* 45–49.

9

Value Differentials and Their Importance in Counseling American Indians

Joseph E. Trimble

It's not a pleasant article to read. In the beginning you're curious as the story about the "psychotic" Navajo male unfolds. The author, Douglas Jewel (1952), takes you through an eleven-month ordeal detailing the circumstances leading to an eventual diagnosis of catatonic schizophrenia. Then, without much warning, you discover that the main problem, if indeed there was a "problem," was one of misunderstanding between the clinical staff and the "patient"—no one at the hospital could recognize that the young male Navajo was speaking his indigenous language! As an afterthought, Jewel emphasizes the need for practitioners to become more sensitive to the covert personality dynamics of their patients.

The theme is not new. Anthropologists as far back as Franz Boas, Bronislaw Malinowski, and William Sumner reminded us of the importance of introducing strict controls to prevent ethnocentric interpretation. Recent attempts by linguists to apply "discovery procedures" to everyday human activities provide a notable example. Moreover, ethnographers are ever mindful that "any explanation of behavior which excludes what the actors themselves know, how they define their actions, remains a partial explanation that distorts the human situation" (Spradley, 1979, p. 13).

Distortions of the human situation are frequent enough in practical everyday interpersonal exchanges, let alone when one encounters people from unique cultural backgrounds. Problematic cross-cultural encounters, however, take on a different, perhaps more perplexing circumstance when one seeks help from a counselor who similarly happens to reflect a different socio-cultural perspective. For many American Indians, there are additional interpersonal, interethnic problems as well—a situation due largely to counselors' lack of experience and knowledge and reliance on stereotypes and preconceived notions. How counseling might be more effective for the American Indian client is therefore the theme of this chapter.

Counseling and the American Indian

Conventional counseling techniques are often inappropriate for use with certain American Indians, especially ones from more traditionally oriented communities (Spang, 1965; Red Horse et al., 1978). Some Indians, like many first-time clients, simply don't know what to expect, and their subsequent silence and apparent nonattentiveness are construed by the counselor as hostility (Jilek-Aall, 1976). Other Indians, more familiar with counseling, conform their behavior to the counselor's ethnocentric expectations of "good client behaviors" (cf. Goldstein & Stein, 1976). In the latter instance, little if any conflict-reduction or problem solving occurs as the client is merely role playing and not being helped by the relationship. In either instance, an internalization of appropriate client-like behavior fails to occur, presumably resulting from the incompatibility between the counselor's technique and the client's cultural orientation.

Some close parallels exist between the counseling of American Indians and the research of a cultural anthropologist. Each recognizes the importance of cultural sensitivity, appropriateness, relevance in information-gathering techniques, and cooperation from their respective clients. Both require permission from their clients to proceed with the arrangements. They differ, however, in who seeks out whom; the anthropologist typically seeks out the client, but in counseling the client (usually) seeks out the counselor.

Like the anthropologist, counselors of American Indians need to be attentive and sensitive to tribal heterogeneity and degree of acculturation (Carlson, 1975). The core of the problem, though, is not simply one's ability to recognize variations but the appropriate and timely use of communication and empathic strategies (Attneave, 1969; Youngman & Sadongei, 1974).

Focusing on heterogeneity and degree of acculturation is no small matter. Further, the appropriate and strategic use of empathic techniques is underscored. With many American Indian clients, the intricacies and vicissitudes of culture simply expand the number of variables the counselor must consider. The use of certain counseling techniques may be questionable in certain instances. For example, use of nondirect client-centered approaches has proved disastrous for some counselors. Many young Indians are not socialized to expound on inner thoughts and feelings. Thus reliance on a client's ability to achieve insights would be a mistake, in particular with the more traditional groups (Dinges et al., 1981).

Providing alternative techniques for use in counseling American Indians is viewed as one solution to circumventing intercultural problems of this kind. Thus far, however, few culturally appropriate techniques have been developed. Youngman and Sadongei (1974) recommend that counselors in the Southwest focus on traditional mannerisms to guide their interactions with Indian youth. Jilek-Aall (1976) and Attneave (1969) urge clinicians to focus on family dynamics, and Attneave points out that family network counseling actually mobilizes relatives and friends into a social force which serves to counteract client depersonalization and isolation. Jilek-Aall suggests that the use of mythological themes in storytelling can provide a medium whereby the client can identify symptoms by expressing personal feelings towards story themes.

While the use of alternative strategies can promote more positive counselor-client interactions, the issue of recognizing variable psycho-cultural phenomena particular to American Indians needs more attention. Cross-cultural understanding can be facilitated if counselors recognize the importance of identifying and comprehending the role of values and the process of values. The remainder of this chapter will thus focus on values, their differential status among some Indians and non-Indians, and the discriminating relationship of value preferences of two samples of American Indians.

Value Differences and the American Indian

Recognition of value and belief differences is one major outcome of intergroup contact. Heightened contact and conflict tend to intensify the differences in value orientations between contact groups. Often the contact eventuates with persons at different levels of understanding, especially when one or the other group occupies a dominant position over the other.

Intergroup contact frequently results in differential assessments of themes, motives, and functions of values and beliefs. A member of one group may evaluate the foreign element in ethnocentric terms and perceive the exotic as a reflection of one's own behavior; confusion and error then follow. An example will clarify this point. A Lower Elwha Indian woman in Washington's Olympic Peninsula region sent her grandson off to school with a big lunch. The non-Indian teacher, assuming that the lunch had been prepared for the child, made him eat all the lunch. What the teacher failed to understand was that, contrary to her expectations, the child had brought the lunch to share with other children. When the child returned home, he asked his grandmother not to fix that kind of lunch again.

Value Identification Hampered by Diversity

Recognizing that Indian groups are different from non-Indian groups, one seeks to ascertain how certain values differ. Unfortunately, a complete catalogue of value differentials is not available despite the attempts of social scientists to develop one. Any such effort would be hampered by the diversity of Indian groups themselves. To begin with, one would have to differentiate among Indians residing on reservations, in rural nonreservation communities, in small towns, and in large metropolitan areas. Next would be the task of listing tribal differences. Altogether the process would be interminable. The United States Bureau of Indian Affairs (BIA) recognizes 478 tribes. Beyond these are 52 identifiable groups or tribes that are Indian but are not recognized as such. Each tribe considers itself distinct from others even if the difference is only nominal.

Just as there are tribal and village differences, there are a multitude of distinctions among Indians and Alaska Natives; for example, the geocultural region where one is raised, his tribal language and degree of usage, the extent of intermarriage among one's family, the acceptance of traditional or contemporary life-style preferences. Arising from this thought is the question of who or what is American Indian. For many non-Indians it is an image of a person with black hair and eyes, brown skin, and high cheek bones. For others it is this plus the added attributions of clothing and hair styles that were characteristic of Indian life a century ago (cf. Trimble, 1974), a physical description which is in part true.

Unlike other ethnic, national, or minority groups in the United States the American Indian has a legal definition. Basically, the BIA defines an American Indian as a person whose Indian blood quantum is at least one-fourth; any less than that the person is not legally Indian. This formula alone has enormous implications for both Indian self-identity and the identification of Indians by non-Indians.

There are variations in the BIA definition. For example, some tribes have set a lower Indian blood quantum such as one-eighth or one-sixteenth in order that more persons could take advantage of tribal benefits. One tribe in Oklahoma, after receiving a land claim adjustment, allowed that, regardless of blood quantum, if a person could prove lineage, he or she was entitled to a share. Some who cared little and in no way identified with the tribe benefited financially.

The Bureau of the Census has not complied with the hard-and-fast criterion of the BIA. It uses a form of self-enumeration, where census-takers will occasionally check with neighbors for verification. Census Bureau criteria are more a kind of social-cultural affiliation than of a legal, sanguinolent one.

For many Indians and non-Indians, a person is not Indian unless he or she is of pure Indian blood—a full-blood. Any offspring of a mixed marriage was typically an outcast in the communities of both parents; "half-breed" (a pejorative term in some areas) usually implied nonacceptance of the person. In the Sioux language such a person was *iyeska* (one who talked many languages or had "mixed blood"). Originally the term was descriptive. It then took on pejorative connotations. Recently, it has been losing its punch and taking on a humorous slant.

The real issue in the United States centers on the matter of Indian identification.[1] For many, it is difficult to accept someone as Indian who happens to possess light hair, blue eyes, and fair skin. More often than not such persons are not accepted, regardless of the extent to which they may have been reared in a traditional Indian manner.

Closely aligned with the definition is the matter of preferred identification with one's American Indian background. Many Indians are raised away from their ancestral land and, as a result, are not familiar with the full range of life-style orientations and local customs. Nonetheless, identity with their heritage is vitally important and such persons may go to great lengths to emphasize their ethnic and tribal background. The importance of identification, therefore, is often critical in enabling one to maintain a strong sense of self-worth.

Maintenance of identification with things "Indian" takes on many seemingly uniform characteristics. Wearing beadwork and jewelry and dressing "western" are generally thought of as accepted pan-Indian forms of identification. Marginal persons may even braid their hair and occasionally sport a small feather or two tied to a hairlock. Paraphernalia is only one way of emphasizing identity. Other behavioral forms such as speech patterns, humor, and gesture, are often displayed in social settings.

Both identification and definitional criteria are important in determining who is an American Indian. But the foregoing discussion still begs the question. "Who, then, is an Indian?" asks Frances Svensson (1973). "At its heart," she continues, "is a state of being, a cast of mind, a relationship to the Universe. It is undefinable" (p. 9).

Some General Orientations

As a construct, values can be understood and examined from a number of perspectives. Psychology and anthropology have contributed immensely to clarifying and describing the construct. In general terms, values are "what is wanted, what is best, what is preferable [and] what ought to be done" (Scheibe, 1970, p. 42). Values reflect one's wishes, desires, goals, passions, or morals. More concisely, values can "define for an individual or for a social unit what ends or means to an end are desirable" (English & English, 1958).[2] It would seem, therefore, that listing the constructs which reflect "ends or means" would suffice to establish the values of any group. In view of the extensive tribal and individual variations of American Indians, however, such listing would hardly know where to begin.

It seems that the next best approach would be to list those Indian values that Indians recognize as differing most from those of the dominant culture. Bryde (1972) developed such a list of basic value differences between the two cultural groups. The list, which was compiled from the general responses he had received from his Sioux informants, is briefly annotated as follows:

- Present-oriented versus future-oriented: The Indian lives in the present. He is not concerned about what tomorrow will bring, but enjoys now. The non-Indian lives for tomorrow, constantly looking to and planning for the future.
- Lack of time consciousness versus time consciousness: Many tribal languages have no word equivalent to the English word. For the Indian there is always time to get things accomplished even if not completed today. The non-Indian's life, on the other hand, is governed almost entirely by time. Those who are prompt are respected and those who are not are usually rejected and reprimanded.
- Generosity and sharing versus personal acquisitiveness and material achievement: The Indian gets in order to give. The one who gives the most commands the most respect. By contrast, the non-Indian is judged by what he has, so that material achievement means acquiring many possessions, which in turn carry the hope of social mobility.
- Respect for age versus emphasis on youth: The Indian respects a person who has knowledge of the people and the world around him. The older Indians are respected for their wisdom and knowledge. The non-Indian society places a greater importance on youth, an emphasis seen daily on television and in politics, for example.
- Cooperation versus competition: The Indian learns to get along with others and values working with others. In the Indian group there is conformity, not competition. The non-Indian believes that competition is essential. Progress results from competition and lack of progress may be synonymous with lack of competition. Every aspect of daily living in the non-Indian culture is quite competitive.
- Harmony with nature versus conquest over nature: Nature, in the Indian view of the world, is indivisible and a person is only a part of that one thing. The Indian accepts the world and does not try to change it. The non-Indian attempts to control the physical world, to assert mastery over it—the more control over nature, the better.

Zintz (1963, p. 175) provides another value list drawing comparisons between Anglo-Caucasian and Pueblo groups. His list identifies the basic value differences as follows:

Pueblo	Anglo
Harmony with nature	Mastery over nature
Present time orientation	Future time orientation
Explanation of natural phenomena	Scientific explanation for everything
Follow the old ways	Climb the ladder of success
Cooperation	Competition
Anonymity	Individuality
Submissiveness	Aggression
Work for present needs	Work to get ahead
Sharing wealth	Saving for the future
Time is always with us	Clock-watching
Humility	Win first prize if at all possible
Win once, but let others win also	Win all the time

A comparison of the Bryde and Zintz lists reveals agreement. Many Indians similarly would concur with the general content of both lists. There also exist areas of consensus suggesting the possibility of some universal patterns of behavior for which persons must find solutions. Kluckhohn and Strodtbeck (1961) and Kluckhohn (1953) narrowed down the seemingly inexhaustible array of general possibilities to three universal value perspectives: man-nature orientation (master over nature, subjugation to nature, and harmony with nature); time orientation (temporal past, present, and temporal future); and relational orientation (status and power positions along lineal orientations, group consensus, and individualism). The possibility of universal reactions to value orientations was supported by Osgood and his colleagues (1966). They showed that a number of words are evaluated positively across many cultures and posess the same intrinsic meaning. Since words are closely linked to ways of thinking and behaving, Kluckhohn's position receives support from psycholinguists.

Attempts to develop generalized value orientations grounded in salient intergroup characteristics can be challenged, however. Because of ethnic and tribal pride, individuals will strongly argue for uniqueness. For example, Aberle (1951, pp. 95–96), in his psychosocial analysis of a Hopi individual, discussed those values that make up what the Hopi construe as the ideal person. For all intents and purposes, it is the word *hopi* itself, which usually is translated as "peaceful." To be *hopi*, one must adhere to the values of (a) strength, including self-control, wisdom, and intelligence; (b) poise, tranquillity, or "good" thinking; (c) obedience to the law, which includes cooperation, unselfishness, responsibility, and kindness; (d) peace or the absence of aggressive behavior; (e) protectiveness or preserving all life forms; and (f) health. A person who follows the opposite values of the *hopi* is typically referred to as a *kahopi*, "not *hopi*." That person is usually thought of as a witch or a "two-hearted" person.

Further complicating the creation of a generalized Indian value perspective is the likelihood that diversity and tribal identification produce much greater differentials in values than one might expect. Tefft (1967), for instance, used a slightly modified version of the Kluckhohn value orientations and found more differences between tribal groups than between Indians and Caucasians. Moreover, his Arapaho student sample showed more disagreement over preferred values in contrast to the Shoshone and Caucasian samples combined. Similar, but less profound, are the findings of Helper and Garfield (1965); using a generalized semantic differential technique, they found "some differences" in value content between Indian and white groups.

Diversification can also result from the degree of contact one group has with another. Often the contact group seeks feedback concerning out-group expectations and attributions. Berreman (1964) found that Aleuts involve themselves in what he calls "evaluation group alienation." They perceive that Caucasians dislike them. As a consequence, when Aleuts are in the presence of Caucasians, they assume roles which differ markedly from their typical behavior in an effort to compromise. The roles often serve to reinforce the perceived expectations that Caucasians have of them, sometimes reinforcing general Indian stereotypes. Chance (1965), in support of this, found that the St. James Cree act more "Indian" (i.e., as they thought the whites wanted them to act) when they are in town than when they are in their own village.

It is often difficult to separate out the differences between role expectations and value orientations, as one is invariably reflected in the other. Behavior can often be construed as representative of what is expected of a person. At the same time, the behavior can be thought of as reflective of a value orientation. Typically, behavior and cognition are combined in many ethnographic studies and subsumed under the general term of *ethos*. Thus, in the interpretation of indigenous group behavior, one is never certain of the actual meaning—is the interpreted value a value or indicative of an expected role? Honigmann (1949) has applied such a perspective in his study of the Kaska in Northwestern Canada. His findings suggest that the Kaska "ethos" of strong emotional constraint, inhibition of emotional expression in interpersonal relations, and apathetic withdrawal from or mistrust of others is related to their low density of population, isolation, and general style of life, characterized by hunting and trapping. This may or may not be indicative of what some would call traditional Kaska values. Alternatively, they may be values that developed as a result of Kaska fear of social contact and acculturation.

In either case, they also could be viewed as simply functional values arising out of the Kaska's remote ecosystem.

Persistence and Change

Values and traditional personality characteristics tend to persist in spite of the variations in social contact and acculturation (Brown, 1969). The return of conservative patterns, unconscious persistency, and generosity have been identified among Cherokees and certain Plains Indians (Meekel, 1936; Devereux, 1951; Gulick, 1960). Schusky (1970, p. 115) noted that differences persisted between Caucasians and Lower Brule Dakotas. He stated that "one readily observes personality differences between Indians and whites . . . on first acquaintance the young seem excessively quiet. Although this shyness lessens with greater familiarity, children are quite reserved before adults, waiting to be 'spoken to before speaking.' Whites frequently comment on the good behavior of Indian children in this respect." Freyre (1956) also noted that the practice of and value placed on mercy killing still persists among certain Eskimo groups (who come under the definition of American Indian), despite Caucasians' insistence that such is murder and Eskimos who commit euthanasia should be punished.

Despite the apparent persistence of certain traditional Indian values, there are individual Indians who experience a great deal of conflict in attempting to internalize alien values. The mere presence of a contact group is known to create some value conflicts. In reference to the Teton Dakota, Macgregor (1970, p. 99) related that "in this environment the basic personality has become almost schizophrenic. Individuals were torn between desires to gain status and role outside the reservation and to enjoy warm, stable and positive interrelations by remaining at home. Through failure to realize either goal, many of the younger generation slipped into a life of apathetic resignation and passivity . . . ."

The same disruption in values apparently can occur when an Indian leaves the reservation for a short period of time. Vogt (1951) found that many Indian veterans who had returned to the reservation from a term in the armed forces had modified their value orientations. Some veterans had adopted a concern for future time that went beyond that which the Navajo traditionally values, and had taken a position that a person controls nature rather than the other way around. Vogt further indicated that those Navajo males who tended to accept Caucasian values were characterized by personal conflicts and feelings of insecurity.

Similar value conflicts emerge for the Indian who leaves the reservation and takes up residence in urban communities. There is typically a strong tendency for urban Indians to retain their "Indianness," while struggling with the almost daily contact with the dominant culture. In so doing, an urban Indian typology has emerged which places an emphasis on internalizing values indicative of Indians in general. Invariably these values are elaborations with modifications of typical tribal values and are more characterized by pan-Indian ideologies. The stretching of the tribal values to accommodate conflict with Caucasian values has produced what White (1970) has called "the lower class 'culture of excitement.' " In his studies of lower-class Sioux in Rapid City, South Dakota, he found that Indian values may reflect the ideal but the behavior may suggest different intracultural dimensions depending upon the situation. One cannot then infer the value from the role or the role from the value, because the intrinsic value of any behavior is situational. This may well be an explanation for the discrepancies in Tefft's findings on Arapaho-Shoshone values, as well as those of Berreman (1964), Chance (1965), and Honigmann (1949) mentioned earlier.

Ablon (1971) collected data on fifty American Indian and Samoan families who relocated from their native homes to a West Coast city. She found that the Indian family members, not the Samoans, have difficulty in adjusting to the urban setting because of an involuntary choice to relocate. There were also a "natural reticence" and tendency to withdraw from encounters. Shyness or "natural reticence," presumably a value preference, was challenged by encounters with other urban residents—especially with those who did not share this orientatation. Kennitzer (1973), in a study of nine "urbanized" Dakota Indians, found dissonance reduction to be a major problem, attributing it to new challenges, forced behavior, and conflicts with cognitively based value preferences.

Conflicts of value orientation are not unavoidable when Indians relocate to urban areas. Affiliation, maintenance of traditional ceremonials, and opportunities to visit native homes may reinforce value retention. "Stayers," those who stay in cities, not "leavers," can retain tribal-based values if their expectations for goal attainment are realized (Graves & Arsdale, 1966). Put another way, if someone voluntarily leaves his or her rural or reservation home for the city and experiences the sense of achieving goal aspirations (e.g., finding a suitable home, landing a respectable job, and being successful at it), the greater the likelihood that basic values will not change substantially. Presumably those who stay are more willing to let go of some basic cultural orientations and learn and internalize those that will assist them in adapting to the new life-style. To the contrary, "leavers" may recognize that certain culturally rooted life-style preferences are not appropriate for city life; rather than change their perspectives, they leave.

The relationship between acculturation, value preferences, and mental health is important in counseling settings (Bigart, 1972; Hallowell, 1950). An interaction occurs that can produce the kind of personal confusion that requires counseling and maybe even psychotherapy. Change, whatever the form and source, is an integral part of maintaining value preferences.

Some Measurement Concerns

Value conflicts may not be attributed strictly to intergroup relations. Rather, they may arise from procedures used to measure and assess values and thus may in part be psychometric artifacts. These issues are not just applicable to the measurement of values, especially at an intercultural level, but are equally applicable to the assessment of psychosocial characteristics.

A limited number of scales and inventories is available to assess values directly. For intercultural research there are even fewer. In most cases, the available scales assess the presence or absence of a value or the magnitude of the value determined by the respondent's interpretations (cf. Manaster & Havighurst, 1972; Zavalloni, 1980). Some of the representative scales are reflected in the work of Allport, Vernon, and Lindzey (1951) who developed a scale to assess six rather general values orientations. Peck (1967) developed sentence completion scales to differentiate between value systems of Mexican and American youth. Kluckhohn (1953; 1961) developed the Value Orientation Inventory to assess values among the Southwestern Pueblos and tribes. She believes, however, that the Inventory is applicable to all groups. Similarly, Morris (1956) developed a "Ways to Live" scale for use in explicit cross-cultural settings. Rokeach (1973) holds to a similar thesis, but has expanded his Rokeach Value Survey to include two sets of eighteen descriptive and evaluative values which have *explicitly* stated universal implications.

To assess single trait-type values, some investigators have developed instruments to tap achievement-orientation, internal-external control, powerlessness, religiosity, etc. Few investigations provide for meaningful research involving situational or contextual influences and value preferences and expressions.

Identifying the value placed on need-achievement is the central theme of a number of interesting studies with Indian groups. Through an intensive content analysis, McClelland and Friedman (1952) found recurrent imagery towards achievement and innovation, suggesting that this group is high in *n ach* (need achievement). Parker (1962), utilizing McClelland's need-achievement measures, found that Ojibwa are much more oriented towards individual achievement than are the Eskimos. Lantis (1953) found similar orientations among Eskimos, which Parkers's findings tended to support. These findings indicate that some Indian groups are more achievement oriented than others, particularly in view of the value findings of Bryde and Zintz listed earlier.

A few studies focus on the use of scales to relate value perspectives to life-style influences. For example, Spindler and Spindler (1957), in their

now classic account of Menomini personality types and degree of acculturation, emphasize the influence that sociocultural development has on
forming new and varying value perspectives. Goldschmidt and Edgerton
(1961), with the aid of an eleven-picture scale, substantiated the Spindlers' thesis. In a related study, Bahr and Chadwick (1974), using the
Wilson-Patterson Scale, found that assimilation (one of Spindlers' categories), racial intolerance, and conservatism are related. Traditional Indian values, they maintain, oppose conservative values, and conservatism is typically an indicator of racial intolerance.

Some Research Findings

Arguments and criticisms of the limited number of value scales focus on
cultural appropriateness and bias. Few if any investigators have developed scales using Indian samples as a reference group or norm group. In
1973 this criticism prompted me, together with a team of investigators,
to explore value orientations as perceived and identified by a relatively
heterogeneous sample of American Indians.

In the first phase of the study, some twenty Indians identified value
orientations as conceptualized from their tribal and individual perspective.[3] This procedure occurred in a two-day roundtable type discussion.
An analysis of the discussion content produced a number of common dimensions or clusters. Items were prepared reflecting the cluster content
and then pretested on a sample of one hundred Indians in Oklahoma.
They were then subjected to an intensive review by the twenty-member
committee. The original value categories included generosity and sharing, ability to relate to others in a nonevaluative manner, integrity, responsibility, and respect for individuality. For ease in handling and interpretation, these five categories were expanded to seven: kindness,
honesty, self-control, social skills, social responsibility, reciprocity
(altruism), and independence.

Following review and analysis of field test results, the scale was presented to 791 American Indians from five different sections of the United
States. Items were presented to the randomly selected respondents by indigenous interviewers. Each item was accompanied by six alternatives
and laid out in standard Likert scale fashion. Average responses for the
five samples and the seven subscales are presented in Table 1.

An inspection of the aggregate mean responses reveals some interesting
patterns. The close agreement for all five groups in the seven scales indicates that overall and site-by-site the respondents felt that representative
values were good human qualities; the scale ranged from 1 (very good
thing to do) to 6 (very bad thing to do). Variations in agreement and endorsement occurred between subscales. While the seven value subscales
are broad enough to be generalized to many subcultures, they contain
elements germane to American Indians.

TABLE 1
Comparative Average Responses to the Social-Value Scales

Sample Site	N	Social Values Scales						
		Kindness	Honesty	Self-control	Social skills	Social responsi-bility	Reciprocity	Independence
Eastern Reservation	75	2.13(.68)	2.55(.52)	2.10(.63)	1.68(.58)	3.55(.61)	2.45(.55)	2.53(.49)
Northern Plains Reservation	58	2.61(.74)	3.12(.83)	2.29(.60)	2.26(.64)	3.48(.50)	2.25(.55)	2.34(.43)
Southwest Pueblo	21	2.23(.72)	2.87(.68)	2.28(.74)	1.86(.64)	3.24(.53)	2.56(.46)	2.55(.53)
Community College	586	2.43(.69)	2.72(.55)	2.19(.63)	1.98(.64)	3.41(.74)	2.56(.49)	2.69(.52)
Military Base	51	2.52(.70)	2.72(.59)	2.25(.61)	2.00(.68)	2.42(.72)	2.89(.52)	2.67(.53)
Total	791	2.41(.70)	2.74(.59)	2.19(.63)	1.97(.65)	4.43(.71)	2.52(.51)	2.64(.52)

NOTE: Standard deviations are presented in the parentheses following the mean responses.

TABLE 2
Distinctive Factor Patterns of Value Scales

Factor 1: Variance accounted for, 79.2%			
Kindness	(.65)	Reciprocity	(.62)
Honesty	(.48)	Social Skills	(.66)
Social Responsibility	(.35)		

Factor 2: Variance accounted for, 20.8%	
Independence	(.53)

We can justifiably assume that the seven value scales share a common theme, but that they measure only a portion of tribal- and village-specific Indian values. A factor analysis of the seven scales produces two factor dimensions. The first dimension contained the kindness, honesty, self-control, social skills, social responsibility, and reciprocity scales, while the independence scale loaded on the second factor. Table 2 shows the distinctive factor patterns.

Factor 1 shows that the subscales are more than likely tapping common values. Independence, too, may be a value; however, its properties may be more or less distinctive than the several values found on factor 1—a topic worthy of additional study. Indeed, the entire set of value items merits further study, perhaps expanded to explore more specific value preferences.

Comparison of Values Between Indian and Non-Indian Samples

It is a matter of empirical concern whether value differences and preferences exist between samples of Indians and non-Indians. In 1971, in an attempt to assess this possibility, I conducted an exploratory study with a sample of high school students from southeastern Oklahoma. This setting was chosen for several reasons. First, the 84 Indians, most of whom were of mixed blood, were receiving educational financial assistance from the Bureau of Indian Affairs. Second, some were boarded at the school, others lived with Indian or non-Indian families in the community, and some were indigenous to the area, living with their biological family; the non-Indian student sample lived in and around the community. Third, there was a definite social mixing of the two groups. The Indian sample represented a wide variety of tribal affiliations with the majority coming from the Creek, Cherokee, Choctaw, Chickasaw, and Seminole Nations, the predominant groups in the area.

A 40-item sentence completion instrument developed by Peck (1967) and Peck and Michalis (1968) for use with Mexican youth was selected to assess value preferences. The instrument was administered to the entire student body of the small school, with the intent to determine its sensitivity to differentiating value preferences for Indians and non-Indians. The sentence stems were analyzed by two judges according to the criteria developed by Peck (1967). A two-group, step-wise, linear, discriminant-function analysis was used to treat the data (Overall & Klett, 1972). Of the 40 items, 31 were adequate to discriminate significantly between the two groups (F[31, 185] =1.5, $p < .05$). According to the mean responses of the 217 subjects on the 40 stems, 50 of 84 Indians were classified as rural, nonreservation Indians while 103 of 137 non-Indians were classified in this way ($X^2 = 30.26$, $p < .001$).

This procedure produced patterns similar to those reported by Peck and Michalis (1968). Specifically, the non-Indian mean responses were similar to the normative data that they provided. A factor analysis of the 40 stem responses produced the same factor dimensions recorded in the Peck and Michalis materials. Based on these findings, we concluded that the scale was at least tapping the dimensions in our group which were intended during its development.

The basic intent of the responses for the groups represented is listed below in terms of representative patterns. The mean generalized (coded) response is presented for each group as follows:

STEM: If I lose most of the time at playing a game, I _____.
NON-INDIAN RESPONSE: "would try another game" or "start something else"—a general substitute or compensation for the activity. INDIAN RESPONSE: "would feel bad" or "would get a little upset"—a general negative depressive or anxious effect.

STEM: When I get mad, I _____. NON-INDIAN Response: "get mad at myself" or "feel terrible"—a general negative depressive or anxious effect. INDIAN RESPONSE: "sulk" or "am grouchy"—a general repressed hostile or aggressive effect.

STEM: When there is something difficult to do, I _____. NON-INDIAN RESPONSE: "go find someone to help me" or "ask the teacher"—a general request for aid or advice. INDIAN RESPONSE: "do it depending on who tells me to" or "don't do it unless I want to"—a general compliance conditional on the circumstances.

STEM: I really get angry when _____. NON-INDIAN RESPONSE: "I see someone mistreated" or "someone is cruel to a dog"—a general mistreatment of people or animals. INDIAN RESPONSE: "I do something bad" or "I do something unsatisfactorily"—a general reaction to one's own behavior or shortcomings.

The discriminant function findings and the responses presented above clearly illustrate that the sentence completion scale is sensitive to aggregate value preferences expressed by two different cultural groups and that there are salient differences in value preferences between the Indian and non-Indian groups.

The significant finding in this exploratory study is not the responses given, but rather the nature of the Indian subjects who gave the responses. The Indians were not representative of one tribe, nor were they "reservation-types." Most of them had close contacts with non-Indians and consequently had to deal with non-Indian values at one level or another. Through all of this interaction, a different value system has been retained somewhat intact in spite of the influence of the dominant culture; but, at the same time, the value system has probably undergone a change from tribal-specific values to a more generalized set of rural pan-Indian values.

It can be concluded that even in a relatively integrated environment two salient sets of response patterns can be differentiated, each indicative of a cultural dimension. Whether they are *values* is academic. The key point is that many of the Indian subjects did not "look Indian"—did not possess the stereotypical Indian physical characteristics—but culturally or "legally" most of them were Indian. To the untrained or insensitive eye, some of those students would not have been identified as Indian. If this misidentification were to occur in a counseling setting (and it has), the results could have unfortunate if not tragic consequences.

What can counselors do if they misidentify? Certainly recognizing the error and discussing the implications with the client would be useful. In some situations it might even be advisable to ask the client if he or she wants to continue the relationship, given the (innocent) lack of awareness of one's preferred ethnic identification.

The lack of awareness may also be the client's fault. For some reason, he may not want to share his cultural heritage with the counselor. Some clients fear that many thoughts and actions may be misunderstood or that the counselor's cultural sensitivity cannot be trusted. Moreover, many American Indians prefer not to identify and would just as soon "pass" as someone from another group, in many cases, preferably a group more "Anglosized."

Finally, it should go without saying that counselors can avoid misidentifications by including ethnic items in the intake interview or making them a part of the initial visit. While this suggestion makes most sense, many counselors often underemphasize the importance and significance of ethnic identification.

Values, Self-perception, and Counseling

Psychologists have convincingly established a relationship between self-image and the process and effects of counseling (Rogers & Dymond,

1954). Usually persons who seek counseling hold a rather negative and sometimes distorted image of themselves. A diminished sense of well-being, dissatisfaction with one's life experiences, perceived need for changes in life-style preferences, and lack of perceived self-acceptance are just a few factors that have been associated with negative self-imagery (cf. Wells & Marwell, 1976).

It could be argued that the strength of value orientations, especially those endorsed by normal healthy functioning individuals, is directly connected to the degree of self-perception. This would be consistent with the long-standing assumption that self-perception influences one's decisions and behavior (Wylie, 1974). Specifically, then, we may ask two questions. First, are persons (American Indians) with high positive self-perceptions more likely to take a stronger, firmer stand on social values than those with moderate or negative self-perceptions? Second, if so, what are the implications for understanding the role of values in counseling American Indians?

To answer the first question, we obtained responses to a 65-item self-regard scale consisting of six subscales: (1) self-esteem, (2) self-acceptance, (3) self-control, (4) avoiding self-development, (5) approach self-development, and (6) self-utilization.[4] Development of the scale followed procedures similar to those used in preparing the values scale discussed earlier.

Composite scores for the six self scales were calculated by summing responses from the 791 respondents, who were described earlier. These participants were then ranked according to their composite self-perception scores; 198 of them fell into the "high-positive quartile," while 213 were placed in the "moderately negative" quartile, or the twenty-fifth and seventy-fifth quartiles, respectively.

An answer to the first question was obtained by comparing the individual social-value scale scores of the two "high" and "low" groups of respondents and analyzing them using appropriate analysis-of-variance statistical procedures.

Table 3 presents the average scores of the high and low groups for each social value, derived F values from the analysis, and corresponding significance values. Results show that the "high" self-perceivers tend to endorse kindness, honesty, self-control, social skills, social responsibility, and reciprocity more significantly than do the "low" self-perceivers.

While these findings for six of the seven values contribute to understanding the relationship between self-perception and values among some American Indians, they must be considered separately. In almost every instance, the value endorsements of both groups are in the positive direction (score of 1 is high, 5 is low), although one group may indicate a stronger endorsement than the other. Thus, the results give at least a par-

TABLE 3
Average Ratings of Social Values by High and Low Self-Perception Groups

Group	N	Kindness	Honesty	Social Skills	Social Responsi-bility	Reciprocity	Independence
				Social Values Scales			
"High" self-perception	198	2.16(.75)*	2.63(.80)	1.76(.72)	1.62(.75)	1.65(.50)	2.27(.60)
"Low" self-perception	213	2.70(.75)	3.05(.61)	2.21(.69)	2.12(.91)	2.12(.62)	2.19(.55)
$F =$		46.89	32.19	38.37	33.92	65.39	1.42
Significance level†		.0001	0	0	0	0	.25

*Standard deviations.
†Probability of F value being greater than a chance event. Zeros are shown in most cases; however, the actual significance values are so small that free expression is not necessary. The margin of error in the significance is more like 1 in 10,000 or greater.

tial answer to the question. Those Indians who perceive themselves positively do tend to feel more strongly about certain values than those who perceive themselves less positively.

Knowledge of the strength of value convictions can be a useful counseling tool. Presumably a client seeks counseling to reduce personal confusion and conflict. Having a negative self-perception can suggest the existence of unstable value orientations, especially those useful in unscrambling or reducing conflict. A counselor might aid the client by reviewing the substance of the client's values along his or her valuing process. With some care a counselor can assist the client in examining the existing relationship between the values, the problem, and ways to bring them into perspective.

Through a clarification and analysis of client values, both counselor and client may discover that it is *a value* that prompts the initial difficulty. A client's perceived inability to acknowledge, respond to, and deal with the value conflict may contribute to feelings of inadequacy and diminished self-worth. Of course, recognizing the source of value conflict may be compounded by the fact that the client comes from a distinctly different culture than the counselor's. On the other hand, there probably are times when clients and counselors from the *same* cultural group have difficulty isolating the conflicting sets of values.

Recognition of value differences, therefore, should not be the only concern of counselors of Indians; strength and degree of endorsement of principal value preferences must be considered as well. The association between self-perception and value preferences can be reasonably strong. Clients who tend to have relatively weak or negative value preferences may not perceive themselves in a positive light. By emphasizing the strengthening of value preferences, counselors may assist in improving a client's self-perception and, in the long run, contribute to promoting positive mental health.

Summary and Conclusion

A few fundamental positions have been taken in this chapter. First, it is argued that cultural anthropologists and counselors of Indians share a number of perspectives, and that both are often in situations where analysis and interpretation of human behavior *can* be distorted. They can also experience interethnic conflicts in working with their respective clients. Second, counseling some American Indians can be a presumptuous enterprise. Many clients simply may not know the expectations, nor understand the intent of counseling as prescribed by the dominant society, nor recognize the need for professional assistance when informal community-based helping networks are perceived as more beneficial. Imposing prescriptions and expectations on the counseling process *can* be diametrically opposed to certain cultural specific life-style orientations and preferences.

A discussion of some American Indian value orientations constituted a third but principal theme. The measurement of value listings and conflicts has produced findings of basic value dimensions among Indians. Additional analyses of the same data show that self-perceptions and degree of value endorsements can vary widely, both within and between groups.

This chapter emphasizes the need for counselors to concentrate on value preferences rather than preconceived images or notions about Indians. Being able to identify value preferences can provide counselors with insights into cultural variations. Many clients, for example, will not resemble the typical physical characteristics of Indians; being sensitive to cultural processes like value orientations rather than to physical characteristics can facilitate the recognition of cultural differences.

Understanding American Indian clients can be enhanced if counselors realize the importance of life-style preferences and orientations. Strength of value preferences play important parts in shaping the way Indians perceive themselves and relate to others. As clients, therefore, Indians should be given ample opportunity to emerge and grow within the counseling context under their own terms and from their own conceptual frame of reference.

To avoid discrepant interpretations, misguided recommendations, and myopic analyses, counselors should be aware of the limitations of their personal value preferences and their counseling styles. Counselors can encourage Indian clients to bring other Indians into the counseling setting to help clarify their perspectives and orientations. The counseling dyadic setting is not as sacred for Indians as it typically is for many Anglos. Use of a third person provides a "cultural punch" (Opler, 1957), a kind of support system for both counselor and client. Through the course of counseling the counselor might encounter substitutes in language usage (Krapf, 1955) which may reflect specific culturally based methods of communicating when one is under duress. Colloquial speech patterns and tribal dialects may be used to express certain feelings or to recreate perceived problematic situations.

This technique of inviting other Indians into the therapy sessions obviously calls for a modification of the customary two-person relationship. The specific aim is to intensify the counselor's understanding of the Indian's frame of reference. Many Indians are not accustomed to self-analysis, nor is there a familiarity with the process of discussing emotional conflicts with a non-Indian. Sharing difficulties with others or allowing others to assume the counselor's role may allow the counselor to play a self-effacing role. Prompted by their need to understand, counselors will be confronted with their own set of values, personal and applied. Progress can then be achieved in stabilizing the relationship, and the subsequent process of understanding and mutual growth can proceed with fewer difficulties.

There are dangers inherent in working with clients from other cultures. The counselor knows that the client is different, not only because he or she may act out the stereotype of expected behavior, but also *because* the client does belong to another culture. The counselor, by becoming so engrossed in the cultural differences that lie hidden in the client's every sentence or gesture, might completely *ignore the problem*. This can occur to even experienced intercultural counselors who may not be aware of their unintended fascination and preoccupation (cf. Trimble, 1975) with the client.

Notes

1. Identification of Indians (Canadian, American, Mexican, and South American) represents a major problem, especially in countries where federal services and support are provided. Recently the term "white Indian" has come into use. Such persons are those who have a non-Indian parent. These mixed-blood Indians are usually not thought of as being "indigenous" or "Indian."

In 1979 a United States government agency initiated a study to work up a fairly detailed but pervasive definition of an American Indian. As of the writing of this chapter the results are not yet available.

2. Quite often social scientists attempt to draw fine distinctions among attitudes, beliefs, ideals, and values. To present even a cursive review of the salient distinctions and characteristics of the constructs would be cumbersome and prove futile in the end. Nonetheless, the reader should be aware that there are distinctions.

3. The committee of twenty Americans Indians reflected a broad range of interests, ages, geocultural regions, residential patterns, and degree of acculturation. For example, they ranged in age from 18 to 55, were bilingual, and came from reservations and rural and urban communities in Oregon, New Mexico, North Carolina, Florida, South Dakota, Oklahoma, Minnesota, Colorado, and Wisconsin. Most had high school educations and worked in some capacity with their respective Indian communities. By no means was the group "representative" of American Indians. Instead, the group composition *reflected* a reasonable approximation to the *status* of most contemporary American Indians.

4. A major study of the self-perception of a sample of American Indians includes an extensive description of value scales, the self-scales together with scales assessing alienation and certain personality correlates (Trimble, 1979).

References

Aberle, D. F. The psychosocial analysis of a Hopi life-history. *Comparative Psychology Monographs*, 1951, *21*(1), 80–138.

Ablon, J. Retention of cultural values and differential urban adaptation: Samo-
    ans and Americans Indians in a West Coast city. *Social Forces*, 1971
    (March), *49*, 385–393.
Allport, G. W., Vernon, P. E., & Lindzey, G. *A study of values: A scale for mea-
    suring the dominant interest in personality (ref. ed.). Boston: Houghton
    Mifflin Co., 1951.*
Attneave, C. L. Therapy in tribal settings and urban network intervention.
    Family Process, 1969 (September), 8, 192–210.   *392. 05 F2I2*
Bahr, H. M., & Chadwick, B. A. Conservatism, racial intolerance, and attitudes
    toward racial assimilation among whites and Indians. *Journal of Social
    Psychology*, 1974, *94*, 45–56.
Berreman, G. D. Alienation, mobility, and acculturation: The Aleut reference
    group. *American Anthropologist*, 1964, *66*, 231–250.
Bigart, R. J. Indian culture and industrialization. *American Anthropologist*,
    1972, *74*, 1180–1188.
Brown, J. E. The persistence of essential values among North American Plains
    Indians. *Studies in Comparative Religion*, 1969 (Autumn), *3*, 216–225.
Bryde, J. F. *Indian students and guidance.* Boston: Houghton Mifflin Co., 1972.
Carlson, E. J. Counselling in native context. *Canada's Mental Health*, 1975, *23*,
    7–9.
Chance, N. Acculturation, self-identification, and adjustment. *American Anthro-
    pologist*, 1965, *67*, 372–393.
Devereux, G. *Reality and dream.* New York: International Universities Press,
    1951.
Dinges, N., Trimble, J., Manson, S., & Pasquale, F. Social ecology of counseling
    and psychotherapy with American Indians. In A. J. Marsella & P. Peder-
    sen (Eds.), *Cross-cultural counseling and psychotherapy: Foundations,
    evaluation, cultural considerations.* Elmsford, New York: Pergamon,
    1981.
English, H. B., & English, A. C. *A comprehensive dictionary of psychological
    and psychoanalytical terms: A guide to usage.* New York: David McKay
    Co., 1958.
Freyre, G. *The masters and the slaves.* New York: Alfred A. Knopf, 1956.
Goldschmidt, W., & Edgerton, R. B. A picture technique for the study of values.
    American Anthropologist, 1961, *63*, 26–47.
Goldstein, A. P., & Stein, N. *Prescriptive psychotherapies.* New York: Pergamon
    Press, 1976.
Graves, T. D., & Arsdale, M. V. Values, expectations and relocation: The Navajo
    migrant to Denver. *Human Organization*, 1966 (Winter), *25*, 300–307.
Gulick J. *Cherokees at the crossroads.* Chapel Hill, North Carolina: Institute for
    Research in Social Sciences, 1960.
Hallowell, A. I. Values, acculturation and mental health. *The American Journal
    of Orthopsychiatry*, 1950 (October), *20*, 732–743.
Helper, M. M., & Garfield, S. L. Use of the semantic differential to study accul-
    turation in American Indian adolescents. *Journal of Personality and Social
    Psychology*, 1965, *2*, 817–822.
Honigmann, J. J. *Culture and ethos of Kaska society* (Yale Publications in An-

thropology, No. 40). New Haven, Connecticut: Yale University Press, 1949.

Jewell, D. P. A case of a "psychotic" Navajo Indian male. *Human Organization*, 1952, *11*, 32–36.

Jilek-Aall, L. The Western psychiatrist and his non-Western clientele. *Canadian Psychiatric Association Journal*, 1976, *21*, 353–359.

Kemnitzer, L. S. Adjustment and value conflict in urbanizing Dakota Indians measured by Q-sort techniques. *American Anthropologist*, 1973, *75*, 687–707.

Kluckhohn, F. R. Dominant and variant value orientations. In C. Kluckhohn & H. A. Murray (Eds.), *Personality in nature, society, and culture*. New York: Alfred A. Knopf, 1953.

Kluckhohn, F. R., & Strodtbeck, F. L. *Variations in value orientations*. New York: Harper & Row, 1961.

Krapf, E. E. The choice of language in polyglot analysis. *Psychoanalytic Quarterly*, 1955, *24*, 343–357.

Lantis, M. Nunivac Eskimo personality as revealed in the mythology. *Anthropological Papers of the University of Alaska*, 2, 1953.

Macgregor, G. Changing society: The Teton Dakotas. In E. Nurge (Ed.), *The Modern Sioux: Social systems and reservation culture*. Lincoln: University of Nebraska Press, 1970.

Manaster, G., & Havighurst, R. *Cross-national research: Social-psychological methods and problems*. Boston: Houghton Mifflin, 1972.

McClelland, D. C., & Friedman, G. A. A. A cross-cultural study of the relationship between child rearing practices and achievement motivation appearing in folk tales. In G. E. Swanson, T. M. Newco , & E. L. Hartley (Eds.), *Readings in social psychology*. New York: Holt, Rinehart & Winston, 1952.

Meekel, H. S. *The economy of a modern Teton Dakota community*. New Haven, Connecticut: Yale University Press, 1936.

Morris, C. *Varieties of human nature*. Chicago: University of Chicago Press, 1956.

Opler, M. K. Group psychotherapy: Individual and cultural dynamics in a group process. *American Journal of Psychiatry*, 1957, *114*, 433–438.

Osgood, C. E. Language universals and psycholinguistics. In J. H. Greenberg (Ed.), *University of language* (2nd ed.). Cambridge, Massachusetts: M.I.T. Press, 1966.

Overall, J. E., & Klett, C. J. *Applied multivariate analysis*. New York: McGraw-Hill, 1972.

Parker, S. Motives in Eskimo and Ojibwa mythology. *Ethnology*, 1962, *1*, 517–523.

Peck, F. R. A comparison of the value systems of Mexican and American youth. *Revista Interamericana de Psicologia*, 1967, *1*(1), 41–50.

Peck, F. R., & Michalis, E. *ITEC instrument manual: Sentence completion instruments—child version* (Coping Styles and Achievement: A Cross-National Study of School Children, Working Paper). Unpublished manuscript, University of Texas at Austin, 1968.

Red Horse, J. G., Lewis, R. L., Feit, M., & Decker, J. Family behavior of urban American Indians. *Social Casework*, 1978, 59, 67–72.

Rogers, C., & Dymond, R. F. *Psychotherapy and personality change*. Chicago: University of Chicago Press, 1954.

Rokeach, M. *The nature of human values*. New York: Macmillan Co., The Free Press, 1973.

Scheibe, K. E. *Beliefs and values*. New York: Holt, Rinehart & Winston, 1970.

Schusky, E. L. Culture change and continuity in the Lower Brule community. In E. Nurge (Ed.), *The modern Sioux: Social systems and reservation culture*. Lincoln: University of Nebraska Press, 1970.

Spang, A. Counseling the Indian. *Journal of American Indian Education*, 1965 (October), 5, 10–15.

Spindler, G. D., & Spindler, L. S. American Indian personality types and their sociocultural roots. *Annals of the American Academy of Political and Social Science*, 1957, *311*, 147–157.

Spradley, J. P. *The ethnographic interview*. New York: Holt, Rinehart & Winston, 1979.

Svensson, F. *The ethnics in American politics: American Indians*. Minneapolis: Burgess, 1973.

Tefft, S. K. Anomie, values and culture change among teen-age Indians: An exploration. *Sociology of Education*, 1967 (Spring), 145–157.

Trimble, J. E. *Say goodbye to the Hollywood Indian: Results of a nationwide survey of the self-image of the American Indian*. Paper presented at the 82nd annual convention of the American Psychological Association, New Orleans, Louisiana, September 1974.

Trimble, J. E. The intrusion of Western psychological thought on Native American ethos: Divergence and conflict among the Lakota. In J. W. Berry & W. J. Lonner (Eds.), *Proceedings of the Second International Conference of the International Association for Cross-Cultural Psychology*. Netherlands: Swets and Zeitlinger, 1975.

Trimble, J. E. *Self-perception and the American Indian*. Book in preparation, 1979.

Vogt, E. Navajo veterans: A study of changing values. *Papers of the Peabody Museum of Archeology and Ethnology*, 1951, *41*, (no. 1).

Wells, L. E., & Marwell, G. *Self-esteem: Its conceptualization and measurement*. Beverly Hills: Sage, 1976.

White, R. A. The lower-class "culture of excitement" among the contemporary Sioux. In E. Nurge (Ed.), *The modern Sioux: Social systems and reservation culture*. Lincoln: University of Nebraska Press, 1970.

Wylie, R. *The self-concept: A review of methodological considerations and measuring instruments*. Lincoln: University of Nebraska Press, 1974.

Youngman, G., & Sadongei, M. Counseling the American Indian child. *Elementary School Guidance and Counseling*, 1974, 8, 273–277.

Zavalloni, M. Values. In H. Triandis & R. Brislin (Eds.), *Handbook of cross-cultural psychology, Vol. 5: Social psychology*. Boston: Allyn & Bacon, 1980.

Zintz, M. V. *Education across cultures*. Dubuque, Iowa: William C. Brown & Co., 1963.

10

Psychotherapy and
the Foreign Student

A. A. Alexander
Marjorie H. Klein
Fikré Workneh
Milton H. Miller

This chapter is concerned with the experience of the foreign student in the United States who seeks psychotherapeutic help and with the experience of his psychotherapist. Our general statements about treating foreign students in psychotherapy stem from our clinical contacts with foreign student outpatients and psychiatric inpatients in the University of Wisconsin Hospital setting, as well as from the wider perspective of ongoing research into the adaptational processes of foreign students on campus (e.g., Klein, Alexander, Tseng, Miller, Yeh, Chu, & Workneh, 1971). Indeed, our research findings and contacts with our "nonpatient subjects" have provided an invaluable frame of reference for the clinical work, and we have attempted here to synthesize some of the most salient of our own and others' work. One way of bridging the cultural barriers in therapy is to know the background, hopes, concerns, and the day-to-day campus life of the nonpatient foreign student. Additionally these factors can be related to a variety of physical health problems, and some of our findings on these relationships are reported. Since our contacts with foreign students have been primarily clinical (the student as "patient") or investigative (the student as "subject" or interviewee), our experience has not been directly that of counselor-client. The hope, however, is that the principles and findings enunciated here will be as relevant to the counseling situation as they are to psychotherapy and useful to the non-clinician and clinician both. Our emphasis and experience is also within the context of non-Western students in a Western culture; thus, the suggestions we make cannot be expected to travel well to the home cultures of the students. The chapter in this volume by Wohl thoroughly addresses the question of exporting Western psychotherapy.

Research on Adaptation

Briefly summarized, our research has shown that the vast majority of non-Western Third World students—nonpatients and patients alike—feel vulnerable during much of their time in the United States. In addition to suffering culture shock when dealing with external matters such as differences in food, climate, language, mannerisms, and communication, these students also suffer from status change and status loss. Most non-Western foreign students have been academically successful at home and are professionally well established. Suddenly they face intense academic pressures and adjustments and a painful social vulnerability as well. Having lost cultural and personal structure on separating from the home country and feeling fearful about making contact with Americans, very few are successful in establishing close relationships with American peers. Instead, they often create a conational "subculture," which recapitulates the home setting and provides necessary support but which also results in barriers to deep intercultural contact (Klein, Alexander, Tseng, Miller, Yeh, & Chu, 1971).

In making the transition from favored professional or student at home to the less-favored student role in the United States, Asian students themselves give highest priority to academic adjustment. They consider interpersonal happiness more as a luxury (Chu, Yeh, Klein, Alexander, & Miller, 1971). A questionnaire survey was made of 252 Third World students as they first registered at the Foreign Student Reception Center at the University Wisconsin campus (Klein, Miller, & Alexander, 1974). Asked about their goals while in the United States and the problems they anticipated, nearly 90 percent of those students responding stated that their most important goal was obtaining professional training; 80 percent sought a specific degree. The desire for personal involvement with Americans or curiosity about the culture was secondary. Only 15 to 25 percent ranked interpersonal goals high, and only 5 percent expressed strong desires to learn about American culture and government. Only in the professional context were interpersonal contacts given emphasis. Forty-six percent of the respondents stated that "finding out how their professional colleagues worked" was a very important goal.

Specific problems these students anticipated also reflected these practical concerns and the dominance of professional academic goals. Finances, course arrangements, academic performance, and living arrangements were expected to be greater problems than were homesickness or making and establishing social contacts.

The secondary status assigned to social contact with Americans was more clearly illustrated in a follow-up (spring term, $n = 59$) questionnaire study of Far Eastern students from the larger survey and in the results of over 40 interviews (each lasting more than two hours) carried out with students from Taiwan, Hong Kong, and Ethiopia. In both these samples, the recurrent finding was one of isolation from the American culture and the maintenance of a rather exclusive or close relationship with a supportive conational subculture. Only half of the Asian subsample expressed any initial interest at all in contact with Americans. Fewer (33 percent for the Far Easterners, 26 percent for Southeast Asians) expected these contacts to be intimate. In person and on paper, these subjects—in response to questions concerning expectations of and interpersonal problems anticipated with Americans—revealed what might be called the stereotypical view that Americans would be superficially friendly but would not be open to the kind of intimate, interdependent friendship based on mutual consideration and trust that was valued at home.

Turning specifically to the questionnaire responses for the 59 students who were willing to be followed up after six months at the University, we found that despite the presence of Americans in the students' housing and work settings, only one-third of the respondents reported a substantial level of friendship with Americans. Instead, there was widespread disillusionment with the quality of interpersonal relationships. Only half of the respondents reported making as many friends over the year as they would have wished; 14 percent reported making no friends. Consistent with the initial expectations, Americans were described as being difficult to know, with some showing little interest in contact with foreign students.

The importance of the conational subculture as a barrier to contact with the host culture was clarified in additional studies of Taiwanese and Koreans on the Wisconsin campus. The Taiwanese study was a questionnaire survey of members of a self-defined subculture, a student social organization. The sample contained 44 respondents—30 males and 14 females (wives of male students). Most had been in the United States for one year or more, with 11 percent having been here for over four years. When asked about the presence of Americans, conationals, and other foreign students in housing, most respondents indicated that they lived with or near Americans. However, responses to other questions regarding the frequency of various social activities with Americans and with conationals indicated a clear preference for the conational groups (see Table 1). Comparing their casual contacts (talking about studies or daily events) with their more personal contacts (talking personally, going out, or eating together), we found no difference in the rate of casual contacts with Americans versus conationals but found a substantial difference in the rate of personal contacts. As Table 1 indicates, personal contact with Americans was rare. For example, 87 percent reported that they either never or rarely ate with Americans, 7 percent reported that they ate with them occasionally, and only 3 percent reported a frequent sharing of

TABLE 1

Frequency of Social Contact with Americans and Conationals, as Reported by Taiwanese Respondents (n = 44)

Item	Rarely or Never	Occasionally	Frequently	No Response
Personal Contact				
Personal Talk				
Americans	64	5	20	11
Conationals	29	29	32	9
Go Out Together				
Americans	83	13	0	3
Conationals	57	34	4	5
Eat Together				
Americans	87	7	3	3
Conationals	27	41	27	5
Casual Contact				
Talk about Studies				
Americans	7	33	65	3
Conationals	23	23	50	4
Talk about Daily Events				
Americans	11	27	55	7
Conationals	5	29	61	5

NOTE: Figures represent percentages of the total. Rarely or never = less than once a month or never; occasionally = several times a month; frequently = several times per week or daily.

meals with Americans. Looking at the whole range of activities, we found that for the modal respondent, the only activities carried out weekly with Americans were superficial talks about classes or daily events, with all other discussions—from those covering politics to home and family and personal activities—occurring either less than once a month or never. All such discussions were carried out with conationals on either a weekly or several-times-monthly basis for most respondents.

Another study of Korean students by Bae (1971) revealed the role of value orientation in social adjustment. A range of social activities similar to that listed in Table 1 was included in the questionnaire and grouped for scoring purposes into casual, friendly, and intimate. Although there was no relationship between the respondents' traditional Korean values and the frequency of either casual or friendly relations with Americans, there was a strong association for intimate contacts involving the sharing of important personal experiences. Only those Korean students who were low in traditional Korean values reported substantial levels of intimate involvement with Americans. Patterns of contact with fellow Koreans were the reverse. Again, there was no difference among the respondents when their attitudes were grouped according to traditional values for the frequency of casual or friendly activities, but the high-tradition-value group reported more intimate activities with Korean friends. This difference also emerged in a direct comparison between the high and low value groups; highly traditional students report more intimate activities with Koreans than with Americans; low-tradition students report more activities with Americans than with Koreans. This same pattern of findings was reported for other kinds of contacts, such as relationships with professors and the frequency of organized extracurricular activities with American and Korean groups.

If it is true, as the above studies suggest, that wide differences in values serve as barriers to intercultural friendships, it is then important to consider under what conditions persons are able to overcome these barriers. To comprehend that persons who disassociate themselves from home country values are more easily able to move into the American culture is not sufficient to understand exactly how the barrier is crossed. For example, previous work with Japanese respondents (Bennett, Passin, & McKnight, 1958) reported that the alienated Japanese student, despite expressing an interest in identifying with Americans, was clearly unable to sustain satisfying relationships and became bitter and disillusioned with both home and American groups. In contrast, the results of our follow-up study of 59 Asian students described earlier suggest some positive correlates of intercultural contact (see Table 2). Here we see that while initial motivation for friendship was not predictive of the number of American friends reported, what might be labelled as self-confidence factors were predictive. The more American friends respondents reported as having in the spring, the more likely they were to have few problems, anticipated then or experienced later, in getting along with Americans and in understanding or speaking English. Among the "outcome variables" reported in the lower portion of Table 2, we see that the frequency of American friendships was associated with the respondent's general sense of well-being and confidence, including feelings of having made satisfying friendships over the year, of not being lonely, and of having done well academically.

We summarize the implications of these research findings for psychotherapeutic contact with non-Western foreign students as follows:

1. Warm, intimate international contacts are the exception rather than the rule for these foreign students on a large American campus.
2. Those who bridge the barrier may be special—may be less strongly identified with home country values and may be relatively high in self-confidence and in communication skills.
3. Those who remain estranged from Americans and who continue to be oriented towards a home country subculture are both more traditional and more inhibited and shy socially.

TABLE 2
Factors Related to Number of Close American Friends As Reported by Asian Students (n = 59)

Variables	Correlation With Number of American Friends Reported	
	r	p Value*
Predisposing Variables (Measured on Arrival)		
Motive		
Strength of Goal to Get Involved with Americans	.01	NS
Degree of Intimacy Desired with Americans	.19	NS
Confidence		
Anticipated No Problems in Getting Along with Americans	.28	.05
Anticipated Few Problems in Understanding or Speaking English	.23	.05
Process Variables (Measured in Spring)		
Lived With or Near Americans	.44	.01
Actually Reported No Difficulty Speaking English	.24	.05
Actually Reported No Difficulty Understanding English	.30	.05
Actually Reported No Difficulty Having Behavior Understood	.16	NS
Found Americans Friendly	.25	.05
Had Few Problems Making Friends with Americans	.24	.05
Outcome Variables (Measured in Spring)		
Overall Level of Self-Confidence High	.23	.10
Satisfied with Ability to Make Friends Here	.31	.05
Not Lonely	.25	.10
Satisfied with Degree Progress	.33	.05
Satisfied with Courses	.31	.05
Satisfied with Studying	.32	.05
Satisfied with Overall Academic Performance	.23	.10
Satisfied with Help Received for Problems	.27	.05

*One-tailed p values given for relationship predicted in advance; two-tailed p values for other variables, including outcome variables; NS = Not significant.

Physical and Psychological Health during the Sojourn

Our clinical experience has led us to view both physical and psychological problems as indicators of maladaptation. We have observed that students in emotional or physical trouble experience themselves as deviant in both worlds: ties with the home world are lost and at the same time they sense failure to function in the new world. The conational subculture, or the student's image of home, is not strong enough to soften the impact. We have also observed that while persons have different motives and needs for the sojourn (e.g., maintenance of home country identification versus cross-cultural adaptation), it is the failure to meet these needs that leads to psychological or physical pain. (The distinction between alloplastic and autoplastic adaptation, discussed by Wohl in this volume, becomes palpable with these students.) Thus in this section our focus is on the relationship between motivational, background and personal resource patterns, and a variety of health problems.

Cross-cultural stress can be mild or severe. Indeed, we view it as a continuum of stress reactions to experienced conflict, varying from the mild and nagging dysphoria and heightened sense of vulnerability that we all experience when traveling abroad, to extremes of depression, fear, and suspicion that are manifested clinically. The basic experience seems to have common, universal elements: there is usually a feeling of depression or dysphoria, a sense of loss and threat, with anxiety reflected both in fears of others and in an increased self-consciousness. Within this, there is also usually a heightened sense of somatic concern. It is this modality of the experience that is the major focus of the data to follow.

As background, some theoretical comments are in order. First, with regard to the depressive component of culture shock, several current theories of depression suggest a special risk for travelers. Views of depression-as-loss are consistent with the loss of social anchorage, loss of status, and disruption of basic social skills and ties with loved ones. It is rare indeed that one moves whole, that is, taking all sources of self-esteem intact and recreating familiar support systems in a new social context. When it can be done—for example, through the presence of home country subcultures as we have discussed earlier—culture shock, and particularly its depressive aspect, can be minimized. When this loss cannot be minimized, or when the sojourner wishes to leave the home culture behind and actively encounter the new culture, the risk for depression may be greater. The recent applications of the learned helplessness model for depression are also germane (e.g., Seligman, 1974). One way to describe what changes in intercultural travel is to speak of the breakdown of habitual contingent relationships between stimulus and response, between behavior and its consequences in the social context. At home the effective person knows, usually implicitly, the rules that guide social interactions, so that one can control the responses of others. Abroad, one must learn new rules and until this takes place, the visitor is plunged into a state of helplessness—that of the ineffective person with no control over reinforcement. It takes social skills to learn new rules and to get reinforcement from new settings. An obvious example of the problem is the adaptation almost all foreign students must make when dealing with the opposite sex in this country, as compared to the rituals of the home country. A fuller examination of role learning as a coping strategy for foreign students is given by Pedersen (1977).

Other key components of the foreign experience are heightened self-consciousness on one hand, and increased concern with others' reactions and intentions, on the other. The feeling that "everyone is looking at me and my mistakes" and the sense that "they will use and exploit me" are common experiences. What is important is that they may readily lead to somatic concern and psychosomatic vulnerability. Concern with the self, in the absence of involving relationships with others, creates a heightened awareness of natural physiological arousal or stress reactions (e.g., tachycardia, or rapid heart beat, in new situations). Other concerns may stem from the depressive experience—feelings of retardation, insomnia, or fatigue. Fears of illness may be further reinforced as the inevitable digestive upsets are combined with concerns for adaptation, to emerge as worries about contamination by strange food and germs.

Thus we would argue that the psychological experience of culture shock has a strong somatic component; the feelings involved have somatic effects, and this facet of the experience may become especially salient for persons who do not tend to think in psychological terms.

In a survey of all student health service visits made in one week in December by all University of Wisconsin students, we found no difference in overall health service utilization for American and non-Western foreign students. However, looking at visits by organ system and type of complaint involved, we did find significant differences in rate of visits as follows: the foreign students had more gastro-intestinal complaints (38 % as opposed to 17 % for American students), more complaints classified as generalized or undifferentiated (12 % versus 6 %), more visits for psychosomatic complaints (19 % versus 7 %), and more pain complaints (19 % versus 5 %). Overall, the foreign students had a frequency of 2.5 times as many such symptoms. There was, however, no difference in the rate of psychiatric complaints.

Other studies of the utilization of psychological, psychiatric, and counseling services on this campus indicated, however, that Third World students are not likely to take their stress-related problems to these sources of help. In one sample group of 491 foreign students followed over a five-year period, we found only 35 who used either psychiatric, psychological, or counseling services, and only 3 who became psychiatric inpatients. At the same time this group made 360 student health service visits for psychosomatic or psychiatric complaints. This rate of 7.6 percent over five years or 1.5 percent on a year-to-year basis can be compared with overall utilization rates of 2.6 percent for the psychiatric outpatient, 2 percent for counseling services, and with the estimate that one out of five native-born students seeks some sort of help for mental health problems over his or her stay at the university. Finally, there is no evidence to suggest that the rate of psychotic breakdown, or suicide, is greater for non-Western students. A review of all inpatient records for foreign students suggests, though, a heavy concentration of acute paranoid and severe depressive episodes. This is consistent with other studies and suggests that there are typical patterns when foreign students do succumb to stress (Tseng & Hsu, 1970; Yeh, 1972; Zunin & Rubin, 1967).

In general, then, our research and clinical experiences with non-Western foreign student patients in the United States suffering from medical or emotional problems have indicated the following:

1. Foreign students are a high risk group, under considerable stress.
2. This stress is more likely to be experienced in the form of physical complaints than psychological complaints.
3. Foreign students are more likely to seek medical than psychological help, with the latter sought only after all other resources have been exhausted.
4. There is considerable commonality to foreign student psychosomatic and emotional problems.

Psychotherapeutic Intervention

With these findings as background, we, as clinicians, are able to assume that when the international student seeks help (by self or referral) with emotional problems, then this person is likely to be in greater need of help than his American counterpart. There are a variety of reasons why this may be true. Students from Eastern and African cultures do not tend to gravitate towards professional help with the same alacrity as do Americans. The home culture has rarely offered similar resources so they have no familiarity with them. The home value system often is such that the need itself for professional help, even while overseas, would constitute a loss of status in the eyes of fellow nationals and the student himself. Treatment is typically delayed even further because many non-Western cultures have elaborate networks for dealing with psychological stress through family, peers, and social structures that are approximated locally. Finally, the person and his fellow nationals are reluctant to attract the attention of what they see as the "authorities," for fear of damaging their student status and the national image of their own country. Racial barriers may also be operative, though perhaps less so in foreign students than in American-born minorities. (For a fuller discussion of this dimension, see the Vontress chapter in this volume; Henderson, 1979; and Atkinson et al., 1978.)

While these factors serve as barriers to the entrance of the foreign patient to the North American mental health system, some may also serve as coping or therapeutic measures. For example, the impulse of fellow nationals to cluster around, support, and protect one of their number who seems to be in trouble is often sufficient support for a successful, albeit limited, survival in the alien culture. It is only when the members of a cultural subgroup become overly protective of a seriously depressed, paranoid, or schizophrenic friend that their support becomes a liability. The person then grows worse, attempts (but rarely completes) suicide, disappears, or becomes so troublesome and embarrassing to the home group that they abandon and disassociate themselves from him, thereby compounding his troubles. This is most often the situation when a foreign student is brought to our psychiatric inpatient service. Even in less extreme cases, however, we have found our foreign outpatients have already exhausted their familiar resources and are in need of more than a psychological Band-Aid. The only exceptions to this general rule are when the foreign student becomes involved with an overly excitable administrator, advisor, or professor. The authority's intolerance for cultural or characterological differences is often translated into a misperception of psychopathology in the student. Dependence may be interpreted as psychological weakness, passive-aggressiveness as alienation, autonomy as irresponsibility, shyness as depression, privacy as paranoia. Treatment in such cases takes on a family therapy flavor in which the goals are to open up communication channels between the student and his advisor, rather than to modify the behavior of the designated patient.

Communication Barriers in Therapy

All who have worked with foreign students are acutely aware that the stakes are higher in therapeutic contacts with international students because, if therapy is unsuccessful, the almost inevitable result is the enforced return of that student—disgraced, wounded, and often professionally dead-ended—to his home country. The therapist's awareness of this is essential to a successful therapeutic beginning.

The therapist must also be especially aware of his own feelings when attempting to relate to foreign students. First impressions and gut reactions may be dreadfully misleading in intercultural encounters. The assumption that there is a common ground of shared experience or the notion that this level of similarity is the only path to understanding is a myth, as Stewart stresses in Chapter 3. We must take the time and care to empathize with differences, to learn the latent messages in intercultural communications, and to bring our intellectual as well as our emotional awareness to bear upon these encounters (cf. Walz & Benjamin, 1978, for an example specific to counseling). Too often we have found that, with our own psychiatric trainees, the intercultural difficulties which the visitor experiences in establishing relationships in the host culture and which have added to psychological distress, are recapitulated in the therapeutic encounter. The students from the Far East, in our experience, tend to enter therapy looking scared, reserved, and passive. This is not unusual in any beginning therapy; what is different is that this pattern of behavior often does not change over time. North American therapists may interpret passivity in a North American patient as resistance, but when they encounter passivity in an Asian patient, they may simply feel frustrated, blocked, and eager to find ways to terminate. For a variety of reasons, an Asian will maintain reserve long after the American patient will have "let it all hang out." American therapists in such relationships then tend to doubt their skill, the patient's motivation, or the possibility of overcoming "cultural differences." The result then is an end to the relationship, which for the foreign patient may be one more encounter in a long list of nongratifying contacts with the "foreigners."

What the therapist needs to keep in mind is not that the patient is uncommunicative or uncooperative, but that the therapist must take time to learn the different cues and signs by which the patient is communicating. Therapists must also learn to recognize when they are presuming anything and then try not to presume. For example, as with all patients, the presenting symptom may be merely a symbol or cover for unspoken difficulties; however, the patient may be using a different code book than the one the therapist knows. Therapists working with foreign patients must become sensitized to the importance of, and the patience required for, social ritual in the ancient cultures from which many of the patients have come. Relatively speaking, Western societies value "getting to the point," "telling it like it is," being "open and genuine." Patients from Eastern cultures have spent too many years developing their own formalized ways of "getting to know" one another and accepting the limits to a relationship to be able to discard them because their therapist may be urging it as healthy. (The extreme case would be the attempt to employ encounter techniques with foreign patients.) The therapist must guard against interpreting patient ritual or reserve as guardedness. Passivity may well be the patient's accepted and appropriate way to relate to authority; to do otherwise, in his system, would constitute not only impropriety but also an aggressiveness or a hostility unknown to him. Further, the patient most often expects an authoritarian, supportive, directive role of the therapist and may see the absence of these qualities as the therapist's lack of concern. Much of American psychotherapy has within it, both in technique and values, the importance of stripping away the "style" of a patient, of confronting, of challenging, of laying open the patient's dynamics—all of which may be a disgrace for the foreign patient (and for some Americans too). Being urged to open up by the person who should be helping him to save face is often more confusing to the patient than he can tolerate.

If a therapist cannot tolerate his own frustration at not knowing what is happening with his patients, he too will give up, convinced that the patient is too alien or inscrutable to be reached or too reluctant to try behaviors that the therapist knows to be therapeutic (such as confrontation or catharsis). When the therapist and patient reject cultural differences between them, they often reject each other as people. Yet our experience with international students has taught us that, above all, the needs, the feelings, the vulnerabilities that we experience as people are the same the world over. Cues are different, values are different, styles are different, communication patterns are different, but the people are the same (Miller, Yeh, Alexander, Klein, Tseng, Workneh, & Chu, 1971). A reject-

ing mother, with no surrogates, will likely have the same pathological effect anywhere. Schizophrenia is as easily recognizable in Benares, Addis
Ababa, and Taipei as it is in Chicago, even though there are still many
questions about different etiologies in different cultures (Draguns, 1973;
Torrey, 1973; World Health Organization, 1973). Psychological trauma
is handled universally by mechanisms such as withdrawal, depression,
regression, denial, and the like; however, what is traumatic and what
defines withdrawal vary widely around the world. (Could one talk
meaningfully of "primal scene" to a patient who grew up in a family living nine to a room?) The need for self-esteem is also universal, though the
ways it is played out may vary greatly. The Asian student in the United
States, for example, has within his identity much more of the homeland,
student status, family, minority status, and future responsibilities and
obligations than does an American student. Such a student has less concern about autonomy and independence and much less stake in rebel-
lion. Yet, when his identity is threatened, this student is no less distressed
than is an American student. Therapists must not mistake the values or
the style for the person. They must not assume the Western way to mental health is the only way. In psychoanalytic terms, one would say that a
therapist dealing with foreign patients is in danger of developing a countertransference to the cultural differences. Therapists, like all of us when
our authority or expertise is threatened, may respond with anger or
dogma. Therapists, when faced with what by Western standards may be
seen as excessive dependency, may be frightened or feel manipulated.
These and similar factors may bring the therapist to the point where his
answer and stance are "I must teach this patient to handle his problems
in the way I know works best—the Western way."

Situational Factors Versus Personal Problems

The foregoing has consisted largely of what not to do. To move on to specific modes of intervention with foreign patients, we might start with the
importance of considering situational aspects in the treatment. Whereas
some therapies emphasize keeping the real world outside the door of the
office, it is especially important to focus on it with foreign patients. For
most foreign students, this is often the first time in their lives that the
day-to-day world has not automatically carried them along. They find
academic structure and expectations to be vastly different from the home
country where the university system, families, professors, and their
government often collaborated to keep them moving along. As well as
being much more academically adrift and unsure of how to proceed, the
foreign student patient may also be having specific problems with language (in lectures or readings), with subject matter for which he is ill-
prepared, with academic authority figures, and with the American edu-

cational system itself. Financial and other practical aspects of the patient's situation must also be fully explored. The loss of anchorage inherent in moving from one culture to another only heightens anxiety, self-consciousness, paranoia, vulnerability, and concern with status. This has been documented, as have the reactions of depression, withdrawal, and somatization. (The work of Tseng, 1975, is a recent example with Chinese.) The therapist should not hesitate to recommend or intervene where appropriate in these practical issues, since they are likely to have a significant effect on the psychological status of the patient. The therapist's efforts in these regards will also serve to reassure the patient on what may be his worst fear—that he is not worth saving. We have yet to find a patient who resents such participation on the therapist's part, since that is often the very expectation they came with.

Conational Support

Another very important therapeutic step may be the active involvement of the patient with the conational network. Whereas the absence of contact with conationals may be pathognomonic, reinstatement of contact can be enormously therapeutic if orchestrated properly. The therapist is often in a uniquely critical position to be the agent for such rapprochement, since to the patient he may appear to be an ally who can ask and arrange for such a contact when the patient no longer feels justified to do so. The therapist is also seen by the friends of the patient as an authority who both certifies the patient's worth and is taking responsibility for him, thereby relieving the conational group of some doubts and fears. On smaller campuses where there may not be many conationals, the arranging even of an introduction to a professor of the same background, or a local businessman, or a friend of a friend, can be beneficial.

Encounters with Strangers

In contrast, we have found that group therapies, or inpatient milieu approaches, often have little or no therapeutic impact on foreign students. When placed in the midst of several Americans, the foreign patient tends either to comply with what he imagines will please, or to withdraw. Group functions or exercises are seen as lacking in dignity and intimacy. The personal pride of the foreign patient runs against the psychological stripping which communal therapies require. The foreign patient's difficulty in discerning the structure implicit in the host culture's modes of interaction may be further compounded in the typical therapeutic setting. When our patient groups have dealt specifically with one another's behaviors, our foreign student patients have tended to feel insulted, demeaned, and attacked. In many of the cultures from which they came, to volunteer one's own response to what someone else is doing (outside of the defined social order) is beyond the bounds of good taste. The therapist must never underestimate the sense and importance of dignity to the foreign student patient. To have others pry into your affairs, to be urged to be open and informal, is not only threatening but demeaning as well.

Specific behavior therapy approaches, if properly presented, can be of value in the treatment of foreign student patients. Yet a behavioral program instituted without considerable orientation and explanation will probably end in failure. In the first place, to enlist the understanding or cooperation necessary for proper behavioral analysis required to develop the program would be difficult. The patient would not see the relevance of questions basic to the analysis and might simply give whatever answers he believes the therapist wishes to hear. But more importantly, by the time the foreign patient has reached therapy he may have gone beyond specific target problems and is primarily seeking (but not asking for) warm, human, interpersonal contact. If that is first achieved, behavioral approaches may be tried and may fit in quite well with the task-oriented approach of many foreign students. But the relationship aspects of the therapeutic intervention must always precede the behavioral ones.

Medication

The use of psychotropic medicines is similarly complicated. We have found a general pattern in which medications are prescribed more frequently for foreign student patients than for their American counterparts; these same medications, though, are taken with less regularity by foreign students. It is, of course, easier to prescribe a drug than to bridge cultural, language, and interpersonal difficulties. This message is not lost to the patient, who will often abjure the drug along with the professional contact itself. There is the added difficulty that unless the therapist has taken the time and endured the stress of coming to understand this particular patient, the medication tried may not be appropriate—a conclusion that the patient may reach long before the therapist does. This is especially a problem where there may be side effects to the medication. These must be anticipated and discussed with foreign patients, especially if such side effects may upset the patient's ability to study or work.

On the other hand, if a sense of trust and understanding is first developed, foreign patients will be eager and responsible in regard to medication. Such approaches are familiar to them—that is, a knowledgeable authority dispensing the specific remedy for their trouble—and are less demanding than interpersonal contact. The patient is not being asked to explore his own interior with a Westerner's map, and is not being asked to bare his soul in an unseemly manner; he will be eager to please someone he trusts. In sum, medication therapies are effective if they are not perceived by the patient as a dismissal but rather the authoritative answer to problems in the context of a secure relationship.

To Stay or To Return

One of the most agonizing issues a therapist may have to confront with a foreign student patient is the question of whether or not the patient should return home before completing studies. It sometimes becomes clear that a return to family, familiar environs, and cultural structure, and the sanctuary that they represent, is the only therapeutic option. Invariably, however, the patient's consideration of that option raises appropriate fears of failure, of abrogation of a promise to be a special person (in his mind or that of the family), and of the possibility of disqualification from progress within the home country's professional or governmental system. In spite of these concerns, some patients unconsciously or privately may have concluded that this is their best option, but cannot bring themselves publicly to say so. The patient may then be waiting, and hoping, for the therapist to put this into words. In any case, the therapist should discuss these matters openly from both the practical and psychological points of view. Speaking the unspeakable most often has a reassuring effect, and once again the weight of the therapist's authority can counterbalance to some degree both the patient's sense of responsibility in the matter and the validity of the decision. As with most fears, anticipation and honest consideration can contribute to mastery. Some smoothing of the return can often be effected by the therapist. Acute symptoms should be treated. Separation from local friends must be worked through. The cooperation and understanding of professors and deans can be obtained, so that letters or certificates for academic work already completed can be transmitted to relevant governmental or private agencies. Communication with the student's family before the return can be encouraged, and countrymen who have had either successful or unsuccessful foreign sojourns themselves can be enlisted. But most essential of all is a full, open, practical, and honest consideration of the meaning of the return to the patient and the inherent legitimizing of the decision and the feelings about it.

Summary

In making and establishing therapeutic contact with a foreign student patient, the therapist must do the following:

1. keep in mind that it has not been easy for the patient to have come for help;
2. remember that on initial contact, what to the therapist might be construed as openness and honesty may be to the patient an invasion of his privacy;
3. *not* assume that he intuitively or automatically understands the meaning, source, or significance of symptoms, feelings, or styles;

4. be aware of his own responses to a person from another culture, so that he can work at bridging cultural gaps and not contribute to them;
5. never underestimate the foreign patient's sense of both national and personal pride and the threat to it that is represented by the situation in which the patient now finds himself;
6. take care that he does not rely on cant or bluster when communication becomes difficult, or when he does not understand or agree with the value system of the patient;
7. above all, forego the temptation to define therapeutic movement in American terms or attempt to "Americanize" the foreign patient;
8. never lose sight of the foreign patient as an individual—unique, distinct, and nobody's stereotype.

Client-patient roles differ from culture to culture and clients must be educated in what to expect and what to do. But more importantly, helper roles differ too, and we must learn to be more flexible in how we are willing to play them. Just as we may vary treatment techniques to fit specific problems, we must vary the way we mobilize and shape the nonspecific factors of the helping relationship to fit the cultural style of the client. The therapist must accommodate the foreign student patient to that person's own culture—the one he carries with him. While there are a few persons who seek to expand their identity through intercultural experiences, they rarely seek out therapists to help them do so. More likely the issue for foreign patients will be to reestablish a concept of themselves with which they can once again be comfortable. We must recognize that therapists carry real and considerable power with these patients, and this power must be used against the patient's problems rather than against the client's sense of self.

References

Atkinson, D. R., Maruyama, M., & Matsui, S. Effects of counselor race and counseling approach on Asian Americans perceptions of counselor credibility and utility. *Journal of Counseling Psychology*, 1978, 25, 76–83.

Bae, C. K. *The effects of traditional Korean values on social adjustment and brain drain of the Korean students in the USA.* Unpublished doctoral dissertation, University of Wisconsin, 1971.

Bennett, J. W., Passin, H., & McKnight, R. K. *In search of identity: The Japanese overseas scholar in America and Japan.* Minneapolis: University of Minnesota Press, 1958.

Chu, H. M., Yeh, E. K., Klein, M. H., Alexander, A. A., & Miller, M. H. A study of Chinese students' adjustment in the U.S.A. *Acta Psychologica Taiwanica*, 1971, no. 13, 206–218.

Draguns, J. Comparisons of psychopathology across cultures. *Journal of Cross-Cultural Psychology*, 1973, 4, 10–47.

Henderson, G. (Ed.). *Understanding and counseling ethnic minorities.* Springfield, Illinois: C. Thomas, 1978.

Hsu, J., & Tseng, W. Intercultural psychotherapy. *Archives of General Psychiatry,* 1972, *27,* 700–705.

Klein, M. H., Alexander, A. A., Tseng, K., Miller, M. H., Yeh, E., & Chu, H. Far Eastern students in a big university: Subcultures within a subculture. *Bulletin of the Atomic Scientists,* 1971, *27,* 10–19.

Klein, M. H., Alexander, A. A., Tseng, K., Miller, M. H., Yeh, E., Chu, H., & Workneh, F. The foreign student adaptation project: Social experiences of Asian students in the U.S. *Exchange,* 1971, *6,* 77–90.

Klein, M. H., Miller, M. H., & Allexander, A. A. When young people go out in the world. In W. P. Lebra (Ed.), *Youth, socialization, and mental health* (Vol. 3 of Mental Health Research in Asia and the Pacific). Honolulu: University Press of Hawaii, 1974.

Miller, M. H., Yeh, E., Alexander, A. A., Klein, M. H., Tseng, K., Workneh, F., & Chu, H. The cross-cultural student: Lessons in human nature. *Bulletin of the Menninger Clinic,* 1971, *35,* 128–131.

Pedersen, P. Role learning as a coping strategy for displaced foreign students. Presented at American Psychological Association Annual meeting, San Francisco, 1977, and in G. V. Coelho (Ed.), *Uprooting and Development.* New York: Plenum, 1980.

Seligman, M. E. Depression and learned helplessness. In R. J. Friedman & M. M. Katz (Eds.), *The psychology of depression: Contemporary theory and research.* Washington, D.C.: V. H. Winston, 1974.

Torrey, E. F. Is schizophrenia universal? An open question. *Schizophrenia Bulletin,* 1973, *7,* 53–59.

Tseng, W. The nature of somatic complaints among psychiatric patients: The Chinese case. *Comprehensive Psychiatry,* 1975, *16,* 237–245.

Tseng, W., & Hsu, J. Chinese culture, personality formation and mental illness. *International Journal of Social Psychiatry,* 1970, *16,* 5–14.

Walz, G. R., & Benjamin, L. (Eds.). *Transcultural counseling: Needs, programs and techniques.* New York: Human Sciences Press, 1978.

World Health Organization. *International Pilot Study of Schizophrenia.* Geneva: WHO, 1973.

Yeh, E. Paranoid manifestations among Chinese students studying abroad: Some preliminary findings. In W. P. Lebra (Ed.), *Transcultural research in mental health* (Vol. 2 of Mental Health Research in Asia and the Pacific). Honolulu: University Press of Hawaii, 1972.

Zunin, L. M., & Rubin, R. T. Paranoid psychotic reactions in foreign students from non-Western countries. *Journal of American College Health Association,* 1967, *15,* 220–226.

PART FOUR

Research
and Practical
Considerations

11

Behavioral Approaches to Counseling across Cultures

Howard N. Higginbotham
Junko Tanaka-Matsumi

This chapter advances a behavioral model for effective cross-cultural counseling.[1] First, we outline the basic components of behavioral intervention from a cross-cultural perspective. Behavioral assessment is contrasted with traditional psychiatric diagnosis as the basis for clinical intervention. Second, we clarify three key issues and questions that come up in cross-cultural therapy: ethical considerations, cultural legitimacy for intervention, and evaluation of therapeutic efficacy. In the behavioral approach treatment assumptions are overtly stated and treatment goals are guided by client and group values rather than theoretical standards of "normality." The behavioral assessment emphasizes functional interrelationships between the client's behavior and the sociocultural environment. Treatment success can be evaluated clearly by reference to specific behavioral targets and culture-specific norms of adjustment. In short, behavior modification stipulates basic cross-cultural research questions.[2]

Third, we demonstrate the applicability of the behavioral approach to two important cross-cultural problems: counseling minority Americans and foreign students, and attempts to reduce stress experienced by overseas sojourners and refugees. Throughout this chapter, we direct attention to the assessment of cultural factors in the definition of changeworthy behaviors and prevailing modes of intervention in the community.

Cross-Cultural Behavior Modification

Behavior modification, since its introduction as a systematic clinical orientation (Eysenck, 1959; Staats, 1963; Ullmann & Krasner, 1965; Wolpe, 1958), has demonstrated its effectiveness in changing the behavior of diverse populations in numerous psychiatric, educational, and community settings (e.g., Bandura, 1969; Leitenberg, 1976). Behavioral techniques prove effective beyond differences in therapist variables (Kazdin & Wilson, 1978). Moreover, their breadth of application far outreaches that of the traditional psychiatric medical model from which the behavior modification movement departed (Kazdin, 1978; Krasner, 1971; Ullmann, 1969). These gains were produced by shifting analytical attention from solely intra-individual variables to functional and reciprocal relationships between the person's behavior and the environment (Bandura, 1977). Recent interest in studying the relationship between behavior and the sociophysical environment (Proshansky, Ittelson, & Rivlin, 1976) and the development of an interactional model of personality (Draguns, 1979; Endler & Magnusson, 1977; Mischel, 1973; Statts, 1980) prompt cross-cultural therapists to recognize that client welfare is more effectively served through the assessment of cultural variables.

Ullmann and Krasner (1969, p. 244) define behavior therapy as "treatment deducible from the sociopsychological model that aims to alter a person's behavior directly through application of psychological principles." Contemporary behavior therapy includes both the application of learning principles (e.g., Eysenck, 1959; Wolpe, 1969) and empirical findings from experimental and social psychology (e.g., Bandura, 1969; Goldstein, Heller, & Sechrest, 1966; Krasner & Ullmann, 1973). Basic social learning principles (e.g., reinforcement, punishment) are applicable to all persons regardless of their ethnic or cultural background (Staats, 1975). The aim of behavior therapy is educational. Clients are taught role behaviors consistent with the expectations of their sociocultural environment. Thus, there is a need to study cultural variables in the context of individual assessment.

Behavior modification has been applied in a number of regions including Europe, Mexico, Japan, South America, Australia, New Zealand, and Southeast Asia (Ardila, 1978; Higginbotham, 1979c; Kazdin, 1978; Sheehan & White, 1976). This cross-cultural development in the application of behavior modification has led us to recognize that behavior modification programs cannot be isolated from the social and cultural contexts in which they are implemented (Bandura, 1974; Franks, 1969; Magaro, Gripp, & McDowell, 1978; Staats, 1968). Training programs in behavior modification must include assessment of cultural variables (Queroz, Guilhardi, & Martin, 1976) so that cross-cultural therapists can act flexibly and plan interventions suited for particular persons in their own culture (Ullmann & Tanaka-Matsumi, 1978). At the same time, therapists must be cautious not to make the error of conceptualizing "culture" as an isolated and fixed entity and assume that persons similar in one respect are also similar in other respects (cf. Kiesler, 1966; Skinner, 1953, p. 424). Differences in customs and manners per se are not of interest. Instead, the primary concern is the functional interrelationships among individual, environmental, and cultural variables, and how these relationships influence the person's social adjustment. Within the cultural context, behavior modification emphasizes individual assessment (Hersen & Barlow, 1976) and treatment procedures tailored to each person (Goldstein & Stein, 1976).

When therapists work with persons from diverse cultural backgrounds, it is important to consider therapist variables. Behavior therapists have been criticized as being "mechanical" (London, 1972) or "implacable" experimenters (Wachtel, 1973). However, they have actively studied the outcome effects of relationship factors like client expectancy as specific therapy conditions. For example, they have investigated treatment credibility (Borkovec, 1973; Goldstein, 1973; Kazdin & Wilcoxon, 1976) as opposed to nonspecific or general therapy processes (Strupp, 1970). Higginbotham's (1977) review of client expectancy in cross-cultural psychotherapy underscored the significance of evoking and maintaining anticipation of appropriate and successful treatment. Independent of specific techniques applied, cross-cultural behavior therapists must attend to culture-relevant role behaviors during client contact if they wish to establish an effective helper-client relationship (Wilson & Evans, 1976).

Problems of Psychiatric Diagnosis

Cross-cultural studies indicate that the current psychiatric classification system fails to reliably assess the nature of maladaptive behavior (e.g., Draguns, 1977; Draguns & Phillips, 1971). Symptom classification does not provide essential data regarding those sociocultural conditions under which problem behaviors are acquired and labeled as deviant (Tanaka-Matsumi, 1979b). In fact, cross-cultural differences are found in evaluative judgments of mental health professionals (Cooper, Kendell, Gurland, Sharpe, Copeland, & Simmons, 1972; Katz, Cole, & Lowrey, 1969; Leff, 1973; Townsend, 1978). Further, even within the same culture, there is no single community criterion for mental illness (Westmeyer & Wintrob, 1979). Each culture develops norms for expected social behavior and judges what behaviors are called "abnormal" (Ullmann & Krasner, 1975).

The process of labeling a person is a complex social act involving the interaction of the client's behavior, those who observe him, and the specific setting within a given culture (Bandura, 1969). Cross-cultural therapists must attend to the social meaning and interpersonal context accompanying presenting problems (Langer & Abelson, 1974; Rosenhan, 1973; Temerlin, 1968). Information regarding culture-specific taxonomies of deviant behavior is useful to cross-cultural work when specific behavioral correlates are identified (Resner & Hartog, 1970; Tanaka-

Matsumi & Marsella, 1976). For example, Carr's (1978) analysis of the cognitive-behavioral factors underpinning *amok*, a Malay behavioral disorder of violent aggression, provides an effective alternative approach to traditional psychiatric diagnosis (cf. Kiev, 1972). In short, cross-cultural therapists need an assessment procedure that incorporates contextual factors associated with problem behaviors.

Functional Analysis of Behavior and Behavior Change Techniques

The behavioral orientation eschews symptom classification methods in cross-cultural work (e.g., Kiev, 1972; Yap, 1974). It focuses instead upon specific behaviors—including cognitive and emotional responses—and their treatment. The three major components of behavioral analysis include person variables (e.g., emotional-motivational, language-cognitive, sensori-motor [Staats, 1975]), his behavior, and the situation. Assessment of the interrelationship among these three factors is termed *functional analysis* (Kanfer & Saslow, 1969).

There are three basic steps in functional analysis. First, the therapist investigates the nature of the client's presenting problem. Although problems may vary across cultures, the behavior assessment always focuses on specific, observable behavioral events in the client's current life. The therapist asks how frequently the presenting problem occurs and what specific behaviors need change. Many clients tend to first describe their problems with subjective, vague, and global terms. For example, the client may report, "I am anxious and cannot work." The task is to find out in what situations the client feels "anxious" and what he does in such situations. The therapist clarifies the precise nature of "anxiety" in this process. Also, even though the client reports anxiousness, its frequency and severity often varies during the course of the day and week in response to identifiable events.

Second, the therapist examines the conditions under which problem behaviors were acquired and specifies their maintaining variables. The therapist calls attention to the events preceding and following the target behavior. Antecedent events include such personal and social influences as what the person was doing immediately prior to the target behavior, whether or not there were people around at that time, and how others responded to the client's problematic actions. At the point of self-referral it is especially important to find what the client is saying to himself or herself about the problem and whether or not the client's own thoughts influence its occurrence (Meichenbaum, 1977).

Cross-cultural differences and similarities in social reactions to unusual behaviors have been reported. For example, Al-Issa's (1977) review of sociocultural factors in "hallucinations" found cultures where people are allowed to hallucinate without negative social consequences. In the West hallucinations are considered disturbing and deemed indicants of severe psychopathology. Often, stigmatizing labels such as "schizophrenic" are applied to those who admit hallucinating. Abad, Ramos, and Boyce (1977) suggest that among Puerto Ricans, temporary experiences of "visual imaginings or auditory sensations of hearing one's name being called, knocking at the door, or strange noises about the house" relate to religious beliefs (p. 27). In the United States these experiences can be inappropriately diagnosed and result in unnecessary hospitalization for Puerto Ricans. Functional analysis would be able to clarify the frequency, severity, and culture-related conditions of these hallucinations.

Personal status variables—age, sex, socioeconomic status, occupation —and other culturally relevant factors are included in the functional analysis because they provide norms for expected behaviors and add general assessment information. Individual differences in abilities for developing alternative social behaviors, beliefs-values-interests, and other attributes like language-cognitive skills (Staats, 1975) are evaluated when they are appropriate to specific target problems. Above all, behavior therapists focus on what the person actually does or fails to do in response to situations (Mischel, 1968).

Beyond pinpointing events preceding and following the target behavior, assessment also examines what the person has done in the past to cope with his problem. This appraisal yields information regarding the range of client coping skills and helps the therapist to suggest alternative coping behaviors for similar problem situations (Meichenbaum, 1977; Novaco, 1975).

Third, after changeworthy behaviors are specified and baseline assessment is completed, techniques are selected in conjunction with the client's desire to produce behavior change. The objective nature of behavior therapy, which specifies target behaviors and therapeutic conditions, permits accurate monitoring of treatment effectiveness. Many techniques are available for changing behavior. Bandura (1969), Kanfer and Goldstein (1974), and Kanfer and Phillips (1970) provide excellent descriptions and evaluations of these methods. By using specific techniques, behavior modification emphasizes changing the consequences of maladaptive responses. For example, Lewinsohn (1974) calls attention to the influential role of social consequences for behaviors looked upon as "depressed" in Western countries. These behaviors are often maintained by reinforcing consequences such as sympathy and other types of interpersonal attention. These consequences are likely to prolong the duration of depressive thoughts and acts. Ullmann and Krasner (1975) point out that people who maintain a depressed repertoire are in fact assuming a cultural role. Depressive behaviors can be reduced in frequency by removing sympathy and attention and shifting rewards to more positive behaviors, including activities that the person previously enjoyed doing.

Recently, cognitive behavior modification extended behavior therapists' repertoire (Meichenbaum, 1977; Staats, 1972). This orientation
provides procedures for assessing task-irrelevant self-statements, teaching self-instruction methods for enhancing attentional control, and for-
mulating generalizable problem-solving methods. Goldfried and Goldfried (1975) view cognitive change methods within the broad context of
self-control. They state that "the ultimate objective is to provide individuals with skills for regulating their own behavior" (p. 114). Interestingly,
this objective is in alignment with the reported aims of Eastern religions'
self-regulation techniques like transcendental meditation, yoga, and
trance inducement (Shapiro & Zifferblatt, 1976). Processes governing
self-control common to cognitive behavior modification and the Asian
systems await further elaboration. However, when self-control procedures specify concrete operations and are methodologically sound (Thoresen & Mahoney, 1974), they deserve cross-cultural application and
evaluation.

In addition to assessing client-presenting problems and selecting
changeworthy behaviors, cross-cultural behavior therapists face broader
sociocultural questions. Therapy procedures take place within the social
context of a given culture. In a culture where individual treatment is uncommon, behavior therapists should employ change strategies using
group variables so that the individual is not isolated. Bandura (1977b, p.
116) notes that societies differ in the extent to which reinforcers are
structured on an individual or collective basis. Social systems in which
people are rewarded or punished in terms of their individual actions are
thought to stimulate self-restraint and self-interest orientations. To
achieve a sense of shared responsibility among people, societies are required where collective contingencies subordinate self-interest to group
welfare so that all members are affected by each other's actions.
Gallimore and his colleagues (Gallimore, 1974; Gallimore, Boggs, & Jordan, 1974) capitalize on group affiliation of Hawaiian children in designing classroom environments. Rewards are made contingent upon
group rather than individual performance. Guthrie, Masangkay, and
Guthrie (1976) studied child malnourishment in a Filipino village and
found it related to early socialization practices by child caretakers. The
interaction among socialization practices, eating habits, and the child's
current cognitive-behavioral status enters the behavior therapist's decisions regarding selection of target behaviors and collaborators who can
influence identified clients.

Furthermore, just as socialization practices and values differ among
groups, the effectiveness and delivery of different reinforcers vary depending upon the person's culture-specific learning history (Gallimore,
Weiss, & Finney, 1974; Schultz & Sherman, 1976; Staats, 1975). For example, persons socialized to expect immediate results of their actions

may be easily discouraged if their efforts don't pay off. Cross-cultural behavior therapists thus evaluate the client's immediate problem behaviors within the social networks of his or her culture.

Behavior Change Agent

Behavior influence is maximized when the person acquires new adaptive behaviors in those settings where they are actually required. Tharp and Wetzel (1969) trained "mediators" to use social reinforcement to reduce undesirable behaviors of predelinquent children in the community. Qualified behavior therapists acted as consultants indirectly influencing the target population. Training behavior change agents has proved effective in such areas as behavioral management of children at home (Patterson, 1974) and in the classroom (Buckley & Walker, 1970), hospitalized psychiatric patients (Paul & Lentz, 1977), and youth in community settings (Fo & O'Donnell, 1974). Mediators exercise a much higher degree of client influence than the therapist by virtue of the power of their continuing relationship with the client. Therapists are initially outside the network of the client's social relations. They must establish a relationship with the client even though it is often circumscribed, temporary, and overshadowed by a host of competing relationships (Higginbotham, 1976). Tharp and Wetzel's (1969) triadic model views therapy as a chain of interconnected interpersonal influences. Treatment effectiveness is assessed by baseline changes in the behavior of both the mediator and the client. The strength of the triadic model lies in the enhancement of generalization and maintenance of behavior change.

Cross-cultural counseling must consider whether or not the use of mediators is practical and agreeable with the client culture's prevailing mode of helping. In one instance where mediators were deemed valuable, elementary school teachers were able to improve the on-task behaviors of Hawaiian children by using social reinforcement procedures in the classroom (Tanaka-Matsumi & Tharp, 1977). This experience suggests that cross-cultural education problems can be improved by looking at educational settings as planned environments with trained mediator-teachers (Jordan & Tharp, 1979). Whom to select and train as behavior influencers is also influenced by cultural factors (Bavermeister & Jamail, 1976). Proper use of community resources is a prime area for further investigation relevant to all situations of culture learning.

In sum, cross-cultural behavior therapists focus directly on specifiable behaviors assessed through functional analysis. In the context of the client culture, culture-related variables, such as group evaluative norms, significant others, effective reinforcers, and methods of administering behavior techniques, assume heavy emphasis. These assessments are necessary in order to increase the power of social influence and bring about desirable behavior change in the client.

Issues and Dilemmas in Cross-Cultural Intervention

Having illuminated the fundamentals of the behavioral approach, we examine this model's utility towards resolving the problems in cross-cultural intervention. These questions include the ethics of behavior change efforts, the cultural legitimacy of clinical methods, and evaluation of treatment efficacy and research variables.

Ethical Considerations

Three ethical considerations are prominent and have been enunciated fully by several others (cf. Draguns, 1981; Higginbotham, 1979a, Korman, 1974). First, therapy is an acculturation process. Cultural sentiments underlying therapeutic methods are transmitted in a context of intense culture learning. The counselor subtly shapes the client into a theoretically predetermined problem conception, then suggests treatment measures to improve such problems (Meichenbaum, 1976). For example, studies indicate that client progress is associated with convergence towards the therapist's own set of values and attitudes (e.g., Kessel & McBrearty, 1967; Meltzoff & Kornreich, 1970). Second, to ensure ethical practice, the clinician's competency must indicate a thorough knowledge of the culture within which he operates. Conversely, as stated at the APA Vail Conference on Professional Training, it is unethical for a professional to offer services to members of a culture group in which he lacks expertise (Korman, 1974). Third, if Western-derived treatments are applied to non-Western populations without proved effectiveness, such procedures may lead to unethical malpractice. In fact, it is presumptuous to export clinical technology when its credibility is under debate in the parent culture (Bergin & Lambert, 1978), and when the underlying mechanisms of behavior change have not been fully specified (Kazdin & Wilcoxon, 1976). Unfortunately, those offering consultation to mental health planners in non-Western regions and indigenous professionals themselves readily apply Western-derived treatments in the absence of cross-cultural validation (Higginbotham, 1979c).

Behavior therapy addresses these ethical issues directly. It does so in part by focusing on the client's immediate social context in selecting treatment goals and behavior influence methods, and by emphasizing an objective assessment of client behavior change. On a more fundamental plane, behavior therapists insure ethical conduct by proceeding with client contact only after they obtain *informed consent* from the client or his or her significant others. Behavioral procedures for the most part appeal to "common sense" and are credible (Kazdin & Wilcoxon, 1976). That is, they are apparent, understandable, and demonstrable in the treatment course. In the cross-cultural arena informed consent also has implications for the client's active participation in goal establishment.

This is particularly so with foreign students. The counselor should warn that changes in value system, world view, and social behaviors promoting adjustment to the host culture may not be compatible with those of the home country.

Cultural Legitimacy

To achieve community legitimacy and acceptance, a therapeutic system must accommodate to four principal criteria (Higginbotham, 1976). These include culture-specific definitions of deviancy, accepted norms of role behavior, expectations of social influence techniques, and approved behavior change agents. Psychological service systems which fail to accommodate along these dimensions are discontinuous with the client's social network and such systems are likely to induce culture change (Higginbotham, 1979b).

Culture-specific Deviancy

As stated earlier, each culture group decides for itself which human actions in what situations by whom constitutes behavioral abnormality (Carr, 1978; Draguns, 1980; Marsella, 1979). Indigenous nosologies which judiciously classify deviant acts according to criteria of severity, etiology, prognosis, and effective cures are documented for diverse peoples (Chen, 1970; Kunstadter, 1975; Lieban, 1973). The behavioral approach, sensitive to the nuances in cultural conceptions of disorder, stipulates that deviancy involves a value judgment. No behavior per se is deviant—the social label is applied by group members observing violations of social expectations.[3] Instead of theoretical criteria of abnormality, the behavioral approach determines changeworthiness and selects target behaviors based upon key cultural considerations: client role and status, attributes of the problem behavior (frequency, duration, intensity), the time and setting in which it takes place, the consequences, and the reason for the behavior as perceived by observers (Bandura, 1977; Fabrega, 1971; Ullmann & Krasner, 1975).

Culture-specific Goals

Behavior therapy honors culture-specific goals of individual adjustment. The socially accepted roles and standards of interpersonal relations become salient criteria for selecting therapy goals. Therapy attempts to resocialize the client towards his own cultural "areté"—i.e., the behavioral qualities a person should ideally possess according to community norms (cf. Goldschmidt, 1971). However, using areté as the outcome standard should be balanced against ethical considerations of individual rights, client consent and choice, and the long-range benefits for the person and his significant others in a changing environment (Harshbarger & Maley, 1974).

Culture-specific Therapists

The third culture accommodation dimension involves the use of means of social influence expected by that community. Each group has various recognizable rituals and techniques to resolve individual problems. Client exposure to expected therapy models has the effect of increasing hope and faith of problem relief. Heightened prognostic expectancies counter demoralization and hopelessness and motivate the client to stay in therapy and follow counselor instructions (Higginbotham, 1977). Procedures of reinforcement, modeling, extinction, and discrimination are assumed to underlie customs and practices concerned with evoking, maintaining, and altering culture members' social behavior across cultures. For example, Naikan therapy in Japan prescribes unique role behaviors (e.g., reverence for one's parents) but influences clients by using social conditions and techniques common to behavior therapy (Tanaka-Matsumi, 1979a).

Culture-specific Therapist Models

A major question in recent years is who is qualified or competent to serve as the change agent for different ethnic groups (Higginbotham, 1979c). Should the helper be a professional, paraprofessional, nonprofessional, peer, or what? When "mediators" (Tharp & Wetzel, 1969) are necessary to change client behavior, the therapist selects one based on the person's availability for influence and supervision by the therapist, his or her ability to behave consistently vis-à-vis the client's problem behavior, and the mediator's recognition as a legitimate source of influence in the client's environment for the problem under consideration (Higginbotham, 1976).

What are the necessary and sufficient "therapist" qualities that enable him or her to exercise maximum social influence towards the client and generate anticipated treatment success? Is therapeutic attraction restricted to indigenous helpers and professionals who share the client's geographic, ethnic, socioeconomic, and racial background? Does rapport develop only when client and therapist hold a mutual set of values, expectations, and disorder definitions (Goldstein, 1981)? Ruiz and Casas in this volume advocate counselor bilingualism and biculturalism as requirements for working with American Chicanos. Supporting half of this formula, Draguns (1981) cautions that even for bilinguals, use of second language is tricky. That is, fleeting allusions, nuances of intonation and meaning, can be lost upon the recipient unless he or she is attuned to the subtleties of the specific cultural language usage. Goldstein (1981), on the other hand, cautions against eliminating potential helpers based on these static factors. Instead, "concern ought to be with the functional, pro-outcome skills of a given counselor, and how such skills may be most effectively enhanced. At this early stage of a young specialty, none save the most volitionally encapsulated and monoculturally oriented ought to be ruled out" (Goldstein, 1981). The behavioral approach remedies these problems by specifying therapy goals and closely observing client performance rather than relying upon the uncertain efficacy of talk therapies. In conclusion, it is necessary to investigate empirically which treatment variables account for observed outcome when cultural criteria are used as success indices.

Treatment Efficacy and Research Needs

The field of cross-cultural counseling should stand or fall on its ability to demonstrate the viability of its procedures (Higginbotham, 1979a, p. 65). Behavior therapy's strength as a model for cross-cultural counseling lies in its advanced methods for evaluating environmental conditions by means of functional analysis and recording the client's behavior change due to treatment factors. Therapy is conceptualized as a single-subject experiment which includes a continuous monitoring of treatment variables and target behaviors. Moreover, behavioral interventions follow culture-specific assessments: community judgments of disorder, prosocial behaviors (treatment goals), expected behavior modification tactics, and appropriate mediators for assisting service delivery. Behavioral culture assessment permits a legitimate intervention plan continuous with the client's life-style, social values, and with mechanisms of community control.

Earlier we referred to therapist characteristics for successful cross-cultural counseling. We turn again to this question with a comprehensive specification of the conditions to bring about desirable change in persons who do not share their counselor's cultural background. The literature is replete with competing notions of why cross-cultural counseling is inherently prone to failure. A partial list includes such factors as patient-therapist "barriers" of social values, culture, and language (D. W. Sue, 1976; Vontress, 1969); cognitive or behavioral incongruity (Carkhuff & Pierce, 1967; Edwards & Edgerly, 1970; Wohl, 1981); resistance (Alexander, Workneh, Klein, & Miller, 1981); negative countertransference and stereotypic therapist responses to their clients (Atkinson, Morten, & Sue, 1979; Bloombaum, Yamamoto, & James, 1968; Safilios-Rothschild, 1969); and incongruent therapy expectations (Goldstein, 1973; Higginbotham, 1977).

A social learning analysis suggests a more parsimonious explanation of treatment failure and provides a means of overcoming it as well. Careful inspection of the social processes involved in work with clients from unique cultures reveals conditions that predictably elicit "countercontrol" (Goldfried & Davison, 1976) or "resistance" to behavior change. Five potential attributes provoke the client to initiate countercontrol efforts: (1) treatment is sought only as a last resort and under pressure from authorities, family or friends; (2) the absence of choice negates personal commitment and responsibility to therapy procedures, inhibiting self-directed efforts to change attitudes and behavior (cf. Collins & Hoyt, 1972); (3) the perceived threat to individual freedom by someone (e.g., "the therapist wants me to give up my cultural identity and act like a middle-class American") elicits "psychological reactance" (Brehm, 1966)—the tendency to resist actively being influenced by that person and to regain freedom; (4) the counseling environment may not provide cues necessary to elicit compliance, especially if the therapist, as a member of a distinct group, lacks attractiveness and persuasion because of his or her cultural ignorance and biased attitudes; and (5) violations of client's pre-therapy expectations of counselor's qualities and techniques diminish client anticipation of success; consequently the client is unwilling to follow the therapist's instructions and instead seeks to escape from the situation not returning for additional sessions.

The social learning approach identifies several factors potentially useful for enhancing the influence of the therapist, although continued research is necessary to validate them for different cultural groups. First, enhancement of the therapist's interpersonal attraction contributes significantly to an attenuation of client resistance (Goldstein, Heller & Sechrest, 1966). Lott and Lott (1972) assert that a liked person can function as a reinforcer with the capacity to shape and maintain the behavior of the other. Other researchers have stated that under conditions of high interpersonal attraction, client-therapist communication is more persuasive: cognitive and emotional states are more willingly communicated and understood more accurately, and the client pays better attention to and remembers therapist instructions (Wilson & Evans, 1976). In short, the client is more willing to model himself or herself after the therapist's behavior. Moreover, as Staats (1975) explains, high interpersonal attraction increases the therapist's ability to function as a discriminative or eliciting stimulus for the client's behavior change and as a reinforcing stimulus for strengthening that change.

Goldstein and his colleagues, in their early work, studied the effects of dissonance-arousal procedures on attraction (Goldstein, 1962; Goldstein, Heller, & Sechrest, 1966). Attraction was increased by having the patient role-play situations incompatible with resistance (e.g., carrying out therapist's instructions); by exposing the patient to information counter to resistant attitudes (e.g., "overhear" another patient praising the therapist's skills); and by overcompensating the client for his or her participation in therapy (e.g., scheduling additional "special" sessions) (Goldstein, Heller, & Sechrest, 1966). In a recent paper, Goldstein (1975) summarized these and other effective relationship enhancers:

The helper-client relationship may be enhanced by direct statements to the client about the helper's likability (structuring); by the client's observation of a counterpart expressing attraction to the helper, or helper observation of a counterpart expressing attraction to a client (imitation); by a client hearing other clients rate a helper as attractive (comformity pressure); by describing the helper to the client as someone of considerable expertness, experience, and accomplishment, or by surrounding the helper with various signs and symbols of such expertness and achievement (status); or by the facilitative conditions of helping behaviors actually offered the client by the helper (e.g., empathy and warmth) (Goldstein, 1975, p. 41).

A second avenue to enhance client influencibility lies in the identification of variables which evoke client expectations of positive treatment effects—prognostic expectations. Countercontrol is effectively handled by elevating the client's prognostic expectations and increasing his faith in the techniques used because these conditions influence selective attention to therapist instructions (Lick & Bootzin, 1975). Expectancies elicit positive emotions such as hope and delight which help counteract anxiety, depression, and helplessness (Frank, 1973). Moreover, as expectations of cure are perceived by others, the person receives confirmation from his social environment that the treatment is likely to succeed. This enables the individual to shed the "sick role" and assume other instrumental roles within his or her social group. It is evident that cross-cultural research is now needed to establish for different groups the most salient components of pretherapy expectations which predict prognostic expectancies. A study is now underway by the authors comparing Thai, Japanese, Hawaiian, and New Zealand populations on various expectation components.

Higginbotham (1977) reviewed the various means through which clients can be induced to believe that appropriate help is forthcoming. These include socialization interviews for teaching clients their role in therapy; therapist manners aimed at fostering liking, respect, and trust; and matching patients with therapists based on certain similarities. According to Goldstein (1975), matching procedures are based, first, on identifying real attributes of helpers and clients which are relevant to how well they relate. Second, these attributes are measured in counseling participants. Third, participants are matched into optimal pairs based on these measurements. Five optimal matches were tentatively found: (1) helper and client maintain congruent expectations of the in-therapy role behaviors each participant enacts; (2) both participants are strongly confident that the results of their meeting will produce positive treatment outcome; (3) helper and client hold in common social, cultural, racial, and economic backgrounds; (4) client and helper overlap in cognitive style, including their use of language, conceptual complexity, extrover-

sion-introversion, objectivity-subjectivity, flexibility, and social awareness; (5) both participants are complementary or reciprocal in their need
to offer and receive belongingness, interpersonal control, and emotional
closeness (Goldstein, 1975, p. 42).

To review, cross-cultural counseling situations are replete with cues
for evoking client countercontrol efforts which diminish the chances of a
positive outcome. Behavioral approaches mediating client resistance
and enhancing influencibility are twofold. The procedures increase the
therapist's attractiveness as a model by changing client attitudes towards him or her; and they identify variables controlling prognostic expectancies and arrange cues either through socialization interviews or
helper-client matching, which elevates hopefulness and anticipated success. The most promising procedure, however, is to take advantage of
cultural assessment of problem definitions, goals, tactics, manners, and
roles expected in therapy. Therapists could be trained to undertake cultural assessment as preliminary to clinical intervention and skillfully use
the appropriate social influence techniques with clients from unique
groups.

Two Cross-Cultural Problems Addressed by Behavioral
Approaches: Counseling American Minorities and
Sojourner Stress

Minority Groups

To elucidate a behavioral approach to cross-cultural counseling, we present an analysis of problems experienced by minority groups and overseas sojurners. Authors in this volume (Ruiz & Casas; Vontress) and
others (Atkinson, Morten, & Sue, 1979; Walz & Benjamin, 1978; S. Sue,
1977) have aptly described the cultural insensitivity of existing mental
health services and their steadfast avoidance by many minority groups.
American minority people and foreign students underutilize formal psychological services for several important reasons. First, ethnic clients
historically received poorer quality care when they sought help and experienced less satisfactory outcomes (S. Sue, 1977). They were often assigned nonprofessional helpers and received treatment requiring less
staff involvement—that is, medication. Second, Padilla, Ruiz, and Alvarez (1975) identified inflexible intake procedures, long waiting lists, and
geographic isolation of the clinic from those it serves. Similarly, mental
health centers which do not have culturally and linguistically competent
workers are frustrating to help seekers who are unable to comprehend
clinic operations nor communicate readily their reasons for seeking help.

The traditional, middle-class model of counseling itself has drawn the
sharpest criticism for its irrelevance to the requirements and life-styles of
minority and non-Western clients. The most glaring deficiency in tradi-

tional counseling for minorities noted by Atkinson, Morten, and Sue (1979) is its intrapsychic view. This view sees dysfunction as the consequence of intrapersonal disorganization rather than societal forces, hence change should be at the individual level conforming to a single standard of normality. The counseling role according to such a model is nonequalitarian and office-bound. This perpetuates the very socialization process which creates barriers between culturally different persons.

Another major factor is the service user's attitudes towards receiving psychiatric care. Research with foreign students indicates that they have a deep apprehension towards clinic attendance except as a desperate last resort. At home, their families try to hide problems from public view because a stigma is attached to being in need of psychiatric care. It is associated with shame, loss of status, and among foreign students fear of being sent home as a failure.

Clinicians working with minority groups have recently recognized the use of behavioral methods as a viable alternative to traditional counseling. They see it as meeting the special requirements of low income and ethnically different clients (Atkinson, Morton, & Sue, 1979; Draguns, in press; Goldstein, 1973; Padilla, Ruiz, & Alvarez, 1975; Rappaport, 1977). When we review these clinicians' independent observations of their therapeutic experiences with blacks, Native Americans, Mexican Americans, and Asian Americans, there are several clear conclusions. Minority group clients desire a "guidance-nurturant" oriented intervention. They want the helper to take an active, directive role and give them explicit directions on how to solve problems and bring immediate relief from disabling distress (Goldstein, 1973). Foreign students who don't find an authoritative, supportive, and directive therapist may interpret the lack of these qualities as the therapist's indifference to their suffering (Alexander, Klein, Workneh, & Miller, 1981). Further, Vontress (1979) asserts that counselors must immediately make clear what, how, and why they intend to do what is planned in therapy in order to reduce uncertainty experienced by clients and their families. Moreover, Smith (1978) posits that the black social experience emphasizes immediate gratification. In essence, minority group clients and foreign students alike are looking for straightforward solutions to concrete and immediate problems that are generating stress crisis in their lives. Therefore, counseling modes which rely on introspection, reflection, and extensive client verbalization to lay open and eventually reorganize one's thinking style and feelings do not meet the needs of minority groups.

Behavior therapy, in contrast, is goal-directed. It is structured into step-by-step procedures through which therapists teach appropriate social skills which can be practiced in the social context of the client's activities. Goldstein (1973) formulated Structured Learning Therapy as explicitly responsive to the needs, preferences, and environmental realities of the poor. Target skills were selected following an assessment of the important deficits observed in lower socioeconomic clients. These targets included self-control, interpersonal stress rehearsal, frustration tolerance, tolerance of ambiguity, need achievement, and accurate affective perception. Behavior change techniques were matched to learning methods familiar to these clients. Structured Learning Therapy proceeds as follows:

> [T]he patient is provided with numerous, specific, detailed, and vivid displays of the specific interpersonal or personal skills we are seeking to teach him (i.e., modeling); he is given considerable opportunity, training and encouragement to behaviorally rehearse or practice the modeled behavior (i.e., role playing); and he is provided with positive feedback, approval, or reward as his enactments increasingly approximate those of the model (i.e., social reinforcement) (Gutride, Goldstein, & Hunter, 1973, p. 408).

Overseas Sojourners

An extensive literature has evolved describing the environmental stressors and adjustment reactions experienced by foreign students, Peace Corps Volunteers, refugees, and other sojourners as they strive to cope with new surroundings (e.g., Brein & David, 1971; Jones & Popper, 1972; Liem & Kehmeier, 1980; Taft, 1977). For foreign students the primary worry is academic difficulties (Sharma, 1973), reflecting collateral problems of language and past educational experience. This is predictable for persons who have made a substantial financial and personal investment towards the successful completion of degree studies. Foreign students are reluctant to allow personal considerations (e.g., getting used to local customs, homesickness, financial problems, making friends with host nationals, participating in campus activities) to get in the way of their studies, although there is some indication that extensive social interaction with local citizens facilitates sojourner satisfaction (Brein & David, 1971; Ferguson, 1979).

Refugees, such as the nearly 300,000 Indochinese who have sought security in the United States since 1975, confront a more profoundly disturbing array of adjustment obstacles than sojourning foreign students. Recent articles point out the intense plight of these "persons without a homeland" and the adverse psychological consequence of their flight from Southeast Asia (Aylesworth, Ossorio, & Osaki, 1979; Ferguson, 1979; Liem & Kehmeier, 1980; Nguyen, 1977; Rahe, Looney, Ward, Tung, & Liu, 1978). Two overarching obstacles to successful resettlement for Vietnamese in Hawaii, for example, are their inability to speak English and the unavailability of suitable jobs, especially for non-English speakers (Nguyen, 1977). Even more psychologically painful is the bereavement and guilt of having left loved ones and friends behind whose fate remains unknown—the "survivor syndrome." Loss of wealth and social status by many refugees, who are forced to seek menial jobs, lead to reduced self-esteem and confidence. Sex role reversal is another humiliating experience for unemployed male household heads whose wives and daughters, never expecting to be income providers, find it easier to secure employment. Elderly Vietnamese are especially prone to stress. They lack language skills, are unable to contribute to family welfare, are forced to receive charity which they despise as begging, and are without the comfort and guidance of their religious leaders.

Another unreclaimable loss is the practice of ancestor worship (Liem & Kehmeier, 1980). Traditionally, Vietnamese were devotedly attached to the tomb sites of their ancestors where they went for prayer and dialogue with their forebears. Lacking this contact, some refugees are lonely and feel incapable of making decisions without ancestral advice. Last, we cannot overlook acts of racism and hostility directed towards the new arrivals by some Americans fearful of their own economic security. Such acts compound resettlement woes and increase refugee adjustment reactions of depression and isolation (Aylesworth, Ossorio, & Osaki, 1979).

Overseas sojourners, in short, experience a "cultural shock" in their struggle to cope with an unfamiliar culture (see Pedersen's chapter in this volume). The term "culture shock" itself has been given at least six different meanings since Oberg (1958) coined it to describe the experience of anthropologists who must learn to handle the violation of social reality implicit in unfamiliar norms, values, and mores (Taft, 1977). The behavioral approach provides a comprehensive appraisal of culture shock. Culture shock is a maladaptive response to a new situation where previous learning is inadequate for coping with the novel environment. Situational and social cues are regularly associated with specific response outcomes (desirable or undesirable), and these cues have come to serve as activators and guides for action (Bandura, 1977). Sojourners, however, can no longer be certain which cues predict what kind of outcomes. The inability to anticipate events correctly—the discontinuity between one's behavior and expected consequences—evokes frustration. It has implications for coping behavior, changes in perceived self-efficacy, and overgeneralization about negative aspects of the host culture (Bandura, 1977b). Defensive or self-protective behavior aims at reducing a person's feeling of vulnerability brought on by the heightened emotional arousal to an unpredictable environment. Avoidance or defensive behaviors persist unless the person is reexposed to the situation. Consistent avoidance behavior prevents the person from learning that the real circumstances have changed (Bandura, 1977b, p. 62). Unfortunately, situational events that occur only coincidentally in conjunction with aversive outcomes may become associated with them as well. Inappropriate defensive behavior may arise when the sojourner overgeneralizes from events actually associated with unpleasant experiences to similar but innocuous events (Bandura, 1977b, p. 78).

Hence, the person with culture shock may come to see a great deal of "danger" in the new environment and come to avoid a broad array of cultural circumstances which might otherwise be found positive. The consequences are harsh self-judgment and negative self-concept. Clinicians recognize the self-defeating and escalating effects of ruminative doubts regarding one's ability to cope. Bandura (1977a, 1979) and Staats (1968; 1975) postulate that expectation of personal efficacy is critical to behavior change. An efficacy expectation is the conviction that one can successfully perform an action required to produce desired outcomes. The strength of that sense of effectiveness determines whether a person will tackle difficult tasks, give up easily, or simply avoid even trying. In short, persons with culture shock learn that their formerly adaptive behaviors and skills are no longer effective.

Remediation of culture shock involves new social learning. Two complementary approaches have been suggested (Brein & David, 1971; David, 1976; Taft, 1977). First, the sojourner may undertake the process of culture learning and acquire those intercultural skills which will enable him or her to attain positive effects and avoid negative effects in the new environment. One must learn those features of the new environment that predict the consequences for different courses of action (Bandura, 1977b). This learning is similar to conducting a functional analysis of behaviors in the new environment, so that one can learn what behavior leads to desirable consequences in a foreign cultural setting. Persons learn to recognize appropriate cues in a novel culture and enhance their intercultural skills based on trial-and-error learning, by imitating the behavior of host culture members, or acquiring the rules of interaction from observations (Taft, 1977). Sojourner preparation programs, in contrast, make use of knowledgeable models (like returning Peace Corps Volunteers) and guided practice in simulated host country settings (Brislin & Pedersen, 1976). Models with bicultural skills teach newcomers to act appropriately in diverse settings and on different occasions in role-playing situations. In short, receiving instructions under conditions of host culture simulation (e.g., Peace Corps training in mock villages [Trifonovitch, 1973] or Triandis' [1975] "culture assimilator") or from seasoned sojourners prepares persons for what to expect and how to cope within a new culture. Such programs teach the newcomer to act in such a way that members of the host culture will respond positively.

The second major avenue for remediating culture shock is through attentuation of unpleasant experiences. This is accomplished by transferring positive reinforcers from home, acquiring new reinforcers in the host setting, neutralizing unpleasant events through desensitization procedures, or making them enjoyable through repeated association with pleasant experiences. David (1976) provides a comprehensive assessment format for counselors to help sojourner clients attain reinforcers and avoid punishers. Four questions are asked: What are your sources of reinforcement back home? Are there any events which might occur but have not that would act as reinforcers? How many potential reinforcers are available in the host culture? What events in the host culture can be used as reinforcers during predeparture training—that is, how can you anticipate good things happening and rehearse your experience with them?

The counselor-trainer is able to focus on specific anticipated problems from the assessment of reinforcers and potentially unpleasant events. His or her task becomes fourfold. First, the counselor assists the client in transferring potential reinforcers to the new culture, especially during the first few months. In planning and preparing the continuance of key reinforcers, it is wise to consult previous sojourners to see if they are already available there (e.g., there *are* golf courses in Japan). Second, new reinforcers are developed if old ones cannot be easily transferred (e.g., tennis courts are unavailable in Kuching, but cricket ovals are plentiful). It is wise to choose new reinforcers compatible with host country values and legal strictures. Third, the counselor prepares the traveler for possible aversive events. Some of these are concrete (e.g., men and women sharing the same toilet facilities), while others are more abstract (e.g., devaluation of individual autonomy). Knowing what the client dislikes and being aware of problems encountered by similar sojourners, the counselor warns what to expect, how to prepare for it, or appropriate avoidance strategies. However, repeated and graduated exposure to initially unpleasant events may soon reduce anxiety related to specific events, especially if it is arranged under otherwise pleasant circumstances.

In sum, the behavioral approach analyzes "culture shock" into specific experiences and behaviors of the individual in a new environment. By identifying situations in which the person faces problems, the therapist guides him or her to learn new skills that help reduce stress and increase opportunities to engage in reinforcing behaviors. This approach is therefore directed towards training people in appropriate social skills and by disseminating culture-related information in a systematic manner.

Summary and Conclusion

In light of an increasing interest in developing an effective helping system for culturally different clients, the present chapter advocates the applicability of behavior modification procedures to cross-cultural issues. While the traditional psychiatric model assumes the universality of psychopathology, the behavioral approach directly assesses the nature of maladaptive behavior in the client's sociocultural context. The behavioral approach emphasizes specific conditions: the client's cultural conception of problem behaviors, setting specific goals in therapy, arranging conditions to increase the client's expectation of therapy success, and making use of appropriate social influence agents, such as mediators in the community. By doing so, the behavioral approach resolves the issues of cultural legitimacy in intervention and ethical procedures, both of which have been debated critically in the field of cross-cultural counseling.

When working with culturally different clients, the behavior therapist makes a systematic effort to minimize "countercontrol" and maximizes the chance of success. Culture-specific definitions of client problems form the basis for judging the effectiveness of behavior-change techniques. Behavior modification draws heavily upon social-learning principles and empirical findings derived from laboratories. The therapist designs new learning situations for the client to acquire alternative role behaviors. To achieve this end, the present chapter closely examines the empirical literature and lays out conditions under which therapist social influence can be maximized.

After reviewing basic issues in cross-cultural behavior modification, the present chapter gives a comprehensive reappraisal of the experience called "culture shock," a now familiar concept to cross-cultural psychologists. Culture shock is a series of experiences in which the person is unable to use formerly effective coping skills in a new environment and consequently loses self-confidence. This problem has been noted by clinicians counseling overseas sojourners and minority group clients. The authors call attention to a variety of training programs developed specifically to teach these individuals how to handle themselves in a new environment to avoid aversive consequences.

Throughout this chapter the authors have emphasized identifying specific conditions under which the therapist can bring about desirable behavior change in the client. Behavior modification procedures meet the challenge of clarifying the social influence processes that are observed across cultures.

Notes

The authors would like to thank Leonard Burns for his helpful comments on an earlier draft of this chapter.

1. In this chapter the term "behavioral approach" signifies those major concepts and procedures associated with operant behaviorism, the psychosocial influence model, social behaviorism, and social learning theory. The authors recognize the operational and sometimes theoretical diversity of these distinct learning models. Yet for purposes of this chapter (and with apologies to their proponents), we have subsumed them under the generic label the "behavioral

approach," recognizing their common origins in experimental studies of learning processes.

2. The philosophy underlying the behavioral approach is the commitment to empiricism and scientific method for describing and understanding human behavior. The "bias" promulgated by this perspective is therefore one of objectivism, recourse to observable phenomena, parsimony of inference, and reliance upon rational, hypothetical-deductive processes for explaining natural events.

3. The authors do recognize, on the other hand, that there is a noteworthy convergence across cultures in the identification and labeling as deviant those social behaviors which communities see as most disturbing to their respective members.

References

Abad, V., Ramos, J., & Boyce, E. Clinical issues in the psychiatric treatment of Puerto Ricans. In E. R. Padilla & A. M. Padilla (Eds.), *Transcultural psychiatry: An Hispanic perspective*. Los Angeles: Spanish Speaking Mental Health Center, University of California at Los Angeles, 1977.

Alberti, R. E., & Emmons, M. L. *Your perfect right*. San Luis Obispo, California: IMPACT, 1974.

Alexander, A. A., Workneh, F., Klein, M. H., & Miller, M. Psychotherapy and the foreign student. In P. B. Pedersen, J. G. Draguns, W. J. Lonner, & J. E. Trimble (Eds.), *Counseling across cultures* (rev. & expanded ed.). Honolulu: University Press of Hawaii, 1981.

Al-Issa, I. Social and cultural aspects of hallucinations. *Psychological Bulletin*, 1977, *84*, 570–587.

Ardila, R. Behavior modification in Latin America. In M. Hersen, R. M. Eisler, & P. M. Miller (Eds.), *Progress in behavior modification* (Vol. 6). New York: Academic Press, 1978.

Atkinson, D. R., Morten, G., & Sue, D. W. *Counseling American minorities*. Dubuque, Iowa: William C. Brown, 1979.

Aylesworth, L. S., Ossorio, P. G., & Osaki, L. T. Stress and mental health among Vietnamese in the United States. In R. Endo, S. Sue, & N. Wagner (Eds.), *Asian-Americans: Social and psychological perspectives*. Palo Alto: Science and Behavior Books, 1979.

Bandura, A. *Principles of behavior modification*. New York: Holt, Rinehart & Winston, 1969.

Bandura, A. Behavior therapy and models of man. *American Psychologist*, 1974, *29*, 859–869.

Bandura, A. Self-efficacy: Toward a unifying theory of behavior change. *Psychological Review*, 1977, *84*, 191–215. (a)

Bandura, A. *Social Learning theory*. Englewood Cliffs: Prentice-Hall, 1977. (b)

Bavermeister, J. J., & Jemail, J. A. Teachers as experimenters and behavior engineers: An extension and cross-cultural replication. *Inter-American Journal of Psychology*, 1976, *10*, 41–45.

Bergin, A. E., & Lambert, M. The evaluation of therapeutic outcomes. In S. L. Garfield & A. E. Bergin (Eds.), *Handbook of psychotherapy and behavior change*. New York: John Wiley & Sons, 1978.

Bloombaum, M., Yamamoto, J., & James, Q. Cultural stereotyping among psychotherapists. *Journal of Consulting and Clinical Psychology*, 1968, *32*, 99.

Borkovec, T. D. The role of expectancy and physiological feedback in fear research: A review with special reference to subject characteristics. *Behavior Therapy*, 1973, *4*, 491–505.

Brehm, J. W. *A theory of psychological reactance*. New York: Academic Press, 1966.

Brein, M., & David, K. H. Intercultural communication and the adjustment of the sojourner. *Psychological Bulletin*, 1971, *76*, 215–230.

Brislin, R. W., & Pedersen, P. *Cross-cultural orientation programs*. New York: Gardner Press, 1976.

Buckley, N. K., & Walker, H. M. *Modifying classroom behavior: A manual of procedures for classroom teachers*. Champaign, Illinois: Research Press, 1970.

Carkhuff, R. R., & Pierce, R. Differential effects of therapist race and social class upon patient depth of self-exploration in the initial clinical interview. *Journal of Consulting Psychology*, 1967, *31*, 632–634.

Carr, J. Ethno-behaviorism and the culture-bound syndromes: The case of *amok*. *Culture, Medicine and Psychiatry*, 1978, *2*, 269–293.

Chen, P. Y. C. Classification and concepts of causation of mental illness in a rural Malay community. *International Journal of Social Psychiatry*, 1970, *16*, 205–215.

Collins, B. E., & Hoyt, M. F. Personal responsibility-for-consequences: An integration and extension of the "forced compliance" literature. *Journal of Experimental Social Psychology*, 1972, *8*, 558–593.

Cooper, J. E., Kendell, R. E., Gurland, B. J., Sharpe, L., Copeland, J. R. M., & Simmons, R. *Psychiatric diagnosis in New York and London*. London: Oxford University Press, 1972.

David, K. H. The use of social learning theory in preventing intercultural adjustment problems. In P. Pedersen, W. J. Lonner, & J. G. Draguns (Eds.), *Counseling across cultures*. Honolulu: University Press of Hawaii, 1976.

Draguns, J. G. Advances in the methodology of cross-cultural psychiatric assessment. *Transcultural Psychiatric Research Review*, 1977, *14*, 125–143.

Draguns, J. G. Culture and personality. In A. J. Marsella, R. Tharp, & T. Ciborowski (Eds.), *Perspectives in cross-cultural psychology*. New York: Academic Press, 1979.

Draguns, J. G. Psychopathology. In H. C. Triandis & J. G. Draguns (Eds.), *Handbook of cross-cultural psychology* (Vol. 6). Boston: Allyn & Bacon, 1980.

Draguns, J. G. Cross-cultural counseling and psychotherapy: History, issues, current status. In A. J. Marsella & P. Pedersen (Eds.), *Cross-cultural counseling and psychotherapy: Foundations, evaluation and cultural considerations*. Elmsford, New York: Pergamon, 1981.

Draguns, J. G., & Phillips, L. *Psychiatric classification and diagnosis: An overview and critique*. Morristown, New Jersey: General Learning Press, 1971.

Edwards, B. C., & Edgerly, J. W. Effects of counselor-client cognitive congruence on counseling outcome in brief counseling. *Journal of Counseling Psychology*, 1970, *17*, 313–318.

Endler, N. S., & Magnusson, D. (Eds.). *Interactional psychology and personality.* Washington, D.C.: Hemisphere Publishers, 1976.

Eysenck, H. J. Learning theory and behavior therapy. *Journal of Medical Science,* 1959, *105,* 61–75.

Fabrega, H., Jr. Medical anthropology. In B. J. Siegel (Ed.), *Biennial review of anthropology.* Palo Alto, California: Stanford University Press, 1971.

Ferguson, B. *Vietnamese refugee adjustment in Honolulu.* Unpublished master's thesis, University of Hawaii, 1979.

Fo, W. S. O., & O'Donnell, C. R. The buddy system: Effects of community intervention program for youth with nonprofessionals as behavior change agents. *Journal of Consulting and Clinical Psychology,* 1974, *42,* 163–169.

Frank, J. D. *Persuasion and healing.* Baltimore: Johns Hopkins University Press, 1973.

Franks, C. M. Introduction: Behavior therapy and its Pavlovian origins: Review and perspectives. In C. M. Franks (Ed.), *Behavior therapy: Appraisal and status.* New York: McGraw-Hill, 1969.

Gallimore, R. Affiliation motivation and Hawaiian-American achievement. *Journal of Cross-Cultural Psychology,* 1974, *5,* 481–492.

Gallimore, R., Boggs, J. W., & Jordan, C. *Culture, behavior and education: A study of Hawaiian Americans.* Beverly Hills, California: Sage Publications, 1974.

Gallimore, R., Weiss, L. B., & Finney, R. Cultural differences in delay of gratification: A problem of behavior classification. *Journal of Personality and Social Psychology,* 1974, *30,* 72–80.

Goldfried, M. R., & Davison, G. C. *Clinical behavior therapy.* New York: Holt, Rinehart & Winston, 1976.

Goldfried, M. R., & Goldfried, A. P. Cognitive change methods. In F. H. Kanfer & A. P. Goldstein (Eds.), *Helping people change.* New York: Pergamon Press, 1975.

Goldfried, M. R., & Kent, R. N. Traditional versus behavioral personality assessment: A comparison of methodological and theoretical assumptions. *Psychological Bulletin,* 1972, *77,* 409–420.

Goldschmidt, W. Areté—Motivation and models for behavior. In I. Galston (Ed.), *The interface between psychiatry and anthropology.* New York: Brunner/Mazel, 1971.

Goldstein, A. P. *Therapist-patient expectancies in psychotherapy.* New York: Pergamon Press, 1962.

Goldstein, A. P. *Structured learning therapy.* New York: Academic Press, 1973.

Goldstein, A. P. Relationship-enhancement methods. In F. H. Kanfer & A. P. Goldstein (Eds.), *Helping people change.* New York: Pergamon Press, 1975.

Goldstein, A. P. Expectancy effects in cross-cultural counseling. In A. J. Marsella & P. Pedersen (Eds.), *Cross-cultural counseling and psychotherapy: Foundations, evaluation and cultural considerations.* Elmsford, New York: Pergamon, 1981.

Goldstein, A. P., Heller, K., & Sechrest, L. B. *Psychotherapy and the psychology of behavior change.* New York: John Wiley & Sons, 1966.

Goldstein, A. P., & Stein, N. *Prescriptive psychotherapies.* New York: Pergamon Press, 1976.

Guthrie, G. M., Mansangkay, Z., & Guthrie, H. A. Behavior, malnutrition, and mental development. *Journal of Cross-Cultural Psychology,* 1976, 7, 169–180.

Gutride, M. E., Goldstein, A. P., & Hunter, G. F. The use of modeling and role playing to increase social interaction among asocial psychiatric patients. *Journal of Consulting and Clinical Psychology,* 1973, 40, 408–415.

Harshbarger, D., & Maley, R. G. (Eds.). *Behavior analysis and systems analysis: An integrative approach to mental health programs.* Kalamazoo, Michigan: Behaviordelia Inc., 1974.

Hersen, M., & Barlow, D. H. *Single case experimental design.* New York: Pergamon Press, 1976.

Higginbotham, H. N. A conceptual model for the delivery of psychological services in non-Western settings. In R. W. Brislin (Ed.), *Topics in culture learning,* 1976, 4.

Higginbotham, H. N. Culture and the role of client expectancy in psychotherapy. In R. W. Brislin & M. P. Hamnett (Eds.), *Topics in culture learning,* 1977, 5, 107–124.

Higginbotham, H. N. Cultural issues in providing psychological services for foreign students in the United States. *International Journal of Intercultural Relations,* 1979, 3, 49–85. (a)

Higginbotham, H. N. Culture and mental health services. In A. J. Marsella, R. Tharp, & T. Ciborowski (Eds.), *Perspectives in cross-cultural psychology.* New York: Academic Press, 1979. (b)

Higginbotham, H. N. *Delivery of mental health services in three developing Asian nations: Feasibility and cultural sensitivity of "modern psychiatry."* Doctoral dissertation, University of Hawaii, 1979. *Dissertation Abstracts International,* in press. (c)

Jones, R. J., & Popper, R. Characteristics of Peace Corps host countries and the behavior of volunteers. *Journal of Cross-Cultural Psychology,* 1972, 3, 233–245.

Jordan, C., & Tharp, R. G. Culture and education. In A. J. Marsella, R. Tharp, & T. Ciborowski (Eds.), *Perspectives in cross-cultural psychology.* New York: Academic Press, 1979.

Kanfer, F. H., & Goldstein, A. P. (Eds.). *Helping people change.* New York: Pergamon Press, 1975.

Kanfer, F. H., & Phillips, J. S. *Learning foundations of behavior therapy.* New York: John Wiley & Sons, 1970.

Kanfer, F. H., & Saslow, G. Behavioral diagnosis. In C. M. Franks (Ed.), *Behavior therapy: Appraisal and status.* New York: McGraw-Hill, 1969.

Katz, M. M., Cole, J. D., & Lowrey, H. A. Studies of diagnostic process: The influence of symptom perception, past experience and ethnic background on diagnostic decisions. *American Journal of Psychiatry,* 1969, 125, 937–947.

Kazdin, A. E. *Token economy.* New York: Plenum Press, 1977.

Kazdin, A. E. *History of behavior modification.* Baltimore: University Park Press, 1978.

Kazdin, A. E., & Wilcoxon, L. A. Systematic desensitization and nonspecific treatment effects: A methodological evaluation. *Psychological Bulletin,* 1976, *83,* 729-758.

Kazdin, A. E., & Wilson, G. T. *Evaluation of behavior therapy: Issues, evidence and research strategies.* Cambridge, Massachusetts: Ballinger, 1978.

Kessel, P., & McBrearty, J. F. Values and psychotherapy: A review of the literature. *Perceptual and Motor Skills,* 1967, *25,* 669-690.

Kiesler, D. Some myths of psychotherapy research and the search for a paradigm. *Psychological Record,* 1966, *65,* 110-136.

Kiev, A. *Transcultural psychiatry.* New York: Free Press, 1972.

Korman, M. National conference on levels and patterns of professional training in psychology: Major themes. *American Psychologist,* 1974, *29,* 441-449.

Krasner, L. Behavior therapy. In P. H. Mussen & M. R. Rosenzweig (Eds.), *Annual review of psychology.* Palo Alto, California: Annual Reviews Inc., 1971.

Krasner, L., & Ullmann, L. P. *Behavior influence and personality.* New York: Holt, Rinehart & Winston, 1973.

Kunstadter, P. Do cultural differences make any difference? Choice points in medical systems available in northwestern Thailand. In A. Kleinman, P. Kunstadter, E. R. Alexander, & J. R. Gale (Eds.), *Comparative studies of health care in Chinese and other societies.* Washington, D.C.: U.S. Department of Health, Education and Welfare, 1975.

Langer, E. J., & Abelson, R. P. A patient by any other name . . . ! Clinician group differences in labeling bias. *Journal of Consulting and Clinical Psychology,* 1974, *42,* 4-9.

Leff, J. Culture and the differentiation of emotional states. *British Journal of Psychiatry,* 1973, *123,* 299-306.

Leitenberg, H. *The handbook of behavior modification and behavior therapy.* Englewood Cliffs: Prentice-Hall, 1976.

Lewinsohn, P. M. A. A behavioral approach to depression. In R. J. Friedman & M. M. Katz (Eds.), *The psychology of depression: Contemporary theory and research.* New York: John Wiley & Sons, 1974.

Lick, J., & Bootzin, R. Expectancy factors in the treatment of fear: Methodological and theoretical issues. *Psychological Bulletin,* 1975, *82,* 917-931.

Lieban, R. W. Medical anthropology. In J. J. Honigmann (Ed.), *Handbook of social and cultural anthropology.* Chicago: Rand McNally, 1973.

Liem, N. D., & Kehmeier, D. F. The Vietnamese. In J. F. McDermott, W. S. Tseng, & T. W. Maretzki (Eds.), *People and cultures in Hawaii* (2nd ed.). Honolulu: University Press of Hawaii, 1980.

London, P. The end of ideology in behavior modification. *American Psychologist,* 1972, *27,* 913-920.

Lott, A. J., & Lott, B. E. The power of liking: Consequences of interpersonal attitudes derived from a liberalized view of secondary reinforcement. In L. Berkowitz (Ed.), *Advances in experimental and social psychology* (Vol. 6). New York: Academic Press, 1972.

Magaro, P. A., Gripp, R., & McDowell, D. *The mental health industry: A cultural phenomena.* New York: John Wiley & Sons, 1978.

Marsella, A. J. Cross-cultural studies of mental disorder. In A. J. Marsella, R. Tharp, & T. Ciborowski (Eds.), *Perspectives in cross-cultural psychology.* New York: Academic Press, 1979.

Meichenbaum, D. A cognitive-behavior modification approach to assessment. In M. Hersen & A. Bellack (Eds.), *Behavioral assessment: A practical handbook.* New York: Pergamon Press, 1976.

Meichenbaum, D. *Cognitive behavior modification: An integrative approach.* New York: Plenum Press, 1977.

Meltzoff, J., & Kornreich, M. *Research in psychotherapy.* New York: Atherton Press, 1970.

Mischel, W. *Personality and assessment.* New York: John Wiley & Sons, 1968.

Mischel, W. Toward a cognitive social learning reconceptualization of personality. *Psychological Review,* 1973, *80,* 252–283.

Nguyen, C. *Research paper on the resettlement of Vietnamese in the state of Hawaii.* Honolulu: Vietnamese and Indochinese Volunteer Assistance, Inc., March 1977.

Novaco, R. *Anger control: The development and evaluation of an experimental treatment.* Lexington, Massachusetts: Heath & Co., 1975.

Oberg, K. *Culture shock and the problem of adjustment to new cultural environments.* Washington, D.C.: U.S. Department of State, Foreign Service Institute, 1958.

Padilla, A. M., Ruiz, R. A., & Alvarez, R. Community mental health services for the Spanish-speaking surnamed population. *American Psychologist,* 1975, *30,* 892–905.

Patterson, G. F. Interventions for boys with conduct problems: Multiple settings, treatments, and criteria. *Journal of Consulting and Clinical Psychology,* 1974, *42,* 471–481.

Paul, G., & Lentz, J. *Psychosocial treatment of chronic mental patients.* Cambridge, Massachusetts: Harvard University Press, 1977.

Proshansky, H. M., Ittelson, W. H., & Rivlin, L. G. (Eds.). *Environmental psychology* (2nd ed.). New York: Holt, Rinehart & Winston, 1976.

Queiroz, L. O. S., Guilhardi, H. J., & Martin, G. L. A university program in Brazil to develop psychologists with specialization in behavior modification. *The Psychological Record,* 1976, *26,* 181–188.

Rahe, R. H., Looney, J. G., Ward, H. W., Tung, T. M., & Liu, W. T. Psychiatric consultation in a Vietnamese refugee camp. *The American Journal of Psychiatry,* 1978, *135,* 185–190.

Rappaport, J. *Community psychology: Values, research, action.* New York: Holt, Rinehart & Winston, 1977.

Resner, G. R., & Hartog, S. Concepts and terminology of mental disorder among Malays. *Journal of Cross-Cultural Psychology,* 1970, *1,* 369–381.

Rosenhan, D. L. On being sane in insane places. *Science,* 1973, *197,* 250–258.

Rosenthal, D. Changes in some moral values following psychotherapy. *Journal of Consulting Psychology,* 1955, *19,* 431–436.

Safilios-Rothschild, C. Psychotherapy and patient's characteristics: A cross-cultural examination. *International Journal of Social Psychiatry,* 1969, *15,* 120–128.

Schultz, C. B., & Sherman, R. H. Social class, development and differences in reinforcer effectiveness. *Review of Educational Research*, 1976, *46*, 25-59.

Shapiro, D. H., & Zifferblatt, S. M. Zen meditation and behavioral self-control: Similarities, differences and clinical applications. *American Psychologist*, 1976, *31*, 519-523.

Sharma, S. A study to identify and analyze adjustment problems experienced by foreign non-European graduate students enrolled in selected universities in the state of North Carolina. *California Journal of Educational Research*, 1973, *24*(3), 135-146.

Sheehan, P. W., & White, K. D. (Eds.). *Behavior modification in Australia*. Parkville, Victoria: Australian Psychological Society, 1976.

Smith, W. D. Black perspectives on counseling. In G. R. Walz & L. Benjamin (Eds.), *Transcultural counseling: Needs, programs and techniques*. New York: Human Sciences Press, 1978.

Skinner, B. F. *Science and human behavior*. New York: Macmillan, 1953.

Staats, A. W. *Complex human behavior*. New York: Holt, Rinehart & Winston, 1963.

Staats, A. W. Social behaviorism and human motivation: Principles of the attitude-reinforcer-discrimination system. In A. G. Greenwald, T. C. Brock, & T. M. Ostrom (Eds.), *Psychological foundations of attitudes*. New York: Academic Press, 1968.

Staats, A. W. *Child learning, intelligence, and personality*. New York: Harper & Row, 1971.

Staats, A. W. Language behavior therapy, a derivative of social behaviorism. *Behavior Therapy*, 1972, *3*, 165-192.

Staats, A. W. *Social behaviorism*. Homewood, Illinois: Dorsey Press, 1975.

Staats, A. W. "Behavioral interaction and interactional psychology." Theories of personality: Similarities, differences, and the need for unification. *British Journal of Psychology*, 1980, *71*, 205-220.

Strupp, H. H. Specific vs. nonspecific factors in psychotherapy and the problem of control. *Archives of General Psychiatry*, 1970, *23*, 393-401.

Sue, D. W. *Barriers to effective cross-cultural counseling*. Paper presented at the Cross-Cultural Counseling Conference, East-West Center Culture Learning Institute, Honolulu, Hawaii, August, 1976.

Sue, S. Community mental health services to minority groups: Some optimism, some pessimism. *American Psychologist*, 1977, *32*, 616-624.

Taft, R. Coping with unfamiliar cultures. In N. Warren (Ed.), *Studies in cross-cultural psychology*. London: Academic Press, 1977.

Tanaka-Matsumi, J. *Naikan therapy: A transcultural view*. Unpublished manuscript, Department of Psychology, University of Hawaii, December, 1975.

Tanaka-Matsumi, J. Cultural factors and social influence techniques in Naikan therapy: A Japanese self-observation method. *Psychotherapy: Theory, Research and Practice*, 1979, *16*, 385-390. (a)

Tanaka-Matsumi, J. Taijin Kyofusho: Diagnostic and cultural issues in Japanese psychiatry. *Culture, Medicine and Psychiatry*, 1979, *3*, 231-245. (b)

Tanaka-Matsumi, J., & Marsella, A. J. Cross-cultural variations in the phenomenological experience of depression: I. Word Association Studies. *Journal of Cross-Cultural Psychology*, 1976, 7, 379–396.

Tanaka-Matsumi, J., & Tharp, R. G. Teaching teachers of Hawaiian children: Consultation and training strategies. In R. Brislin & M. Hamnett (Eds.), *Topics in culture learning*, 1977, 5.

Temerlin, M. K. Suggestion effects in psychiatric diagnosis. *Journal of Nervous and Mental Disease*, 1968, *147*, 349–359.

Tharp, R. G., & Wetzel, R. J. *Behavior modification in the natural environment.* New York: Academic Press, 1969.

Thoresen, C. E., & Mahoney, M. J. *Behavioral self-control.* New York: Holt, Rinehart & Winston, 1974.

Townsend, J. M. *Cultural concepts and mental illness.* Chicago: University of Chicago Press, 1978.

Triandis, H. Culture training, cognitive complexity and interpersonal attitudes. In R. Brislin, S. Bochner, & W. Lonner (Eds.), *Cross-cultural perspectives on learning.* New York: Halstead, 1975.

Trifonovitch, G. On cross-cultural orientation techniques. *Topics in Culture Learning*, 1973, *1*.

Ullmann, L. P. Behavior therapy as a social movement. In C. M. Franks (Ed.), *Behavior therapy: Appraisal and status.* New York: McGraw-Hill, 1969.

Ullmann, L. P., & Krasner, L. *Case studies in behavior modification.* New York: Holt, Rinehart & Winston, 1965.

Ullmann, L. P., & Krasner, L. *A psychological approach to abnormal behavior.* Englewood Cliffs: Prentice-Hall, 1969 (1st ed.), 1975 (2nd ed.).

Ullmann, L. P., & Tanaka-Matsumi, J. On training for behavior modification. *Japanese Journal of Behavior Therapy*, 1978, *3*, 47–53 (in Japanese).

Vontress, C. E. Cultural barriers in the counseling relationship. *Personnel and Guidance Journal*, 1969, *48*, 11–17.

Wachtel, P. L. Psychoanalysis, behavior therapy, and the implacable experimenter: An inquiry into the consistency of personality. *Journal of Abnormal Psychology*, 1973, *82*, 324–334.

Walz, G. R., & Benjamin, L. *Transcultural counseling.* New York: Human Sciences Press, 1978.

Westermeyer, J., & Wintrob, R. "Folk" criteria for the diagnosis of mental illness in rural Laos: On being insane in sane places. *American Journal of Psychiatry*, 1979, *136*, 755–761.

Wilson, G. T., & Evans, I. M. Adult behavior therapy and the therapist-client relationship. In C. M. Franks & G. T. Wilson (Eds.), *Annual review of behavior therapy.* New York: Brunner/Mazel Publishers, 1976.

Wohl, J. Intercultural psychotherapy: Issues, questions, and reflections. In P. B. Pedersen, J. G. Draguns, W. J. Lonner, & J. E. Trimble (Eds.), *Counseling across cultures* (rev. & expanded ed.). Honolulu: University Press of Hawaii, 1981.

Wolpe, J. *Psychotherapy by reciprocal inhibition.* Palo Alto, California: Stanford University Press, 1958.

Wolpe, J. *The practice of behavior therapy.* New York: Pergamon Press, 1969.

Yap, P. M. *Comparative psychiatry: A theoretical framework.* Toronto: University of Toronto Press, 1974.

12

Psychological Tests and Intercultural Counseling

Walter J. Lonner

Psychological testing is often an important part of the counseling process, especially in the United States and many other Western countries. However, in the counseling of students from various cultural or ethnic groups, one critical question needs to be asked before testing is initiated: To what extent can Western-based psychometric devices effectively bridge the gap that may exist between the culture where the tests originated and the culture from which the client has come? With this question serving as our major concern, this chapter will consider problems that are associated with the use of tests, inventories, checklists, and other assessment devices that are found in the offices of mental health practitioners and other human services personnel who work with personal, vocational, and academic adjustment problems of persons from diverse ethnic minorities and foreign backgrounds. Little specific mention will be made of problems associated with such widespread testing programs as the Graduate Record Examinations or similar national programs at the elementary and secondary level (such as the Iowa Tests of Basic Skills). The reason for this omission may be obvious: such purely academic-oriented measures perform quite a different function than do clinical or psychological tests. Moreover, those who administer such academic- or achievement-type testing programs to students from different cultural backgrounds no doubt take into consideration such matters as differentials in previous schooling, language competencies, and other factors that may place people from different cultural backgrounds at a disadvantage when they are exposed to unfamiliar testing materials. For example, the Educational Testing Service, which administers many achievement-type testing programs, has been aware of these kinds of problems for years.[1] Most of the points raised in this chapter, though, may be validly generalized to certain problems associated with the use of such purely academic-type tests.

The points to be discussed will have varied applicability to "foreign," "minority," or "ethnically different" persons. The point of departure for "different" would be the white middle-class population of the United States, that is, the cultural group the vast majority of psychological tests was geared to in the first place. However, it cannot be assumed that foreign or ethnically different persons always depart from this reference group. Some foreign students, for example, from Canada or Great Britain, may more closely resemble the typical American college student than do students from a variety of subcultures within the United States. For instance, it might reasonably be expected that a student from Liverpool, going to school in the United States, will be more familiar with tests and their uses than a member of the Navajo nation or the Mexican American community in New Mexico. The non-American student, especially at the college level, systematically does not represent the modal citizen of his or her country. Rather, he or she may be quite cosmopolitan, and may also know more about the United States than does the typical student from Schenectady or Omaha. In some instances, the same may be true of students who come from certain minority groups within the United States.

Where a psychological test is used to elicit information from clients who come from cultures or subcultures that have not been systematically represented in the initial stages of test development, there are several issues that must be considered. In other words, we can return once again to the central theme of the chapter: To what extent can Western-based tests effectively step across cultural boundaries so that they may be useful adjuncts in counseling across cultures?

Issues in Psychological Testing That Are Applicable to the Assessment and Counseling of Culturally Different Students

Several books and journal articles that have appeared during the past decade have addressed problems asociated with intercultural assessment. These sources offer generally cautious evaluations, implying that many earlier attempts to devise "culture-fair" tests or attempts to extend various culture-bound tests to people from other cultures have been, at best, modest successes and, at worst, miserable failures. The root of this problem was nicely stated by Frijda and Jahoda (1966), who argued that for a test to be truly fair it had to be either equally familiar or equally unfamiliar to all. As either option is impossible, bias is inherent in all tests, a situation not likely to change.

One of these books, by Triandis, Vassiliou, Vassiliou, Tanaka, and Shanmugam (1972), explains various extensions of semantic differential methodology (Osgood, May, & Miron, 1975) in the measurement of subjective culture (or ways in which people evaluate and perceive others in particular cultural milieus). For example, Triandis et al. pinpointed both antecedents and consequents of behavioral dispositions, or tendencies of people from a given culture to behave in predictable ways. They also assessed the manner in which different cultural roles affect the behavior of those from other cultures. Triandis (1975) gave a different treatment of the basic rationale. There he discussed isomorphic versus nonisomorphic behavior, and how behavioral scientists in applied settings may benefit from the work done with various "cultural assimilators." Cultural assimilators (see Triandis, 1976, chap. 2) are training devices aimed to help others become more familiar with "other culture" roles, values, behavioral intentions, and so forth. Another book, by Manaster and Havighurst (1972), surveyed problems associated with the use of scales to measure values and personality. A third volume, edited by Cronbach and Drenth (1972), concerns the adaptation of "mental" tests (i.e., intelligence or ability tests) for use in other cultures. The book by Brislin, Lonner, and Thorndike (1973) discusses a wide range of methodological problems in cross-cultural psychology. It includes several chapters of direct relevance to the assessment of personological variables in intercultural counseling. The volume by Samuda (1975) concerns itself with problems in the psychological testing of American minorities. Finally, the most recent and most theoretical and practical threatment of the topic is the comprehensive chapter by Irvine and Carroll (1980).

The following topics are paramount when assessing psychological test data across cultures, or when selecting a test for use in another cultural setting:

1. the distinction between constructs and criteria;
2. the establishment of equivalence;
3. the nature of the test stimuli, including verbal as well as nonverbal material;
4. the exporting of norms;
5. response sets;
6. the tendency to infer deficits from test score differences; and
7. the cultural isomorphism of Western-based tests and the motives for taking them.

The Distinction Between Constructs and Criteria

Psychological constructs, when used interculturally, may be viewed as the "givens" inferred by psychologists which characterize and compare humans on assumed universal dimensions. Some of the more popular constructs are intelligence, anxiety, need for achievement, psychological sexuality, dependency, aggression, and other personological variables.

Criteria, on the other hand, are usually the points of evidence or proof in empirical research. Criteria usually involve measurable levels of performance or functioning that may be suggestive of the underlying construct being assessed. Psychological tests have often been described as either construct-related (that is, they relate to all or part of some psychological theory and are therefore called theoretical) or criterion-referenced (that is, they depend upon empirically established relationships and are not necessarily associated with any particular psychological theory). This distinction has been used by Anastasi (1976) and to some extent by Cronbach (1976), the two most widely used books on psychological testing in the United States. Since it may be invalid to assume that psychological constructs constitute a universal template (owing to indigenous thought or value systems, for example, or because most constructs have been developed and inferred by Western scientists), the use of construct-related tests could result in an inappropriate attribution of a construct to a person whose culture of origin may not foster the development of, or may not value, the Western-based construct. In the jargon of cross-cultural methodologists, this is "imposing an etic"—assuming a construct to be valid everywhere, or at least in the new cultural setting. The counterpart of "etic" is "emic," a term used to describe the nature of the construct from within that culture only. (For a discussion of the emic-etic distinction, see Berry, 1969; Price-Williams, 1974; Lonner, 1979.) Using a similar rationale, the same researchers may maintain that criteria are not transferable from one culture to another.

Consider an example using the popular construct of intelligence. Intelligence is an unequivocal panhuman characteristic. All cultures have a word for it, and even the most radical cultural relativist would hesitate to deny its veridicality as a powerful source of human variation. However, the actual behavioral connotations or ramifications of intelligence vary significantly across cultures. In the West, for example, intelligence is usually associated with being smart (knowledge of many things) and fast (ability to relate these known things rapidly to others). Among the Baganda people of Uganda, however, the concept of intelligence, *obugezi*, is associated with wisdom, slow thoughtfulness, and social propriety; it is not important to be fast, but it is important to be right (Wober, 1974).

Thus, the conservative solution would be to develop tests based on locally (within culture) conceived constructs, with locally valid criteria to "prove" the existence of the construct. Berry (1972) has called this approach "radical cultural relativism," as opposed to its extreme, which may be called universal construct ubiquity. Obviously, the radical extreme would lead to the dilemma of rendering comparisons across cultures impossible; every group of people would have its own noninterchangeable set of constructs and attendant criteria. Carried to an existential extreme, this line of thought would mean that every person would have his own set of constructs and criteria, a concept not unfamiliar to the counseling orientation of phenomenological theorists like Carl Rogers and George Kelly. More technically, this translates into ipsative (nonnormative) scales, in which the one and only reference point for the measurement of the construct is locked into each culture separately. Thus, the metric used within one cultural group would be noncomparable with another group's metric. The same would hold for individual persons within one culture.

A more reasonable way to view the problem would be to assume a high extensional agreement among behavioral scientists (as well as in a client-counselor dyad) as to what a construct is; how criteria document the construct's *particular* cultural manifestation may vary. For example, a counselor and his client may agree that shyness (extensionally validated by both as at least a personality adjective) is one of the client's characteristics. The counselor, knowing the overt manifestations and social or personal ramifications for shyness in his own culture, may falsely attribute these criteria to his client. However, for the client (and unknown to or overlooked by the counselor) shyness may be based on criteria that are more appropriate in an Alpine village or a Navajo village. The word shyness would be agreed upon, but its culturally determined referents would not (see Zimbardo, 1977, for evidence of cultural variations of shyness). Such differentials are probably used extensively in many intercultural counseling encounters as a ploy, or as a "foot-in-the-door," leading to more effective learning of feeling or affect on the part of both the client and the counselor. Discussing the nature of shyness and its behavioral characteristics in both the client's and the counselor's cultural experiences may lead to a more proper location of the phenomenology of the emotion.

Because of such problems associated with criteria and their cultural variations, many have concluded that criteria-based tests (such as the Minnesota Multiphasic Personality Inventory) are inappropriate for intercultural use. On the other hand, tests developed on the basis of some culturally invariant construct or construct system are more defensible for use, since they would bridge the gap that exists between the culture of the client and the culture of the counselor. Later in the chapter this problem will arise again in a discussion of the MMPI and several other personality assessment techniques.

The Establishment of Equivalence

Related to the construct-versus-criteria problem is the concern for establishing equivalence across cultures. It should be clear that if equivalence of tests is established across cultures, then these stable bases would permit substantial confidence in making intercultural comparisons. However, tests seldom completely satisfy certain standards that have been adopted by cross-cultural methodologists as goals.

Four types of equivalence have received most of the attention by methodologists. The first of these is *functional equivalence*. Cultural artifacts, institutions, rituals, roles, and so forth are variable throughout the world. However, since every society or cultural group must exercise basic functions in order to survive (Aberle, Cohen, Davis, Levy, & Sutton, 1950), comparativists are obliged to find the common ground among these cultural prerequisites before using tests to measure the presence of traits in one culture as opposed to others. One cultural group's sign of status, for example, may be a small herd of cattle; another group's functional counterpart may be a pickup truck and a chain saw; a third group's equivalent may be a trip to the Virgin Islands. Or, as Przeworski and Teune (1970) have so colorfully put it: "For specific observation a belch is a belch and nepotism is nepotism. But within an inferential framework a belch is an 'insult' or a 'compliment' and nepotism is 'corruption' or 'responsibility.' " Thus tests used across cultures should be tapping into the same functional characteristics. If they do not, then conclusions drawn from making comparisons of test scores could be flawed.

Conceptual equivalence operates at the level of the individual while functional equivalence operates at the level of the group. Conceptual equivalence is concerned with the meaning that persons attach to specific stimuli such as test items. This form of equivalence is at the root of the generally held opinion, mentioned earlier, that it is impossible to develop a truly culture-fair test. Such a test, it has been argued, would have to contain items that are either equally familiar or equally unfamiliar to everyone. In the first situation, the stimulus object, word, or sentence would have to be so ubiquitous that virtual uniformity of exposure would be guaranteed (Coca-Cola comes close to the ideal). In the second situation, one would have to go to another planet to find test material that would be totally unfamiliar to all. However, certain projective tests (see below) often make the claim that their stimuli (e.g., inkblots) are uniformly unfamiliar to everyone and thus culture-free. Inkblots, however, are not equally unfamiliar to all people, but they may tend in the direction of being relatively ambiguous, which is a different matter. Without test items that are conceptually equivalent and, at the same time, have relevance to functionally equivalent cultural indicators, interpretations of responses may be sheer guesswork.

A variant of conceptual equivalence is *linguistic*, or translation, *equivalence*. As implied, this form of equivalence must deal with equilibrating words and sentences on tests, questionnaires, interviews, and so forth so that the same meaning is communicated. This potentially complex area is so important that many people have contributed to a growing set of guidelines (see Brislin [1976] for one of the more recent treatments of the entire area of translation and its numerous problems and possible solutions). Back-translation is a term for a method with which the serious user of tests across cultures should have some familiarity. In back-translation, one takes a sentence in the first (or originating) language, translates it into the "target" language, and then has a native speaker of the target language return the translation through a bilingual interpreter. For example, if the phrase "A stitch in time saves nine" were translated, back-translated, and further refined so as to come back unscathed in meaning (that is, a little preventive maintenance now will save considerable work in the future), then a successful back-translation would have been accomplished (and so would a measure of functional equivalence, you may have noticed).

The fourth type of equivalence has been called *metric equivalence* (see Poortinga, 1975a, 1975b, for details). The points to be emphasized here are that tests and measures should be functionally equivalent, that is, they should measure the same behavioral property in different groups of people. Tests and measures should in addition be *score equivalent:* they must measure some concept or construct both quantitatively and qualitatively. A test should be measuring the same things, and at the same levels, when employed in other cultural contexts.

Sechrest, Fay, and Zaidi (1972), it should finally be mentioned, discussed the issues of equivalence in terms of the idiomatic, grammatical-syntactical, experiential, and conceptual. They also refer to what they call the paradox of equivalence. The paradox, as Sharma (1977) correctly points out, is as follows: If a test is to yield comparable results across cultures in order to demonstrate equivalence, then as it becomes more equivalent the less likely will cultural differences be found. If, on the other hand, one looks primarily for cultural differences and ignores the problem of equivalence, then the greater the likelihood of finding cultural differences. In the latter case, however, the differences that are found may reflect inadequacies in the establishment of equivalence rather than real cultural differences. The problem can be stated another way, compatible with a classical anthropological problem associated with making comparisons across cultures: As a test item or stimulus diffuses into (is carried to) another culture, its form, function, and meaning may vary in unknown and perhaps unpredictable ways.

The Nature of Stimuli: Verbal Versus Nonverbal

It has long been assumed, probably incorrectly, that tests employing the use of nonverbal stimuli are relatively unambiguous and hence more appropriate for intercultural use. Many tests, for example, use figurative analogies, mazes, and other formats which assume that abilities, intelligence, and even personality can be assessed more fairly across cultural groups if the widely variable linguistic dimension is transcended. As discussed later, this assumption has resulted in the wholesale and often careless use of projective tests interculturally, such tests having their own methodological problems (Abel, 1973; Lindzey, 1961; Spain, 1972). The same may be true of such tests as Raven's Progressive Matrices and Cattell's Culture-Fair Intelligence Test, both of which are saturated with nonverbal content.

Research on cultural and ecological influences on perceptual and cognitive style has shown that these factors can influence the way in which simple stimuli are interpreted. A classic example is a study by Hudson (1960), who investigated the ways in which different groups of individuals in both black and white South Africa interpreted simple line drawings. This work ushered in a great amount of intercultural research in the psychology of visual perception (see Deregowski [1980] for an extensive review, and Segall [1979] for an overview of the ways in which culture and ecology affect visual perception). These rather esoteric and experimental studies have minimal direct relevance for the counseling of persons from other cultures. Nevertheless, they do give us insights into an extremely important psychological process and force us to exercise caution when nonverbal stimuli are used in psychological tests. Many things might be "going on" perceptually of which we have scant or no awareness, even as we assume an invariance of process. For example, it has recently been suggested (Roth, 1978) that the reasoning used in the solution of verbal puzzles or analogies is the same type of reasoning used in the solution of nonverbal puzzles or analogies. Thus it may be illusory to assume that nonverbal tests are more fair than verbal tests simply because the former have been stripped, on the surface, of the verbal-cultural factor.

As mentioned earlier under the establishment of equivalence, it should not be assumed that verbal material—words, phrases, and sentences found in personality and intelligence tests—have the same meanings to all persons everywhere, even if they can read English well. Western-based tests and inventories, particularly those developed in the United States, are liberally endowed with subtle idioms. Before rather technical advances in translation procedures became available (Brislin, 1970; 1976), many tests were translated literally, word-for-word, without adequate attention paid to accuracies in meaning in the context of the idioms and meanings of other languages. Sechrest, Fay, and Zaidi (1972) have summarized a wide assortment of problems associated with the translation of testing and other material for cross-cultural use.

The Exportation of Norms

Test norms based on one cultural group should not be considered valid for other cultural groups. Norms, of course, include the use of percentile ranks and other reference points based on the proportion of students who meet various levels of criterion performance. Unless there is strong evidence for the invariability of such performance, one must "de-center" the various rankings and adjust the levels of performance on the basis of other factors. For example, an Eskimo student's score placing him at the fiftieth percentile using external norms could, with adjustments for language and educational differentials, place him at the seventy-fifth percentile when considering his own group. A useful example of how psychometric adjustment of test scores can lead to better culture-fairness has been given by Thorndike (1971). The basis of these adjustments was briefly explained in this way (Brislin, Lonner, & Thorndike, 1973):

> Fairness (may be approximated or developed) by setting levels of test performance that will qualify applicants or students from diverse cultural groups in proportion to the percentage of those in the groups who reach a specified level of criterion performance. Neither mean test scores nor mean criterion values alone would be used as indicators of "superior" or "inferior" performance. Different regression lines for each group as the lines relate to the same levels of criterion performance across groups would be instrumental in guiding one's use of the word "fairness."

Nor should comparisons with national norms in any country be considered valid unless invariance across cultures can be established. Without some common reference point—an external and neutral level of criterion performance, for example—sets of norms developed independently in two or more countries are just that—independent measures. Numerous researchers have used norms of convenience in comparative research, especially in the area of personality measurement. Good examples of this questionable procedure include the numerous attempts to compare the MMPI data extracted from a small number of subjects from a foreign country or ethnic group with the anchoring United States data and norms (see below). If scores are nearly identical, the intercultural extension of one set of norms may be valid. But if more than one set of scores or norms departs from the pattern of the second set of scores or norms, the less confidence one can have in interpreting the significance of the differences. Segall, Campbell, and Herskovits (1966), in their well-known investigation of visual illusions, were confident that their comparisons of perceptual and ecological processes affecting illusion susceptibility were making sense because they found such small differences between groups of subjects from many cultures. When these small differences occurred, they were generally in line with ecological hypotheses advanced by Segall et al. Had the differences been widely discrepant, a failure to communicate with the subjects (about the nature of the task, clarity of the directions, and so on) would have been the more plausible reason for score differentials. Thus, the closer norms or scores across

cultures "fit," the more likely those norms are comparable, since frequent cross-norm points of articulation could not be due to statistical error or the failure to communicate.

An example may help to explain how these articulating scores can
build confidence in the use of a particular test among diverse groups of
foreign students. The United States' Strong Vocational Interest Blank
(SVIB), used in both translated and untranslated forms for possible extension to other countries, yielded few significant occupational scale differences among subjects from nine Western nations (Lonner & Adams,
1972). Since a large number of interest scale differences were possible,
the essential uniformity of profiles across all countries suggests that the
inventory did about the same job of measuring interests in all the countries sampled. Had there been many significant differences, two conclusions could have been drawn: first, the scales yielding the significant differences were obviously not comparable across countries, and second, a
number of the concordant scales may have been articulated across countries purely by chance. Thus, not knowing which, if any, of the scales
may have accurately measured interests across two or more countries,
the entire array of cross-national profiles would have had to be dismissed
as too dangerous to salvage for valid interpretative purposes.

Response Sets

In the psychological testing literature there are many response sets
(sometimes referred to as response styles) that could affect test scores.
The response set of *acquiescence*, for instance, generally refers to the
tendency of a subject to agree (or its reverse, to disagree) with extremes,
usually on attitude statements. Some foreign students taking tests may
tend to say yes out of politeness, for instance. Asian students' disposition
comes to mind as one quick and stereotyped example of this phenomenon. The response set of *social desirability* refers to the tendency of subjects to answer in the direction they consider to be the more socially
favorable alternative. Other response sets include *evasiveness* (unwillingness to commit oneself) and *carelessness* (the making of inconsistent judgments). A brief summary of response sets and the types of instruments in
which each can most liberally be found has been given in Fiske (1970).
Another problem, called *extreme response style*, was the focus of a cross-
cultural study by Chun, Campbell, and Yoo (1974).

Unless a psychological test or other data-gathering device has a built-
in sensor to detect the presence of response sets, any one of these response
sets may affect the final score. Any client from another culture will likely
possess an assortment of cultural values and general culture-originating
personality factors that predispose him to respond in ways that appear
unique to a United States psychologist or counselor. For example, people

who have been conditioned not to take a middle-of-the-road position will likely respond infrequently to the "?" in the "Yes-?-No" response format frequently found in personality tests. Such dispositions could lead to distorted or inflated responses, especially if the test has not been normed on the culture of which the student is a member. Thus, a critical step to be taken before unusual or bizarre profiles or scores are interpreted would be to ascertain how response sets may have influenced the results. If they are even slightly suspect, the safest alternative would be to ignore altogether the results rather than to try to bend interpretations around them.

Response sets tend to invalidate test scores in terms of uniculture norms. However, there may be times when the response sets themselves could be helpful in assessing particular aspects of a student's personality or attitudinal dispositions. For example, it may be of significant interest to discuss with the client his or her reasons for responding in unexpected ways, and these stated reasons may give clues to ways in which the client approaches life situations.

The above possibilities necessitate a brief summary of a methodological controversy that for many years has surrounded response sets and response style. As Anastasi (1976, p. 520) has pointed out, research on these response tendencies has gone through two principal stages. They were first considered irrelevant, a merely unwanted source of error variance. Attempts were therefore made to adjust test formats or scoring procedures in order to minimize these effects. Later they were regarded as indicators of personality dispositions, worthy of study in their own right. For instance, Crowne and Marlowe (1964) developed an argument that the response set or *social desirability* (or responding to inventories and tests in a manner so as to put up a good front) is related to a person's need for social approval and avoidance of criticism. Block (1965) and Rorer (1965) can be consulted for arguments that response sets or styles are not critical factors affecting test scores. On the other side of the coin are those who suggest that response styles cannot be dismissed simply as sources of error variance or methodological artifacts (e.g., Jackson & Messick, 1958; Bentler, Jackson, & Messick, 1972).

The Tendency to Infer Deficits from Test Score Differences
Counselors should be wary of the tendency to overinterpret test score differences, a situation in which the test interpreter is generally motivated to account for lower scores (which may, for example, suggest pathology, lowered intelligence, or some other deficiency). Typically, personality tests are constructed so as to scale both the highs and lows of personality functioning (see below). Hence, any tendency to overinterpret these tests may be to make high scores higher than they really are; similar tendencies may exist for lower scores. Overinterpretation by clinicians is

difficult to avoid, for they naturally want to construct a coherent and complete picture of a client's personality. Nature abhors a vacuum; counselors abhor incomplete information about their client.

When a member of a culture different from one's own does not do well on standard intelligence tests or on the tasks requiring mental gyrations designed by psychologists, then reasons for the differences advanced by test interpreters may fall into an artificially imposed deficit column. Cole and Bruner (1971) have not overstated the case when they noted that intelligence tests tell us what people cannot do, but fall short in telling us what they can do (for informative reviews of culture and cognitive, perceptual, and intellectual processes, see Berry & Dasen, 1974; Cole & Scribner, 1974; Serpell, 1976; Pick, 1980; Price-Williams, 1980). An example given by Cole (1975) exemplifies the potential problem. His remarks stem from his reaction to numerous research findings that many people throughout the world fail on tasks designed to measure whether or not the Piagetian notion of conservation has been reached (e.g., a "nonconserving" person may report that there is more water when it is poured from a single tall beaker into a series of shorter beakers). Cole writes:

> Are we to believe that aborigine adults (who may earlier have failed to convince the researcher that they can "conserve" water) will store water in tall thin cans in order to have more water? . . . Do they think they lose water when they pour it from a bucket into a barrel? I am tempted to believe that they would have disappeared long ago were this the case.

The same point is valid for the more standard ability tests that may be imposed on foreign students. Unless compelling corroborative evidence from varied external sources suggests that test scores are valid, no inferences suggestive of deficits in ability or in personality should be drawn. Scores on psychological tests are, of course, incomplete representations of a person. But test scores are certainly better than nothing at all. One may argue that reasonably good tests given under optimal conditions to students from different cultural backgrounds are in fact more reliable initial representations of behavioral predispositions than is an initial interview or other information of a highly subjective nature.

The Cultural Isomorphism of Western-based Tests

By the time an American youngster has graduated from high school, he has taken dozens of tests designed to measure his personality, abilities, achievement, intelligence, and potential for success in college or in the occupational world. These tests, especially those of intelligence and school achievement, are isomorphic to the competitive, technological, and success-oriented West; that is, they are part of the system and are good forecasts of what is to come in the academic and business world. Not only are most students from most countries unfamiliar with psychological tests, but the tests may be a parody of whatever may be isomorphic to measures of academic performance or promise in their own countries.

In the context of determining levels of intellectual functioning among American ethnic groups, psychologists generally concede that the primary source of tested differences in intelligence lies in the subject's level of motivation. (See Labov, 1970, for an excellent example of how a researcher can elicit good responses from minority group children by examining which factors in a testing or interview situation are important to the subject.) When a member of a minority group sees no likely payoff for taking assorted tests, why should he bother? In a similar vein, Pedersen (1971) has found evidence in the literature suggesting that a foreign student's motivation to learn English is correlated with his desire to integrate with the American community or to remain in the United States after his education. A payoff is what drives the student to English proficiency.

The analogue source of variability between American and foreign college students likely can be accounted for by two dimensions—a familiarity–unfamiliarity dimension and a differential culture–test isomorphism dimension.

Attempts to Resolve One or More of the Issues

We have now briefly surveyed seven problem areas associated with intercultural testing. It is now appropriate to discuss a few ways that testing experts have tried to circumvent these problems.

There have been numerous attempts, for example, to minimize the Euro-American bias in many psychological assessment instruments. By devising tests that contain stimuli—both verbal and nonverbal—that cut across cultural lines, or by adequately norming existing tests on subjects from many cultures, testers may be able to make more valid comparisons of test scores across cultures. But realistically, the problems may never be fully resolved. Nevertheless, those who wish to examine these problems in more complete detail are invited to consult the recent works, mentioned earlier, that address themselves to these problems and to related methodological concerns. These books have surveyed in considerably more depth than I have in this chapter the problems of testing, adaptation, and interpretation.

It may be instructive and informative to consider some examples of some tests that have enjoyed at least moderate success among persons from various cultural backgrounds. A brief review of some tests that have been designed to measure intelligence or specialized abilities will be followed by a more extensive look at a handful of personality-type tests. At the end of the chapter projective techniques will receive separate attention.

Intellectual Assessment

The Cattell Culture-Fair Intelligence Test is one of several attempts to develop a measure of general intelligence through the use of nonverbal material (see Brislin et al., 1973). It consists of various forms, but the format is consistent: items require the subject to complete a series, to classify objects that belong together, and to complete patterns that amount to figurative analogies. The Cattell Culture-Fair may exceed some tests in its alleged comprehensiveness in tapping various intellectual dimensions, but it certainly does not exceed the Kohs Blocks or the Raven Matrices for sheer usage. Both of these popular tests capitalize on spatial-perceptual relations; both are assumed to be good indices of the general or "g" conception of intelligence. They have been useful largely because they are fun to take. All children like to play with blocks, and with the Kohs, children merely have to construct patterns by following diagrams. Similarly with the Raven Matrices. The test is nearly self-administering and it is engrossing. People seem to enjoy solving the nonverbal problems which they face.

The Kohs Blocks, Raven Matrices, and other spatial-perceptual tests and tasks have been used extensively across cultures in attempts to measure and understand cultural variations in Witkin, Dyk, Faterson, Goodenough, and Karp's (1974) concept of psychological differentiation. It has been hypothesized and supported by research in a number of cultural settings that certain cultural and ecological factors foster the development of a field-independent cognitive style (where characteristics of autonomy, a great sense of separate identity, and nonconformity are more apt to be found). On the other hand, some cultures foster the development of relatively undifferentiated individuals, who are termed field-dependent. The cognitive style of field dependence characteristically is associated with such traits or tendencies as group orientation, conformity, and a relatively low sense of separate identity. As one may surmise from this brief description of traits found on either end of this continuum, people who score high on Kohs Blocks, Raven Matrices, and similar tests are found to be more field independent. This cognitive style dimension, which cuts across intellectual, social, and personality domains, has received a great deal of cross-cultural attention. The reader may want to become familiarized with this popular construct and its concomitant cultural and subcultural variations (see Berry, 1976; Witkin & Berry, 1975; Witkin & Goodenough, 1981).

The D-48 Test is an interesting nonverbal test of intelligence for the simple reason that it cuts across linguistic and cultural lines by using the format of the domino, which has been around for more than four thousand years. Hence the domino may be among the more familiar stimuli among cultures. The researcher Domino (1968) reported on the use of various tests with foreign students from twenty-one countries. He showed that of four culture-fair intelligence tests employed, the D-48 correlated best with grades and was easiest to administer. With test construction logic similar to the logic used in the construction of the D-48, the Perceptual Acuity Test (Gough & McGurk, 1967) may be regarded as a useful tool for intercultural comparisons. It capitalizes on types of visual illusions, responses to which are known to vary according to cultural and ecological factors (Segall et al., 1966).

Standard intelligence tests like the Wechsler Adult Intelligence Scale or the Stanford Binet (see Anastasi, 1976; Cronbach, 1976) have been used abundantly across cultures, with varying degrees of success. Their use has been so extensive that we cannot afford the luxury, in this chapter, to devote much space to the numerous reasons for their successes and failures. However, largely as a reaction against the alleged and implicit cultural unfairness of the Wechsler and similar tests (which invariably contain such questions as "When is Washington's birthday" and "Who wrote the *Iliad?*"), there have been several attempts to develop intelligence tests that are as fair to specific minority groups in the United States as the Wechsler is "fair" to the affluent white. One of these is called the BITCH test, an acronym for Black Intelligence Test of Cultural Homogeneity (or Black Intelligence Test Counterbalanced for Honkies, if one wishes to be in an aggressively humorous mood). Another test goes by the title of the Chitling Test, referring to a popular item on the menu of a traditional and perhaps stereotyped American black family. Both tests have the same rationale: items can be developed which measure the levels of intelligence in a particular cultural milieu (for example, most white Americans are not as aware of Booker T. Washington's birthday as they are of Abraham Lincoln's; also, in black English, most whites do not know that to be "bad" is really "good"). These "tests" have made their point: every ethnic group has its own slang, idioms, heroes, and cultural legacies. This point can be proven ad infinitum, but valid intercultural comparisons could not be made via the use of tests unless at least some of the items common to tests are first identified.

The Assessment of Personological Variables

The assessment of intelligence across cultures poses serious problems of definition, method, and interpretation. Personality testing across cultures is fraught with at least the same type of difficulties. The field of culture and personality, in fact, is currently in a state of flux and confusion, as cogently stated by Draguns (1979a; 1979b). By briefly taking a look at several popular personality measures, including their underlying assumptions and cross-cultural applications, we may gain a better contextual understanding of the problems associated with the appraisal of personality variables in other cultural contexts. Five measures will be considered: *Cattell's 16 PF Test*, the *Minnesota Multiphasic Personality Inventory* (MMPI), the *California Psychological Inventory* (CPI), the *Locus of Control Scale*, and the *State-Trait Anxiety Inventory*.

Cattell's 16 PF Test purports to measure 16 personality factors or traits. The source traits (so named because Cattell believes them to be at the basic source of human personality functioning) were identified through the technique of factor analysis. A diversity of data, coming from questionnaires, personal history documents, autobiographical statements, and other sources, were factor-analyzed. The result is the 16 PF, which measures the extent to which persons are high or low on each of these scales (e.g., reserved versus outgoing, trusting versus suspicious, and relaxed versus tense).

The 16 PF is one of the products of Cattell's theory of personality (Cattell & Dreger, 1977), a theory that is based upon many years of statistical endeavors. Since Universal Indices have been assigned to each of the sixteen factors, it is evident that Cattell and his associates believe these factors to be interculturally valid. Thus in using the 16 PF, one would be tempted to interpret scale similarities as confirmation of the convergence of source traits and scale differences as evidence of true cultural differences.

The *Minnesota Multiphasic Personality Inventory* (MMPI). A vast literature and colorful history surrounds the MMPI, which is one of the most widely used and controversial paper and pencil personality tests ever devised. Its original intent was to measure the extent to which an individual's responses to the 566 items (e.g., "I love to go to dances" or "I have had some very unusual religious experiences") were like the responses of individuals who fell into discrete psychiatric groupings such as hypochondriacal reactions, schizoid or paranoid tendencies, or manic depressive disorders. The logic here was that deviations of personality paralleled the so-called medical model; the early German psychiatrist Emil Kraepelin used this model to develop a psychiatric taxonomic system, an influence which is still felt in clinical practice. Nowadays the names of the scales are not nearly so important as the configuration of responses to the items when the profile is interpreted. However, the logic now used is similar to the logic of the medical model: people who show similar patterns in personality dysfunction or in poor adjustment to crises tend to respond in highly similar ways to the items. Graham (1977) and Duckworth (1979) have written two of the more recent books that outline the essence of the MMPI and its contemporary usage.

In some ways the MMPI can be considered inappropriate for use across cultures. It started with a Western system of psychiatric classification, its original normative groups came primarily from small groups of University of Minnesota hospital patients (and, for contrast, visitors to the hospital), and it is essentially atheoretical or criterion-oriented. In other ways, however, the MMPI can be considered an excellent cross-cultural assessment device, at least on a continued exploratory basis. First, it is unlikely that an infinite plasticity of personality disorganization or dysfunction exists (Draguns, 1980); some commonality is likely to be found if not already evident. Second, the mountains of MMPI data that have been accumulated give clinicians and researchers one of the richest storehouses of psychometric data ever amassed (over 70 translations of the MMPI are in use). Third, as patterns of complaints and disorders as well as systems of diagnosis diffuse across and within cultures, there may be an increasing tendency to view both symptom and diagnosis in universalistic dimensions (Draguns, 1980).[2]

A number of investigators have considered problems associated with the cross-cultural use of the MMPI (e.g., Lanyon, 1968; Glatt, 1969; Kadri, 1971; and Gynther, 1972). Gynther's can be singled out as an informative presentation of numerous problems associated with the use of the MMPI in cultures other than where it was developed. His concern was whether or not the MMPI can be viewed as a source of discrimination rather than a true and accurate measure of adjustment. In his review of the literature, Gynther concluded that small but consistent differences in the black versus white scores represent differences between blacks and whites in values, social expectations, perceptions, and roles rather than differences in adjustment. His review suggests that the principal value held by blacks is "distrust of society or social cynicism," a finding similar to those of Triandis (1976), who used an entirely different method to measure black versus white differentials in the perception of the social environment. In other words, Gynther and Triandis may have identified an important factor that differentiates blacks from whites in how they cut up the pie of experience. It is likely that any ethnic or minority group, in any nation-state, has, in general, different perceptions and expectations.

Two recent books concern the extension of the MMPI to populations which were not represented in the original norming process. One, a *Handbook of Cross-National MMPI Research* (Butcher & Pancheri, 1976), is totally devoted to the topic. A very useful guide, the *Handbook* examines a variety of issues surrounding the use of the MMPI in other countries (e.g., translation problems, norms, international cooperation, and so forth). It also presents a useful summary of computerized services, ongoing projects, and prospects for the future use of the MMPI. A more recent volume (Butcher, 1979) contains two chapters that are relevant to the scope of this chapter. One of them, by Butcher and Clark, discusses ongoing MMPI work on an international scale. The other chapter, by

Gynther, is rich with information concerning MMPI use with the major ethnic minority groups in the United States. It updates and goes beyond his 1972 paper (cited above); his search of the literature led him to conclude that black-white personality differences on the MMPI are real and substantial.

The *California Psychological Inventory* (CPI) is a 480-item self-report measure of 18 personality dimensions (such as dominance, sociability, responsibility, self-control, and femininity). While many of its items come directly from the MMPI, Gough, the developer of the CPI, claims that the items tap important dimensions of social interaction that occur every day. These "folk concepts," as Gough calls them, are "aspects and attributes of interpersonal behavior that are to be found in all cultures and societies, and that possess a direct and integral relationship to all forms of social interaction" (Gough, 1968, p. 57). Thus, unlike the development of the MMPI and many other personality inventories, one factor considered during the development of the CPI was its potential usefulness in a variety of cultural settings, both in the United States and abroad. A comprehensive CPI handbook has been compiled by Megargee (1972).

Several CPI scales have received considerable attention across cultures; this attention usually focuses on whether or not selected scales are invariant across cultures. The Femininity (Fe) scale, for instance, was studied in Japan by using 600 students in a Japanese university (Nishiyama, 1975). Since 30 of the 38 scale items which make up the Fe scale yielded differences in the same direction as in the original normative group, the author concluded that the scale is sufficiently robust for use in Japan. Similar conclusions have been reached by individuals studying the Fe scale, and other scales, in many different countries.[3]

The *Locus of Control Scale*, otherwise known as the I-E Scale (Internal–External), is a popular, quick method to measure the "locus of control" of reinforcement. The method was originally developed by Rotter, a social psychologist, who suggested that some persons, by virtue of the nature of the social environment that fosters achievement and autonomy, can be characterized as "internals"—that is, reinforcement comes from within the individual since they control the environments where reinforcement is random or capricious; an "external" may believe that fate, luck, or chance is the rule of thumb in life (Rotter, 1966). This construct led to the development and widespread use of the I-E Scale. The I-E Scale consists of 29 items, 23 of which are scored in order to give the individual a score of from 0 to 23, with higher scores being in the external direction. The saliency and popularity of this construct has resulted in two books (Phares, 1976; Lefcourt, 1976) and many articles. Scales for use with children have been developed, as have alternate adult scales.

Locus of control, however, is likely shaped and packaged differently in other groups. Numerous studies have examined the nature of the I-E Scale in a variety of sociocultural settings, subjecting the responses to factor and other statistical analyses. The results of these studies suggest that when subjects from widely differing cultures are given the scale, their responses might form their own unique clusters. The reason underlying such different clustering can be traced to differing perceptions of the social, political, and interpersonal environment. For example, Nagelschmidt and Jakob (1977) gave the I-E Scale to a sample of Brazilian women. Two factors, "externality" and "fatalism," emerged, casting doubt (as have many other studies) over the unidimensionality of the construct as originally conceived. Munro (1979), in his examination of the Scale's factor structure among blacks and whites in Africa, found marked similarity of the "control cognitions" of the two groups. Munro suggests that the modification of the content of the Scale should be attempted "to explore the qualitative differences in cognitions about events which have more immediate importance in the personal, social, and vocational lives of people in various cultures" (1979, p. 171). Finally, Jones and Zoppel (1979) have presented evidence suggesting that the I-E Scale lacks equivalent meaning between blacks in Jamaica and blacks in the United States.

The *State-Trait Anxiety Inventory* (STAI), the last paper-and-pencil personality-type test we will consider, is one of nearly a hundred measures that have been developed to assess the psychological construct of anxiety. As a basic human emotion, anxiety (alternately called threat, fear, dread, stress, and sometimes panic in the psychological literature) is perhaps the most common affect that the counselor will witness in his clients. Spielberger, a clinical psychologist, developed the STAI as a measure of anxiety as both a general personality trait which may permeate a person's entire personality fabric and as a state, or a momentary and situationally induced property of emotional functioning (see Spielberger, 1972; 1975). The STAI is enjoying increased usage, primarily in research on anxiety as a psychological process, across cultures. For example, the book edited by Spielberger and Diaz-Guerrero (1976) contains research reports concerned with the use of the inventory among the French, Turkish, Greeks, Italians, Canadians, Swedes, and groups of persons of Spanish and Mexican ancestry. The construct of anxiety was also important in the consideration of personality development in the United States (Austin, Texas) and Mexico City (Holtzman, Diaz-Guerrero, & Swartz, 1975).

Spielberger and his collaborators intend to develop anxiety inventories that are useful for both intra- and intercultural application and research. In so doing, they need to take into account the *etic* (universal) dimensions of anxiety as well as its *emic* (culture-specific) characteristics. They need also to take into account other problems, such as the hypothesized unidimensionality of the construct. Recall that in the brief discussion of Rotter's Locus of Control Scale, many studies suggest that the construct is multidimensional. In the age of interaction, one must consider the person-by-situation-by-time nature of personality functioning (Endler & Magnusson, 1976; Mischel, 1979). However, as the best developed measure of cross-cultural anxiety, the STAI merits consideration by those who wish to gain a better appreciation of this nebulous and important emotion.

In his report concerning the measurement of anxiety, Sharma (1977) summarized several major methodological problems associated with the use of anxiety scales for making cross-cultural comparisons. To some extent the problems Sharma identified are common among all attempts to measure personological variables interculturally. Thus it is appropriate to close this section by mentioning once again some major problems that stand in the way of counselors who wish to use tests in making comparisons across cultures, or who wish to assess the characteristics of one person.

Sharma discussed problems of translation, a topic we examined earlier in this chapter. He also identified two other problems. One is the familiar problem of interpretation. Since cross-cultural comparisons are plagued by several confounds (e.g., language is confounded with culture, as are test-taking attitudes), it is often difficult to draw many strong conclusions when all that one has are test scores. Therefore, methodologists (e.g., Campbell, 1969) recommend a "plausible rival hypothesis" approach when conducting cross-cultural research. This approach suggests that researchers be constantly vigilant concerning potential alternative ways to explain their data, in addition to the hypotheses they are actually testing. Also, support for test scores from nontest sources should be sought. This could lead to a triangulation of results, thereby increasing explanatory power and perhaps offering some validity for tests or other assessment devices.

The other problem pointed out by Sharma concerns situation variables. Different situations, such as actual physical danger, ambiguous circumstances, and daily routines, will evoke different levels of anxiety for different people, and these factors can vary widely across cultures as well. Perhaps one can generalize from research on anxiety and extend the same kind of cautionary note to most other types of testing, especially in the personality domain.

The Special Case of Projective Techniques

For fifty years or more, many attempts have been made to study interrelationships between culture and personality or psychopathology by projective methods. A special sort of psychological test, one common characteristic of projectives is that they tend to maximize rather than minimize stimulus ambiguity. Hence it is assumed that any meaning given to the stimuli is a function of how the subject projects his wants, needs, anxieties, or dispositions into his response. In other words, responses are assumed not to be a function of uniformly perceived properties of stimuli, a situation that is the opposite of what would be desired in intelligence or ability testing. Typical projectives include the Rorschach inkblots, the Thematic Apperception Test, and completion-type tests which may, for instance, require the subject to respond briefly ten or twenty times to the sentence, "I am . . . ." Rabin (1968) classified and discussed a great variety of projective methods, and Reynolds and Sundberg (1976) document some contemporary trends in the use of projectives, which seem to be on the decline.

The most likely reason for this decline is that these clinical methods have generally been under siege during the past fifteen or twenty years (Lindzey, 1961; Molish, 1972; Spain, 1972), especially in the cross-cultural arena. With so much concern about their validity and reliability, skepticism has inhibited their use. Lindzey points out the following characteristic flaws in cross-cultural research employing projective methodology: (1) Inferences drawn from projectives have often been contaminated by knowledge of other data or information outside the testing situation; (2) Investigators have tended to use subjective impressions when relating projective data and inferences derived from ethnographic sources; (3) Many features of the testing situation could have affected the results of the tests; (4) Factors such as age, sex, and education, as well as alternative hypotheses concerning the results, are seldom mentioned in published reports; (5) The examiner's influence on test performance is usually left unaccounted for; (6) Problems of sample comparability across cultures have been largely ignored; (7) Methods of scoring and interpretation have depended heavily upon procedures developed in the United States and Europe and extended uncritically to cross-cultural studies; (8) Few studies have tried to integrate findings derived from projective techniques with data derived from other, more traditional anthropological techniques; (9) There have been tendencies to treat group averages as descriptive of the entire group, which ignores widespread intracultural individual variation; and (10) Little evidence is available suggesting that there is much accumulation of sophistication and wisdom in using projectives. (See also Brislin, Lonner, & Thorndike [1973] and Holtzman [1980] for brief summaries of the shortcomings pointed out by Lindzey.)

Obviously, any single study that has employed projective methodology would certainly not be guilty of committing all of the above errors. Also, by inserting "psychological test" or "interview data" in the place of "projectives," we can see that all forms of inferential material gathered from individuals in varied cultural settings have great flaw potential. In spite of these potential pitfalls, there are many adherents who fully support and even extol the virtues of projectives. One representative supporter is the anthropologist DeVos. DeVos (1976) asserts that those who consider comparative research with projectives as impossible are frequently those self-styled authorities who may never have had first-hand experience with projectives in one culture let alone several cultures. In defense of their use, DeVos believes that projectives can be validly used in other cultural settings, since they can tap into nonorganic (learned) personality patterns that are a function of "universally recognizable capacities in human beings that go through a process of maturation" (p. 285). DeVos argues that the tendency to think rationally and the propensity to "regress" to "pre-causal cognitive patterns under emotional duress or stress" are universal, as is the capacity for altered states of consciousness. That being the case, he therefore argues against relativism and for comparativism when assessing components of maturation, including social adaptation or personal adjustment. Consequently, projective-based studies which tap these universal sources of human processes of adaptation can extract useful data that other methods may miss.

One of the advantages of projectives (and ironically one of their disadvantages as well, when considering the desire for a high degree of standardization in tests) is their seemingly endless potential for modification. For example, Edgerton (1971) studied four East African tribes, with respect to variations in their levels of adaptation. Part of his project involved an examination of values that these tribes differentially held. To study their values, Edgerton prepared four drawings, one for each culture, depicting a total of nine social situations or interpersonal encounters. The essential content of the drawings was the same; variations took into consideration local clothing, hairstyle, and facial features so as to capitalize both on the emic features of the separate sets of drawings and the etic nature of the values the pictures were designed to assess. Similarly, many attempts have been made to ethnicize the Thematic Apperception Test. Many of these modifications are summarized in Brislin et al. (1973); a search in social psychiatric or cross-cultural journals will yield contemporary examples of these attempts to develop more culturally relevant stimulus materials.

Various other modifications and applications of numerous projectives are briefly summarized in Holtzman's (1980) review of the cross-cultural use of projective methodology. Holtzman devoted a significant portion of that review to a contrast between the Rorschach inkblots and his own test, the Holtzman Inkblot Techniuqe (HIT). The Rorschach technique, as Holtzman points out, poses serious problems for cross-cultural research. The same problems would be of concern to anyone working in a cross-cultural counseling setting. Standard Rorschach procedure is as follows: (1) responses are elicited from the ten inkblots, five in black and white and five in various colors; (2) the subject tells the examiner what he sees while the examiner writes down the responses; and (3) the subject is asked to look at each inkblot again, and this time a "detailed inquiry" about the percepts takes place.

Interpretations of the responses to the Rorschach, often of a psychoanalytic nature, are then attempted. Such interpretations require intimate knowledge of psychoanalysis and, if used in other cultures, a detailed knowledge of the culture. The psychometric weaknesses of the Rorschach and the influence of situational factors in both the subject's responses and the examiner's interpretation have restricted its use in cross-cultural counseling.

Thus Holtzman and his colleagues developed the HIT to overcome the shortcomings of the Rorschach while retaining the better features of the method. The HIT consists of two parallel forms, each containing 45 matched inkblots. There are two practice cards common to both forms. Only one response per card is requested of subjects and a simple, standardized inquiry follows each response. Objective scoring procedures and criteria have resulted in psychometric properties that exceed those of the Rorschach. Moreover, the similarity of factor structures across cultures, as well as the availability of impressively accurate computerized interpretations of basic personality variables, suggest that Lindzey's (1961) trenchant criticisms of projectives—which are now twenty years old—may be quite overstated in view of recent work with the HIT.

Although the HIT has been used in numerous cross-cultural research projects, its most extensive use has been among American and Mexican nationals, and Mexican Americans (see especially Holtzman, Diaz-Guerrero, & Swartz, 1975). Gamble's (1972) review of the HIT, part of which is concerned with its cross-cultural validity, concluded with strong support for this version of inkblot perception as a means of studying personality. From the contemporary perspective of cross-cultural counseling, the use of the HIT can therefore be encouraged, if indeed the use of projective methods is indicated in a particular case. At the same time, the ongoing examination of the validity of the HIT and other projectives must be encouraged and demanded. The inherent subjectivity, from both the subject's and the examiner's perspective, involving stimuli that may or may not have common meaning across cultures, suggests that projectives may always promise more hope for truly common and valid bases of cross-culturally useful data than they will produce.

Summary

Psychological tests have traditionally been important adjuncts to the counseling process. With the increased interest in counseling persons who come from different cultural backgrounds, counselors must be aware of certain problems associated with the cross-cultural use of psychological tests. In this chapter we have considered seven problem areas associated with the use of tests in other cultural settings, or with people who have been socialized in cultures different from those of the counselor. Several cross-culturally useful tests were briefly described; these tests are representative of more or less "culturally appropriate" measures in the intelligence-abilities domain as well as the personality area. A discussion of projective techniques and methodology was also presented.

This review is intended neither as an endorsement nor a condemnation of the psychological assessment of persons from cultural backgrounds different from the counselor's sphere of experience. Many counselors, psychiatrists, and other mental health workers have never used tests routinely. The difficulties associated with their use across cultures will serve only to reinforce their preference to use the interview, medical reports, academic records, or other means to develop a dossier of information for the mutual benefit of this professional interaction. Among others, however, psychological tests are considered extremely important, for they lend themselves to the collection of data in a systematic and standardized fashion and can therefore supplement information gathered about the client by other means. The chapter is, then, addressed to routine and potential users of psychological tests, alerting them to some of the more persistent obstacles that should be overcome before psychological test data can be considered as useful as desired in cross-cultural counseling.

Notes

1. A good source of information about ongoing international research on tests and testing problems is the Educational Testing Service's *International Newsletter*.

2. A recent international conference on personality assessment was devoted essentially to the cross-cultural use of the MMPI (Butcher, Hama, & Matsuyama, 1979). Although this is a valuable collection of papers, the publication may be hard to find in a library. Professor James N. Butcher of the University of Minnesota Department of Psychology may be contacted about its availability.

3. Counselors and researchers who are interested in learning more about the CPI and its current applications may want to write the Institute for Personality Assessment and Research at the University of California at Berkeley, which is the center of activity in CPI matters.

References

Abel, T. M. *Psychological testing in cultural contexts.* New Haven, Connecticut: College and University Press, 1973.

Aberle, D. F., Cohen, A. K., Davis, A. K., Levy, M. J., & Sutton, F. X. The functional prerequisites of society. *Ethics*, 1950, *60*, 100–111.

Anastasi, A. *Psychological testing* (4th ed.). New York: Macmillan, 1976.

Bentler, P. M., Jackson, D. N., & Messick, S. A rose by any other name. *Psychological Bulletin*, 1972, 77, 109–113.

Berry, J. W. On cross-cultural comparability. *International Journal of Psychology*, 1969, 4, 119–128.

Berry, J. W. Radical cultural relativism and the concept of intelligence. In L. J. Cronbach & P. J. D. Drenth (Eds.), *Mental tests and cultural adaptation*. The Hague: Mouton, 1972.

Berry, J. W. *Human ecology and cognitive style: Comparative studies in cultural and psychological adaptation.* Beverly Hills: Sage/Halsted, 1976.

Berry, J. W., & Dasen, P. R. (Eds.). *Culture and cognition.* London: Methuen, 1974.

Block, J. *The challenge of response sets.* New York: Appleton-Century-Crofts, 1965.

Brislin, R. W. Back-translation for cross-cultural research. *Journal of Cross-Cultural Psychology*, 1970, 1, 185–216.

Brislin, R. W. (Ed.). *Translation: application and research.* New York: Gardner Press, 1976.

Brislin, R. W., Lonner, W. J., & Thorndike, R. M. *Cross-cultural research methods.* New York: John Wiley & Sons, 1973.

Butcher, J. N. (Ed.) *New developments in the use of the MMPI.* Minneapolis, Minnesota: University of Minnesota Press, 1979.

Butcher, J. N., Hama, H., & Matsuyama, Y. *Proceedings of the Sixth International Conference on Personality Assessment.* Doshisha University, Kyoto, Japan, July 1979.

Butcher, J. N., & Pancheri, P. *A handbook of cross-national MMPI research.* Minneapolis, Minnesota: University of Minnesota Press, 1976.

Campbell, D. T. Perspective: Artifact and control. In R. Rosenthal & R. Rosnow (Eds.), *Artifact in behavioral research.* New York: Academic Press, 1969.

Cattell, R. B., & Dreger, R. M. (Eds.). *Handbook of modern personality theory.* Washington, D.C.: Hemisphere, 1977.

Chun, K., Campbell, J., & Yoo, J. Extreme response style in cross-cultural research: A reminder. *Journal of Cross-Cultural Psychology*, 1974, 5, 465–480.

Cole, M. An ethnographic psychology of cognition. In R. W. Brislin, S. Bochner, & W. J. Lonner (Eds.), *Cross-cultural perspectives on learning.* New York: John Wiley & Sons, Halsted, 1975.

Cole, M., & Bruner, J. S. Cultural differences and inferences about psychological processes. *American Psychologist*, 1971, 26, 867–876.

Cole, M., & Scribner, S. *Culture and thought: A psychological introduction.* New York: John Wiley & Sons, 1974.

Cronbach, L. J. *Essentials of psychological testing* (4th ed.). New York: Harper & Row, 1976.

Cronbach, L. J., & Drenth, P. J. D. (Eds.). *Mental tests and cultural adaptation.* The Hague: Mouton, 1972.

Crowne, D. P., & Marlowe, D. *The approval motive: Studies in evaluative dependence.* New York: Wiley, 1964.

Deregowski, J. B. Perception. In H. C. Triandis & W. J. Lonner (Eds.), *Hand-*

book of cross-cultural psychology, Vol. 3: Basic Processes. Boston: Allyn & Bacon, 1980.

DeVos, G. A. The interrelationship of social and psychological structures in transcultural psychiatry. In W. P. Lebra (Ed.), *Culture-bound syndromes, ethnopsychiatry, and alternate therapies.* Honolulu: University Press of Hawaii, 1976.

Domino, G. Culture-free tests and the academic achievement of foreign students. *Journal of Consulting and Clinical Psychology,* 1968, *32,* 102.

Draguns, J. G. Culture and personality. In A. J. Marsella, R. Tharp, & T. Ciborowski (Eds.), *Cross-cultural perspectives on psychology.* New York: Academic Press, 1979. (a)

Draguns, J. G. Culture and personality: Old field, new directions. In L. Eckensberger, W. Lonner, & Y. Poortinga (Eds.), *Cross-cultural contributions to psychology.* Lisse, The Netherlands: Swets and Zeitlinger, 1979. (b)

Draguns, J. G. Psychopathology. In H. C. Triandis & J. G. Draguns (Eds.), *Handbook of cross-cultural psychology, Vol. 6: Psychopathology.* Boston: Allyn & Bacon, 1980.

Duckworth, J. *MMPI interpretation manual for counselors and clinicians* (2nd ed.). Muncie, Indiana: Accelerated Development, Inc., 1979.

Edgerton, R. B. *The individual in cultural adaptation.* Berkeley: University of California Press, 1971.

Endler, N., & Magnusson, D. (Eds.). *Personality at the crossroads.* Washington, D.C.: Hemisphere, 1976.

Fiske, D. W. *Measuring the concepts of personality.* Chicago: Aldine-Atherton, 1970.

Frijda, N., & Jahoda, G. On the scope and methods of cross-cultural research. *International Journal of Psychology,* 1966, *1,* 109-127.

Gamble, K. R. The Holtzman inkblot technique: A review. *Psychological Bulletin,* 1972, *77,* 172-194.

Glatt, K. M. An evaluation of the French, Spanish, and German translations of the MMPI. *Acta Psychologica,* 1969, *29,* 65-84.

Gough, H. G. An interpreter's syllabus for the California Psychological Inventory. In P. McReynolds (Ed.), *Advances in psychological assessment.* Palo Alto, California: Science and Behavior Books, 1968.

Gough, H. G., & McGurk, E. A group test of perceptual acuity. *Perceptual and Motor Skills,* 1967, *24,* 1107-1115.

Graham, J. R. *The MMPI: A practical guide.* New York: Oxford University Press, 1977.

Gynther, M. White norms and black MMPIs: A prescription for discrimination? *Psychological Bulletin,* 1972, *78,* 386-402.

Hall, C. S., & Lindzey, G. *Theories of personality* (3rd ed.). New York: Wiley, 1978.

Holtzman, W. H. Projective techniques. In H. C. Triandis & J. W. Berry (Eds.), *Handbook of cross-cultural psychology, Vol. 2: Methodology.* Boston: Allyn & Bacon, 1980.

Holtzman, W. H., Diaz-Guerrero, R., & Swartz, S. D. *Personality development in two cultures.* Austin, Texas: University of Texas Press, 1975.

Hudson, W. Pictorial depth perception in subcultural groups in Africa. *Journal of Social Psychology*, 1960, 52, 183–208.

Irvine, S., & Carroll, W. K. Testing and assessment across cultures: issues in methodology and theory. In H. Triandis & J. Berry (Eds.), *Handbook of cross-cultural psychology, Vol. 2: Methodology*. Boston: Allyn & Bacon, 1980.

Jackson, D. N., & Messick, S. Content and style in personality assessment. *Psychological Bulletin*, 1958, 55, 243–252.

Jones, E., & Zoppel, C. Personality differences among blacks in Jamaica and the United States. *Journal of Cross-Cultural Psychology*, 1979, 10, 435–456.

Kadri, Z. N. The use of the MMPI for personality study of Singapore students. *British Journal of Social and Clinical Psychology*, 1971, 10, 90–91.

Labov, W. The logic of non-standard English. In F. Williams (Ed.), *Language and poverty*. Chicago: Markham Publishing Co., 1970.

Lanyon, R. I. *A handbook of MMPI group profiles*. Minneapolis: University of Minnesota Press, 1968.

Lefcourt, H. M. *Locus of control: Current trends in theory and research*. New York: John Wiley, 1976.

Lindzey, G. *Projective techniques and cross-cultural research*. New York: Appleton-Century-Crofts, 1961.

Lonner, W. J. Issues in cross-cultural psychology. In A. J. Marsella, R. Tharp, & T. Ciborowski (Eds.), *Cross-cultural perspectives on psychology*. New York: Academic Press, 1979.

Lonner, W. J., & Adams, J. L. Interest patterns of psychologists in nine Western nations. *Journal of Applied Psychology*, 1972, 56, 146–151.

Manaster, G. J., & Havighurst, R. J. *Cross-national research: Social-psychological methods and problems*. Boston: Houghton Mifflin Co., 1972.

Megargee, E. I. *The California Psychological Inventory handbook*. San Francisco: Jossey-Bass, 1972.

Mischel, W. On the interface of cognition and personality: Beyond the person-situation debate. *American Psychologist*, 1979, 34, 740–754.

Molish, B. Projective methodologies. *Annual Review of Psychology*, 1972, 23, 577–614.

Munro, D. Locus of control attribution: Factors among blacks and whites in Africa. *Journal of Cross-Cultural Psychology*, 1979, 10, 157–172.

Nagelschmidt, A., & Jakob, R. Dimensionality of Rotter's I-E scale in a society in the process of modernization. *Journal of Cross-Cultural Psychology*, 1977, 8, 101–111.

Nishiyama, T. Validation of the CPI Femininity Scale in Japan. *Journal of Cross-Cultural Psychology*, 1975, 6, 482–489.

Osgood, C. E., May, W., & Miron, W. *Cross-cultural universals of affective meaning*. Champaign, Illinois: University of Illinois Press, 1975.

Pedersen, P. *A proposal for the use of multi-lingual resources in education of non-English speaking foreign students through non-degree, problem-oriented curricula offerings in one or more foreign languages*. Paper presented at

302 _Lonner_

the NAFSA-CBIE International Conference, University of British Columbia, May 1971.

Phares, E. J. _Locus of control in personality._ Morristown, New Jersey: General Learning Press, 1976.

Pick, A. Cognition: Psychological perspectives. In H. C. Triandis & W. J. Lonner (Eds.), _Handbook of cross-cultural psychology, Vol. 3: Basic Processes._ Boston: Allyn & Bacon, 1980.

Poortinga, Y. H. Limitations on intercultural comparison of psychological data. _Nederlands Tijdschrift voor de Psychologie,_ 1975, _30,_ 23–39. (a)

Poortinga, Y. H. Some implications of three different approaches to intercultural comparison. In J. W. Berry & W. J. Lonner (Eds.), _Applied cross-cultural psychology._ Amsterdam: Swets and Zeitlinger, 1975. (b)

Price-Williams, D. R. Cognition: Anthropological perspectives. In H. C. Triandis & W. J. Lonner (Eds.), _Handbook of cross-cultural psychology, Vol. 3: Basic Processes._ Boston: Allyn & Bacon, 1980.

Price-Williams, D. R. Psychological experiment and anthropology: The problem of categories. _Ethos,_ 1974, _2,_ 95–114.

Przeworski, A., & Teune, H. _The logic of comparative social inquiry._ New York: Wiley, 1970.

Rabin, A. I. _Projective techniques and personality assessment._ New York: Springer, 1968.

Reynolds, W. M., & Sundberg, N. D. Recent research trends in testing. _Journal of Personality Assessment,_ 1976, _40,_ 228–233.

Rorer, L. G. The great response-style myth. _Psychological Bulletin,_ 1965, _63,_ 129–148.

Roth, D. Raven's matrices as cultural artifacts. _Newsletter of the laboratory of comparative human cognition,_ Center for Human Information Processing, University of California at San Diego, 1978, _1,_ 1–5.

Rotter, J. Generalized expectancies for internal versus external control of reinforcement. _Psychological Monographs,_ 1966, _80_ (1, Whole No. 609).

Samuda, R. J. _Psychological testing of American minorities._ New York: Dodd, Mead, 1975.

Sechrest, L., Fay, T. L., & Zaidi, S. M. H. Problems of translation in cross-cultural research. _Journal of Cross-Cultural Psychology,_ 1972, _3,_ 41–56.

Segall, M. H. _Cross-cultural psychology: Human behavior in global perspective._ Monterey, California: Brooks/Cole, 1979.

Segall, M. H., Campbell, D. T., & Herskovits, M. _The influence of culture on visual perception._ Indianapolis: Bobbs-Merrill Co., 1966.

Serpell, R. _Culture's influence on behavior._ London: Methuen, 1976.

Sharma, S. Cross-cultural comparisons of anxiety: Methodological problems. _Topics in Culture Learning,_ 1977, _5,_ 166–173.

Spain, D. H. On the use of projective techniques for psychological anthropology. In F. L. K. Hsu (Ed.), _Psychological anthropology_ (new ed.). Cambridge, Massachusetts: Schenkman Publishing Co., 1972.

Spielberger, C. D. Anxiety as an emotional state. In C. D. Spielberger (Ed.), _Anxiety: Current trends in theory and research_ (Vol. 1). New York: Academic Press, 1972.

Spielberger, C. D. The measurement of state and trait anxiety: Conceptual and methodological issues. In L. Levi (Ed.), *Emotions—Their parameters and measurement.* New York: Raven Press, 1975.

Spielberger, C. D., & Diaz-Guerrero, R. (Eds.). *Cross-cultural anxiety.* Washington, D.C.: Hemisphere, 1976.

Thorndike, R. L. Concepts of culture-fairness. *Journal of Educational Measurement*, 1971, 8, 63–70.

Triandis, H. C. Culture training, cognitive complexity and interpersonal attitudes. In R. W. Brislin, S. Bochner, & W. J. Lonner (Eds.), *Cross-cultural perspectives on learning.* New York: John Wiley & Sons, Halsted, 1975.

Triandis, H. C. (Ed.). *Variations in black and white perceptions of the social environment.* Champaign, Illinois: University of Illinois Press, 1976.

Triandis, H. C., Vassiliou, V., Vassiliou, G., Tanaka, Y., & Shanmugam, A. V. *The analysis of subjective culture.* New York: John Wiley & Sons, 1972.

Witkin, H. A., & Berry, J. W. Psychological differentiation in cross-cultural perspective. *Journal of Cross-Cultural Psychology*, 1975, 6, 4–87.

Witkin, H. A., Dyk, R. B., Faterson, H. F., Goodenough, D. R., & Karp, S. A. *Psychological differentiation.* Potomac, Maryland: L. Erlbaum Associates, 1974.

Witkin, H. A., & Goodenough, D. R. *Cognitive styles: Essence and origins.* New York: International Universities Press, 1981.

Wober, M. Towards an understanding of the Kiganda concept of intelligence. In J. W. Berry & P. R. Dasen (Eds.), *Culture and cognition.* London: Methuen, 1974.

Zimbardo, P. *Shyness: What it is and what to do about it.* Reading, Massachusetts: Addison-Wesley, 1977.

13

Research and Research Hypotheses About Effectiveness in Intercultural Counseling

Norman D. Sundberg

In their classic book on personality and culture, Kluckhohn and Murray (1953) reminded us of a basic principle: Every person in different ways is like all persons, like some persons, and like no other persons. This perplexing mixture of similarities and differences underlies the problems of cross-cultural counseling and psychotherapy. The counselor meeting a client for the first time encounters these three aspects in one person—the universal, the group-specific, and the unique. The counselor, too, has these tripartite characteristics. As such, the counseling pair meets in a particular context, and they interact in a social and physical setting with its own history and relationships. Counseling itself is part of Western culture, though it probably has parallels in every society that has ever existed. "Culture is a great storehouse of ready-made solutions to problems which human animals are wont to encounter" (Kluckhohn & Murray, 1953, p. 54). Counseling, in a sense, is a cultural solution to personal problem solving.

This intermixture of universality, group similarity, and uniqueness is not easily untangled and presents many difficulties for research on intercultural counseling and its effectiveness. Almost all research depends on comparisons—condition with condition, person with person. Thus, research concentrates most on group contrast phenomena and ignores both the universal and the unique. Seldom do we think about what we share with others. Like newspaper reporters, social scientists tend to look for the unusual. Even statistical procedures are designed so that they document probable differences rather than commonalities, and the bias of journals seems to be against articles finding no differences, that is, confirming the null hypothesis. Likewise, dealing with uniqueness has never been a strong point in personality research despite Allport's longtime advocacy (1937) and Tyler's continuing concern for individuality

(1978). It is difficult to strike a balance between the two dangers of being overly concerned with group and cultural differences and being not concerned enough—between over-differentiation and under-differentiation. We shall return to these problems of similarity and commonality later in this chapter.

Research on the effectiveness of intercultural counseling and psychotherapy has been meager. A tabulation of articles in four relevant psychology journals in recent years reveals only 3 percent that have any recognition of cultural factors in titles and less than 1 percent that include research on psychotherapy or counseling which consciously involves cultural or ethnic factors. This scarcity raises serious questions about the generalization of claimed principles across ethnic or national groups. The general literature does contain several overviews of ideas, examples, and sources for hypotheses on intercultural counseling research. Representative of these are works done by Atkinson, Morten, and Sue (1979), Henderson (1979), Lebra (1972), Marsella, Tharp, and Ciborowski (1979), Marsella and Pedersen (1981), Pedersen, Lonner, and Draguns (1976), Sanua (1966), Torrey (1972), and Walz and Benjamin (1978). In addition, Lorion (1978) provides a good review of the relation of therapy to conditions of low status and poverty, and King (1978), Strauss (1979), and Triandis and Draguns (1980) present reviews of social and cultural aspects of psychology. In line with recent attention to this so-called *Age of Depression*, it is interesting that other chapters in this book (Alexander, Klein, Workneh, & Miller, and Ruiz & Casas) report studies showing acute paranoia and depression common among foreign students, and depression a core problem with Chicanos. Manson and Kinzie (Manson, 1979) also report depression as very common among American Indians and Indochinese refugees. Role stress and evaluation ambiguity also seem to be related to psychopathology in Cuban refugees (Naditch & Morrissey, 1976).

Here the focus will be on those aspects of one-to-one counseling that are most relevant to intercultural and inter-ethnic work. The crucial questions are these: Does the fact that the client and counselor differ in cultural background make for differences in the effectiveness of the counseling? And what special problems may arise or what special opportunities exist in the process of cross-cultural counseling research? It would seem that the greatest value of doing research under intercultural conditions as opposed to the usual monocultural conditions lies in the possibility for studying the effects of similarity-diversity and for determining how universally applicable are our counseling theories and techniques. The variations in expectations, frames of reference, adaptation processes, and communication style offer excellent natural opportunities for experiments if we can record and analyze our observations effectively.

In the usual one-to-one counseling situation, the five major components are the context, the client, the counselor, the mode of interaction, and the topic or problem. Intercultural considerations can affect any or all of these. If one takes the first three, the following possibilities exist: (1) The client and counselor are from different backgrounds and are working in the cultural setting of the counselor—a student from Nigeria, for example, seeing a Caucasian American counselor in an American college. (2) the client and counselor are different but are working in the homeland of the client—a student in India consulting a visiting American professor, or an American client seeing an immigrant Filipino psychologist in the United States. (3) The client and counselor differ from one another in culture and are interacting within a third setting—an Iranian student seeing a Hungarian refugee psychologist in an American counseling center. All three of these situations may be accompanied by a variation in mode of interaction, for example, nondirective, information giving, behavior modifying, or psychoanalytic. Finally, the topic of discussion or action may vary—a financial problem, career planning, depression, or male-female relations. Intercultural considerations come into play when there are variations related to social background, values, and customary activity patterns in any of these five aspects. This chapter emphasizes national and language differences and applications with foreign students, but obviously most of the same considerations would apply to within-country ethnic differences and to other kinds of clients. Research on black-white counseling problems in the United States is relevant to research on foreign students and vice versa. Techniques and theory developed for one kind of difference may well be tried with another. These ideas of difference also may apply to other counseling contrasts—generational, sexual, handicapping, and status differences. It is likely, from past research, that one difference is so powerful that it overrides many others—namely socioeconomic differences, which are tied to both poverty and education (Lorion, 1978).

Communication and Counseling

Of particular importance in intercultural counseling is effectiveness of communication. Communication is important in all counseling, but in the cross-cultural interacting dyad or system, there are many more opportunities for errors in understanding the spoken or nonspoken language. We can think of messages encoded and decoded in the two personal systems by means of "codebooks" which are only partially congruent. Schumacher, Banikiotes, and Banikiotes (1972) have shown that linguistic compatibility between black students and white counselors in high school is quite low. Of particular importance are individual differences in cognitive differentiation as Triandis, Vassiliou, Vassiliou, Tanaka, and Shanmugam (1972) have pointed out in discussions of subjective culture—the way a group using a mutually understandable dialect perceives the social environment. Some groups differentiate and achieve fine degrees of meaning in areas that others differentiate grossly. For instance, desert-dwelling Bedouins have hundreds of words having to do with camels, whereas Americans have hundreds of words having to do with automobiles. In order for a Bedouin to talk about camels with an American or an American to talk about automobiles with a Bedouin in some meaningful detail, much teaching and learning would be necessary. Similarly, some cultures and ethnic groups are highly verbal about human relations and feelings, whereas others speak little about such things. Leff (1973) demonstrated through an analysis of international psychiatric data that patients from less developed countries (and blacks in the United States and United Kingdom admitted to public hospitals as compared with whites of equal socioeconomic status) showed less differentiation of emotions and higher correlations among anxiety, depression, and irritability. Some investigators (Raskin, Crook, & Herman, 1975; Westbrook, Miyares, & Roberts, 1978), however, have found few differences in presenting symptoms and problems between blacks and whites. Obviously, this area needs more research. It does seem reasonable to assume that two parties in a cross-cultural discussion live with varying levels of differentiation about particular topics, and they are sometimes likely to feel bewildered, bored, powerless, or unsure in communication.

Triandis, Vassiliou, Vassiliou, Tanaka, and Shanmugam (1972) hypothesized that two persons will interact effectively with each other if they overlap substantially in their subjective cultures and if they are matched so that they make similar differentiations. Torrey (1972) stresses a similar idea of shared world view as one of the major components of all forms of "psychotherapeutic" helping in various cultural forms. However, it is possible for both persons (client and counselor) to obtain highly congruent understandings which may be unrealistic and ineffective. Medicine men and quacks, no matter how respected and effective with psychosomatic disorders they may be, cannot treat glaucoma or smallpox as effectively as can modern health-care givers. Within the usual clinical and counseling settings, however, the problem is often one of fitting the treatment to the assumptive framework of the clients. Illustrating this concern for congruence, Szapocznik, Scopetta, Aranalde, and Kurtines (1978) concluded that the Cuban emphasis on authority, family, and present time activity in comparison with Anglo American values suggested that the therapist select structural family therapy as a model. This form of treatment was advocated earlier by Minuchin, Montalvo, Guerney, Rosman, and Schumer (1967) for use with Puerto Rican adolescents; it involves manipulation of the present "ecology of living" of the family.

In counseling the counselor and client give each other verbal and nonverbal guidance about what is important and what is not important, and thus they establish a relative mutuality of meanings. As anthropologists and psychologists point out, cultures vary with respect to how each fosters nonverbal as well as verbal interaction between people (e.g., Birdwhistell, 1970; Boucher, 1979). Traditional Japanese girls, for instance, may not look males in the eye; for a Westerner accustomed to eye contact, this behavior can be disconcerting and may be misinterpreted. Some American Indian and Micronesian groups comprehend the direct gaze as threatening under certain conditions. (I have found it to be an interesting training technique to use role playing in which the "counselor" is told that looking closely into someone's face is seen as anger or giving "the evil eye." Most people feel it extremely disconcerting to lose the customary feedback from direct observation.)

Of particular importance for the counseling interaction is the attitude towards listening. In Vontress's chapter in this book, one learns that cultural backgrounds, and especially noisy and crowded home conditions, predispose some clients not to listen to words but to notice actions which imply emotions. Understanding the degree of cultural emphasis on verbal expression and verbal control of behavior seems particularly important in therapy.

Cultural differences may also enter into the allowances made by the counselor for discrepancies between behavior and self-report on the part of the client. Promises to return for another appointment, punctuality, and all manner of contractual behavior will be violated or incompletely fulfilled (in the eyes of the Caucasian middle-class American) by people of different cultural and ethnic backgrounds. There are, of course, great individual differences between thought and action and in the carrying out of promises and plans, to which the counselor should also be sensitive.

Hypotheses for Research

The purpose of this section is to propose some hypotheses leading towards research in intercultural counseling. Although I call them hypotheses, it might be better to think of some as "proto-hypotheses," as they are far from having operational definitions. Many will be similar to those found for any kind of counseling. That similarity is to be expected, since, as I will argue in conclusion, counseling cross-culturally must share much with counseling in general. Smith, Burlew, Mosley, and Whitney (1978, pp. 159–160) have expressed a similar view through their listing of the necessary minority counselor characteristics: rapport, empathy, interest, appreciation of the minority culture, understanding of special terms and language, knowledge of the person's community, and awareness of problems of living in a bicultural world.

One basic assumption underlying all of these hypotheses is that each person involved in the intercultural counseling dyad has the three components mentioned at the start of this chapter: universal human components shared with all human beings, group-related components shared with certain other human beings, and unique components particular to each individual.

Another assumption is that there is an optimum number of shared components important for effectiveness of the counseling interaction. The optima for different content areas are yet to be determined. For instance, the counseling pair must share some way of communicating verbally or nonverbally, but beyond a certain level of command of the language it is unlikely that further knowledge adds much to effectiveness in counseling. Knowing fifty thousand words of German may add little to a counseling dialogue in German beyond what would be said if one only knew twenty thousand words.

A third assumption is that the purposes of counseling or psychotherapy are to be found in systems away from the client-counselor interaction itself. It could be argued that a rewarding experience in the dyadic session is sufficient in itself; the actors would not expect more than what happens at a good party and would leave the session with a sense of enjoyment. One could even argue that society should provide such opportunities for entertainment and encounter, but such an objective is not usually what clients, counselors, or taxpayers expect from a counseling service. The purpose of the artificial counseling setting is to affect either the personal system of the client or the interactional systems of the client outside the counseling session. There should be trans-situational effects. In many cases counseling activity itself must go beyond the office-based dyadic interaction. (For further discussion of assumptions and systems-possibility-developmental theory, see Sundberg, 1977; and Sundberg, Tyler, & Taplin, 1973.)

The following is a series of five areas of important research in intercultural counseling. Each will present some relevant hypotheses—fifteen in all.

A. *Mutuality of Purposes and Helping Expectations*

The process of arriving at expectations for what is to be gained from counseling is particularly important in intercultural work. These intercultural expectations are on a continuum with those in same-culture contacts, but such expectations will be influenced by cultural factors. The first hypothesis has to do with the symbolic and practical meaning of entry into the counseling system itself. In addition to individual motives for contacting the counseling service, the counselor should be aware of the socialization of the person as regards seeking help. It is likely that individual members of different cultural and ethnic groups vary in their willingness to come to strangers for help and in their sense of comfort with the bureaucratic aura of services. (Outreach services are designed "to go to the people," but even they must be concerned with the atmosphere of entry.) One study (Webster & Fretz, 1978) indicates that American college students of several ethnic backgrounds (Asian, black, and white) all tend to prefer family or relatives as the first source of assistance with both educational-vocational and emotional problems. They go to the university counseling center only as a third choice for educational-vocational problems and as a fifth choice for emotional problems. Ethnic differences were not strong in this study, but other studies (e.g., Andrulis, 1977; Sue & Sue, 1974; Sue & Kirk, 1975) have shown significant differences in usage of counseling by different minority groups; it would seem that research in non-American settings or with non-American populations might show greater divergencies in service usage. Jackson (1976) has argued that there is an African genesis in the attitudes of blacks towards seeking help; the underlying world view is unlike the dichotomous Western mode of thought and bias towards rationality and quantification. Jackson suggests an authoritative reaching out to bring in blacks with problems. Higginbotham's excellent review (1977) of client expectations also emphasizes the need to understand why clients come for services. Degree of acculturation among minority groups affects acceptance of majority American attitudes and practices; for instance, Connor (1975) concluded from a study of third generation Japanese Americans that they had moved towards general American norms, and Buriel (1975), Knight and Kagan (1977), and Knight, Kagan, Nelson, and Gumbiner (1978) found that later generations of Mexican Americans approximate American norms more than did earlier generations in regard to competitiveness and field independence. Goldstein's work (reviewed by Lorion, 1978) emphasizes that therapist expectations are critical at the start of work with lower-income patients. Since the early part of counseling involves establishment of rapport and trust, the counselor has to be particularly attuned to the client's feelings about meeting with a strange expert and attitudes towards revealing private emotions. One proto-hypothesis coming from a review of these several reports and research projects can be stated as follows:

1. Entry into the counseling system will be affected by cultural background, acculturation, and socialization towards seeking help; counselor awareness of such cultural screening—the likely feelings and symbolic meaning of help seeking—will enhance the effectiveness of the counseling program.

Studies of the symbolic meaning of help seeking may be particularly fruitful. One might hypothesize that minority members coming in to counseling will unconsciously see themselves as threatened in a one-down power relationship; for instance, the black client may be ambivalent about the white counselor because whites symbolize oppression. Furthermore, the "helpee role" will be related to how psychological problems or disorders are viewed in the client's culture—how passive one is to be in the presence of the knowledgeable or powerful helper. Understanding parallel or similar roles in the culture—going to a healer, presenting a problem to a member of the family—will help the counselor understand the client from a contrast culture.

A second hypothesis has to do with congruence of purposes, one of the primary concerns of all counseling. Cultural differences in expectations are likely to create incongruence, and the greater the incongruence, the more difficult it will be to establish trust, confidence, and mutual attraction. One of the ideas frequently mentioned in regard to native healing is the manner in which the curer meets the expectations of the "patient" (e.g., Carstairs, 1955; Torrey, 1972). Among those expectations, common acceptance of goals would be particularly important. The second hypothesis is as follows:

2. The more similar the expectations of the intercultural client and counselor in regard to the goals of counseling, the more effective the counseling will be.

Not only in regard to goals but also to techniques, process, and relationship, the client and the counselor have expectations that are implicit and explicit before their first meeting and that develop further as the counseling sessions progress. Socialization for dependency, customs of restricting personal communications to the family circle, and attitudes towards social hierarchy are relevant. Another important variable is the symbolic nature of the counselor in the culture-of-origin or the culture-of-residence (such as priest, healer, parental figure, scientist, or outcast). Grey (1965) suggested, in discussing his experiences counseling in India, that counselors should be trained to cope with the client's expectations about authority and decision making. Benfari (1969) found that primitive societies which foster a large degree of childhood dependence had person-oriented healers, whereas societies that socialized for low dependence did not. Atkinson, Maruyama, and Matsui (1978) found that directive counselors were rated as more credible and approachable than nondirective ones by Asian Americans. Aronson and Overall (1966) and Overall and Aronson (1963) found that low-income patients expected stronger, more supportive therapy than comparison groups; these findings are questioned by Lorion (1978), although other studies did find the lowest socioeconomic status level to have less understanding of therapy than others. Low-income people are not necessarily of a different culture, but it is striking how often findings about Americans in poverty

approximate the findings of minority and Third World situations, perhaps because the power imbalances are similar. Related to power considerations is the orientation towards locus of control—whether within
the person or in the surrounding environment; Sue (1978) presents some
interesting hypotheses about differing cultural world views regarding internal and external attributions of control and responsibility; oppression
occurs when the counselor blindly imposes another view on the client.
Expectations are also affected by mass media; the almost universal
availability of television may be bringing about a new commonality of
expectations about helper-helpee relationships and procedures (Wahl,
1976). Tan (1967), in one of the few studies of intercultural expectancies,
found that both American and foreign students tended to be more authoritarian than were graduate students in counseling training in two
American universities; foreign students who had been in the United
States longer were more similar to American students. In the study in
Miami mentioned earlier (Szapocznik et al., 1978), it will be recalled
that a greater value was placed on hierarchical relations among Cubans
than among Anglos; consequently, therapists were expected to be more
effective if they brought the families in to the center and in general exerted strong control. Another variable receiving much attention in recent years is self-disclosure (e.g., Jourard, 1971), a procedure which
would seem to be basic to most mainstream American counseling approaches. Because of its seeming importance for counseling, self-
disclosure deserves more extensive cross-cultural research attention.
(However, it is likely that self-disclosure, much vaunted by the dominant
professional subculture, may itself be culturally interactive; there are
positive features to such defense mechanisms as denial, as Lazarus
[1979] says, and it seems eminently reasonable that revealing one's problems in counseling may not be appropriate for some people in some
situations.) In any case, congruence and understanding seem important
as stated by the following hypothesis:

3. Of special importance in intercultural counseling effectiveness is the
   degree of congruence between counselor and client in their orientations towards dependency, authority, power, openness of communication, and other special relationships inherent in counseling.

Common understanding of purposes is more important in some instances than in others. A counselor could help someone from another culture with a minor problem more easily than he could help someone from
his own culture with a serious problem. Minor problems are more likely
to be alleviated by the simple provision of information, or they may just
"go away." The clarity of communication is likely to relate to the effec-

tiveness of the contact. The more the "problem" can be identified clearly and targeted, within reason, the more likely both parties may be satisfied with the results. This thinking leads to another hypothesis:

4. The more the aims and desires of the client can be appropriately simplified and formulated as objective behavior or information (such as specific tasks or university course requirements), the more effective the intercultural counseling will be.

This hypothesis suggests that the intercultural counselor should be prepared to use multiple channels for communication. Brochures, printed explanations, graphic portrayals, and films of procedures for handling problems may be of much more value in intercultural counseling than in ordinary counseling. The counselor may also need to teach the other-culture client specific skills for handling specific situations. It should be noted, however, that the simplification and use of supplementary materials should only be used when relevant to the client's needs and not as an escape from facing crucial emotional issues.

B. Developing the Counselor's Intercultural Understanding and Communication Skills

In any system, but particularly in the counseling interaction, communication is important. A sensitivity to what the other person is trying to convey verbally and nonverbally and an ability to respond to that communication are the cornerstones of counseling and psychotherapy. In the intercultural context, we can assume there is always some language problem. Early language learning seems to be related to expression of feelings. Achebe (1960, p. 45) illustrates this in his novel about a young Nigerian who has just returned from college in London:

> Obi was beginning to feel sleepy and his thoughts turned more and more on the erotic. He said words in his mind that he could not say out loud even when he was alone. Strangely enough, all the words were in his mother tongue. He could say any English word, no matter how dirty, but some Ibo words simply would not proceed from his mouth. It was no doubt his early training that operated this censorship, English words filtering through because they were learnt later in life.

The book *Cross-Cultural Anxiety* by Spielberger and Diaz-Guerrero (1976) presents reviews of language learning which corroborate Achebe's characterization. Saying taboo words in one's mother tongue is more anxiety-provoking than pronouncing them in a second language. In personal counseling, the counselor should know something of the early socialization of the client. Thus, another hypothesis follows:

5. The more personal and emotion-laden the counseling becomes, the more the client will rely on words and concepts learned early in life, and the more helpful it will be for the counselor to be knowledgeable about socialization in the client's culture.

The counselor's learning could come about before or during the counseling sessions. Obviously the counselor needs to be open to learning. Some studies have shown that prejudicial attitudes are associated with ineffective counseling (e.g., Millikan, 1965; Millikan & Patterson, 1967) and that psychotherapists may hold cultural stereotypes as does the general population (Bloombaum, Yamamoto, & James, 1968). Sometimes prior knowledge is an impediment; the counselor may think he knows more than he does, and the result is a less individualized approach. Of course, there are many advising and guidance situations where a large amount of knowledge of cultural background is not necessary; for example, if the focus is on a sharply defined financial or academic information problem, detailed examination may confuse the issue or alienate the client. In some situations (e.g., with non-English speaking refugees), an interpreter may be necessary. Kinzie (1972) points out problems with interpreters from his experience in Malaysia but concludes they have proven their worth. Counselors may occasionally want to use interpreters to sit in on counseling sessions not only to serve as informants about a particular client's cultural meanings but also to provide training in intercultural or interethnic counseling.

In general, learning from the client about his or her background is a necessary part of counseling. In an interview survey of counselors' successes and failures in working with other-culture clients, one of my students (Bengur, 1979) found that the willingness to learn and to request information about practices relevant to the client's problems came up repeatedly as a helpful technique.

Counselor sensitivity—the ability to place oneself in the role of the client and to empathize with the client's feelings and environmental context—is crucial. In intercultural work, the counselor must be sensitive to the meanings and connotations of language, both in the client's culture and in the contextual culture surrounding the interaction. Words carry different emotional charges and bring different images to persons of different cultures. Likewise, nonverbal aspects of communication enter into the understanding of feedback and reinforcement patterns. Americans often misinterpret as "no" the slight twist of the head which, in India, signifies "yes" or "agreed"; in bazaars Americans have been known to walk away thinking a haggling proposal has been rejected until the shopkeeper calls them back. Relevant to this illustration, Rubin (1976) surveyed ways of saying "no" in different cultures. Hall (1966; 1979) has pointed out that Arabs are much more likely than are northern

Europeans to push and touch in public, that is, to invade the "personal bubble" of strangers. Such information is of importance to both client and counselor in interpreting experience in a foreign culture. Within the counseling session itself, the study of nonverbal aspects of movement and use of space could prove to be an interesting contribution to basic knowledge as some scientists suggest (Birdwhistell, 1970; Boucher, 1979; Hall, 1966).

Different cultures are also likely to vary in free associations. For instance, one study (Shaffer, Sundberg, & Tyler, 1969) found that samples of adolescents in India listed many more words related to food than did Americans; another study (Bates, Sundberg, & Tyler, 1970) showed that Indians reveal much less aggressive and humorous content in drawings than do Americans. Tanaka-Matsumi and Marsella (1976), in their study of associations to words for depression, found that Japanese nationals gave more external and somatic responses, such as "rain" or "headache," whereas Americans, including Japanese Americans, associated more internal mood states, such as "loneliness." Johnson (1973) found that foreign students varied widely in the number and kinds of adjectives they used to characterize Americans and other nationalities. The amount of feedback from clients to counselors or among fellow counseling group members in discussion groups is affected by culture. Ogawa and Weldon (1972) reported, for instance, that Japanese Americans respond less to other speakers than do Caucasian Americans, and they attributed the difference to the Japanese norm of *enryo*, shyness or restraint.

Despite the many problems inherent in intercultural communication, one must remember that some immigrants have been highly successful psychotherapists and counselors, for example, many of those psychologists and psychiatrists who fled the Nazis in the 1930s and 1940s. Their success may, however, demonstrate certain commonalities in Western culture as well as a refined sensitivity to other persons. Emotional sensitivity might be measurable (Davitz, 1964; J. Hall, Rosenthal, Archer, DiMatteo, & Rogers, 1978; Sundberg, 1966) and intercultural emotional sensitivity appears to be also potentially assessable. One likely way in which intercultural awareness and empathy in the counselor might be increased would be for him or her to study the arts of other places (Adinolfi, 1971), especially drama, films, and novels, since they often deal with intense emotionality.

An obvious hypothesis that arises from these considerations is as follows:

6. The effectiveness of intercultural counseling will be enhanced by the counselor's general sensitivity to communications, both verbal and nonverbal, and by a knowledge of communication styles in other cultures.

Reviewing the research, H. C. Smith (1966, p. 177) stated that "most of what we have learned about people we have learned informally. The sensitive people are simply those who have learned the most. The most sensitive person is the most highly motivated, most open to new experiences, most ready to participate in learning about them, and most able to assess the adequacy of what he has learned." Communication sensitivity may be related to language-learning ability (Sundberg, 1966), to the sex of the counselor (i.e., women are reputedly more aware of interpersonal nuances), to knowledge and experience in at least one or two cultures other than one's own, to interest and motivation for understanding other cultures, to skill in paraphrasing and reflection of feeling in interviews, and, with specific clients, to some similarity of early experiences, socioeconomic background, and occupational experiences. The likely importance of many of these relationships suggests the use of peers and conationals for counseling.

A related hypothesis concerns the background of the counselor. A biographical inventory and tests of knowledge might be used to measure relevant intercultural abilities. Carkhuff and Pierce (1967) have shown, in a frequently quoted study, that client-counselor similarity in race results in more willingness for self-exploration. However, the several reviews of differences (Griffith, 1977; Harrison, 1975; Higginbotham, 1977; Sattler, 1977) present a mixed picture, which we will discuss in more detail later. Most studies have been limited to nonclient samples and analogue situations; few are concerned with training and its effects. Training programs aimed at expanding the awareness and intercultural response repertoire of counselors, such as those of Pedersen (1977; 1978), seem very promising. These programs alert the counselor not only to different assumptions and problems in the contrast culture, but they also facilitate sensitivity to the unspoken biases of one's own culture. Analogue studies by Berman (1979) and Woods and Zimmer (1976) demonstrate how counseling skills and verbal operant conditioning might be studied in mixed racial interaction. The latter study, incidentally, found no significant black-white differences in conditionability, but Berman found blacks tended to use more active expression skills whereas whites used more attending skills. Selection as well as training should be considered for multicultural counseling competence. Presumably a person's experience and interest demonstrated by previous close and favorable cross-cultural contacts would relate to counseling effectiveness. Lorion (1978) discusses various forms of therapist preparation for work with low-income clients, many ideas of which would apply to cross-cultural situations. These considerations lead to the following proposal:

7. Specific background and training in cross-cultural interactions similar to the counseling one and an understanding of the day-to-day

living problems in other relevant cultures as compared with one's own will enhance the effectiveness of intercultural counselors.

Though that hypothesis would seem intuitively to be correct, its actual testing will likely reveal many subtle problems. The quality of experience and training and not just the quantity is of importance.

C. Developing the Client's Intercultural Attitudes and Skills

The other side of the coin in counseling is the preparation and development of the client so that he or she may participate effectively in the counseling interaction and the counseling program. Expectations and purposes have already been mentioned. The counselor must also give consideration to teaching specific skills to clients and to utilizing relevant attitudes and skills already present in the client's repertoire.

While it is generally advisable "to meet the client where she or he is" by special outreach programs or by procedures which are congruent with cultural expectations, sometimes to adapt the activities of a busy counseling service to the style of interaction to which the client is accustomed is not possible. The counselor may have to work with the client in developing an understanding of the counselor's point of view and in preparing for participation in the counseling process. With some clients, it may be necessary to explain the counseling process carefully, with frequent use of such techniques as paraphrasing and perception checks. For intense counseling, the client may need to be taught to speak what is on her or his mind in a relaxed manner; in other words, to develop the skills required to play the counseling role. With lower-class clients, Strupp and Bloxom (1973) reported the successful use of role-induction film for psychotherapy, and Heitler (1973) found an "anticipatory socialization interview" produced marked improvement in group therapy. These investigators were teaching clients what to expect in counseling and how to participate in the process. Lorion's review of research (1978) found pretreatment preparation for therapy with disadvantaged patients to be consistently favorable; he points out that this pretreatment for clients needs to be paralleled by preparation of therapists for work with special clienteles. The hypothesis which grows out of these considerations is as follows:

8. The less familiar the client is with the counseling process, the more the counselor or the counseling program will need to instruct the client in the skills of communication, decision making, and transfer to outside situations.

In the development of skills for survival in a bicultural or multicultural world, assessment tools have come under considerable recent attack.

This extensive field will not be covered in this review, but readers would do well to note that special cautions must be applied in the use of tests (see Lonner's chapter in this book, and discussions in Smith et al., 1978). Probably entirely new approaches need to be developed to improve the understanding of minority and cross-cultural functioning.

D. *Cultural Considerations of the Client's Areas of Action*

So far we have been looking mainly at characteristics of the client and counselor and their interaction. Off-stage characteristics—the external environment, daily life as it pertains to intercultural considerations— deserve attention here. In this regard, four factors are salient: cultural assumptions about choice and decision making, the client's reference groups, the process of adapting to intercultural stress, and choice of arenas of action.

Early family influences, religious groups, schools, and mass media inculcate cultural values, many of which are implicit and go unquestioned. Among these is a set of assumptions about choice and possibilities, that is, strategy and openness in searching for possibilities, priority for alternatives, and the responsibility and manner of making life decisions. Cultures vary in the emphasis placed on individual autonomy and on parental responsibility. For instance, in traditional India, as Sundberg, Sharma, Rohila, and Wodtli (1969) have demonstrated, the father is typically the authority who makes the choices for his adolescent children's future occupation and marriage. Knowledge of the constraints and opportunities in Third World countries is important if one is to assist many clients in career planning. Yeh (1972) demonstrates the family components involved in diagnosing and treating depression and paranoia in Chinese students studying abroad. He notes that paranoia may be treated better after the student returns home. Beliefs about the timing of life's events is critical. For instance, Hindu beliefs emphasize that certain roles should be taken up at various stages in one's life, culminating in a withdrawal from the world—something quite different from Western beliefs. Timing-related customs have a direct bearing on the immediate counseling interaction as well. This includes the keeping of appointments and the degree of punctuality, as well as the length of acquaintance time before business agreements are reached (Hall & Whyte, 1960). A hypothesis (which follows the primary injunction for cross-cultural therapy by Torrey, 1972) may be stated as follows:

9. The effectiveness of intercultural counseling will be increased by mutual knowledge of the values and assumptive framework of the culture of the client's origin in relation to the cultures of the present and future fields of action.

The matter of knowledge, however, requires caution. A little information sometimes can be a hindrance if it leads to "type-casting," or stereotyping, or misinterpretations. Greater knowledge may help only in understanding groups, but not necessarily individuals. More helpful would be a learning attitude towards the most relevant intercultural phenomena. A learning attitude is closely related to sensitivity, as mentioned in an earlier hypothesis. Several of the books already mentioned could be used in training for knowledge of other cultures, and intercultural learning propensities could be defined operationally by attitudes and problem-solving tests (e.g., Triandis, 1976, chap. 2). Of incidental interest here is the research by Matarazzo and Wiens (1977) with police applicants; the researchers found no overlap between blacks and whites on scores for knowledge of black dialect terms. Besides the obvious need to hire black policemen who understand the dialect, these results suggest that white policemen who were relatively familiar with black dialect might be selected for cross-cultural work.

Another significant element in understanding a client is acquaintance with and use of the reference groups that the client considers important. With whom does the person identify? Whose judgments about worth and status are accepted? Who will be important to the client in the future? In traditional cultures, the family, the neighborhood, and the caste or clan are important. In modern urban settings, professional or work groups exert greater influence, and the nuclear family plays a more central role than does the extended family. The study by Cottrell (1973) of cross-national marriages in India found that international life-styles had already been established by the couples before they married. These couples who lived mainly in urban settings judged themselves by "sophisticated" standards rather than by more traditional Indian values. Being highly select, foreign students on an American campus are more likely to fit into the modern and international setting than the traditional one (see Gordon, 1964, pp. 224–232). Some are eager to become a part of the reference group of Americans or of other students rather than to conform to home-country norms. Stecklein, Liu, Anderson, and Gunararatne (1971) found that foreign students are most likely to seek out other foreign students to help them solve personal problems, and Antler (1970) indicated that commiseration with conationals is more important than with Americans. Boyd, Shueman, McMullan, and Fretz (1979) describe training for psychological support groups for minority college students. My experience indicates that three norms or reference groups for foreign students should be taken into account: the host country (e.g., American), the native country, and those who try to relate to both "worlds"; good indices for deciding which group is appropriate for the student seem to be language usage and number of friends in each category.

Counselors may find that they can use conationals or "co-ethnics" of the client either as consultants, co-counselors, or peer counselors. The counselor should recognize potential pitfalls, however, since conationals may have their own disabling biases and may impede the client's adaptation to the host culture and eventual independence. In spite of these cautions, a well-chosen, well-trained conational is likely to be most helpful. The influence of persons of similar background relates to the strength of identification with the ethnic or cultural group. Jackson and Kirschner (1973) found that those who designated themselves "Afro Americans" or "blacks" more often preferred a counselor of African descent than did those who referred to themselves as "Negro" or "colored." Ruiz, Padilla, and Alvarez (1978) analyzed the different degrees of commitment to cultural values among Spanish-speaking and surnamed Americans. That a person continues to use the ethnic language is a fair index of identification with the minority group, they found. Stress is greatest for those who are in transition from one culture to another and who are trying to gain acceptance either in the Anglo or Hispanic culture. These several foregoing considerations lead to the following hypothesis:

10. Intercultural counseling is enhanced by the knowledge of the client's degree of identification with the relevant cultures and the use of cultural reference group members who are most important for the client.

How an individual adapts to another culture has long been of interest to anthropologists and psychologists. The overused term culture shock signifies a difficult period of depression and anxiety that follows the initial enthusiasm of the first few weeks in a new and strange country. The newcomer is not yet able to control or predict the new system. In addition, he or she may be physically ill and unable to find familiar food. Students are often homesick and lack social supports. Traveling professors and businessmen usually suffer a change of status in moving to a new country. (Sometimes, however, when they are treated with much deference and have servants, they enjoy an increase in status.) Conway (1969) and Sundberg (1973) discussed different phases of sojourner satisfaction and their respective implications for advisors and institutions. Zain (1965), in a survey of foreign students, found a U-shaped adjustment curve, with a high initial adjustment for those who had been in the United States less than six months, a high adjustment again after three years, but poorer adjustment in between. The counselor must be sensitive to basic physical needs and must assist the client in getting in touch with others who have successfully gone through the initial adjustment. Along the way there may be a challenge to home values and mores. The counselor must think through the ethical implications of challenging a foreign student's culture-related values. Many young male foreign students in America mention their difficulty in understanding the availability of American girls, their revealing clothes, and their apparently provocative behavior, and the portrayals of femininity on television and in the cinema. In a period of youth and young adulthood, identity and values are in the process of formation. With the loss of familiar social supports, some young people become disoriented. Another aspect for both foreign and minority (perhaps most) students is the tension regarding change with one's family. Rodriguez (1979) poignantly describes the bittersweet pride of poorly educated Mexican American parents as their child advances in college but grows apart from the family. Chapters in Lebra (1972) illustrate other mental health concomitants of migration and culture change. Older graduate students and sojourners may have their immediate families with them; spouses and children may then be exposed to cultural stress and the whole family will be a potential concern for counseling.

It is likely that persons who have previously made a successful transition from one environment to another—from a small town to a city or from one country to another—will be better able to deal with other change and culture shock. This problem of adaptation to a new environment applies also to reentry problems to one's own native land. Brislin and Van Buren (1974) have reported a program specifically aimed at training international sojourners to "worry" constructively and to expect problems when they return home. The counselor, in the role of community organizer, can do something about the orientation of students for both entry and return. With all these considerations in mind, the following hypothesis is proposed:

11. The effectiveness of intercultural counseling is increased by counselor awareness of the process of adaptation to the stress and confusion of moving from one culture to another (system boundary crossing) and by consideration of the skills required to gain mastery over the new system.

A major factor in counseling for the "arena of action" is whether or not the client intends to stay in the host culture. Sometimes the purpose of counseling is to help a foreign student client make a choice between remaining or returning. There are probably many personality differences between remainers and returners, especially if these persons have come from high-contrast cultures such as those found in most of the Asian and African countries.

Most counseling will be oriented towards the short-range problems of the client. In a college situation, the arena of action will likely center on immediate problems dealing with language, academic work, and fi-

nances (Benson & Miller, 1966). Johnson's research (1971) with international clients led him to conclude that these persons should be thought of
as students first, not foreigners. The study found international students'
morale was high during vacations and low during examinations; the investigators concluded that, contrary to popular belief, foreign students
have greater difficulty in adapting to academic work, not to American
culture. In another chapter in this book, Alexander et al. report studies
showing that foreign students' goals are concerned mostly with professional and academic training, not involvement in American life-style
and relationships. The degree of involvement, however, is relative to the
maintenance of traditional values. (Whether these considerations about
foreign students apply to in-country cross-ethnic counseling is an open
question.) The following hypothesis is proposed:

12. Effective counseling requires a consideration of both the present liv-
    ing situation and the future arena of action, its focus determined by
    the goals and priorities of the client and an exploration of the bicul-
    tural or multicultural nature of these situations.

*E. Universality, Group Commonality, and Uniqueness in Intercultural
Counseling*

Counseling is a social institution in America and Europe. Every culture
probably has some method for handling individual problems that are
not easily solved by the social structure. Frank (1974), Kiev (1964), and
Torrey (1972) found common elements between helping procedures in
modern and premodern societies. Torrey's four pan-cultural commonalities are most widely noted: (1) shared world view leading to labeling of
the disorder (the "Rumpelstiltskin effect"), (2) benevolent personal qualities in the therapist or healer, (3) the patient's expectations for being
helped, and (4) certain specific techniques, such as catharsis and interpretation. Draguns (1975) adds a fifth characteristic, that of therapy as a
universally special, intense, and removed experience in high contrast to
daily living; Frank (1974) points out that the locale, or setting, usually is
clearly designated as a place of healing or help. Counseling and similar
processes produce a refuge from society. In previous interaction with the
surrounding system, the client has lost out in the judgment of self
(regarding sociocultural expectations) or in the judgment of society. He
or she is out of step. The counselor typically provides a socially approved
antithesis to mainstream society, offering a confidential, noncritical acceptance in which the client can talk about weaknesses and dependence
and about taboo topics such as hate, sex, and egotism. One adviser of
foreign students summed up his many years of experience as regards an
adviser's required virtue: patience.

Within the American professional subculture there are several theorists and researchers who have pointed to commonality among different schools. Fiedler (1950), for instance, found that expert therapists from different schools, as compared to novices, held much in common, especially with regard to communication skills. Schofield (1964) pointed to the commonality of the basic human dimension of nonjudgmental friendliness in psychotherapy. Gilmore (1973, p. 116) referred to the somewhat different terminology of Rogers, Tyler, Truax, and Carkhuff, who each identified similar desirable characteristics in a counselor: empathic understanding, positive and nonpossessive acceptance, and sincerity. Behavior therapists also talk of the importance of positive reinforcement as the client moves towards target behaviors. Well-designed studies by various investigators (e.g., Zeiss, Lewinsohn, & Muñoz, 1979) have shown that several major kinds of therapy produce improvements over those found with a control group, but that the therapies do not differ significantly in effectiveness; so-called "nonspecific" factors are the effective agents. Bandura (1977) argues that the essential ingredient in all therapeutic change is the client's increased sense of self-efficacy; this view reflects that of Frank (1974), emphasizes demoralization as the root cause of disorder and restoration of a sense of mastery or competence as the key element in change. As pointed out in the chapter on foreign students (cf. Miller, Yeh, Alexander, Klein, Tseng, Workneh, & Chu, 1971), the feelings and needs of people seem to be the same around the world, though the surface behavior, life-styles, and communication patterns may differ. It may be that an analysis of commonalities in different theories will also lead to the discovery of commonalities across cultures in the helping process. Such potential universality remains to be carefully specified and measured. All of these ongoing considerations of commonality across clients and across theories lead to the following hypothesis:

13. Despite great differences in cultural contexts, language, and in the implicit theory of counseling process, a majority of the important elements of intercultural counseling is common across cultures and clients. These elements include such counselor characteristics as a tolerance for anxiety in the client, a manifest positive flexibility in response to the client, a reasonable confidence in one's information and belief system, and an interest in the client as a person.

Just as there are universal processes that will be shown by research, there are counseling techniques or tactics that may be especially useful within a given culture. Kiev (1969; 1972) and Torrey (1972), while identifying some universals, also question the transcultural generalizability of Western psychiatric practices. (Torrey warns of "mental imperialism.") There may be several principles for differentiating between cultures. Prince (1969), for instance, posits that cultures favoring internal controls promote insight-oriented therapy while cultures relying on external controls prefer more directive therapies. The use of charms and magic incantations to cure diseases would seem ridiculous to most Westerners, but their use is very helpful in certain cultures. (We prefer colored pills, comfortable offices, and other trappings.) Western professionals working in non-Western settings differ in the degree they believe mental health practice should be bent to meet local belief systems (Draguns, 1975). The difference between the universal and the culture-specific is likely to parallel the difference between abstract general laws of learning and problem solving and the specific content, tactics, and symbols used in studies of specific languages. Berry's (1969) suggestions for differentiating etic (transcultural or universal) and emic (in-culture) characteristics help clarify the general purposes (see also Lonner, 1979). This obvious hypothesis may be stated:

14. Culture-specific modes of counseling will be found that work more effectively with certain cultural and ethnic groups than with others.

Finally, an overriding caution in counseling is that the counselor should not treat the client as a "foreigner" or as a "stereotype" but as an individual person with his or her own unique background and own personal resources. The preceding hypothesis interrelates with this, calling to mind the profound principle posited by Prince (1976) that for the most part people heal themselves spontaneously. On their own, they seek special, helpful situations provided by the culture (such as conversations with friends, religious ceremonies, cathartic expression in sports, and in some cultures dissociated trance states). People will often have their own individual therapeutic procedures, e.g., their pleasant activities to counteract depression (Lewinsohn, 1975). The person chooses a unique way of life from his preceived opportunities and foreseen possibilities (Tyler, 1978). The psychologist needs to respect the person's unique history, resources, strengths, and ability to use available cultural resources as well as acts of self-management and self-help. Such attention to the individual, however, should not obscure the fact that cultures vary in the emphasis they place on assertion of individuality. Many American Indian and Mexican groups have norms which stress cooperation and self-effacement. In general, white Americans and other Western-oriented people are more individualistic in their attributions in contrast with Third World peoples who are more oriented towards societal concerns and traditions. Berman (1979) demonstrated that white Americans, when explaining personal problems, focused almost exclusively on the individual as opposed to the society. Blacks, on the other hand, were more equally distributed in their attributions. These ideas lead to the final hypothesis about the special character of each person:

15. Intercultural counseling will be effective to the extent that the counselor views the client as an individual with his or her own competencies and resources for "self-righting" during difficulties.

Fifteen hypotheses have been mentioned under five headings. As stated earlier, they would be more properly called proto-hypotheses, since the constructs and propositions must yet be sharpened and assessment methods identified or developed to measure the variables. It is hoped, however, that they will provide stimuli towards bringing cultural considerations into counseling theory building and research. It remains to be seen whether some of these hypotheses are in themselves culture-bound.

Similarities and Differences in Personal Systems

Throughout our discussion remains the question of how one measures similarities between counselor and client, and how well each knows the cultures, values, and social environment of the other. One general hypothesis in psychotherapy and counseling might be stated as follows: As the amount of shared client and counselor expectations, knowledge, and interests increases, the probable success of counseling also increases.

Counseling is a multivariate research problem. A number of statistical methods need to be used for comparing processes, people, and situations, and the problem of getting sufficiently large samples when there are so many variables is a serious one. (For methods of pattern comparison, see Bolz, 1972, pp. 161–260; Cronbach & Gleser, 1953; Wiggins, 1973.) The problem of establishing differences and similarities across cultures adds further complications (see reviews by Brislin, Lonner, & Thorndike, 1973; Lonner, 1979; Poortinga, 1975; Triandis, Malpass, & Davidson, 1973). Methodologies relevant to the emic-etic distinction (Berry, 1969) and problems of comparison and functional equivalence are also discussed by Lonner (1979; and in this book). The problem is also one of human categorization (Rosch, 1975).

For highest priority, I would choose research on similarities of expectations in counseling, for this topic is close to the very reason for counseling. The research should emphasize not only initial goals and interests, but also the process by which people arrive at an agreement to work together. When expectations are clear and congruent, the need for extensive similarity in other ways is less essential. Analogies can be made with other "contract" situations. In cashing a check, it does not matter if the bank teller is foreign-born or local-born, white or black, young or old, male or female, as long as the request is understood and the money handed over. In an inquiry about location of services or where to apply for assistance, the important thing is mutual understanding of the question and ability to deliver the answers. Much of intercultural advising and guidance has this practical aspect, and even personal counseling shares this feature. A training program for intercultural counselors should not ignore the importance of imparting realistic financial, educational, and procedural information, even though many "sophisticated" counselors prefer to become immersed in the more personal and "juicy" aspects of social and sexual relations, emotions, and strange customs.

There are obvious physical and behavioral features that influence the occurrence and nature of the first contact. For instance, a sojourner in a strange land is more likely to speak first with someone from the home country. Americans in India unsure of their situation are more likely to talk with available Americans than others. Some Afro Americans prefer going to black counselors, at least initially. Some research on testing has indicated that black interviewees are more open with black interviewers than with Caucasians (Ledvinka, 1971). Grantham (1973) found that disadvantaged blacks preferred black counselors; he also found that they explored themselves in greater depth with female counselors of either color. Vontress (1971) saw the establishment of a common group membership as significant for rapport. Carkhuff's review (1972), while in general agreement with the conclusions just presented, shows that effectiveness in black-white relationships depends on the interpersonal skills of the helpers; and, among some, race is not an issue. Later reviews (Griffith, 1977; Harrison, 1975; Higginbotham, 1977) show mixed results in preferences for same or contrast culture matching, although a more recent study (Thompson & Cimbolic, 1978) again showed how black clients were more likely to take a problem to a black counselor. Research with American blacks does suggest that many of them prefer to talk with black counselors, but with other ethnic groups the preference is much less clear. The degree of salience or importance attached to ethnicity and cultural identity as well as religiosity might be assessed (Bochner & Ohsako, 1977) in trying to understand and match for cross-cultural relations. Parloff, Waskow, & Wolfe (1978) concluded that most of the research to date on racial similarity and differences in therapy and counseling is poor because many studies only use nonclients, analogue situations, and only one interview. Most of the concern has been with whether white counselors can work effectively with minority clients. Jones and Seagull (1977) present an interesting discussion of white guilt and power needs and offer some helpful suggestions; they see the cross-cultural relationship as an example of a general way whereby people of differing values can learn from each other.

A possibility to explore and evaluate is a channeling operation in which first contacts are from the potential client's culture (perhaps specially selected and trained minority or foreign students); these persons could assess the client's needs and refer the client to someone in whom they have confidence. Thus, the counselor would have a kind of seal-of-approval from a member of the counselee's cultural group. But, aside from some individual preferences for first contact, the compatibility of the counseling pair is likely to be of more importance the longer and more intensive the contact. The increasing use of peer-counseling and indigenous paraprofessionals is a reflection of the significance of personal similarity. Training programs in which individuals live and work in the ghettos or other cultural situations may also help to produce a similarity of "cognitive maps."

But the question remains—similarity in regard to what? For most moderate-term and long-term counseling, what actually is important? Goldstein (1978) found research on matching to be poor or conflicting. Compatibility and similarity may be based on many different variables —sex, socioeconomic status, education, handicaps, experience with drugs, and leisure-time interests, to mention a few—in addition to ethnic similarity. Probably more important than study of demographics or external experience is research comparing clients and counselors on their orientations to counseling. (For some work in therapist orientations, see Spilken, Jacobs, Muller, & Knitzer, 1969; Sundland, 1977.) Of relevance here, too, is the question about whether international student clients should be treated as students first, or as foreigners. As mentioned earlier, the former alternative seems to be more important in the eyes of several researchers. The intercultural counselor needs to beware of overemphasizing differences and the exotic (just as the clinical assessor faces the danger of overemphasizing pathology). As discussed by Higginbotham and Tanaka-Matsumi in another chapter, similarity and effectiveness may be enhanced not only by matching but by preparatory training or socialization for counseling.

Problems of Criteria and Programs of Evaluation

Most of the hypotheses in this chapter refer to the effectiveness of counseling. Thousands of pages have been written about the measurement of outcomes of dyadic or small-group counseling and psychotherapy, and thousands of additional pages have been published about evaluation of programs that are relevant to counseling-in-the-large, or community counseling. (For overviews of evaluation, see several chapters in Garfield and Bergin, 1978; Cowen, 1978; Mahoney, 1978; Mintz, Luborsky, & Christoph, 1979; Hadley & Strupp, 1977; and Frank, 1979.) Therefore, it is not necessary to recount here the many kinds of criteria that might be used, such as client reports of satisfaction, counselor ratings, Q sorts, tests, changes in activities, and grade-point averages. (See Benson [1978] for a discussion of criteria for overseas adaptation.)

Probably the best kinds of criteria to evaluate the effectiveness of intercultural counseling would employ several judges to check on perceptions of change or benefit. The instruments used in behavioral assessment and the self-anchoring kind of measurement devised by Cantril seem promising. Also nonobtrusive measures, such as indexes (for foreign students) of campus participation, grade-average improvement, and observation of dormitory behavior, may be appropriate for certain studies.

Large sample research into the effectiveness of intercultural counseling presents serious obstacles. Even a rather sizable number of international students in America, when classified by sex, country of origin, year in college, and whether or not they sought counseling, would produce extremely small numbers in experimental cell breakdowns. The sheer availability of large numbers of minorities in the United States probably accounts for the fact that the vast majority of the studies have employed such samples; yet, as pointed out earlier, even the American cross-ethnic studies have seldom been true experiments with variables basic to counseling and therapy.

There seem to be three other directions for realistic cross-cultural research. One is to retain the goal of obtaining a large sample but to broaden the notion of intercultural status to include the category of marginal clients compared with mainstream clients. Marginal clients might include all those with unusual characteristics and backgrounds, such as minority members, handicapped students, and students who speak poor English. In such a sampling, foreign students might occupy positions on continua, their position based on such factors as communication ability, knowledge of mainstream social customs, and ability to cope with problem situations. The continua might then be related to the larger problems of counseling effectiveness and process.

The opposite direction would involve the study of individuals—one at a time. Allport, Skinner, and other psychologists have found conducting intensive studies of personal documents, performances, and reports of experience to be productive of ideas. Chassan (1976), Davidson and Costello (1969), and Dukes (1967) have suggested ways in which research can be conducted with an N of one. Leitenberg's review (1963) of the major single-case studies and Kazdin's article on design (1978) are probably the most useful for present purposes. The object of the controlled case study is to demonstrate that changes in behavior and self-report co-vary with changes in counseling. The most common designs now are those used with behavior therapy. A baseline of observed behavior is established; a period of intervention follows; then the client and counselor see if the recorded behavior has changed. In order to prove that the intervention made a difference, sometimes the counselor withdraws treatment for a period of time and then returns to the original intervention. For a behavior problem such as the inability to study, a client may be asked to keep a record of the number of half-hours spent studying each day. The intervention may be the positive reward of a five-minute break after each half-hour in which the student may obtain a personally preferred drink.

The application need not be limited to the usual behavioral approaches. Similar research programs can be used with free associations and other verbal behavior. The history of psychology shows examples of outstanding single-case research, for example, Stratton's use of inserted lenses to test visual adaptation, the Kelloggs' study of a chimpanzee they raised in their home, and Jones' reconditioning of Peter's fears. Such intensive study, one by one, of the persons involved in intercultural counseling would gradually build up a shared knowledge, the basic objective of all science.

A third direction for intercultural research would be the recruitment of persons with special cultural backgrounds for experiments that mimic the counseling situation. With contrived counseling, normal people might be used, and large samples of minorities, refugees, foreign sojourners, and other contrast cultural groups might be available, especially if they were paid for participation. (Generalization to realistic counseling situations then needs to be a concern.) Studies of dyadic interaction by analogues, role playing, and simulation of real-life problem solving can shed light on the dynamics of counseling. Research might usefully be conducted on problems of "at risk" populations at an early point, thereby preventing the later need for counseling.

Centers for the systematic collection of intercultural case data would help a great deal in the development of a knowledge base. What is needed is an organized way by which subjects who represent major problems, major countries with high-contrast cultures (such as India, Hong Kong, Iran, and Nigeria, as compared with Western countries), and major cross-ethnic problems may be sampled, so that over time there might be a comparison across methods and outcomes from intensive individual studies. It would be important to conduct parallel studies testing the same processes within different cultural or ethnic communities. This research would check intracultural utility of principles. The intercultural comparisons would be at the level of theories, not at the level of individual and group differences alone. Lonner (1975) has asserted that the best research is multi-method, multi-investigator, multi-cultural, longitudinal, and theory-related. Such complex investigations would require close coordination and a high degree of commitment, and these factors might be provided by a center on intercultural human development.

Community Counseling

Counseling-in-the-large (as opposed to the counseling-in-the-small covered earlier in this chapter) involves indirect approaches to helping persons. It is related to community psychology and community mental health. If psychotherapy is, as Schofield (1964) cleverly says, the purchase of friendship, then the increase of friendly activity towards students and others from different cultures may take the place of counseling in a more formalized setting. Peer counseling (Gravitz & Woods, 1976), support systems (Boyd et al., 1979), friendship families, and other community-related programs no doubt increase the effectiveness of the college and community experience. Reisman and Yamakoski (1974) have shown, however, that a simplistic equivalence of friendship and counseling behavior is not reasonable; their subjects wanted more than the empathic, noninformative communications they receive from friends.

Studies of these programs and their value could be instituted to help to determine the best ways to orient foreign students, relate them to the community, and organize their fellow countrymen for mutual support. Zain's study (1965) led him to conclude that orientation programs are of extreme importance in disseminating realistic information about the academic processes, which are the students' main problems. Mills (1967) found in a survey that foreign students tend to overrate their knowledge of English and their academic preparation, as compared with American administrators' ratings of them. Administrators also believed foreign students need more advising than do American students, and they favored special orientation programs. Strub (1978) has shown how cross-cultural group counseling might be used in tense, mixed racial situations; his evaluation instruments could serve, perhaps with modification, in similar kinds of studies.

Kelly (1970, pp. 183–207), in an article on programs and research for interventions in a community, outlined ways of studying aspects of this problem including the effectiveness of mental health consultation as a radiating process. Intervention would involve sequential assessment of key persons in a community, the students themselves, and the effectiveness of programs to bring about organizational change in meeting such problems or personal crises. The programs aimed at prevention of distress and failure seem to be particularly important for experimentation. Muñoz and Kelly (1975), in providing an introduction to the prevention of psychological problems, pay considerable attention to cross-ethnic problems.

How Widely Applicable is Counseling?

Another way of looking at the intercultural counseling problem is to raise the question about its utility in different cultures and settings. We already know from many accounts about psychotherapy that there are serious questions about its ethnocentric application to other societies (Draguns, 1975). Sanua (1966) pointed out that even our theories and research are ethnocentric. Albee (1977) related psychotherapy to the culture changes accompanying the decline of the Protestant Ethic and the glorification of the self in a consumption-oriented capitalistic society.

For a specific example of problems in application of Western ideas of helping, let us take India. The Indian psychiatrist Neki (1975) pointed out that Western therapy is applicable only to Westernized Indians. One psychiatrist said that it took him five years in India to unlearn what he had learned in five years abroad. For instance, there are great differences between India and the United States in regard to decision making —an important aspect of counseling young people. Compared with American teenagers and college students, Indians seem to have fewer choices in making decisions about their lives (Sundberg & Tyler, 1968). There are several reasons for this: (1) Often for economic survival in India, a person must take whatever work he or she can get, and the opportunities are few; (2) The extended family system exercises strong control over young persons; they cannot make up their minds independently about occupation, marriage, or other things; (3) The traditional "group-isms" about India, as exemplified by the significance of religion, caste, language, and political and social alignments, prevent the individual from choosing freely; (4) The limitations on geographical mobility based on family loyalties and traditions as well as on economic constraints prevent a person from having distant opportunities; (5) The sheer absence of objects of attraction (e.g., television in most places) and the paucity of recreation and other opportunities reduce alternatives for choice; and (6) The lack of physical activity and weakened energy of persons affected by poor nutrition and an occasionally debilitating climate might limit options. Sundberg, Sharma, Rohila, and Wodtli (1969) demonstrated that adolescents' views of decision making in India were much more restricted by family considerations than they are in America. Tyler, Sundberg, Rohila, and Greene (1968) concluded that the degree of external structure, as it exists in educational arrangements in three countries, may be inversely related to internality and individuality in vocational choice making; if the school system splits children into different streams at an early age, the children are less likely to develop cognitively complex structures for life possibilities. Draguns (1975, p. 284) makes a relevant point: "The nature of psychotherapy practiced would also seem to depend upon the structure of the culture in which it occurs and, especially on the 'degrees of freedom' that are open to most of its members."

In addition, the counseling interaction itself is affected by certain cultural factors in India. The concept of privacy and openness is not the same as in America. In both cultures one can talk within the family about certain "family matters," but in India one is less likely to speak the same to outsiders, such as counselors. Family cohesiveness and dominance over personal life requires consideration of family in any decision. If people do seek outside help, the traditional authoritarianism throughout society makes clients more dependent upon a counselor and increases expectations for a strong and decisive role. Being nondirective might mean rejection and lack of interest or inadequacy to the Indian client.

All of these factors, combined with differences in customs and content, make the transfer of counseling to India a serious problem. An intercultural element in counseling in India—that is, an Indian counselor working with a Thai student or an American visiting professor counseling an Indian student—further complicates the situation.

One of the important tasks for future research is the study of "folk counseling" and "natural" systems of problem solving and influence for change in various countries (Frank, 1974; Kiev, 1964; Torrey, 1972). (See MacDonald and Oden, 1977 for interesting case examples of therapy-matching cultural expectations of Hawaiian youths.) The person who would teach or counsel in another country would do well to find out as much as he or she can about the living situations of prospective clients and how they handle personal problems. A visit could help clarify these processes, and the counselor could work within the community to enhance and supplement these processes appropriately, rather than to superimpose imported counseling concepts and practices.

Yet as Kinzie (1978) points out from extensive psychiatric experience in America and abroad, there are many instances in day-to-day psychotherapeutic practice in which one must deal with value systems and social and cultural conditions alien to one's experience. He concludes that intercultural sensitivity and professional competence can provide the basis for useful treatment of a wide variety of disorders among a wide variety of people. A counselor needs to become sensitive to his or her own intercultural scope and limitations; these are important implications for training.

The Ethics and Etiquette of Intercultural Research

Psychologists and other social scientists are becoming aware that their research choices, processes, and reports are not produced in a vacuum. They impinge on subjects' feelings, pride, and way of life. Ethnic groups in the United States and several foreign countries have pointed out the unilateral exploitation and the invasion of privacy of some social science research. The ethical guidelines established by the American Psychological Association for research on human subjects, with their particular attention to the subjects' informed consent of data collection before it is carried out, should be considered for research work elsewhere. In recent years much attention has been given to ethical issues in cross-cultural research (for instance, Berrien, 1970; Lonner, 1979; Tapp, Kelman, Triandis, Wrightsman, & Coelho, 1974). As Higginbotham and Tanaka-Matsumi point out in their chapter on social learning, it is unethical to introduce treatment methods which violate the cultural base of clients.

Beyond the concern for ethical treatment of individual subjects, there are many problems about the propriety of the way research is carried out in intercultural settings. Some general principles include regard for such matters as the following: the provision of benefits for the local participants and native social scientists who help, the use of local experts to participate in the interpretation and publication of results, the provision for feedback to institutions as well as persons, the guarding against "letdown"—the decline in attention (and perhaps crucial financial support) when a program leaves, and the general concern for introducing procedures and ideas that will disrupt the local society. As much as possible one should anticipate the side effects on the local behavioral ecology and take appropriate preventive steps. These and many other professional political and administrative considerations need to be included in an intercultural counseling study.

Still, in spite of all the caveats and complications, intercultural counseling is an exciting and promising area of study. It brings to psychology and other social sciences many opportunities for important learning— how different peoples might understand each other better, how one culture is viewed by another, and new ways of observing our basic human commonalities, similarities, and uniqueness.

References

Achebe, C. *No longer at ease.* New York: Ivan Obolensky, 1960.

Adinolfi, A. A. Relevance of person perception research to clinical psychology. *Journal of Consulting and Clinical Psychology,* 1971, 37, 167–176.

Albee, G. W. The Protestant ethic, sex and psychotherapy. *American Psychologist,* 1977, 32, 150–161.

Allport, G. W. *Personality: A psychological interpretation.* New York: Holt, 1937.

Andrulis, D. P. Ethnicity as a variable in the utilization and referral patterns of a comprehensive mental health center. *Journal of Community Psychology,* 1977, 5, 231–237.

Antler, L. Correlates of home and host country acquaintanceship among foreign medical residents in the United States. *Journal of Social Psychology,* 1970, 80, 49–57.

Aronson, H., & Overall, B. Treatment expectations of patients in two social classes. *Social Work,* 1966, 11, 35–41.

Atkinson, D. R., Maruyama, M., & Matsui, S. Effects of counselor race and counseling approach on Asian Americans' perceptions of counselor credibility and utility. *Journal of Counseling Psychology,* 1978, 25, 76–83.

Atkinson, D. R., Morten, G., & Sue, D. W. *Counseling American minorities: A cross-cultural perspective.* Dubuque, Iowa: William C. Brown, 1979.

Bandura, A. Self-efficacy: Toward a unifying theory of behavioral change. *Psychological Review,* 1977, 84, 191–215.

Bates, B. C., Sundberg, N. D., & Tyler, L. E. Divergent problem solving: A comparison of adolescents in India and America. *International Journal of Psychology,* 1970, 5, 231–244.

Benfari, R. C. Relationship between early dependence training and patient-therapist dyad. *Psychological Reports,* 1969, 24, 552–554.

Bengur, B. *Interviews with counselors about effective and ineffective cross-cultural counseling.* Paper prepared at the University of Oregon, Eugene, 1979.

Benson, A. G., & Miller, R. E. *A preliminary report on uses of the Michigan International Student Problem Inventory in research, orientation and counseling, developing a balanced program and evaluating potential for academic success of/for foreign students.* Unpublished paper, Michigan State University, International Programs Office, May 1966.

Benson, P. G. Measuring cross-cultural adjustment: The problem of criteria. *International Journal of Intercultural Relations,* 1978, *2,* 21–37.

Berman, J. Individual versus societal focus in problem diagnosis of black and white male and female counselors. *Journal of Cross-Cultural Psychology,* 1979, *10*(4), 497–507.

Berrien, F. K. A super-ego for cross-cultural research. *International Journal of Psychology,* 1970, *5,* 33–39.

Berry, J. W. On cross-cultural comparability. *International Journal of Psychology,* 1969, *4,* 119–128.

Birdwhistell, R. *Kinesics and context: Essays in body motion communication.* Philadelphia: University of Pennsylvania Press, 1970.

Bloombaum, M., Yamamoto, J., & James, Q. Cultural stereotyping and psychotherapists. *Journal of Consulting and Clinical Psychology,* 1968, *32,* 99.

Bochner, S., & Ohsako, T. Ethnic role salience in racially homogeneous and heterogeneous societies. *Journal of Cross-Cultural Psychology,* 1977, *8,* 477–492.

Bolz, C. R. Personality types. In R. M. Dreger (Ed.), *Multivariate personality research.* Baton Rouge: Claitor's Publishing Division, 1972.

Boucher, J. D. Emotion and culture. In A. J. Marsella, R. Tharp, & T. Ciborowski (Eds.), *Perspectives on cross-cultural psychology.* New York: Academic Press, 1979.

Boyd, V. S., Shueman, S., McMullan, Y. O., & Fretz, B. R. Transition groups for black freshmen: Integrated service and training. *Professional Psychology,* 1979, *10,* 42–48.

Brislin, R. W., Lonner, W. J., & Thorndike, R. M. *Cross-cultural research methods.* New York: John Wiley & Sons, 1973.

Brislin, R. W., & Van Buren, H. Can they go home again? *Exchange,* 1974, *9*(4), 19–24.

Buriel, R. Cognitive styles among three generations of Mexican American children. *Journal of Cross Cultural Psychology,* 1975, *6,* 417–429.

Carkhuff, R. R. Black and white in helping. *Professional Psychology,* 1972, *3,* 18–22.

Carkhuff, R. R., & Pierce, R. Differential effects of therapist race and social class upon patient depth of self-exploration in the initial clinical interview. *Journal of Consulting Psychology,* 1967, *31,* 632–634.

Carstairs, G. M. Medicine and faith in rural Rajasthan. In B. D. Paul (Ed.), *Health, culture and community.* New York: Russell Sage Foundation, 1955.

Chassan, J. B. *Research design in clinical psychology and psychiatry.* New York: Appleton-Century-Crofts, 1967.

Connor, J. W. Value changes in third generation Japanese Americans. *Journal of Personality Assessment*, 1975, *39*, 597–600.

Conway, R. M. *The psychological effects of cross-cultural experience.* Louvain, Belgium: Université Catholique de Louvain, 1969.

Cottrell, A. B. Cross-national marriage as an extension of international life style: A study of Indian-Western couples. *Journal of Marriage and the Family*, 1973, *35*, 739–741.

Cowen, E. L. Some problems in community program evaluations. *Journal of Consulting and Clinical Psychology*, 1978, *46*, 792–805.

Cronbach, L. J., & Gleser, G. C. Assessing similarity between profiles. *Psychological Bulletin*, 1953, *50*, 456–473.

Davidson, P. O., & Costello, C. G. (Eds.). *N = 1: Experimental studies of single cases.* New York: Van Nostrand Reinhold Co., 1969.

Davitz, J. R. (Ed.). *The communication of emotional meaning.* New York: McGraw-Hill Book Co., 1964.

Draguns, J. G. Resocialization into culture: The complexities of taking a worldwide view of psychotherapy. In R. W. Brislin, S. Bochner, & W. J. Lonner (Eds.), *Cross-cultural perspectives on learning.* New York: Wiley, 1975, pp. 273–290.

Dukes, W. F. N = 1. *Psychological Bulletin*, 1965, *64*, 4–79.

Fiedler, F. E. A comparison of therapeutic relationships in psychoanalytic, nondirective and Adlerian therapy. *Journal of Consulting Psychology*, 1950, *14*, 436–445.

Frank, J. D. *Persuasion and healing: A comparative study of psychotherapy* (rev. ed.). New York: Schocken, 1974. (a)

Frank, J. D. Psychotherapy: The restoration of morale. *American Journal of Psychiatry*, 1974, *131*, 271–274. (b)

Frank, J. D. The present status of outcome studies. *Journal of Consulting and Clinical Psychology*, 1979, *47*, 310–316.

Garfiend, S. L., & Bergin, A. E. (Eds.). *Handbook of psychotherapy and behavior change: An empirical analysis* (2nd ed.). New York: Wiley, 1978.

Gilmore, S. K. *The counselor-in-training.* New York: Appleton-Century-Crofts, 1973.

Goldstein, A. P. Relationship-enhancement methods. In F. H. Kanfer & A. P. Goldstein (Eds.), *Helping people change.* New York: Pergamon, 1975.

Gordon, M. *Assimilation in American life.* New York: Oxford University Press, 1964.

Grantham, R. J. Effects of counselor sex, race and language style on black students in initial interviews. *Journal of Counseling Psychology*, 1973, *20*, 553–559.

Gravitz, H. L., & Woods, E. A multiethnic approach to peer counseling. *Professional Psychology*, 1976, *7*, 229–235..

Grey, A. L. The counseling process and its cultural setting. *Journal of Vocational and Educational Guidance*, 1965, *11*, 104–114.

Griffith, M. S. The influence of race on the psychotherapeutic relationship. *Psychiatry*, 1977, *40*, 27–40.

Hadley, S. W., & Strupp, H. H. Evaluations of treatment in psychotherapy: Naivete or necessity? *Professional Psychology*, 1977, *8*, 478–490.

Hall, E. T. *The hidden dimension.* Garden City, New York: Doubleday, 1966.

Hall, E. T. Learning the Arabs' silent language. *Psychology Today,* 1979, *12*(8), 45–54.

Hall, E. T., & Whyte, W. F. Intercultural communication: A guide to men of action. *Human organization,* 1969, *19,* 5–12. (Reprinted in A. G. Smith [Ed.], *Communication and culture.* New York: Holt, Rinehart & Winston, 1966.)

Hall, J. A., Rosenthal, R., Archer, D., DiMatteo, M. R., & Rogers, P. L. Profile of nonverbal sensitivity. In P. McReynolds (Ed.), *Advances in psychological assessment* (Vol. 4). San Francisco: Jossey-Bass, 1978, pp. 179–221.

Harrison, D. K. Race as a counselor-client variable in counseling and psychotherapy: A review of the research. *The Counseling Psychologist,* 1975, *5*(1), 124–133.

Heitler, J. B. Preparation of lower-class patients for expressive group psychotherapy. *Journal of Consulting and Clinical Psychology,* 1973, *41,* 351–560.

Henderson, G. *Understanding and counseling ethnic minorities.* Springfield, Illinois: Charles Thomas, 1979.

Higginbotham, H. N. Culture and the role of client expectance in psychotherapy. In R. W. Brislin & M. P. Hamnett (Eds.), *Topics in Culture Learning,* 1977, *5,* 197–224.

Jackson, G. G. The African genesis of the black perspective in helping. *Professional Psychology,* 1976, *7,* 292–308.

Jackson, G. G., & Kirschner, S. A. Racial self-designation and preferences for a counselor. *Journal of Counseling Psychology,* 1973, *20,* 560–564.

Johnson, D. C. Ourselves and others: Comparative stereotypes. *International Educational and Cultural Exchange,* 1973, *9*(2–3), 24–28.

Johnson, D. C. Problems of foreign students. *International Educational and Cultural Exchange,* 1971, *7,* 61–68.

Jones, A., & Seagull, A. A. Dimensions of the relationship between the black client and the white therapist: A theoretical overview. *American Psychologist,* 1977, *32,* 850–855.

Jourard, S. M. *Self-disclosure.* New York: Wiley, 1971.

Kazdin, A. E. Methodological and interpretive problems of single-case experimental designs. *Journal of Consulting and Clinical Psychology,* 1978, *46,* 629–642.

Kelly, J. G. The quest for valid preventive interventions. In C. D. Spielberger (Ed.), *Current topics in clinical and community psychology* (Vol. 2). New York: Academic Press, 1970.

Kiev, A. (Ed.). *Magic, faith and healing: Studies in primitive psychiatry today.* New York: Macmillan Co., Free Press, 1964.

Kiev, A. Transcultural psychiatry: Research, problems and perspectives. In S. C. Plog & R. B. Edgerton (Eds.), *Changing perspectives in mental illness.* New York: Holt, Rinehart & Winston, 1969.

Kiev, A. *Transcultural psychiatry.* New York: Macmillan Co., Free Press, 1972.

King, L. M. Social and cultural influences on psychopathology. *Annual Review of Psychology,* 1978, *29,* 405–434.

Kinzie, J. D. Cross-cultural psychotherapy: The Malaysian experience. *American Journal of Psychotherapy,* 1972, *26,* 220–231.

Kinzie, J. D. Lessons from cross-cultural psychotherapy. *American Journal of Psychotherapy*, 1978, *32*, 510–520.

Kluckhohn, C., & Murray, H. A. Personality formation: The determinants. In C. Kluckhohn, H. A. Murray, & D. M. Schneider (Eds.), *Personality in nature, society and culture*. New York: Random House, Alfred A. Knopf, 1953.

Knight, G. P., & Kagan, S. Acculturation of prosocial and competitive behaviors among second and third generation Mexican-American children. *Journal of Cross-Cultural Psychology*, 1977, *8*, 273–284.

Knight, G. P., Kagan, S., Nelson, W., & Gumbiner, J. Acculturation of second and third generation Mexican-American children: Field independence, locus of control, self-esteem and school achievement. *Journal of Cross-Cultural Psychology*, 1978, *9*, 87–97.

Lazarus, R. S. Positive denial: The case for not facing reality. *Psychology Today*, 1979, *18*(6), 44–60.

Lebra, W. P. (Ed.). *Transcultural research in mental health*. Honolulu: University Press of Hawaii, 1972.

Ledvinka, J. Race of interviewer and the language elaboration of black interviewees. *Journal of Social Issues*, 1971, *27*, 195–197.

Leff, J. Culture and the differentiation of emotional states. *British Journal of Psychiatry*, 1973, *123*, 229–306.

Leitenberg, H. The use of single-case methodology in psychotherapy research. *Journal of Abnormal Psychology*, 1973, *82*, 87–101.

Lewinsohn, P. M. The use of activity schedules in the treatment of depressed individuals. In J. D. Krumboltz & C. E. Thoresen (Eds.), *Counseling methods*. New York: Holt, Rinehart & Winston, 1975.

Lonner, W. J. An analysis of the prepublication evaluation of cross-cultural manuscripts: Implications for future research. In R. W. Brislin, S. Bochner, & W. J. Lonner (Eds.), *Cross-cultural perspectives on learning*. New York: John Wiley & Sons, Halsted, 1975.

Lonner, W. J. Issues in cross-cultural psychology. In A. J. Marsella, R. Tharp, and T. Ciborowski (Eds.), *Perspectives on cross-cultural psychology*. New York: Academic Press, 1979.

Lorion, R. P. Research on psychotherapy and behavior change with the disadvantaged. In S. L. Garfield & A. E. Bergin (Eds.), *Handbook of psychotherapy and behavior change: An empirical analysis* (2nd ed.). New York: Wiley, 1978, pp. 903–938.

MacDonald, S. & Oden, C. W. *Aumakua:* Behavioral direction visions in Hawaiians. *Journal of Abnormal Psychology*, 1977, *86*, 189–194.

Mahoney, M. J. Experimental methods and outcome evaluation. *Journal of Consulting and Clinical Psychology*, 1978, *46*, 660–672.

Manson, S. M. Personal communication, September 1979.

Marsella, A. J. Cross-cultural studies of mental disorders. In A. J. Marsella, R. Tharp, and T. Ciborowski (Eds.), *Perspectives on cross-cultural psychology*. New York: Academic Press, 1979.

Marsella, A. J., & Pedersen, A. (Eds.). *Cross-cultural counseling and psychotherapy: Foundations, evaluation, cultural considerations*. Elmsford, New York: Pergamon, 1981.

Marsella, A. J., Tharp, R., & Ciborowski, T. (Eds.). *Perspectives on cross-cultural psychology.* New York: Academic Press, 1979.

Matarazzo, J. D., & Wiens, A. N. Black Intelligence Test of Cultural Homogeneity and Wechsler Adult Intelligence Scale scores of black and white police applicants. *Journal of Applied Psychology,* 1977, *62,* 157-163.

Merluzzi, T. V., & Merluzzi, B. H. Counselor race and power base: Effects on attitudes and behavior. *Journal of Counseling Psychology,* 1977, *24,* 430-436.

Miller, M. H., Yeh, E. K., Alexander, A. A., Klein, M. H., Tseng, K. H., Workneh, F., & Chu, H. M. The cross-cultural students: Lessons in human nature. *Bulletin of the Menninger Clinic,* 1971, 35(March), 128-131.

Millikan, R. L. Prejudice and counseling effectiveness. *Personnel and Guidance Journal,* 1965, *43,* 710-712.

Millikan, R. L., & Patterson, J. J. Relationship of dogmatism and prejudice to counseling effectiveness. *Counselor Education and Supervision,* 1967, *6,* 125-129.

Mills, T. J. *Identification of the academic problems confronting foreign graduate students at the University of Oregon, 1966-67.* Master's thesis, University of Oregon, 1967.

Mintz, J., Luborsky, L., & Christoph, P. Measuring the outcomes of psychotherapy: Findings of the Penn Psychotherapy Project. *Journal of Consulting and Clinical Psychology,* 1979, *47,* 319-334.

Minuchin, S., Montalvo, B., Guerney, B., Rosman, B. L., & Schumer, F. *Families of the slums.* New York: Basic, 1967.

Muñoz, R. F., & Kelly, J. G. *The prevention of mental disorders.* Homewood, Illinois: General Learning Systems, 1975.

Naditch, M. P., & Morrissey, R. F. Role stress, personality, and psychopathology in a group of immigrant adolescents. *Journal of Abnormal Psychology,* 1976, *85,* 113-118.

Neki, J. S. Psychotherapy in India: Past, present and future. *American Journal of Psychotherapy,* 1975, *29,* 92-100.

Ogawa, D. M., & Weldon, T. A. Cross-cultural analysis of feedback behavior within Japanese American and Caucasian American small groups. *Journal of Communication,* 1972, *22,* 189-195.

Overall, B. & Aronson, H. Expectations of psychotherapy in patients of lower socioeconomic class. *American Journal of Orthopsychiatry,* 1963, *33,* 421-430.

Parloff, M. B., Waskow, I. E., & Wolfe, B. B. Research on therapist variables in relation to process and outcome. In S. L. Garfield & A. E. Bergin (Eds.), *Handbook of psychotherapy and behavioral change: An empirical analysis* (2nd ed.). New York: Wiley, 1978, pp. 233-282.

Pedersen, P. The triad model of cross-cultural counselor training. *Personnel and Guidance Journal,* 1977, *55,* 94-100.

Pedersen, P. Four dimensions of cross-cultural skill in counselor training. *Personnel and Guidance Journal,* 1978, *56,* 480-484.

Pedersen, P., Lonner, W. J., & Draguns, J. G. (Eds.). *Counseling across cultures.* Honolulu: University Press of Hawaii, 1976.

Poortinga, Y. H. Some implications of three different approaches to intercultural comparison. In J. W. Berry & W. J. Lonner (Eds.), *Applied cross-cultural psychology.* Amsterdam: Swets & Zeitlinger, 1975.

Prince, R. H. Psychotherapy and the chronically poor. In J. C. Finney (Ed.), *Culture change, mental health and poverty.* Lexington: University of Kentucky Press, 1969.

Prince, R. H. Psychotherapy as the manipulation of endogenous healing mechanisms: A transcultural survey. *Transcultural Psychiatric Research,* 1976, *13,* 115–133.

Prince, R. H. Variations in psychotherapeutic procedures. In A. J. Marsella, R. Tharp, & T. Ciborowski (Eds.), *Perspectives on cross-cultural psychology.* New York: Academic Press, 1979.

Raskin, A., Crook, T. H., & Herman, K. D. Psychiatric history and symptom differences in black and white depressed inpatients. *Journal of Counseling and Clinical Psychology,* 1975, *43,* 73–80.

Reisman, J. M., & Yamakoski, T. Psychotherapy and friendship: An analysis of the communication of friends. *Journal of Counseling Psychology,* 1974, *21,* 269–273.

Rodriguez, R. Going home again: The new American scholarship boy. In D. Atkinson, G. Morten, & D. W. Sue (Eds.), *Counseling American minorities: A cross-cultural perspective.* Dubuque, Iowa: William C. Brown Co., 1979, pp. 149–158.

Rosch, E. Universals and cultural specifics in human categorization. In R. W. Brislin, S. Bochner, & W. J. Lonner (Eds.), *Cross-cultural perspectives on learning.* New York: Wiley, Halsted, 1975, pp. 117–206.

Rubin, J. How to tell when someone is saying "no." In R. W. Brislin (Ed.), *Topics in Culture Learning,* 1976, 61–65.

Ruiz, R. A., Padilla, A. M., & Alvarez, R. Issues in the counseling of Spanish-speaking surnamed clients: Recommendations for therapeutic services. In G. Walz & L. Benjamin (Eds.), *Transcultural Counseling.* New York: Human Sciences Press, 1978, pp. 13–56.

Sanua, V. D. Sociocultural aspects of psychotherapy and treatment: A review of the literature. *Progress in Clinical Psychology,* 1966, *7,* 151–190.

Sattler, J. M. The effects of therapist-client racial similarity. In A. S. Gurman & A. M. Razin (Eds.), *Effective psychotherapy: A handbook of research.* New York: Pergamon Press, 1977.

Sattler, J. M. Racial "experimenter effects" in experimentation, testing, interviewing and psychotherapy. *Psychological Bulletin,* 1970, *73,* 137–160.

Schofield, W. *Psychotherapy: The purchase of friendship.* Englewood Cliffs: Prentice-Hall, 1964.

Schumacher, L. C., Banikiotes, P. G., & Banikiotes, F. G. Language compatibility and minority group counseling. *Journal of Counseling Psychology,* 1972, *19,* 255–256.

Shaffer, M., Sundberg, N. D., & Tyler, L. E. Content differences on word listing by American, Dutch and Indian adolescents. *Journal of Social Psychology,* 1969, *79,* 139–140.

Smith, H. C. *Sensitivity to people.* New York: McGraw-Hill Book Co., 1966.

Smith, W. D., Berlew, A. K., Mosley, M. H., & Whitney, W. M. *Minority issues in mental health.* Reading, Massachusetts: Addison-Wesley, 1978.

Spielberger, C. D., & Diaz-Guerrero (Eds.). *Cross-cultural anxiety.* New York: Wiley, 1976.

Spilken, A. Z., Jacobs, M. A., Muller, J. J., & Knitzer, J. Personality characteristics of therapists: Description of relevant variables and examination of conscious preferences. *Journal of Consulting and Clinical Psychology,* 1969, *33,* 317–326.

Stecklein, J. E., Liu, H. C., Anderson, J. F., & Gunararatne, S. A. *Attitudes of foreign students toward educational experiences at the University of Minnesota.* Minneapolis: University of Minnesota, Bureau of Institutional Research, 1971.

Strauss, J. S. Social and cultural influences on psychopathology. *Annual Review of Psychology,* 1979, *30,* 397–416.

Strub, R. Cross-cultural group counseling and its effect on reducing tension in a racially mixed school. In G. Walz & L. Benjamin (Eds.), *Transcultural Counseling.* New York: Human Sciences Press, 1978, pp. 153–190.

Strupp, H. H., & Bloxom, A. L. Preparing lower-class patients for group psychotherapy: Development and evaluation of a role-induction film. *Journal of Consulting and Clinical Psychology,* 1973, *41,* 373–384.

Sue, D. W. Eliminating cultural oppression in counseling: Toward a general theory. *Journal of Counseling Psychology,* 1978, *25,* 419–428.

Sue, D. W., & Kirk, B. Asian-Americans: Use of counseling and psychiatric services on a college campus. *Journal of Counseling Psychology,* 1975, *22,* 84–86.

Sue, S., & Sue, D. W. MMPI comparisons between Asian-American and non-American students utilizing a student psychiatric clinic. *Journal of Counseling,* 1974, *21,* 423–427.

Sundberg, N. D. A method for studying sensitivity to implied meanings. *Gawein,* 1966, *16,* 1–8.

Sundberg, N. D. Cross-cultural advising and counseling. *Student Services Review,* 1973, *7,* 6–12.

Sundberg, N. D. *Assessment of persons.* Englewood Cliffs: Prentice-Hall, 1977.

Sundberg, N. D., Sharma, V., Wodtli, T. & Rohila, P., Family cohesiveness and autonomy of adolescents in India and the United States. *Journal of Marriage and the Family,* 1969, *31,* 403–407.

Sundberg, N. D., & Tyler, L. E. Adolescent views of life possibilities in India, the Netherlands and the United States. *Student Services Review,* 1968, *3*(1), 8–13.

Sundberg, N. D., Tyler, L. E., & Taplin, J. R. *Clinical psychology: Expanding horizons* (2nd ed.). New York: Appleton-Century-Crofts, 1973.

Sundland, D. M. Theoretical orientations of psychotherapists. In A. S. Gurman & A. M. Razin (Eds.), *Effective psychotherapy: A handbook of research.* New York: Pergamon Press, 1977.

Szapocznik, J., Scopetta, M. A., Aranalde, M. A., & Kurtines, W. Cuban value structure: Treatment implications. *Journal of Consulting and Clinical Psychology,* 1978, *46,* 961–970.

Tan, H. Intercultural study of counseling expectancies. *Journal of Consulting Psychology,* 1967, *14,* 122–130.

Tanaka-Matsumi, J., & Marsella, A. J. Cross-cultural variations in the phenomenological experience of depression: I. Word association studies. *Journal of Cross-Cultural Psychology*, 1976, 7, 379–396.

Tapp, J. L., Kelman, H. C., Triandis, H. C., Wrightsman, L. S., & Coelho, G. V. Continuing concerns in cross-cultural ethics: A report. *International Journal of Psychology*, 1974, 9, 231–249.

Thompson, R. A., & Cimbolic, P. Black students' counselor preference and attitudes toward counseling center use. *Journal of Counseling Psychology*, 1978, 25, 570–575.

Torrey, E. F. *The mind game: Witchdoctors and psychiatrists*. New York: Emerson Hall Publishers, 1972.

Triandis, H. (Ed.). *Black and white perceptions of the social environment*. Urbana: University of Illinois Press, 1976.

Triandis, H. C., & Draguns, J. G. (Eds.). *Handbook of cross-cultural psychology: Psychopathology* (Vol. 6). Boston: Allyn & Bacon, 1980.

Triandis, H. C., Malpass, R. S., & Davidson, A. R. Psychology and culture. *Annual Review of Psychology*, 1973, 24, 355–378.

Triandis, H. C., Vassiliou, V., Vassiliou, G., Tanaka, Y., & Shanmugam, A. V. (Eds.). *The analysis of subjective culture*. New York: John Wiley & Sons, 1972.

Tyler, L. E. *Individuality: Human possibilities and personal choice in the psychological development of men and women*. San Francisco: Jossey-Bass, 1978.

Tyler, L. E., Sundberg, N. D., Rohila, P. H., & Greene, M. M. Patterns of choices in Dutch, American and Indian adolescents. *Journal of Counseling Psychology*, 1968, 15, 522–529.

Vontress, C. E. Racial differences: Impediments to rapport. *Journal of Counseling Psychology*, 1971, 18, 7–13.

Wahl, O. Six TV myths about mental illness. *T.V. Guide*, 1976 (March 13), 4–8.

Walz, G. R., & Benjamin, L. *Transcultural counseling: Needs, program and techniques*. New York: Human Sciences Press, 1978.

Webster, D. W., & Fretz, B. R. Asian American, black and white college students' preferences for help-giving sources. *Journal of Counseling Psychology*, 1978, 25, 124–130.

Westbrook, F. D., Miyares, J., & Roberts, J. H. Perceived problem areas by black and white students and hints about comparative counseling needs. *Journal of Counseling Psychology*, 1978, 25, 119–123.

Wiggins, J. S. *Personality and prediction: Principles of personality assessment*. Reading, Massachusetts: Addison-Wesley Publishing Co., 1973.

Woods, E., & Zimmer, J. M. Racial effects in counseling-like interviews: An experimental analogue. *Journal of Counseling Psychology*, 1976, 23, 527–531.

Yeh, E. K. Paranoid manifestations among Chinese students studying abroad: Some preliminary findings. In W. Lebra (Ed.), *Transcultural Research in Mental Health* (Vol. 2 of *Mental Health Research in Asia and the Pacific*). Honolulu: The University Press of Hawaii, 1972, pp. 326–340.

Zain, E. K. *A study of the academic and personal-social difficulties encountered*

by a selected group of foreign students at the University of Oregon. Unpublished doctoral dissertation, University of Oregon, 1965.

Zeiss, A. M., Lewinsohn, P. M., & Muñoz, R. F. Nonspecific improvement effects
in depression using interpersonal skills training, pleasant activity schedules or cognitive functioning. *Journal of Consulting and Clinical Psychology,* 1979, *47,* 427–439.

Author Index

Subject Index

About the Authors

A. A. Alexander is a professor of psychiatry at the University of Wisconsin Medical School and research associate of the Wisconsin Psychiatric Institute, Madison, Wisconsin. Since 1967, he and his collaborators have been studying the psychological and psychiatric responses involved in intercultural adaptation.

J. Manuel Casas is an assistant professor in the Counseling Psychology Program at the University of California, Santa Barbara. He has worked extensively with ethnic minorities and serves as a consultant to various organizations and corporations who are interested in working more effectively with ethnic minorities. Major areas of interest include the identification of counselor and client variables which affect cross-cultural counseling; effective counseling approaches to use with the culturally different client; and prevailing extrapsychic variables which may contribute to the development of intrapsychic problems among culturally different clients. He has published widely in these areas and is presently conducting an extensive study on the Mexican-American family.

Juris G. Draguns is a professor of clinical psychology at The Pennsylvania State University. He has published extensively on cultural influences upon abnormal behavior and has co-edited *Handbook of Cross-Cultural Psychology. Volume 6: Psychopathology.* His empirical research has involved the comparison of psychiatric symptoms in the United States, Japan, and Latin America as well as among several ethnic groups in Israel and Hawaii. He has taught and served as a consultant in Europe and has held a fellowship at the East-West Center in Honolulu. He is interested in bringing cross-cultural research results to bear upon the practical problems of delivering psychological services in different cultures and in culturally pluralistic settings.

Howard N. Higginbotham presently directs the Community Psychology Program at the University of Waikato, Hamilton, New Zealand. His interest in cross-cultural counseling stems from a broader concern with how culture-specific aspects of psychological helping can be assessed and represented in the design of formal treatment systems within distinct communities. He developed the concept "culture accommodation" to describe this process and it is the theme of several articles and book chapters summarizing fieldwork results from mental health facilities surveyed in Southeast Asia.

Youngsook Kim Harvey, associate professor of anthropology at Chaminade University of Honolulu and assistant clinical professor of psychiatry at the John Burns School of Medicine, University of Hawaii, has been interested in the relationship between culture and mental health both in research and teaching. She has written several articles which reflect this concern; in her recent book, *Six Korean Women: The Socialization of Shamans,* she combines her topical research interest with her keen interest in biography as a methodological strategy for psychological anthropology.

Harry H. L. Kitano is professor of social welfare and sociology, academic assistant to the chancellor, and co-director of the Alcohol Research Center, University of California, Los Angeles. His books include *Race Relations,* 1980; *Japanese Americans: The Evolution of a Subculture,* 1976; and *American Racism* (with Roger Daniels), 1970, all published by Prentice-Hall. He is currently directing a study concerning alcohol drinking patterns of various Asian American groups.

Marjorie H. Klein is a professor of psychiatry at the University of Wisconsin Medical School. She studied the problems of Scandinavian students while she was a doctoral student at Harvard University (Social Relations Department). In 1963, she joined the University of Wisconsin Department of Psychiatry and, with Ford Foundation support, she began the foreign student adaptation project. Her research presently is divided into studying the ways in which foreign students adjust to American campuses and into developing methods by which the results of psychotherapy can be measured objectively.

Walter J. Lonner is a professor in the Department of Psychology, Western Washington University, Bellingham. He is founding and current editor of the *Journal of Cross-Cultural Psychology,* which started in 1970 and has since been a major outlet for research in cross-cultural psychology. He has contributed to the cross-cultural literature, frequently in the form of co-authored and co-edited books. Lonner has worked and studied abroad on two different occasions. With an academic background in counseling, clinical, and educational psychology, he has a continued interest in understanding the interface between these disciplines and multicultural settings.

Noreen Matsushima is a doctoral student in the School of Social Welfare at the University of California, Los Angeles. She is currently engaged in research oriented toward the evaluation of process variables in cross-cultural counseling. Secondary research pursuits include the examination of the effects of socialization on minority women's perceptions of their sexuality.

Milton H. Miller is professor and chairman, Department of Psychiatry, Harbor-UCLA Medical Center, Torrance, California, and regional director, Los Angeles County Department of Mental Health. In his role as regional director he is responsible for the mental health care of a multi-ethnic population of 2.2 million persons. He began his research on intercultural adaptation at the University of Wisconsin and has continued it in both Canada and the United States. He has been active as a consultant for the World Health Organization in Southeast Asia and is currently on assignment in Bangladesh.

Paul Pedersen taught in Asia for six years and counseled foreign students at the University of Minnesota for seven years as an Associate Professor in Psychoeducational Studies. Presently he is director of a National Institute of Mental Health training grant for Developing Interculturally Skilled Counselors, through the Departments of Psychology and Social Work, University of Hawaii, and the East-West Culture Learning Institute. Several publications, workshops, conferences, and a specialized program for intercultural counseling have emerged from the training grant.

Rene A. Ruiz, a clinical psychologist, is currently professor and head, Department of Counseling and Educational Psychology at New Mexico State University. He is the author of more than 50 books, chapters, and articles which focus on the relationship between ethnic minority group membership (especially Hispanic groups) and adjustment, mental health, counseling, psychotherapy, and assessment.

Edward C. Stewart is professor of communication, International Christian University, Tokyo. He brings a wealth of knowledge from his experience in counseling and training Peace Corps volunteers. He has worked in the United States with students from foreign countries who have come to study in American schools. He brings the perspective of the psychology of communication to the problems of intercultural counseling. In addition to his university teaching experience, he has been active as an international consultant for public and private agencies. Through the Human Resources Research Office and elsewhere, he has also published some of the most frequently quoted materials on intercultural training.

Norman D. Sundberg is a professor in the Department of Psychology and the Wallace School of Community Service and Public Affairs at the University of Oregon. He has been director of the clinical psychology training program and the University Psychology Clinic. As a clinical, counseling, and community psychologist, he has taught in both European and Asian university programs. During two Fulbright awards he has consulted and lectured on the development of student services in universities in India. He has published several books and numerous articles and chapters in clinical, counseling, personality, and cross-cultural psychology. He has conducted extensive research projects on adolescent perceptions of possibilities, values, time perspectives, family decision-making, and other characteristics in India, the Netherlands, Australia, and the United States.

Junko Tanaka-Matsumi, an assistant professor of psychology at Hofstra University, received her doctoral degree in clinical psychology from the University of Hawaii. She was an East-West Center degree scholar from Japan, and subsequently was a staff psychologist at Bellevue Psychiatric Hospital and a clinical instructor in psychiatry at New York University School of Medicine. Her primary interests include an application and investigation of social learning approaches to psychological problems in cross-cultural settings.

Joseph E. Trimble, an associate professor in the Department of Psychology at Western Washington University, Bellingham, Washington, is perhaps one of the more active psychologists involved in articulating the mental health problems among American Indians and native groups in general. He has directed numerous multicultural research projects on problems of ethnicity and life-threatening events, has consulted for numerous government and private agencies, and has published many articles on intergroup relationships, with an emphasis in cross-cultural psychology.

Clemmont E. Vontress is professor of education at The George Washington University, Washington, D.C., and is best known for his more than sixty articles, chapters, and papers on the ways in which ethnicity affects the counseling process. He has been active in the leadership of several national organizations and is one of the best known blacks in the field of counseling psychology. He has acted as a consultant to university programs, government agencies, and other organizations on problems relating to intercultural counseling.

Ronald M. Wintrob, professor of psychiatry and anthropology at the University of Connecticut, has been a leader in the field of transcultural psychiatry, both in the United States and abroad. Through the American Psychiatric Association, he has been active in promoting courses on cultural sensitivity in medical schools and among mental health professionals. He has taught in Montreal, Canada, Liberia, and New Zealand.

Julian Wohl, a clinical psychologist, is professor of psychology at the University of Toledo where he served as chairman of the Department of Psychology for 6 years. Most of his professional activity now is divided between psychoanalytic psychotherapy and implications of counseling and psychotherapy in Southeast Asia. He has published several papers on each of these subjects. He held Fulbright lectureships at Rangoon University in Burma and at Chiang Mai University in Thailand.

Fikré Workneh was trained as a psychiatrist at the University of Wisconsin and is now assistant professor of psychiatry at the medical school of The University of Addis Ababa, Ethiopia. His interests range from the problems of foreign students and medical graduates to that of developing the psychiatric services of his homeland.